Balancing Act

A Practical Approach to
Business Events Based Insights

By Kip M. Twitchell

Cover art: *Heavensent*, detail,
By Lane Twitchell, 2007, 48 x 48, cut paper and acrylic polymers on plexi mounted to panel.

Published by CreateSpace.com, a division of Amazon
ISBN 978-0-9915701-0-2

First published in 2011
Edition 1.5.20150131

Dedicated to my mentors
and the SAFR project team members

Contents

Figures

Preface

"I wouldn't give a fig for the simplicity on this side of complexity; I would give my right arm for the simplicity on the far side of complexity."
– Oliver Wendell Holmes.

On May 9, 1996 I called Eric Denna, my college professor nearly 10 years before and a friend. I was working as a consultant implementing large financial reporting systems. As a professor, Eric had done consulting work, but had recently accepted a position as the CIO of a publishing company. We caught up for a few moments, and then I asked him, since he no longer did part-time consulting, what advice he would give a consultant. He pondered for a moment, and then said, "Study history. Every day I am in some meeting and a decision is made and I wonder why it ended up that way. As I dig a little deeper I learn reasons going back multiple years that influence things today. Study history."

This book is in part a history book, describing the principles behind financial reporting. But it is a history book with an eye towards the future. In the fall of 2005, I was having a steak dinner in Buffalo with Rick Roth, my consulting partner at the time and another principal character in this book. As we discussed our current project and some of the problems we were facing, he made this observation about our role on the project, "The true test of an expert is the ability to predict." Rick, who is also a licensed pilot, understood that predicting requires first accurately assessing a position, but second, understanding trajectory and speed by knowing a second position. Knowing where we have been, and where we are will help predict where we are going. "Study history."

Principles are very powerful things. They are neatly packaged nuggets of truth than can be applied to a multitude of situations. Laws which are founded on truth do nothing more than predict outcomes. Early in my education Eric exposed me to a theory called the REA Accounting Model. Although not completely accurate or precise, I refer to this theory as business events-based accounting or business events-based insight.[1] I have found this theory expresses some very powerful principles for financial reporting based upon some natural laws of computing and information systems. The principles aren't limited to financial reporting but instead apply to many types of business reporting, and the computer systems that support it. It could be considered perhaps an alternative approach to the traditional accounting model which goes back hundreds of years. Our computer systems have automated the traditional approach, without considering the implications of alternative approaches.

The principles involved in the theory have been discovered and applied in other areas of computing, but they are not often articulated as principles, or if they are, they are not well-known. Perhaps they are not well-known because accounting and computer theory are both mind-numbingly boring. To help the reader endure such tedium, I have chosen to describe these principles through the story of my career. The lessons come from four primary teachers: Eric L. Denna the Professor, Richard K. Roth the Partner, the project team headed by Jay R. Poulos, and Douglas F. Kunkel the Programmer.

If Jay Poulos is anything, he is practical. At times, I have found him frustratingly practical. But that quality, shared by Rick and Doug, has kept my experiences grounded in what is really possible. So

1. Although various other terms are used throughout this book to describe McCarthy's theory, this book is about the Resources-Events-Agents (REA) account model. As McCarthy noted in this paper's abstract: "Researchers often equate database accounting models in general and the Resources-Events-Agents (REA) accounting model in particular with events accounting as proposed by Sorter (1969). In fact, REA accounting, database accounting, and events accounting are very different. Because REA accounting has become a popular topic in AIS research, it is important to agree on exactly what is meant by certain ideas, both in concept and in historical origin. This article clarifies the intellectual heritage of the REA accounting model and highlights the differences between the terms events accounting, database accounting, semantically-modeled accounting, and REA accounting. It also discusses potentially productive directions for AIS research." Cheryl L. Dunn and William E. McCarthy, *The REA Accounting Model: Intellectual Heritage and Prospects for Progress* The Journal of Information Systems (Spring 1997), 31-51, or at http://www.msu.edu/user/mccarth4/DUNN&MC.htm (Accessed May 2009).

although this book is about a theory, it is not theoretical; it is not academic. This book describes real implementations of a significant portion of the theory over numerous years for well-known companies. It is about the grinding and refining of the theoretical as it meets practical problems, exposing new insights.

"Study history" Eric said. It is good advice because principles are usually additive; it is important to understand the basics of computing before understanding large-scale system implementations. Being clear about bookkeeping is important to understanding the accounting profession. I have determined to write this book so that anyone that has had a basic accounting course and created a spreadsheet can understand the concepts and implications of the ideas.[2] Of course the reader will determine if I have been successful.

I am aware that because of this goal, perhaps the book will please no one. Accountants may find my review of accounting tedious and simplistic at times. Computer scientists may likely make the same complaint about information systems. I doubt anyone will find that it is not comprehensive enough, even though it cannot cover all computer processes or accounting procedures. Some scholars now argue that post-reductionism analysis provides greater insight into the implications of new innovations.[3] Rick has always held that the most effective people are those that are experts in more than just one discipline. Fully understanding the intersection of accounting and computers will yield many more fruits than learning more and more about less and less of either field. People with deep capabilities in multiple disciplines produce the most creative results. This book attempts to expose new principles.

If the basics begin to bog down or bore, it is possible to skip selected sections. For example, the Chapter 8, "REAL Analysis Method," on page 43 describes how to build a business event based system from the ground up as well as some aspects of IT methodology for creating systems. This idea is at the far end of the potential implications of the system. In the balancing act of my career I haven't seen the theory applied at this extreme. Even so, I think it important to understand, particularly if we are attempting to chart where we might be headed. It is also not necessary to read a computer dump as explained in Chapter 38, "Abends," on page 193, but I do believe it is important to appreciate how to do it. Care should be taken, though, at thinking too much material is optional. Many computing textbooks contain made-up computer languages to demonstrate principles. The SAFR details in Part 5 might profitably be approached in this way.

At a dinner with Jay, Doug and Rick in Oregon in the summer of 2008, I said I was exasperated by the constant bickering between the business users of the systems being built and the IT department in charge of building them. Jay said, "Kip, if I was in Finance, I would be angry at the service from IT. Years ago finance was consistently served by IT people who understood accounting. But then IT decided they were responsible for a lot of other things that had no direct benefit to the business organization, and disbanded these knowledgeable groups of people. That was a tremendous disservice to the business." Applying the technology effectively requires understanding the problems being solved.

Doug, as the programmer rather than professor, is not a man taken to thinking much about theory. I was surprised one day to hear him comment with tremendous conviction that the only hope for truly flexible business system architectures lays with the adoption of the principles of a business event based systems. The principles involved are quite wide ranging in their implications. They find connections to data warehousing, business intelligence, ERP systems, parallel processing, code generation, legacy systems conversion, subsystem architecture, and even systems development methodologies.

What was it that Doug saw that was so convincing after years of building systems? Why should anyone invest the time to understand this theory? Let me state briefly what I hope you will understand at the end of this book.

---

2. David McCullough, in writing of the self educated American Revolutionary War general Nathanael Greene said, "It was a day and age that saw no reason why one could not learn whatever was required--learn virtually anything--by the close study of books..." McCullough, David G., "1776" page 23, (Simon & Schuster, 2005).

3. James Burke, *Twin Tracks : The Unexpected Origins of the Modern World*, (Simon & Schuster, 2003).

Part 1 – The Pearl introduces the story line and gives a summary of the implications of the theory by recapping the basic problem and solution. If you want a short summary of the problem and the solution, read Chapter 2, "The Problem," on page 5 and Chapter 3, "The Solution," on page 7. Everyone interested enough in reading some of this book should read this part.

Part 2 – The Professor describes my time in college; introductory courses in computers using the analogy of a business meeting, and basic bookkeeping and accounting using a personal financial system example. It shows that Eric Denna's explanations of what we consider as a very straightforward way of keeping track of money and information actually has a great deal of variability and flexibility to it. Building upon the personal financial system, it shows that multiple choices about how to record the same transactions and produce the same outputs are possible. It proves that a very different approach than debits and credits can be used. It then shows the methodology Eric taught to design a computer system which could actually go even further to redefine the accounting system. People interested in really understanding the heart of the solution need to understand this part.

Part 3 – The Partner introduces Rick Roth, and describes the reasons why the theory isn't implemented more widely. The reasons include confusing the means for the ends, as traditional ways of record keeping in accounting are confused for accounting standards; neglect of a long-known processing paradigm and development of tools to support long-forgotten aspects of it—the batch program as opposed to on-line processing; the adoption of the traditional accounting system or subsystem as the basic architecture for business systems at the expense of scale; how reduction of processing patterns and subsequent industry tool hegemony creates barriers to alternative approaches. It lays the foundation for how an alternative system could be constructed which would balance the demands of today's accounting requirements, but allow the theory to be implemented in a much more full sense, with wide-ranging implications. It shows the consequences of ignoring or being ignorant of these principles. People interested in understanding why traditional approaches to the problem won't work need to understand this part.

Part 4 – The Projects introduces Jay Poulos and the broader SAFR team, and describes the general pattern of how the system has been implemented over the years. It introduces the Scalable Architecture for Financial Reporting, or SAFR, not because the tool is necessary to implement the theory, but because it's development was guided by the theory. Thus understanding it exposes elements of the practical application. This part also discusses what might be termed the SAFR method. This includes practical ways to identify business events from legacy systems and the importance of focusing on the rows of data, not the columns; a practical approach to data cleansing and creating new reference data to support new insights from the events; data capture and management of rules and reference data for loading and extracting data, as well as other steps. Anyone trying to apply the theory to a particular problem needs to understand the steps outlined in this part.

Part 5 – The Programmer describes the solution programmed at its core by Doug Kunkel over 25 years. It begins by outlining the fundamental patterns and functions of a reporting system including select, sort, summarize, and format. It then discusses how to address performance, including single-pass architecture, parallelism, code generation, and process piping. It covers customization, common key data buffering of data, and information generation. Anyone interested in architecting a SAFR solution needs to understand this part.

Part 6 – The Platform describes a working system for one of the world's largest financial institutions built by the next generation of men and women involved in exploring, building for and implementing these concepts. It includes an accounting rules engine, which brings data from source systems and allows Finance to create the additional data needed specifically by Finance; an arrangement ledger, with balance-based and allocation-type processes; general ledger processes, providing control at a summary level and arrangement and general ledger extract processes feeding data to an on-line version of SAFR. It also describes ancillary and supporting functions, including reference data maintenance, platform adjustment and process monitoring, error handling, time zone and scalability factors.

Part 7 – The Plan closes this book with a few words about where all this might be headed. The true test of an expert is one's ability to predict.

Obviously I have been tutored by many people. Yet if this book contains errors, I alone am responsible for them.

Part 1. The Pearl

Chapter 1. Introduction

I sat and listened to Bob Beech describe to a potential customer my and others' decades-long work as an "oystering" process: Within a small, confined environment a problem is worked over and over until a beautiful object appears. Bob was a very good talker. As a boy, I'll bet he was constantly in trouble for talking, and probably for not holding still too. As well as talkative and energetic, Bob was also very smart. He grasped something unique about the solution for a fundamental information systems problem, and could see its much broader application.

Bob was in the midst of trying to save his company from the ravages of the Internet bubble. His company had agreed to own and market this technology. I had worked with his small company for a month, trying to help them understand it and begin to build a market for it.

He wasn't winning the war quickly enough. As I visited his office a month later, I sensed people problems between my team and his. I decided I needed to talk with Bob. Perhaps he didn't understand enough about the history of the tool, or the ideas upon which it was created; as a consultant, those were things I was used to describing a lot. We sat down for a few minutes. It quickly became clear to me that Bob knew a lot more than I did about the state of things. The problem wasn't the history or the technology. It was the finances of his company. After a few minutes, Bob excused himself to go to a meeting with all his employees. I went back to my borrowed cubicle to think.

The company cubicles were already more than three-quarters empty. The building was new, commissioned and leased by Bob's company anticipating continued Internet heyday growth. The interior was painted in bold colors, with high warehouse-like ceilings and spaces for exercise and game rooms. A sign created by a design firm even explained the naming scheme for the conference rooms and cubicle groupings.

It was very quiet sitting in my guest cubicle. The quiet didn't bode well. With only a whisper, how could this company sell the results of that oystering process? But I was still excited to have someone recognize value in the pearl, even if he was desperate for an idea to salvage his company.

While I sat and thought, Bob announced to his employees that he was taking drastic measures to try to save the company; including laying-off most of the employees and stopping work on all other projects except mine.

Later that afternoon, Bob stopped and asked if we could talk a bit more. Given our earlier discussion and the results of my cubicle contemplations, I decided I'd listen a lot more and talk less. Reflecting on it later, I think Bob taking this time when he must have been under tremendous pressure was one of the kindest things anyone had done for me.

Bob started the conversation by telling me what had led him to found the company. He studied medicine, but didn't really like to stick people with needles. He also felt that practicing medicine was not a leveraged activity; it was basically one doctor, one patient. He hoped to have a larger impact. He said he viewed the future of medicine at the intersection between mechanical or bio-technical molecular and digital information. That was why he formed his company. I sensed a real passion when he said, "No matter what happens to this company or anything else, this will be the problem I will be trying to solve."

He asked why I had ended up doing what I was doing. I was surprised by my own reaction. I looked at the floor and realized, perhaps for the first time, or at least never that deeply, that I felt a sense of mission similar to his; a very deep sense of mission. After a momentary pause, Bob quietly suggested that if I felt so strongly, I should try to write the definitive white paper about the concepts. He said there are people that have spent their whole professional lives proving that what is expressed in one such short white paper is really true.

Because of Bob's encouragement, a week later I took a day during my family vacation to visit my alma mater, Brigham Young University. I started by looking up an article a professor had introduced me to, by W. E. McCarthy, Ph.D. in July 1982 *The Accounting Review* entitled "The REA Accounting Model: A Generalized Framework for Accounting Systems in a Shared Data Environment."[4] I spent the day reflecting on what I really understood of the topic, and what insights I could add.

Now, multiple years later, I realize that I am more likely to be in the second group of people Bob described; the ones who spend their lives teasing out all the implications of a paper rather than creating one with a blinding flash of inspiration. This paper is really the foundation of my life's work.

McCarthy's papers generated a body of academic work over twenty plus years. People who hear about the theory say it makes perfect sense to them. It seemed there is something about it that could greatly simplify the business information systems architecture of the world. McCarthy's disciples have seen this potential. Early proponents went so far as to call for a revolution in accounting systems architecture.[5] There was a call to arms, but the fortress of accumulated lines of code and embedded business processes repulsed the attack.

After talking to Bob that day, February 8, 2002, I drove to the airport to fly home. On the way I was asked to join a conference call about a project that would be necessary to help save my own company, a very large company, from suffering the same fate as Bob's. That project would put the theory, and the small team of people I have worked with who believed in it, to the test. It was the culmination of years of practical experience. It was a call to arms of a different kind, and would prove whether the pearl had any value or not.

But my story is getting ahead of itself. Let me attempt to first describe the pearl. Of course to understand a pearl, it is important to know that at the core of a pearl is an irritant—a problem—that causes the oyster to create a pearl. Let's start there.

4. William E. McCarthy, *The REA Accounting Model: A Generalized Framework for Accounting Systems in a Shared Data Environment,* The Accounting Review, Volume LVII, NO. 3 (July 1982) 554-577.

5. Eric L Denna, et al., *Event-Driven Business Solutions, Today's Revolution in Business and Information Technology,* (Homewood, IL: Business One Irwin, 1993).

Chapter 2. The Problem

If you are old enough, think of the world before you had access to an Internet search engine; if you have always had access to the Internet, think of your world without it. Think of the length of time it would take you to answer certain types of questions. For example, if you have to make a purchasing decision, how would you gather information? If you have to travel some place new, how would you receive directions, and how detailed or accurate would they be? What kinds of questions would simply go unanswered, and at what costs?

Having considered the value of rapid access to information, now consider the limits to the types of information available through an Internet search engine. When was the last time you entered a number into a search term, except for an address or a year? It's likely not often. The data we search for in an internet search engine is mostly textual, not quantitative.

Have you ever wondered about the value of the results in the search engine? Don't get me wrong; I am not suggesting there is no value to the information available on the Internet. But consider that, by and large, search engine results are from information people gave away for free, or at most sold for advertising. By definition, the value cannot be consistently high because the highest value data isn't given away or sold at advertising rates.

Lastly, the type of the data, by and large, tends to be what is called unstructured data. The words on this page are unstructured. Structured data, on the other hand, tends to look much more like what is gathered in a spreadsheet, with each row representing an occurrence, and columns headings describing what is in each cell on the row. Race results or donor lists are typical examples of structured data that can be found on the Internet.

The amount of structured data *not* released on the internet likely dwarfs the structured data released. This is because the majority of structured data is deemed high value, and by its nature isn't easily digestible by search engines. Thus it is retained by the owners of the systems that gather it: businesses, governments, and organizations.

So if an Internet search engine provides valuable information, but it tends to be textual, (not quantitative), of questionable or moderate value (rather than consistently high value), and unstructured (rather than structured), then where do we search for quantitative, high value, structured data?

As an individual, the place we most often search for this kind of data is perhaps in our own financial data; your Quicken accounts, or checking or credit card registers. However, most of the time these "searches" are different from an Internet search. We certainly do search periodically for a specific transaction—a single row of data. Perhaps we need to know if we paid a certain bill. If our data was accessible by a search engine, it might be very useful in these situations.

Greater value, however, often comes from using this data in a different way, something a search engine cannot usually help with. This value comes from analyzing the results of your spending or the results of your investing. It answers questions like "Where does most of my money go?" or "How much have I paid in taxes in the last five years?" A search engine cannot answer these types of questions based upon your raw financial data, even if we were to put it on the Internet, because the answers require aggregation.

Aggregation is the process of combining rows of structured data, accumulated over time, to produce a balance. Search engines, by and large, do not do this. Rather they present each occurrence as an answer (and thus the numerous pages of search results from searching common terms). However, seeing each 401(k) transaction or each cell phone payment provides little insight; it is the cumulative results that provide insights.

The business world is not without systems capable of answering quantitative questions. In fact, these are some of the oldest systems in business, the financial systems. They are the bedrock of the capital markets. They are well established, highly controlled and, by and large, very reliable. Unreliability has serious implications for those involved, and eventually gets noted, when earnings are restated or businesses are investigated upon failure.

Yet for all the usefulness of these systems, those that use them consistently would not describe them as having the same simplicity of use as an Internet search engine. Why is that? There are two fundamental reasons.

The first is that when these systems were constructed, they were designed to provide information on a small set of attributes. For example, the General Ledger typically only answers financial questions about legal entities, cost or profit centers and perhaps product or type of customer, etc. A different system must be used to understand performance of departments or individuals; a third for specialized questions about compliance with regulations. And we haven't even touched on systems which accumulate risk, trading positions, or a host of other accumulated financial metrics.

Said another way, it would be as if an Internet search engine indexed all documents on the Internet, but only for the letters A – G, another engine for the letters H – L, another specialized one for the letters M and N, and so forth. Questions which use more than one group of letters cannot be answered by searching just one engine.

The second reason is that decisions about how to aggregate the data were predetermined when the systems were turned on. Some systems accumulate results monthly, others perhaps less frequently and some more frequently. Some accumulate average daily balances, others do simple addition. Once the data is aggregated for one period or using one method, it cannot be "disaggregated" or even converted into another form, since the underlying detail is typically long gone.

Thus although in the last 15 years almost everyone has come to understand the efficiencies that might come with better information from an Internet search engine, quantitative results have not progressed at the same speed. Some have argued that "the epochal shift from qualitative to quantitative perception..." in the late Middle Ages and Renaissance "made modern science, technology, business practices, and bureaucracy possible"[6]. Organizations that recognize that the world is again ripe for a similar leap forward in the ability to effectively use all this quantitative data will be best positioned for the world that will undoubtedly emerge.

6. Alfred W. Crosby, The Measure of Reality: Quantification and Western Society, 1250 – 1600, [Cambridge University Press, © 1997], preface material.]

Chapter 3. The Solution

So what does an Internet search engine for quantitative analysis look like? How must the next generation of systems be constructed to unlock the potential power of quantitative data?

The answer may surprise some. It does not begin from scratch, but rather with today's trusted systems of record—in summary. These systems have been developed over decades, the processes honed through incremental improvements and rigorous quality audits. By and large these systems capture accurate results—in summary. These are today's financial, risk, management, and other similar systems.

The answer continues by finding the detailed business events that feed these existing systems. These detailed business events may go by other names, including economic events, recorded acts of commerce, or perhaps simply transactions. All of today's quantitative analytical systems begin with these events as inputs. When originally captured, these business events contained, or at least had hope of containing or providing the basis for deriving, all the attributes—the letters of the alphabet A through Z—used in the subsequent aggregation and analytical processes that were implemented.

To get to a quantitative analytical engine as powerful as an Internet search engine, we will need to keep these business events at a much lower level of detail than any of the systems we build today. If we want to understand accumulated quantities for occurrences that contain the combinations of A and T, we have to be able to find transactions where A and T occurred together, and then accumulate the quantities.

We cannot approach the problem like many of today's quantitative systems and attempt to accumulate all combinations of events for every combination of A through Z before someone asks the question, and then present the results if that question ever gets asked. If an Internet search engine followed a similar approach, it would be programmed to attempt to anticipate every question that might ever be asked, having all answers stored prefixed by the question: instead of searching for answers, the index would search for questions and then present the stored answers. Imagine the complexity of attempting to anticipate every question, let alone updating all those questions every time something changed on the Internet affecting the stored answers?

Instead, our new and improved quantitative analytical engine, similar to a search engine, must keep the raw materials for answering the questions. Our question can then work with any combination of attributes to select events of interest for analysis. There is no other way.

This introduces a problem though: as we have noted, quantitative analysis is not like an Internet search because these business events must be accumulated. Thus our question typically is not looking for one transaction or event, but the accumulated results of many events. In addition to the steps needed for textual search engine processing, which starts with Select, and a somewhat analogous step of Sort[7], we need the truly unique processing step of Summarize.

These additional steps are performed in the existing systems—using data that has been reduced in size by summarization. These steps require much more computer processing power than the single step of Select. That is because many of the questions require handling many more business events. Many quantitative questions require all the business events for an entire month, quarter, year or more. Even for medium-sized enterprises this might mean several million business events.

Although computers continue to get faster all the time, building a system capable of performing such work can be very, very, very expensive. It would be very expensive for a company to own on their own

7. Search results are sorted so that the most relevant results are presented first. In quantitative analysis, the business events must be sorted not so the most relevant results are on top but rather so that the amounts associated with like attributes—the letters in our analogy—can be accumulated together.

the infrastructure necessary for a private copy of an Internet search engine. Yet as we have noted, the value of this quantitative data is so high that it must be kept within the company—a publicly accessible search engine cannot provide the answers. So each company must establish their own such environment, but how is it possible to ever get to Internet search engine levels of effectiveness for quantitative data?

The answer lies in creating a consolidated "data supply chain." Today's organizations have many systems which capture business events, select relevant events for the questions they are intended to answer, sort those events, and summarize them to provide the answers. This is a "data supply chain". As noted, they have one for the letters A – G, another for the letters H – L, another specialized one for the letters M and N, and so forth. A consolidated data supply chain would capture and keep the business events at a much lower level of detail, and allow selection, sorting, and summarization to be done in response to questions asked of the data for any of the letters.

A consolidated data supply chain would eliminate the cost of maintaining multiple systems all of which accumulate quantitative data, replaced by a single system which serves the data purposes of the other systems. These cost savings, coupled with increased revenues from better decision making, and greater efficiencies and effectiveness from the quantitative search engine approach, will pay for the system for those organizations that undertake to build it.

The SAFR software and teams have been building such systems since before the advent of the Internet. SAFR is: (1) an information and reporting systems theory, (2) refined by 25 years of practical experience in creating solutions for a select group of the world's largest businesses, (3) distilled into a distinctive method to unlock the information captured in business events, (4) through the use of powerful, scalable software for the largest organization's needs, (5) in a configurable solution addressing today's transparency demands.

The Theory

Companies expend huge sums of money to capture business events in information systems. Business events are the stuff of all reporting processes. Focusing reporting systems on exposing business events combinations can turn data into information much more rapidly, with much greater accuracy, and at much lower per report cost than any other available approach.

The Experience

Although analysis of business events holds the answers to business questions, as noted they aren't to be trifled with, particularly for the largest organizations. Reporting processes—particularly financial reporting processes—accumulate millions and billions of business events. In fact, the balance sheet is an accumulation of all the financial business events from the beginning of the company! Such volumes mean that unlocking the information embedded in business events requires fundamentally different approaches. The 25 years of experience of building SAFR in services engagements has exposed, principle by principle, piece by piece, and layer by layer, maybe the only viable way, yet identified after all these years.

The Method

This experience has been captured in a method of finding and exposing business events, within the context of the existing critical reporting processes. It uses today's recognized financial data supply chain, like a compass pointing north, to constrain, inform, and guide identification of additional reporting details. It facilitates definition of the most important questions to be answered, and configuring repositories to provide those answers consistently. It also explains how to gradually turn on the system without endangering existing critical reporting processes.

The Software

The infrastructure software is a hard asset with hundreds of thousands of lines of source code and a feature set rivaling some of the best known commercial software packages.

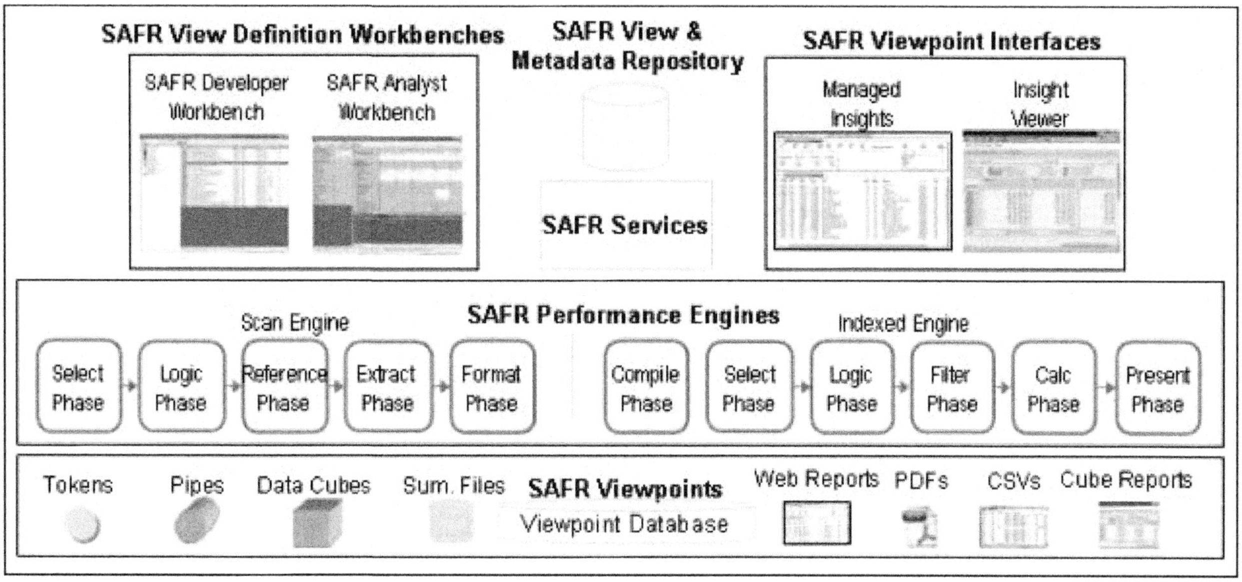

Figure 1. Infrastructure Software Conceptual Framework

The Scan Engine is the heart of SAFR, performing in minutes what other tools require hours and days to do. The Scan Engine is a parallel processing engine, generating IBM z/OS machine code. In one pass through a business event repository, it creates many business event "views" or outputs providing rich understanding. It categorizes, through join processes, the business events orders of magnitude more efficiently than other tools. Built for business event analysis, in numerous tests on existing infrastructure at a number of companies, it has consistently achieved a throughput of a million records a minute. It is highly extensible to complex problems. Desired views are defined in the SAFR Developer Workbench or rule based processes in the SAFR Analyst Workbench or in custom developed applications. The Scan Engine executes as a scheduled process, resolving all specified requests in one execution.

The Indexed Engine provides one at a time view resolution through on-line access to Scan Engine and other process outputs. It uses Scan Engine performance techniques. Reports structure and layout are dynamically defined in the Analyst Workbench. The Indexed Engine creates reports in a fraction of the time required for other tools. Managed Insights users select parameters to drill down to increasing levels of business events, and perform multidimensional analysis through the Viewpoint Interfaces. The Insight Viewer enables discovery of business event meaning in an iterative development mode.

The Solution

The SAFR Infrastructure Software has been configured over a decade for a number of the largest financial services organizations to provide an incredibly scalable Financial Management Solution (FMS).

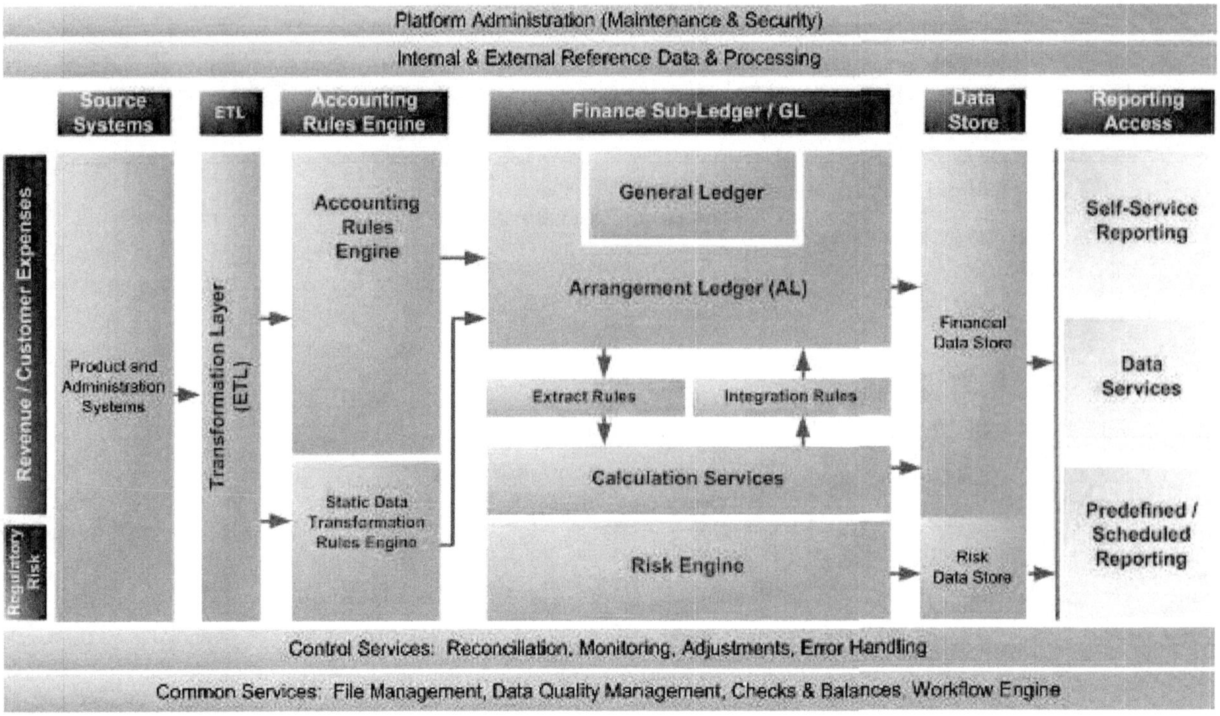

Figure 2. The SAFR Financial Management Solution

The heart of FMS is the Arrangement Ledger (AL). An "arrangement" is a specific customer/contract relationship. The AL, a customer/contract sub-ledger, maintains millions of individual customer/contract level balance sheets and income statements. This incredibly rich operational reporting system supports a large swath of reporting outputs, provided today in summary, with the added benefit of being able to drill down to business event details if needed. Doing so allows pivoting high quality financial numbers by customer, product, risk, counterparty and other characteristics, all reconciled, audited, and controlled.

AL is fed daily business events from the source systems. The business events become complete journal entries at the customer-contract level, in the Accounting Rules Engine. Rules are under control of finance rather than embedded in programs in source systems, enabling Finance to react to changes in financial reporting standards.

The business event journal entries are posted by the Arrangement Ledger on a daily basis, while it simultaneously performs multi-currency, intercompany eliminations, GAAP reclassification, year-end close and other processing. It accepts and properly posts backdated entries, and summarizes daily activity to pass to the General Ledger. The General Ledger provides another control point for the traditional accounting view of the data. The Arrangement Ledger performs reclassification and accepts summary level GL adjustments, keeping the arrangement detail aligned with the summary General Ledger.

AL also accepts customer/contract descriptive information with hundreds of additional attributes to describe each customer-contract, and counterparty or collateral descriptive attributes. This enables "pivoting" financial balances by a nearly unlimited set of attributes, not just the traditional accounting code block. Extract processes produce various summaries, ultimately numbering in the thousands, to support information delivery for not only traditional accounting but also statutory, regulatory, management, and risk reporting. The SAFR one pass capability enables AL to load the repository, generate data, generate new business events, and create extracts all in one process. The SAFR AL outputs are loaded into the incredibly information rich Financial Data Store, and its attendant reporting applications.

Conclusion

The principles built up line upon line in this solution and outlined hereafter will help build the next generation of analytical and reporting systems. These principles include (1) the organizing nature of focusing on the stability of business events, rather than attempting to predict future desired analyses; (2) this in turn demanding greater levels of detail in reporting applications; (3) which delays aggregation processes until much closer to report time; (4) requiring greater scale of processing; (5) which can only be made cost effective by analytical process consolidation; (6) and all of this made practical by the tempering act of summarizing historical business events when necessary—a true balancing act.

There is no other course. These processes are employed in today's systems in a haphazard and crosswise way to the principles involved because they are not recognized and understood. Employing them explicitly in the next generation of systems can fundamentally change decision making processes for individuals and organizations. And it can do so in the near term, having great benefits to society. But these new systems look very different than what we have today.

Understanding these principles requires being grounded in the basics of reporting and analytics, starting with the original such system: accounting. To do that, we need to return to school.

Part 2. The Professor

Accounting was perhaps the first documented reporting process, and almost all types of reporting processes are built upon its ideas and approaches in some measure. It has been highly developed over centuries, and can handle a myriad of needs in sophisticated ways. I believe anyone that is going to deal with reporting processes should understand the basics of accounting, and computers which are now integral to it.

Let me emphasize this point: Understanding accounting will provide insight into all types of reporting and many types of analytical functions.

The following chapters start by explaining these basics, but do not end there. They begin to show that we can change how we have automated these things and satisfy many more needs in a much more efficient manner. Yet doing so requires that the finance systems change fundamentally.

McCarthy, seventeen years after his initial paper, wrote the following about its impact. "REA theory has expanded considerably.... However the rate of this progress and the assimilation of REA work into the mainstream ideas of accounting have not been without problems and impediments." "Completely customized implementation of a new enterprise information system is not a common occurrence..."[8]

Accountants aren't known for their flexibility. At times, they obscure the essence of a matter, citing accounting traditions and standards. If finance people want the information they provide to continue to be relevant, they must consider if alternative approaches are possible to the standard system architecture. The Chapter 6, "Business Events," on page 31 and Chapter 7, "Resources and Agents," on page 39 present a measured approach to considering what really is and is not required.

Eric Denna has written "To assess whether an alternative system architecture is viable to meet the needs of information customers, it is important to focus not on whether the alternative emulates the traditional mode of processing and data storage, but whether it is able to accomplish the desired objectives of the traditional architecture, and much more."[9]

Chapter 8, "REAL Analysis Method," on page 43 presents a view of the theory. This is important as it shows where we may be going. We don't yet build systems this way, but some day we likely will; our needs for better reporting and more flexible systems architecture will drive us there inexorably.

---

8. William E. McCarthy, Semantic Modeling in Accounting Education, Practice, and Research: Some Progress and Impediments Published in: Conceptual Modeling: Current Issues and Future Directions, 1999, pages 147 and 150, http://www.msu.edu/~mccarth4/chen-con.html (April 2008).

9. Anita Sawyer Hollander, Eric L. Denna, J. Owen Cherrington, Accounting, Information Technology, and Business Solutions 2nd ed. (© McGraw-Hill Companies Inc.: 2000) p. 499. Emphasis added.

Chapter 4. Computers

Deciding to major in accounting wasn't very difficult for me. My father had worked as an accountant all my growing-up years. The first time I sensed I liked to deal with data came when I was 20, while serving as a volunteer missionary in Japan for my church. The mission president complained about not being able to read my handwriting. So he gave me a portable typewriter to complete reports. I remember one day completing a report which summarized data from a number of other reports, stopping for a minute, looking at it, feeling a sense of satisfaction at what I had produced, and thinking I could improve the process.

Before returning to college in 1985 after my missionary service, I suggested to my father that my mission president was right about my handwriting; I needed a typewriter. While I was in Japan, personal computers had become widely available. My father suggested we look at them. We went to a newly opened retail computer store on a Saturday morning. The place was packed with people who seemed to know everything about computers. They were buying software, hardware, upgrades and host of other things I hadn't ever heard of. We couldn't get anyone's attention. After moving the mouse around on a demo Apple Computer that I now know badly needed to be rebooted, we gave up and bought a typewriter. The experience left me wondering how all those people knew so much about computers.

Based upon these feelings, I registered for an introductory course in information systems. It gave me a better sense of the history of computers, and how they worked. The professor for the course, Dr. Gary Carlson must have been in his mid-sixties. He was mostly bald with clipped gray hair around the ears, glasses and somewhat portly. I remember his suit pants being just short enough to give the impression he knew a lot about computers. Later I learned he had pioneered the use of computers at the university over many years. It seemed plausible that he could have worked on the first computers. I vaguely remember heroic stories of his meeting the inventors of various languages and hardware innovations. The first day he promised to de-mystify the computer; that we would learn how to turn one on and make it work. And I did, booting up an IBM® PC from a 5¼ inch floppy drive, and writing a paper and making a spreadsheet.

Computer Basics

To understand my experiences with events based accounting theory, one needs to understand three basic components of a computer: the CPU or processor, memory, and disk storage. These might be easiest to understand by using an analogy of a group of people in a meeting. Think of the hard disk as a three ring binder containing minutes of the last meeting, the white board as computer memory, and the CPU as the people in the meeting. When the meeting starts up, one person copies the diagrams and bullet points of the last meeting from the binder onto the whiteboard so that everyone can see them. As the meeting progresses, changes are made to the information on the white board; new things are added, and some erased. At the conclusion of the meeting, the contents of the white board are again copied as minutes into the binder for use in the next meeting.

For the most part, the people don't interact with the binder directly; passing it around for everyone to read would be too slow. Remember this: access to the binder is slow. Likewise, the process of reading and writing data to and from the hard disk is slow. But the binder and hard disk are permanent. Between meetings the whiteboard might be erased or changed. Its contents, like computer memory, are volatile. Computer memory is erased every time the computer is turned off or loses power. Anyone that has lost work on a document when the computer crashed understands that principle. Access to the whiteboard is also quick, as is communication between the people or processors.

So the basic process of computing can be summarized as the processor moving data from the hard disk to memory when starting a program or opening a file, and then back to the hard disk when the data is saved. Once in memory, the data can be modified or new data created by the processors. Accessing data from a disk is many times slower than accessing memory.

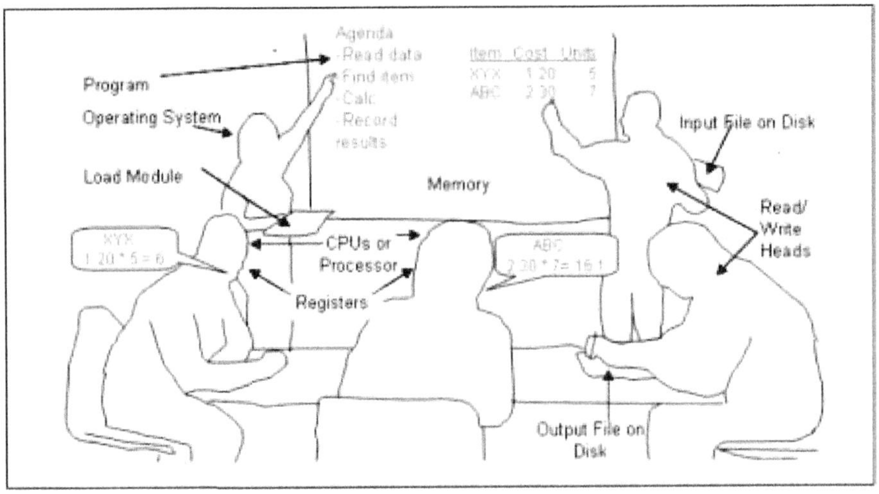

Figure 3. Computer Basics

Processors

Our analogy isn't completely accurate. Unlike humans, processors do not think; they only do what they are told. To correct our analogy imagine that the people need a lot of help to get through the meeting, so some very formal procedures are created, similar to Robert's Rules of Order. The rules say everything that must be done in the meeting, in a very detailed way. The "processors" follow those rules exactly to conduct the meeting. In computers, these procedures are like computer programs. The procedures aren't written in English. They are written in computer languages. After my initial classes with Dr. Carlson, I had classes in programming languages, both BASIC and COBOL. From these I learned how to instruct the computer processors to do very specific tasks.

The amount of work a processor can do is measured by its processing speed. Imagine that in meetings for some reason, people speak in a very rhythmic way. Japanese is a language that actually has an element of time to each syllable. Suppose people in our meeting can say a syllable in exactly a ½ second. To communicate a thought of 40 syllables, 20 seconds will be required. A different set of people in another meeting may be able to say one syllable every ¼ second, thus communicating twice as many syllables in the same amount of time. But this doesn't mean that meeting will accomplish more than our meeting. It depends on the meeting language. If the language for the other meeting is verbose or formal like that used in Congress, such as "I agree that my esteemed colleague's proposal is the proper approach to the problem" (24 syllables) rather than "That's great" (two syllables) for our meeting, our meeting may actually accomplish more even though we speak fewer syllables per second.

Processors work in a similar way, executing so many computer "instructions" per second. Processor speeds are often measured in gigahertz now, megahertz a few years ago, reflecting that they can execute so many billions or millions of computer instructions in one second. But processor speed is only one part of how long a process will take. If the computer program is not efficient, it can waste the speed of the processor[10].

Hard Disk

The process of getting data to and from the disk is similar to writing in a binder. A disk has an "arm" that contains a read/write head. It is somewhat similar to both a pen and an eye, but this pen and eye only work with the binder; they don't write on the white board, don't use a white board marker on the

10. For additional information on computer speeds and instructions, see Chapter 17, "Programming Tools," on page 79.

binder, nor a pen on the white board. The pen can only be writing one thing at a time, and it cannot be reading at the same time it is writing. The person has to correctly position either his or her eyes to the right place in the binder to read, or the pen to the correct location to write. And just as it takes time to flip pages to find open space or find the needed information, it takes time for the disk to spin and be correctly positioned to read or write data.

In these programming classes, I learned that there are two basic ways to access data from the hard disk: sequentially or indexed. Sequential access is the oldest and the simplest. Indexed access is more complex, but more useful for many types of problems. Let's continue the analogy focusing on the binder or notebook to understand the difference. Let's assume the contents of our binder are so valuable we ultimately turn it into a full-fledged book.

Sequential access to a book is simple: pick up the book and begin reading until done. One can stop after a sentence, a page, a chapter, or after completing the entire book. If one finishes the book, everything the book contains will be known. But finding something in the middle of the book can be difficult and time-consuming.

Indexed access is more complex but more useful if we know we are going to pick up the book and try to find something without reading the entire book. But before building an index, one has to have an idea of how it will be used. Will we access our meeting minutes by date? Do the meetings cover multiple topics? If so will an index to a specific topic be important to see how it evolved over time? How detailed should we be about the topics? Should we have an entry for every time a word is used which will make our index very large, or only to the first use within a meeting? Perhaps we need another index to people's names with their associated action items.

Sequential disk access is similar to reading the book from the beginning. Imagine for a minute we have a computer file that has a record for each employee. When I am going to process payroll, I might know that everyone in this file needs a payroll check. It doesn't really matter who I start with. My program can read the first record on the file and using the employee name and salary, calculate the person's payroll for the period. The program then reads the next employee record, and proceeds through the file for every employee on the file. My program has used sequential access.

Indexed access means we have to know much more about the questions we will be asking of the data. The simplest form of indexed access, the form I used in my first programming class, is to know the length of each record. If each person's payroll record is 50 characters[11] and I need the 10th record, I know I can skip 499 characters and start reading the file at the 500th character to obtain that record. This type of index is very simple but not very useful. It would be like knowing that our meetings minutes always take up one and only one page, and we hold them on a regular schedule. We could use these two facts plus the date of the first meeting to know that if we skip 10 pages we would be at the meeting minutes for a certain day. It is indexed access, but very simple.

Use of the minutes over time will probably help determine what indexes we need to create, and even improve when we can't find something. But that time spent searching for something when we can't find it can take a lot of time; and in the world of computers for certain problems, sequential access to the whole thing (like the "find" feature in a word processor) may actually be faster[12].

Memory

If you have ever purchased a home PC, you might know that real memory, the white board in our example, is much smaller than disk storage, orders of magnitude smaller. A personal computer when I was taking these classes would have had 256 kilobytes of memory (256 times about 1000 bytes, or 256,000

11. Rather than "characters" the correct term for computer storage is "byte". One byte often holds one character, but it can under some conditions hold more or less than one character.

12. For more on I/O, see Chapter 18, "Input/Output," on page 83 and on indexes, see Chapter 19, "Select, Sort, Summarize," on page 89.

"characters" in a sense), but 20 megabytes of hard disk space (20 times approximately 1 million bytes).[13] Thus the hard disk could hold 80 copies of what fit in memory; as if the contents of the white board filled one page in our binder, and our binder has 80 pages in it. The amount of disk space available in most PCs has grown faster than the memory available, such that a standard computer today might have 160 times more hard disk than memory. Again, consistent with our analogy, it is easier to add pages to our binder than to add whiteboards to the room.

Computers can be made to look like they have more memory than they do by writing portions of memory to disk that aren't required at the moment. This would be similar to copying the contents of the whiteboard into the binder before starting on a new topic. But remember that working with the memory and the white board is faster than getting data from disk or the binder. Thus a break in the meeting occurs while someone copies all this down in the binder and the contents of the binder for the new topic is copied to the board. This process slows down processing significantly. But it is preferable to bringing the meeting to a halt because of lack of white board space, or having the computer stop processing because of lack of memory.

Certainly there are many more facets to computers. In Dr. Carlson's introductory classes I heard stories about other types of computers than PCs, and my COBOL class did include work on a larger shared machine. But I didn't really understand much about them. I also knew that somehow the instructions I wrote in the computer language—the procedures—were "compiled" into something else that really is what the processor used, but I didn't see the need to understand this in a lot more detail at the time. My interest was not in the computers themselves. It was in the information they provided. I needed to better understand the framework for providing information. I got my wish in my next semester, in studying one of the oldest information frameworks called accounting.

13. "1986: September - IBM announces the IBM PC-XT Model 286, with 640KB RAM, 1.2MB floppy drive, 20MB hard drive, serial/parallel ports, and keyboard for US$4000" from *A Partial History of the IBM Computers* at http://oldcomputers.net/ibm5155.html(Accessed May 2006).

Chapter 5. Accounting

Producing information had provided satisfaction that day on my mission as I typed that report. But the next semester I put down my computer books, and basically forgot the topic as I took an introductory accounting class. These courses seemed to have no dependence upon understanding computers. Yet the steps involved were similarly systematic, as I learned about basic bookkeeping, the systematic procedures of accounting.

The following year I entered the accounting program and began my indoctrination into a very old system of information gathering and reporting. Modern accounting is said to have begun with Luca Pacioli documenting double-entry bookkeeping methods in 1494 AD[14], only two years after America was discovered, and long before the invention of computers. I found the integration of all the steps very interesting, how this approach resulted in information that could be useful and actionable, yet from so many small seemingly disconnected parts.

The Balance Sheet

Financial statements enable understanding a person's or organization's finances. To simplify our discussion, let's focus our discussion on a single family's finances. Imagine your family has never tracked their finances. You have kept the receipts and records for things, but you have never added them up. One day you receive notice from a lender that you have not paid some bill. With this motivation, you immediately go to someone for financial counseling.

The first thing the counselor will want to understand is whether you own more than you owe others. The financial concept that answers this question is net worth. What is owned or legitimate claims upon other people's things are called assets. Financial obligations or potential obligations are called liabilities. Net worth is the difference between assets and liabilities.

The credit counselor will want to categorize, or make a listing of, your assets and liabilities. But even for individuals, listing everything—the couch, the chair, the pen, each type of stock, each credit card, etc. would be very tedious. So groups of similar things are created.

The balance sheet the counselor makes will list

Assets: Things you own

Less Liabilities: Things you owe

Equals Net Worth (for individuals) or Owner's Equity (for a company)

14. John R. Alexander, *The History of Accounting, Association of Chartered Accountants in the US (ACAUS)*, http://www.acaus.org/acc_his.html Accessed May 2006. Also Anita Sawyer Hollander, Eric L. Denna, J. Owen Cherrington, *Accounting, Information Technology, and Business Solutions*, 2nd ed. (© McGraw-Hill Companies Inc.: 2000) 80 - 81, and A. Crosby, *The Measure of Reality: Quantification and Western Society 1250 – 1600*, (Melbourne, Australia: Cambridge University Press, 1997), 202 and 208.

Balance Sheet		As of April 30, 2008		As of April 1, 2008	
Assets					
Checking Account		3,252.26		2,534.00	
Investment 401(k)		58,655.43		57,823.00	
Automobile		23,985.00		23,985.00	
Personal Property		15,245.00		15,245.00	
Home		185,000.00		185,000.00	
	TOTAL ASSETS		286,137.69		284,587.00
Liabilities and Net Worth					
Credit Card Payable		3,824.24		3,483.00	
Auto Loan Payable		16,902.20		17,274.19	
Mortgage Payable		157,067.78		157,377.03	
	TOTAL LIABILITIES		177,794.22		178,134.22
Net Worth		106,452.78		106,452.78	
Net Income For Month		1,890.69			
	TOTAL NET WORTH		108,343.47		106,452.78
	TOTAL LIABILITIES & NET WORTH		286,137.69		284,587.00

Figure 4. Example Balance Sheet

The Income Statement

Balance sheet measures financial position at one moment in time, for example, the morning you went to visit the counselor. Knowing where you are may help alleviate the immediate fear of being bankrupt, but it doesn't help you predict if you will soon be bankrupt. The income statement measures activity over time, or the change between two balance sheets. It helps understand if you are headed to bankruptcy.

When you were born you had no assets or liabilities. So the balance sheet was very, very simple. An income statement that covers your entire life from the day you were born until you went to the credit counselor will start with what you have earned in all your jobs, gifts you have received, interest on that savings bond grandma bought for you. All these are added up as individual sub-categories under the heading of Revenue.

Everything you spend for things you consume are called expenses, for example, tickets to a movie, the bag of chips for a snack, the payment of your phone bill. Certain payments you make are not expenses; they are an investment in an asset. Even though you pay someone to buy a savings bond, you haven't consumed anything; there is value in the thing you bought that you could exchange for something else.

There is a bit of balancing in making these category decisions. You might not consume something immediately, like the food in your kitchen cabinets. Yet because the value of the food is so low, and diminishes quickly as the food is eaten or spoils, it is easier to call it an expense when purchased rather than when consumed. The number of days of rent on a storage unit you have consumed since the last rental check is similar; called an accrued expense.[15]

15. Alternatively, we can record an asset and estimate consumption. Purchasing a car is a good example. The declining value of the car is called depreciation. It is that portion of the car you "consumed" over time. One could calculate the potential sales price car for at the end of each year and record an expense. But consumption of a car isn't really that precise of an activity to record on your income statement. It is usually easier to guess at the expected life of the car, divide the cost of the car by that number, and say you consumed that much each year you had it. Other examples of time-based consumption (earnings can also be estimated for that matter) include calculating how much of your storage unit you have consumed from the date you normally make the payment (say the 15th of the month) to the end of the month. These sorts of calculations are called "accrued" expenses (or revenue).

So, in the end, the income statement the counselor makes will list

Revenue: What you earned

Less Expenses: What you consumed

Equals Net Income or Net Loss

Income Statement		
For the Month of April, 2008		
Revenue		
Salary Revenue	4,487.30	
Gains on 401(k)	481.86	
TOTAL REVENUES		4,969.15
Expenses		
Mortgage Interest Expense	657.03	
Utilities Expense	147.23	
Federal Tax Expense	525.86	
State Tax Expense	105.17	
Auto Insurance Expense	425.00	
Auto Repair Expense	477.73	
Gas Expense	63.51	
Food / Other Expenses	574.00	
Auto Loan Interest Expense	102.94	
TOTAL EXPENSES		3,078.47
NET INCOME		1,890.69

Figure 5. Example Income Statement

Income statements show changes in balance sheets. The "bottom line" of the income statement is often the most important point. Insolvency (more liabilities than assets), as summarized on the balance sheet, is best predicted by expenses being greater than revenues as shown on the income statement. But financial reporting begins with the balance sheet because measuring things at a point in time is easier than calculating the change over time.

This relationship highlights the difference between transactions and balances. You are probably familiar with many of these concepts from simply looking at your checking or savings account statement. On those statements, there is usually a section that says what the balance was at the beginning and end of the month, similar to the balance sheet. There is another section that shows each deposit and withdrawal. These would be included in the income statement. If you add or subtract each of these, they explain the change between the beginning and ending balance.

The Accounting Cycle

Creating these reports once, figuring out one's financial position, is very different from doing this on an ongoing basis. To produce financial statements time and time again, one needs to understand the accounting cycle.

Figure 6. Steps in Accounting Cycle

Execute Business Events

Business events are things like making purchases, earning money, reconciling bank accounts. These are not accounting, per se, but rather the real work of life

Journal Entries

Your accountant would have asked that you provide pay stubs for every pay period, and receipts for every purchase you made. Then she would take these and create journal entries. For example, if you paid for gas with your credit card, she would turn that one receipt into two rows in a notebook that might look like this:

Journal Entry ID	Date	Account Number	Account	Debit/Credit (Sign)	Amount
JE1	08 Apr. 2008	534	Gas Expense	Debit (Increased)	34.93
JE1	08 Apr. 2008	211	Credit Card Payable	Credit (Decreased)	(34.93)

Description: Purchased gas

Figure 7. Example Journal Entry

These two rows are called a journal entry. The accountant would have recorded the Journal Entry ID on the receipt, to show it has been recorded and provide a way to trace the expense into the notebook. They would make similar entries in the notebook for all receipts and pay stubs.

Why two rows? Because bookkeeping, the process of accounting, is based upon the accounting equation. The basis of the Balance Sheet is:

Assets = Liabilities + Owner's Equity

The Income Statement uses this equation:

Net Income = Revenue – Expenses

These equations and recording two rows for everything keeps the system "in balance". It allows bookkeeping to check for errors in recording the information.

If we remove time periods from the equation, or in other words assume that we only produce one Income Statement covering one's entire life, then Owner's Equity = Net Income. Then we can combine the balance sheet and income statement equations:

```
Assets = Liabilities + (Revenue - Expenses)
```

Accounting can actually be done without the use of debits and credits, and many modern systems only use the terms to mean positive and negative.

We can use basic algebra to manipulate the accounting equation.

```
Assets = Liabilities + (Revenue - Expenses)
```

To be:

```
Assets - Liabilities - Revenues + Expenses = 0
```

You'll remember again from basic algebra that you can do anything you like to an equality, such as the accounting equations listed above, as long as you (1) do the same thing to both sides of the equation, or (2) the net result of what you do to one side equals zero. All journal entries have a minimum of two entries to hold to that rule. The effect of the two entries equal zero, one affecting an expense and one a liability for example.

A debit or credit, then, simply indicates if something is positive or negative relative to the natural account sign in the last equation. Cash has a natural debit or positive balance; it is an asset you want to have. A loan has a natural negative sign, or a credit balance, because it is a liability. Debits and credits are completely unnecessary if the users of the financial statements were happy having loans and revenues and even owner's equity reflected as negative numbers. Yes, because of the accounting equation, unfortunately the natural sign for revenues is negative and expenses are positive.

We'll assume our little family example here includes fifty-five rows in 14 different journal entries shown at the end of this chapter.

Chart of Accounts

The accountant determined which categories to track by referring to the chart of accounts. It lists the account number and name, like Cash, and next to it is noted if this is an asset, liability, equity, revenue or expense account.[16]

Acct. No.	Account Title	Acct. Type	Sign	Lvl
100	Total Assets	Asset	Debit	1
110	Current Assets	Asset	Debit	2
111	Checking Account	Asset	Debit	3
112	Investment 401(k)	Asset	Debit	3
120	Fixed Assets	Asset	Debit	2
121	Automobile	Asset	Debit	3
122	Personal Property	Asset	Debit	3
123	Home	Asset	Debit	3
200	Total Liabilities	Liab.	Cred.	1
210	Current Liabilities	Liab.	Cred.	2
211	Credit Card Payable	Liab.	Cred.	3
220	Long Term Liabilities	Liab.	Cred.	2
221	Auto Loan Payable	Liab.	Cred.	3
222	Mortgage Payable	Liab.	Cred.	3
300	Net Worth	Equity	Cred.	1

Acct. No.	Account Title	Acct. Type	Sign	Lvl
400	Total Revenue	Rev.	Cred.	1
410	Revenue	Rev.	Cred.	2
411	Salary Revenue	Rev.	Cred.	3
412	Gains on 401(k)	Rev.	Cred.	3
500	Total Expenses	Exp.	Debit	1
510	Interest Expense	Exp.	Debit	2
511	Mortgage Int. Expense	Exp.	Debit	3
512	Utilities Expense	Exp.	Debit	2
513	Credit Card Int. Expense	Exp.	Debit	3
520	Tax Expenses	Exp.	Debit	2
521	Federal Tax Expense	Exp.	Debit	3
522	State Tax Expense	Exp.	Debit	3
530	Auto Expenses	Exp.	Debit	2
531	Auto Loan Int. Expense	Exp.	Debit	3
532	Auto Insurance Expense	Exp.	Debit	3
533	Auto Repair Expense	Exp.	Debit	3
534	Gas Expense	Exp.	Debit	3
540	Other Expenses	Exp.	Debit	2
541	Food / Other Expenses	Exp.	Debit	3
600	Net Income	Net Inc.	Cred.	1

Figure 8. Sample Chart of Accounts

Accounts are defined for anything you want to see on the financial statement. You could ask the accountant to make accounts for each bank account and each type of stock you had if you wanted. You could in fact make accounts for stock you hoped to someday own. But accounts with no journal entries against them will not show up on the financial statements. This chart of accounts is a little bit like the index; what you will be interested in seeing later is decided beforehand. Journal entries can only be made against these set of accounts.

16. The chart of accounts might also note whether an account had a natural debit or credit sign. This would be used to interpret the journal entries if the sign wasn't used to indicate positive and negatives. It also might be used to multiply revenues and expenses by -1 for presentation on the reports so they are more intuitive.

Accounts, organizations, cost centers, and other reference data can often be expressed as hierarchies. Our simple account hierarchy could be depicted this way.

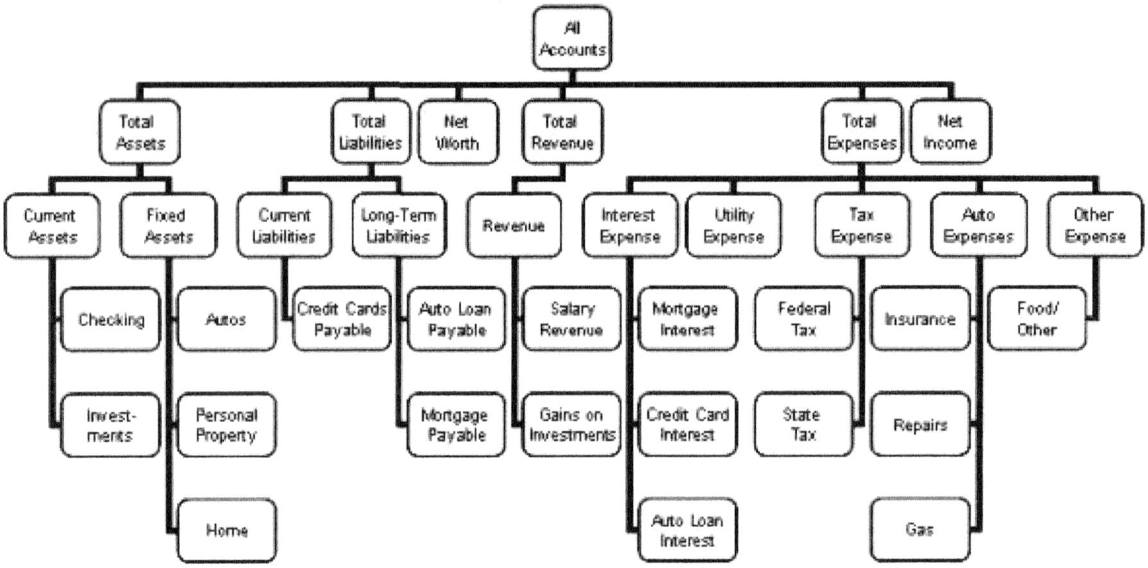

Also note—and this is important—that the chart of accounts has to be established before the first journal entry is recorded for which we want to report results. Everything you want to report on must be decided in advance. Accounts can be changed over time, but seeing historical data at a finer level of detail, for example each individual stock held rather than the lump sum in the investments account, wouldn't be possible from the accounting system records[17].

General Ledger

The notebook in which the accountant wrote the journal entries is called the General Journal. Periodically, she will "post" them to the General Ledger. Let's clarify what we mean by the word post.

A ledger is a summary of journals; in our example the ledger contains only one row for cash. It is a running total of the balance, similar to maintaining a balance in your check register. We would update the corresponding General Ledger account for each account on every row in the General Journal.

For example, the following are the entries that affect the credit card payable account. These are like the individual checks on your checking account statement.

17. Notice that on our chart of accounts the account numbers mirrors the hierarchy of accounts. Our journal entries use only accounts at level 3. The other levels are used to categorize lower level accounts. So even within account, there are more meanings than just one. The level one and two accounts show up on the financial statements. In a more sophisticated financial system, these amounts can be calculated, making production of the financial statements even easier.

Journal Entry ID	Date	Account Number	Account Title	Debit/ Credit	Amount	Description
JE0	01 Apr. 2008	211	Credit Card Payable	Credit	(3,483.00)	Opening Balance
JE1	08 Apr. 2008	211	Credit Card Payable	Credit	(34.93)	Purchased gas
JE6	22 Apr. 2008	211	Credit Card Payable	Credit	(198.78)	Purchased new tires
JE7	22 Apr. 2008	211	Credit Card Payable	Credit	(278.95)	Replaced alternator
JE9	27 Apr. 2008	211	Credit Card Payable	Credit	(28.58)	Purchased gas
JE10	28 Apr. 2008	211	Credit Card Payable	Debit	200.00	Credit card payment

Figure 9. Credit Card Payable Entries for April

The following shows the changes in the general ledger credit card payable balance if these entries are posted on the date of the entry. In other words, this shows the balance for the checking account after each "check" is cashed.

Date	Account Number	Account	Day's Movement or Change	End of Day Balance
01 Apr. 2008	211	Credit Card Payable		(3,483.00)
02 Apr. 2008	211	Credit Card Payable		(3,483.00)
03 Apr. 2008	211	Credit Card Payable		(3,483.00)
04 Apr. 2008	211	Credit Card Payable		(3,483.00)
05 Apr. 2008	211	Credit Card Payable		(3,483.00)
06 Apr. 2008	211	Credit Card Payable		(3,483.00)
07 Apr. 2008	211	Credit Card Payable		(3,483.00)
08 Apr. 2008	211	Credit Card Payable	(34.93)	(3,517.93)
09 Apr. 2008	211	Credit Card Payable		(3,517.93)
10 Apr. 2008	211	Credit Card Payable		(3,517.93)
...				
22 Apr. 2008	211	Credit Card Payable	(477.73)	(3,995.66)
...				
27 Apr. 2008	211	Credit Card Payable	(28.58)	(4,024.24)
28 Apr. 2008	211	Credit Card Payable	200.00	(3,824.24)
29 Apr. 2008	211	Credit Card Payable		(3,824.24)
30 Apr. 2008	211	Credit Card Payable		(3,824.24)

Figure 10. General Ledger Balances for Credit Card Payable

The General Ledger is the ledger that summarizes the results for a company or a significant portion of a company like a division.

Trial Balance

When we want to make a financial statement, first we would list the last row for each account, the current balance, on another sheet of paper. This is called a trial balance. We can test if everything has been recorded correctly by adding up all the balances. The debits should equal the credits; the positive numbers should equal the negative numbers; thus the name trial balance. The accounting equation should also be in balance. If the numbers don't add up we did something wrong. This little step checks our process and gives us all the numbers needed to produce financial statements.[18]

18. Note that this step does not check that everything was recorded. We could have lost receipts, and not made journal entries. Things may be in balance, but not necessarily accurate or complete.

	As of April 30, 2008	As of April 1, 2008
111 Checking Account	3,252.26	2,534.00
112 Investment 401(k)	58,655.43	57,823.00
121 Automobile	23,985.00	23,985.00
122 Personal Property	15,245.00	15,245.00
123 Home	185,000.00	185,000.00
211 Credit Card Payable	(3,824.24)	(3,483.00)
221 Auto Loan Payable	(16,902.20)	(17,274.19)
222 Mortgage Payable	(157,067.78)	(157,377.03)
300 Net Worth	(106,452.78)	(106,452.78)
411 Salary Revenue	(4,487.30)	
412 Gains on 401(k)	(481.86)	
511 Mortgage Interest Expense	657.03	
512 Utilities Expense	147.23	
521 Federal Tax Expense	525.86	
522 State Tax Expense	105.17	
532 Auto Insurance Expense	425.00	
533 Auto Repair Expense	477.73	
534 Gas Expense	63.51	
541 Food / Other Expenses	574.00	
531 Auto Loan Interest Expense	102.94	
Grand Total	0.00	

Figure 11. Sample Trial Balance

Producing the financial statements is a process of pulling each row off the trial balance in order by the account number, and putting them onto another sheet of paper, then using the accounting equations for totals on the balance sheet and income statement.[19]

Closing Entries

We've assumed thus far only one period in our financial reports. We made only one income statement covering your entire life. However, using shorter time periods for the income statement will help to more accurately predict what the future will be. We add an additional step when we want to end one Income Statement period and start another. The income statement accounts are "closed" for the prior period so that the income statement stops accumulating prior activity and shows activity from here forward.[20]

19. Alternatively if the hierarchy is used which contains levels for each of the subtotals on the financial statements, then even the subtotals are calculated and presented as rows of data in the reporting process.

20. Thinking back to the accounting equations, making closing entries is simply making the revenue and expense accounts zero, and making the increase or decrease in equity permanent. There are two ways to do this depending on what our accountant wants to do with the General Ledger notebook for the new income statement period: does she plan to use the same General Ledger notebook she used last period, or start a brand new notebook? The most common way is use the same notebook, to keep the balance sheet totals running. In this case, the trial balance amounts for all income statement accounts are negated and made journal entries, and an entry for the net income made to net worth. That way, when the journals are posted to the General Ledger for the next period, the balance sheet amounts aren't changed—the cash balance from the last day of the month is the same as the first day of the next month—but the income statement amounts are not; income statement accounts start with a balance of zero.

Journal Entry ID	Date	Account Number	Account	Debit/Credit (Sign)	Amount
JE14	01 May. 2008	411	Salary Revenue	Debit (Decreased)	4,487.30
JE14	01 May. 2008	412	Gains on 401(k)	Debit (Decreased)	481.86
JE14	01 May. 2008	511	Mortgage Interest Expense	Credit (Decreased)	(657.03)
JE14	01 May. 2008	512	Utilities Expense	Credit (Decreased)	(147.23)
JE14	01 May. 2008	521	Federal Tax Expense	Credit (Decreased)	(525.86)
JE14	01 May. 2008	522	State Tax Expense	Credit (Decreased)	(105.17)
JE14	01 May. 2008	531	Auto Loan Interest Expense	Credit (Decreased)	(102.94)
JE14	01 May. 2008	532	Auto Insurance Expense	Credit (Decreased)	(425.00)
JE14	01 May. 2008	533	Auto Repair Expense	Credit (Decreased)	(477.73)
JE14	01 May. 2008	534	Gas Expense	Credit (Decreased)	(63.51)
JE14	01 May. 2008	541	Food / Other Expenses	Credit (Decreased)	(574.00)
JE14	01 May. 2008	300	Net Worth	Credit (Increased)	(1,890.69)

Description: April Closing Entries

Figure 12. Sample Closing Entries

The closing entries record the "transfer" of the money from the Income Statement equation to Balance Sheet equation. The following shows the trial balance before and after posting these entries.

	As of April 30, 2008	As of May 1, 2008
111 Checking Account	3,252.26	3,252.26
112 Investment 401(k)	58,655.43	58,655.43
121 Automobile	23,985.00	23,985.00
122 Personal Property	15,245.00	15,245.00
123 Home	185,000.00	185,000.00
211 Credit Card Payable	(3,824.24)	(3,824.24)
221 Auto Loan Payable	(16,902.20)	(16,902.20)
222 Mortgage Payable	(157,067.78)	(157,067.78)
300 Net Worth	(106,452.78)	(108,343.47)
411 Salary Revenue	(4,487.30)	-
412 Gains on 401(k)	(481.86)	-
511 Mortgage Interest Expense	657.03	-
512 Utilities Expense	147.23	-
521 Federal Tax Expense	525.86	-
522 State Tax Expense	105.17	-
532 Auto Insurance Expense	425.00	-
533 Auto Repair Expense	477.73	-
534 Gas Expense	63.51	-
541 Food / Other Expenses	574.00	-
531 Auto Loan Interest Expense	102.94	-
Grand Total	0.00	0.00

Figure 13. Trial Balances after Closing Entries

Recording of new journal entries for May can go on without interruption while the trial balance and financial reports for April are being constructed.

The following fifty five rows make up the journal entries for the sample financial statements, including the closing entries.

Journal Entry ID	Date	Account Number	Account Title	Debit/Credit (Sign)	Amount	Description
JE0	01 Apr. 2008	111	Checking Account	Debit (Increased)	2,534.00	Opening Balance
JE0	01 Apr. 2008	112	Investment 401(k)	Debit (Increased)	57,823.00	Opening Balance
JE0	01 Apr. 2008	121	Automobile	Debit (Increased)	23,985.00	Opening Balance
JE0	01 Apr. 2008	122	Personal Property	Debit (Increased)	15,245.00	Opening Balance
JE0	01 Apr. 2008	123	Home	Debit (Increased)	185,000.00	Opening Balance
JE0	01 Apr. 2008	211	Credit Card Payable	Credit (Increased)	(3,483.00)	Opening Balance
JE0	01 Apr. 2008	221	Auto Loan Payable	Credit (Increased)	(17,274.19)	Opening Balance
JE0	01 Apr. 2008	222	Mortgage Payable	Credit (Increased)	(157,377.03)	Opening Balance
JE0	01 Apr. 2008	300	Net Worth	Credit (Increased)	(106,452.78)	Opening Balance
JE1	08 Apr. 2008	534	Gas Expense	Debit (Increased)	34.93	Purchased gas
JE1	08 Apr. 2008	211	Credit Card Payable	Credit (Decreased)	(34.93)	Purchased gas
JE2	15 Apr. 2008	111	Checking Account	Debit (Increased)	1,752.85	April salary
JE2	15 Apr. 2008	522	State Tax Expense	Debit (Increased)	52.59	April salary
JE2	15 Apr. 2008	521	Federal Tax Expense	Debit (Increased)	262.93	April salary
JE2	15 Apr. 2008	112	Investment 401(k)	Debit (Increased)	175.29	April salary
JE2	15 Apr. 2008	411	Salary Revenue	Credit (Increased)	(2,243.65)	April salary
JE3	17 Apr. 2008	221	Auto Loan Payable	Debit (Decreased)	371.99	Automobile payment
JE3	17 Apr. 2008	531	Auto Loan Interest Expense	Debit (Increased)	102.94	Automobile payment
JE3	17 Apr. 2008	111	Checking Account	Credit (Decreased)	(474.93)	Automobile payment
JE4	17 Apr. 2008	512	Utilities Expense	Debit (Increased)	147.23	Utility payment
JE4	17 Apr. 2008	111	Checking Account	Credit (Decreased)	(147.23)	Utility payment
JE5	20 Apr. 2008	532	Auto Insurance Expense	Debit (Increased)	425.00	Auto insurance payment
JE5	20 Apr. 2008	111	Checking Account	Credit (Decreased)	(425.00)	Auto insurance payment
JE6	22 Apr. 2008	533	Auto Repair Expense	Debit (Increased)	198.78	Purchased new tires
JE6	22 Apr. 2008	211	Credit Card Payable	Credit (Increased)	(198.78)	Purchased new tires
JE7	22 Apr. 2008	533	Auto Repair Expense	Debit (Increased)	278.95	Replaced alternator
JE7	22 Apr. 2008	211	Credit Card Payable	Credit (Increased)	(278.95)	Replaced alternator
JE8	24 Apr. 2008	222	Mortgage Payable	Debit (Decreased)	309.25	House payment
JE8	24 Apr. 2008	511	Mortgage Interest Expense	Debit (Increased)	657.03	House payment
JE8	24 Apr. 2008	111	Checking Account	Credit (Decreased)	(966.28)	House payment
JE9	27 Apr. 2008	534	Gas Expense	Debit (Increased)	28.58	Purchased gas
JE9	27 Apr. 2008	211	Credit Card Payable	Credit (Decreased)	(28.58)	Purchased gas
JE10	28 Apr. 2008	211	Credit Card Payable	Debit (Decreased)	200.00	Credit card payment
JE10	28 Apr. 2008	111	Checking Account	Credit (Decreased)	(200.00)	Credit card payment
JE11	29 Apr. 2008	541	Food / Other Expenses	Debit (Increased)	574.00	Various payments
JE11	29 Apr. 2008	111	Checking Account	Credit (Decreased)	(574.00)	Various payments
JE12	30 Apr. 2008	111	Checking Account	Debit (Increased)	1,752.85	April salary
JE12	30 Apr. 2008	522	State Tax Expense	Debit (Increased)	52.59	April salary
JE12	30 Apr. 2008	521	Federal Tax Expense	Debit (Increased)	262.93	April salary
JE12	30 Apr. 2008	112	Investment 401(k)	Debit (Increased)	175.29	April salary
JE12	30 Apr. 2008	411	Salary Revenue	Credit (Increased)	(2,243.65)	April salary
JE13	30 Apr. 2008	112	Investment 401(k)	Debit (Increased)	481.86	Gains on 401(k)
JE13	30 Apr. 2008	412	Gains on 401(k)	Credit (Increased)	(481.86)	Gains on 401(k)
JE14	01 May. 2008	411	Salary Revenue	Debit (Decreased)	4,487.30	Closing Entries
JE14	01 May. 2008	412	Gains on 401(k)	Debit (Decreased)	481.86	Closing Entries
JE14	01 May. 2008	511	Mortgage Interest Expense	Credit (Decreased)	(657.03)	Closing Entries
JE14	01 May. 2008	512	Utilities Expense	Credit (Decreased)	(147.23)	Closing Entries
JE14	01 May. 2008	521	Federal Tax Expense	Credit (Decreased)	(525.86)	Closing Entries
JE14	01 May. 2008	522	State Tax Expense	Credit (Decreased)	(105.17)	Closing Entries
JE14	01 May. 2008	531	Auto Loan Interest Expense	Credit (Decreased)	(102.94)	Closing Entries
JE14	01 May. 2008	532	Auto Insurance Expense	Credit (Decreased)	(425.00)	Closing Entries
JE14	01 May. 2008	533	Auto Repair Expense	Credit (Decreased)	(477.73)	Closing Entries
JE14	01 May. 2008	534	Gas Expense	Credit (Decreased)	(63.51)	Closing Entries
JE14	01 May. 2008	541	Food / Other Expenses	Credit (Decreased)	(574.00)	Closing Entries
JE14	01 May. 2008	300	Net Worth	Credit (Increased)	(1,890.69)	Closing Entries

This little process, outlined by Luca Pacioli and honed over half a millennium, now is remarkable. Continually doing these steps enables creating financial statements whenever desired. It is nearly mechanical, and perfectly suited to be automated by computers. The output from this process is a paper with words and numbers on it, something perfectly suited as output from a computer. And when this process was put into computers, it wasn't changed at all; the computer simply substituted for the ledger paper. I am amazed that it is such a remarkably enduring information gathering and reporting framework.

Nine months later I ducked as one of my accounting professors expressed his displeasure at the durability of that little system.

Chapter 6. Business Events

Without turning around, Eric Denna threw a chalkboard eraser at me as hard as he could. At least it seemed that hard. It whizzed past my head, bounced off the back wall of the classroom, and dropped onto the floor. Eric was a brand new professor. This was his first course. Perhaps that explains some of his enthusiasm, and the strength of his convictions. From the first day of class I sensed he was ready to change the world. And we were his tools.

I was in my junior year in the accounting program in the fall of 1988, and Eric was my professor for an introductory course in accounting information systems. He had just graduated from Michigan State University. His mentor had been William E. McCarthy and his specialty the REA Accounting Model. REA stood for Resources, Events and Agents. Eric was drilling it into our heads that an accounting system could be constructed without specifically recording revenues, expenses or any of the other accounting system classifications. That would change the definition of the accounting model. He wanted to make sure we understood that. So while he was writing REA on the board to begin the catechism, I flippantly said it was all clear to me: REA stood for Revenues, Expenses and Assets. The eraser was his answer.

The Book of Record

What would accounting be without revenues or expenses? Eric taught us that revenues, expenses, liabilities, assets and owner's equity were simply "classifications," "views" or perspectives of business events that were of interest to the accountants. But other views of these business events exists that were equally valid for other users. By forcing the accounting view of the data on top of the data capture, other uses or views of the data are destroyed. He said there was an entirely different way the system could be constructed to report the same results. He argued that that approach would allow the system to do much more.

What does that mean? Let's start simple by continuing our example, by defining what "the data" is, or perhaps more descriptively, what the "book of record" is. The term "book of record" is used by accountants to define the most important part of the accounting system; that which is audited and found to be accurate in "all material respects." The choices for the book of record from our accounting system are:

1. The information on the balance sheet and income statement,
2. The information on the trial balance,
3. The rows in the General Ledger, or
4. The journal entries.

Options one and two don't make a lot of sense; they are outputs from the book of record, not the book of record. Once the statements are produced they are static and don't change; they are not updated through the accounting cycle.

Most accountants would define the General Ledger (the GL) as the book of record. It is the last step in the accounting cycle before the creation of the trial balance and financial statements. It is an ongoing part of the process.

However, every balance in the GL has to be supported by journal entries. This then suggests that actually the journal entries could be the book of record. Instead of using the General Ledger as the source of producing the trial balance and the statements, it is possible to use the journal entries. But, to use the journal entries as the source of producing the trial balance and the statements, one would need to keep all the journal entries ever created and add them up to produce the trial balance as of a point in time.

Make no mistake; this isn't an easy thing to do. In our personal financial example, if some portion of the cash you have on hand was earned on your first summer job, you would need to have journal entries for it and all the other receipts and expenditures since then to calculate your cash balance today.

That seems a bit unrealistic. But if it were possible, would there be benefits? Does that system do more? Would it allow other "perspectives" or "views" of the financial information as Eric suggested?

Flexible Income Statements

One thing it would enable is creation of income statements for any period of time, eliminating the need for the closing entries. By using the general ledger, an income statement can be produced every day in April, the balances would always start from the first day of the month.

For example, if we wanted our accountant to give us an income statement for an odd period, say April 16th through May 5th, she couldn't use the GL for the income statement balances. Ignoring the closing entry, the following journal entries show that the salary revenue for that period should be $2,243.65.

Journal Entry ID	Date	Account Number	Account Title	Debit/ Credit	Amount	Description
JE2	15 Apr. 2008	411	Salary Revenue	Credit	(2,243.65)	April salary
JE12	30 Apr. 2008	411	Salary Revenue	Credit	(2,243.65)	April salary
JE14	01 May. 2008	411	Salary Revenue	Debit	4,487.30	Closing Entries

Figure 14. Salary Revenue Account Journal Entries

But if the General Ledger were used, it would show zero on May 5th.

Date	Account Number	Account	Day's Movement or Change	End of Day Balance
01 Apr. 2008	411	Salary Revenue		-
02 Apr. 2008	411	Salary Revenue		-
...				
15 Apr. 2008	411	Salary Revenue	(2,243.65)	(2,243.65)
16 Apr. 2008	411	Salary Revenue		(2,243.65)
...				
30 Apr. 2008	411	Salary Revenue	(2,243.65)	(4,487.30)
01 May. 2008	411	Salary Revenue	4,487.30	-
02 May. 2008	411	Salary Revenue		-

Figure 15. Ledger Balances for Salary Revenue Account for April

If we produced the income statement by adding up the journal entries within the date range, rather than from the GL, we could produce this and any other income statement.

Journal entries could be used to generate the balance sheet in a similar manner; the journals can be added up to determine the financial position at any point in time. There is a catch, though. All income statement accounts must also be included in the balance sheet calculation in order to show net worth or retained earnings. This would be necessary if there were no closing journal entries.

If we decided to call the journals the book of record, perhaps we have a bit more flexible reporting system as we have seen. These benefits aren't really all that great. But this way of thinking helps to highlight a key concept, which can lead to even greater flexibility in the accounting system.

Events

The "E" in REA Theory stands for "Event". The idea behind the theory is that events, business events, provide the basis for business reporting. A business event is anything the business wants to plan, execute, control, or evaluate. For example, in our personal financial world, being paid our salary is an event we would likely want to plan, execute by seeing that we actually get paid, control where the money is deposited, and evaluate any deductions taken out such as taxes when we do our income taxes.

It is likely that every journal entry made in our personal financial system is an event; we wouldn't have taken the time to make a journal entry of it if we didn't want to plan, execute, control or evaluate it. Thinking of the journal entries as events helps to understand the theory. Events are sometimes more commonly called transactions.

Transactions Versus Balances

This difference, between viewing the GL or the journal entries as the book of record highlights a key contrast in the approach to financial reporting: the difference between transactions and balances. Balances tend to be a point in time picture, much like the balance sheet. The GL shows the balance for each account after the posting process. The GL balances are immediately informative; there is no calculation to be done to make them useful. However, they aren't very flexible; they are mostly useful for the information they contain at that moment.

Transactions aren't as informative. They can be used as building blocks and combined in many ways to present information. But, they have to be added up to form balances before they become interesting.[21]

To show this graphically, the following are the transactions—the offset side of the journal entries—affecting the credit card payable account.

Journal Entry ID	Date	Account Number	Account Title	Debit/ Credit	Amount	Description
JE0	01 Apr. 2008	121	Automobile	Debit	23,985.00	Opening Balance
JE1	08 Apr. 2008	534	Gas Expense	Debit	34.93	Purchased gas
JE5	20 Apr. 2008	532	Auto Insurance Expense	Debit	425.00	Auto insurance
JE6	22 Apr. 2008	533	Auto Repair Expense	Debit	198.78	Purchased new tires
JE7	22 Apr. 2008	533	Auto Repair Expense	Debit	278.95	Replaced alternator
JE9	27 Apr. 2008	534	Gas Expense	Debit	28.58	Purchased gas

Figure 16. Single Side of Credit Card Payable Account Journal Entries

The following are the resulting balances at the end of each day from posting these transactions to the General Ledger Credit Card Payable Account Balance:

Date	Account Number	Account	Day's Movement or Change	End of Day Balance
01 Apr. 2008	211	Credit Card Payable		(3,483.00)
08 Apr. 2008	211	Credit Card Payable	(34.93)	(3,517.93)
22 Apr. 2008	211	Credit Card Payable	(477.73)	(3,995.66)
27 Apr. 2008	211	Credit Card Payable	(28.58)	(4,024.24)
28 Apr. 2008	211	Credit Card Payable	200.00	(3,824.24)

Figure 17. Credit Card Payable Account General Ledger Balances

What do the general ledger balances tell us? We can see the date, the account number and name, the day's change in the balance, sometimes called the movement, and the balance at the end of the day.

21. A much smaller set of reports are produced with listings of transactions without any modification.

Notice that the number of balances is less than the number of journal entries because we purchased tires and had the alternator replaced both on the same day. From the balances we can't see what we did on that day, just the net effect of all that happened. Another difference is that the journals have a description. Because more than one thing can happen on a day, the description would be meaningless summarized on the ledger.

Why would that be important? Notice that many of the journals deal with the car. Might it be useful to know when we last purchased tires; perhaps we could negotiate a discount if they had not lasted as long as expected? We can find this information on the journal entries, but not on the ledger.

And that is a major point Eric was trying to teach us. More information is available from the journal entries than the ledger. The financial reports aren't geared to tell us about car maintenance; they tell us about money. When we summarize transactions, like we do when we update the ledger, we lose information that might be useful to us or others. The accounting "view" of the data precludes other uses of it.

Balances have an affinity for the balance sheet. Transactions are sometimes called movements, in that they represent the changes in balances. They have an affinity for the income statement—the statement that explains changes in the balance sheet.

These affinities and relationships aren't always so straight forward. Sometimes balances are used as transactions, in that they are manipulated to form new balances and new information as we will see later. And although the income statement shows accumulated "transactions," it is produced as of a specific point in time using revenue and expense balances from the ledger. Thus the distinction between balances and transactions isn't always tidy and our language in describing them isn't very exact, but being able to recognize and use each is important.

Additional Attributes

Thus far in our financial system, we have been interested in one category of "things" called account. In our little financial example, there isn't much question about the "who" is involved. We have assumed that our financial system is just for us as an individual, but business financial systems aren't just for one person. A business is most often composed of groups of people, and the system has to produce reports for these groups. In business, the "who" is very important and a lot of work goes into keeping track of it all. Let's extend our example financial system in perhaps a bit of a farfetched way to show how this impacts the system, and how this can cause balances to become transactions if approached in a particular way.

Let's assume that our financial system is for our family, which is composed of more than one person. Each family member in our little system might use some ID, like a social security number, to record on the journal entries which ones are theirs. In our example, as in many traditional financial systems, a concept of a cost center is used to track the "who".[22]

22. Note that a hierarchy can be applied to the cost center table, the same as with the account table.

Cost Center Number	Cost Center Title	Level
CC100	Family	1
CC110	Dad	2
CC120	Mom	2
CC130	Children	2
CC131	Child 1	3
CC132	Child 2	3

Figure 18. List of Cost Centers

This cost center simply becomes another column on the journal entries containing numbers similar to the Account column. This column would also be added to the General Ledger. Thus when we post entries, we post them to a combination of account and cost center. At any point in time we can find what the balance is for a particular account for a particular cost center by looking in the general ledger. We can then produce a trial balance which is summarized by cost center as well as by account. Using these pieces of information, we can then produce financial statements for each person.

Let's suppose our journal entries for salaries identify whether they are for Dad, Mom or the first child.

Journal Entry ID	Date	Cost Center	Cost Center Title	Account Number	Account Title	Debit/ Credit	Amount	Description
JE0	4/1	CC110	Dad	111	Checking Account	Debit	1,140.30	Dad's Account Balance
JE0	4/1	CC110	Dad	300	Net Worth	Credit	(1,140.30)	Dad's Opening Balance
JE2	4/15	CC110	Dad	111	Checking Account	Debit	788.78	Dad's April salary
JE2	4/15	CC110	Dad	522	State Tax Expense	Debit	26.29	Dad's April salary
JE2	4/15	CC110	Dad	521	Federal Tax Expense	Debit	131.46	Dad's April salary
JE2	4/15	CC110	Dad	112	Investment 401(k)	Debit	87.64	Dad's April salary
JE2	4/15	CC110	Dad	411	Salary Revenue	Credit	(1,034.18)	Dad's April salary
JE12	4/30	CC110	Dad	111	Checking Account	Debit	788.78	Dad's April salary
JE12	4/30	CC110	Dad	522	State Tax Expense	Debit	26.29	Dad's April salary
JE12	4/30	CC110	Dad	521	Federal Tax Expense	Debit	131.46	Dad's April salary
JE12	4/30	CC110	Dad	112	Investment 401(k)	Debit	87.64	Dad's April salary
JE12	4/30	CC110	Dad	411	Salary Revenue	Credit	(1,034.18)	Dad's April salary
JE0a	4/1	CC120	Mom	111	Checking Account	Debit	1,140.30	Mom's Account Balance
JE0a	4/1	CC120	Mom	300	Net Worth	Credit	(1,140.30)	Mom's Opening Balance
JE2a	4/15	CC120	Mom	111	Checking Account	Debit	788.78	Mom's April salary
JE2a	4/15	CC120	Mom	522	State Tax Expense	Debit	26.29	Mom's April salary
JE2a	4/15	CC120	Mom	521	Federal Tax Expense	Debit	131.46	Mom's April salary
JE2a	4/15	CC120	Mom	112	Investment 401(k)	Debit	87.64	Mom's April salary
JE2a	4/15	CC120	Mom	411	Salary Revenue	Credit	(1,034.18)	Mom's April salary
JE12a	4/30	CC120	Mom	111	Checking Account	Debit	788.78	Mom's April salary
JE12a	4/30	CC120	Mom	522	State Tax Expense	Debit	26.29	Mom's April salary
JE12a	4/30	CC120	Mom	521	Federal Tax Expense	Debit	131.46	Mom's April salary
JE12a	4/30	CC120	Mom	112	Investment 401(k)	Debit	87.64	Mom's April salary
JE12a	4/30	CC120	Mom	411	Salary Revenue	Credit	(1,034.18)	Mom's April salary
JE0b	4/1	CC131	Child 1	111	Cash on Hand	Debit	253.40	Child's Account Balance
JE0b	4/1	CC131	Child 1	300	Net Worth	Credit	(253.40)	Child's Opening Balance
JE2b	4/15	CC131	Child 1	111	Cash on Hand	Debit	175.29	Child's April wages
JE2b	4/15	CC131	Child 1	411	Wages Revenue	Credit	(175.29)	Child's April wages
JE12b	4/30	CC131	Child 1	111	Cash on Hand	Debit	175.29	Child's April wages
JE12b	4/30	CC131	Child 1	411	Wages Revenue	Credit	(175.29)	Child's April wages

Figure 19. Cost Center Journal Entries

When we make a trial balance from a ledger that includes cost center as a posted element (a column), it would look like this:

Cost Center	Cost Center Title	Account Number	Account Title	Amount
CC110	Dad	111	Checking Account	2,717.87
CC110	Dad	112	Investment 401(k)	175.29
CC110	Dad	300	Net Worth	(1,140.30)
CC110	Dad	411	Salary Revenue	(2,068.36)
CC110	Dad	521	Federal Tax Expens	262.93
CC110	Dad	522	State Tax Expense	52.59
CC120	Mom	111	Checking Account	2,717.87
CC120	Mom	112	Investment 401(k)	175.29
CC120	Mom	300	Net Worth	(1,140.30)
CC120	Mom	411	Salary Revenue	(2,068.36)
CC120	Mom	521	Federal Tax Expens	262.93
CC120	Mom	522	State Tax Expense	52.59
CC131	Child 1	111	Cash on Hand	603.97
CC131	Child 1	300	Net Worth	(253.40)
CC131	Child 1	411	Salary Revenue	(350.57)

Figure 20. Cost Center Trial Balance

Now we have an interesting problem. We have added cost center to our whole system, and that allows us to produce information at a lower level of detail. But have we lost the ability to produce the summary results? Can our system still produce the consolidated family financial statements we showed in Chapter 5, "Accounting," on page 19 above? The trial balance now has multiple rows for one single account; one row for Dad's checking account and another for the Mom's and a third for the Child's[23]. There is a need to add together these rows before we can place them on the consolidated family financial statement.

This could be accomplished in a couple of different ways. One way would be to create another ledger, a summary ledger. In the summary ledger, we might only have account, and not record cost center, just like the ledger in our example above. We then post each journal entry to two ledgers, once to the detailed ledger, and then once to this summary ledger. We can then produce two trial balances, one from the summary that feeds the consolidated statements, and one from the detailed ledger that feeds the individual statements.[24]

This approach raises an interesting question: Which ledger, the summary or the detail, is the book of record?

Another approach is possible though. We could post only to the detail ledger, and then produce the detailed trial balance that includes cost center like that shown above. We could then take a temporary copy of the last detailed ledger rows and blank out cost center. We could then summarize these rows, by adding together like rows where two people had activity for the same account, to create a new trial balance for the consolidated entries. The new rows would look like the following[25]:

23. Note that the child's account title is "Cash on Hand" but the consolidated Account Title is Checking account. This system allows defining local accounts titles for individual financial statements different from the consolidated accounts.

24. An additional approach would be to use a reporting hierarchy. The net effect of this approach isn't a great deal different than the option of creating the additional entries or another ledger. It is just that these "created entries" using the hierarchy only exist long enough to be used on the report. They may never be actually stored anywhere. But the processing of "rolling up a hierarchy" creates them nonetheless.

25. Note that the bottom three rows are exactly the same amounts as in the original Figure 11 on page 26. The top three rows are not the same amounts because they are affected by other entries not included in the subset of entries in this cost center example. If all the journal entries had been used in the example, the trial balance would be exactly the same as that shown in the Sample Trial Balance.

Account Number	Account Title	Amount
111	Checking Account	6,039.70
112	Investment 401(k)	350.57
300	Net Worth	(2,534.00)
411	Salary Revenue	(4,487.30)
521	Federal Tax Expense	525.86
522	State Tax Expense	105.17

Figure 21. Summarized Cost Center Trial Balance

This second approach is interesting. Here we have taken the balances as of a point in time in the detailed ledger to make transactions that we then summarize to create new balances.

This now raises another interesting question: Which journal entries would be considered the book of record: The detailed journal entries that include cost center, or do we also include the new summary journals we've just created?

This same approach to report on new attributes is used through IT systems; when a new attribute is needed, more detail is created. Yet at report time, the detail has to be summarized out. Today's Finance have need to add attributes like Book Code (IFRS or Local GAAP), products, customer types, even customers for high value accounts. This constant contest, between the need for additional attributes on the one hand and the need for an instantaneous answer on various reports on the other, is what McCarthy and Eric were trying to get at.

Automation

Actually, a third approach is also available. We could add up each of the detailed journal entries, which includes cost center, and create both trial balances, by simply ignoring the cost center value when making the second trial balance. This can be done because we have computers. Eric started to intertwine accounting and my computer classes, and show they had a closer relationship than I had realized.

Adding up all the detailed journal entries each time a report is to be produced would be far too expensive if done manually. In a manual system, the investment in arithmetic has to be retained to produce the next period's report. Balances store this investment; transactions do not. Debits and credits were invented because people are error prone when doing math. They check that the investment made in math today has value tomorrow. However, the low cost and consistent accuracy of computing can make retaining this investment unnecessary, simplifying the entire system. This is at the heart of the whole matter Eric was trying to teach us. Computers make it possible to use transactions with more information on them to produce multiple outputs in a more flexible manner.

Additional options are available for a definition of the book of record besides just the GL or the double-entry journal entries. A different set of "journal entries" could also be considered the book of record. But now we start to depart from the standard process of accounting.

Chapter 7. Resources and Agents

In the midst of my classes with Eric, I continued to have core accounting classes; I continued to be steeped deeper and deeper in the accounting tradition of information gathering and reporting. In these classes I learned about things called subsidiary ledgers, places where particular types of accounting entries are kept. These ledgers helped simplify the accounting process by not requiring the recording of both sides of the journal entries, and recording other items of interest for reporting.

Accounting has a reputation for being inflexible and unbending in the way it is done; creative accounting is something no ethical person aspires to. But that reputation isn't accurate. The number of ways to record the information and produce the reports is very diverse, even within the double-entry system. And if subsidiary ledgers and other ways of recording information are taken into account, the options are even more diverse. Understanding an alternative can help make the REA theory clearer. One of the most common alternative accounting approaches is called singled sided accounting. The use of business events might be confused for this form of accounting. Let's make it clear what this is.

Single Sided Accounting

Single sided accounting as an alternative form of the double-entry accounting system has been around perhaps as long as or longer than the double-entry system and elements of it are very common even in today's financial reporting systems. Take for example the check register in our personal financial system. There is no reason to make two rows to record each check that is written, (1) one that says what liability was decreased or expense incurred, and (2) the other to show the decrease in cash in the checking account. The reason is that almost all the cash side entries would look exactly the same. By definition, recording the expense or liability side of the entries in the checking account register means we can infer what are the credit or debit entries to cash.[26]

These cash rows are called the "offset"; they are just the opposite side and always to the same account. The single sided accounting entries in the check register record our cash transactions and we only make the offset entry to the actual cash account periodically. We might record the offset to the general ledger when we reconcile the checking account monthly to reflect the cumulative effect of the changes in cash. In effect for the double-entry system, we have one massive journal entry posted monthly, where all the things we purchased are one set of rows, all the causes of deposits like our paychecks are the other rows, and the difference between the two is a single row offset increase or decrease in cash.

Now if every transaction we did always involved cash in the checking account, we could make our personal financial system such that we only record half of the rows in all of our entries. But this is too simplistic even for our simple example because we also have credit cards; we need to record how we paid because sometimes we used cash, other times the credit card.

Resources

Eric taught us that the "R" in REA stands for resource. If we were to view the cash or credit cards as a resource, would that change our system? In other words, can we make up a computerized financial system that records the events, and uses resources as a way to get to the financial statements?

Let's see if this system might work. We could decide that:

- Each Balance Sheet account is a Financial Resource
- Financial Resources are used to pay for or accomplish any Financial Event

---

26. Quicken, as a financial tool works this same way as the old hand written check register. By selecting the register within which the entries are made, Quicken infers the other side of the entry.

- Financial Events are Income Statement accounts
- Financial Resources can be transferred from one type to another, thus cash can be used to pay the credit card balance.

	Event ID	Date	Event Type	From Acct	From Account	To Acct	To Account	Amount	Description
1	JE0	01 Apr. 2008	Transfer	300	Capital Investment	111	Checking Account	(2,534.00)	Opening Balance
2	JE0	01 Apr. 2008	Transfer	300	Capital Investment	112	Investment 401(k)	(57,823.00)	Opening Balance
3	JE0	01 Apr. 2008	Transfer	300	Capital Investment	121	Automobile	(23,985.00)	Opening Balance
4	JE0	01 Apr. 2008	Transfer	300	Capital Investment	122	Personal Property	(15,245.00)	Opening Balance
5	JE0	01 Apr. 2008	Transfer	300	Capital Investment	123	Home	(185,000.00)	Opening Balance
6	JE0	01 Apr. 2008	Transfer	300	Capital Investment	211	Credit Card Payable	3,483.00	Opening Balance
7	JE0	01 Apr. 2008	Transfer	300	Capital Investment	221	Auto Loan Payable	17,274.19	Opening Balance
8	JE0	01 Apr. 2008	Transfer	300	Capital Investment	222	Mortgage Payable	157,377.03	Opening Balance
9	JE1	08 Apr. 2008	Event	211	Credit Card Payable	534	Gas Expense	(34.93)	Purchased gas
10	JE2	15 Apr. 2008	Event	113	Payroll Deduction	411	Salary Revenue	2,243.65	April salary
11	JE2	15 Apr. 2008	Event	113	Payroll Deduction	522	State Tax Expense	(52.59)	April salary
12	JE2	15 Apr. 2008	Event	113	Payroll Deduction	521	Federal Tax Expense	(262.93)	April salary
13	JE2	15 Apr. 2008	Transfer	113	Payroll Deduction	112	Investment 401(k)	(175.29)	April salary
14	JE2	15 Apr. 2008	Transfer	113	Payroll Deduction	111	Checking Account	(1,752.85)	April salary
15	JE3	17 Apr. 2008	Event	111	Checking Account	531	Auto Loan Interest Expense	(102.94)	Automobile payment
16	JE3	17 Apr. 2008	Transfer	111	Checking Account	221	Auto Loan Payable	(371.99)	Automobile payment
17	JE4	17 Apr. 2008	Event	111	Checking Account	512	Utilities Expense	(147.23)	Utility payment
18	JE5	20 Apr. 2008	Event	111	Checking Account	532	Auto Insurance Expense	(425.00)	Auto insurance payment
19	JE6	22 Apr. 2008	Event	211	Credit Card Payable	533	Auto Repair Expense	(198.78)	Purchased new tires
20	JE7	22 Apr. 2008	Event	211	Credit Card Payable	533	Auto Repair Expense	(278.95)	Replaced alternator
21	JE8	24 Apr. 2008	Event	111	Checking Account	511	Mortgage Interest Expense	(657.03)	House payment
22	JE8	24 Apr. 2008	Transfer	111	Checking Account	222	Mortgage Payable	(309.25)	House payment
23	JE9	27 Apr. 2008	Event	211	Credit Card Payable	534	Gas Expense	(28.58)	Purchased gas
24	JE10	28 Apr. 2008	Transfer	211	Credit Card Payable	111	Checking Account	200.00	Credit card payment
25	JE11	29 Apr. 2008	Event	111	Checking Account	541	Food / Other Expenses	(574.00)	Various payments
26	JE12	30 Apr. 2008	Event	113	Payroll Deduction	411	Salary Revenue	2,243.65	April salary
27	JE12	30 Apr. 2008	Event	113	Payroll Deduction	522	State Tax Expense	(52.59)	April salary
28	JE12	30 Apr. 2008	Event	113	Payroll Deduction	521	Federal Tax Expense	(262.93)	April salary
29	JE12	30 Apr. 2008	Transfer	113	Payroll Deduction	112	Investment 401(k)	(175.29)	April salary
30	JE12	15 Apr. 2008	Transfer	113	Payroll Deduction	111	Checking Account	(1,752.85)	April salary
31	JE13	30 Apr. 2008	Event	112	Investment 401(k)	412	Gains on 401(k)	481.86	Gains on 401(k)

Figure 22. Financial Events

If we were to create this type of system, it might look like the rows shown in the Financial Events figure above. The signs on the amounts are relative to their impact on the "from" Financial Resource. The trial balance used for our month-end financial statements in the Figure 11 on page 26 can be produced from just these rows. Because the trial balance is the basis for all the financial statements, no other information is needed. Remember, for our family financial example, the double sided entries required 55 rows of data; whereas there are only 31 rows[27] of data here.[28]

Creating such examples seems to have been a cottage industry for those interested in McCarthy's theory in those days; many examples were probably much more elaborate and comprehensive. I believe Eric's doctoral thesis was one example. This approach can be described quite easily to an accountant by noting that almost any Balance Sheet account can be calculated from the Income Statement rows alone. I remember Eric suggesting if we wanted to know what inventory was, we could add up all the goods

27. The number is not exactly half of the 55 rows because not every journal entry in our original system was composed of only two rows and additional rows were added to reflect the use of payroll deduction as a financial resource. Payroll deduction is a balance sheet clearing account, used because no other resource actually received the money before it was used for a financial event: paying taxes and investing in the 401(k).

28. See "Appendix 1: Accounting Model" on page 333.

produced, subtract goods shipped, and the difference are goods on hand. Want to know accounts receivable? Add up all the sales, subtract all the receipts and the difference is accounts receivable.[29]

My simple example is meant to show that an alternative to the traditional accounting model can work; it is not a serious suggestion of the "right" way to build an accounting system. It shows that a system which does not much resemble a double-entry accounting system could be considered the book of record. The primary benefit of my simple system would be many fewer recorded rows. Again, this isn't a big improvement; but perhaps important as we will see later on. Let's see if this system can be extended to make it even more useful.

Agents

The A in REA stands for Agents. Eric taught us that the definition of Agents was the suggested approach to deal with the "who" of accounting.

Cost centers, as discussed in the last chapter, record who inside the organization was responsible for a particular financial transaction. Adding cost center had a ripple effect upon our financial system, requiring either a new ledger or additional types of entries, or new trial balances to produce the different types of reports expected.

Our checking account register is an example subsidiary ledger in which we only make one sided entries, and then periodically make a two sided entry to the general ledger to record the net effect upon cash for a lot of transactions. Early on, well before computers, accountants realized that because only one side of the entry is made in the subsidiary ledger, adding a column to those journals didn't have the same ripple effect through the general ledger. Thus subsidiary ledgers are used to store additional information that is only of limited interest.

McCarthy recognized that a great deal of effort is also spent on recording the external "who" that is involved in a transaction; the "who" beyond that recorded in cost center. Most of this complexity in financial systems is embedded in subsidiary ledgers as well.

Subsidiary Ledgers

Most businesses have at least two types of subsidiary ledgers, accounts receivable and accounts payable, and two types of external agents: customers and vendors. Businesses track how much customers owe in the accounts receivable subsidiary ledger, and how much they owe vendors in the accounts payable subsidiary ledger. The one sided journals used to record these activities and the corresponding subsidiary ledgers are very similar for each.

Each customer or vendor is typically assigned a unique ID. If customers or vendors can have multiple accounts with our business (if we are a bank, one customer might have a checking account and a savings account), we might also have an account number (Note: not a GL account, but a customer or vendor account) recorded at the same time on the subsidiary ledger.

Just like the relationship of the general journal entries to the general ledger, the subsidiary journals are posted to the subsidiary ledger. Thus at any point in time, a particular customer or vendor balance can be found.[30]

This subsidiary journal and ledger approach to the reporting problem has the same benefits and draw backs as the general ledger. The balances are stored to preserve the investment in arithmetic, but we now

---

29. As we have shown with the cash and credit card account, this is true only if each Balance Sheet account is affected by only two Income Statement accounts.

30. Note that similar to the simple REA approach above, the subsidiary ledger also cannot use the inherent double-entry reconciliation. Other mechanisms must be used to ensure all records are recorded properly in a subsidiary ledger.

have multiple possible parts to the book of record, each with some portion of the information we recorded at the time the business event happened.

Alternative Agent Approach

Alternatively, we could eliminate the need for sub-ledgers if we add another two columns to the cost center example above, one for internal agent and another for external agent. We could then use the computer to add up the rows by the columns of interest to produce the report that we want when we want it. This approach shows that the REA model not only makes marginal improvements on the existing reports, such as allowing production of an income statement at any point in time and reducing the number of entries required to produce the report, but it significantly reduces the number of ledgers maintained and intermediate journals needed to post to each of these systems. This change in definition of the book of record has far reaching impacts for how reporting systems are constructed.

The benefits of making this change alone may not outweigh the cost. This approach requires keeping the journal entries from the beginning of time to calculate right now any report we need. So the reduction in the number of systems and subsidiary ledgers may be outweighed by the cost of the engineering needed to make the computer capable of summarizing all that data even if it were kept.

Eric, and the REA theory, suggested there is actually one more possible definition of the book of record: the actual receipts, bank and other statements used to create the journal entries. The real power of the theory is demonstrated when we expand the accounting model to include new types of information. To do that, we will need to analyze our information needs in greater detail. The steps we will follow came in a subsequent class.

Chapter 8. REAL Analysis Method

I couldn't keep myself from needling Eric in later classes as well. A year or so after he introduced me to the event based concepts, I took a database design class from him. I had learned Lotus 1-2-3 the prior semester, and was familiar with the "database" functions of the spreadsheet. It allowed users to select certain rows of data using criteria entered into other rows. I repeatedly pointed out these functions to Eric, and went so far as to create spreadsheet macros that demonstrated the "ability" to do all sorts of database functions. These generated a few laughs from the class when I showed them as part of our project demonstrations, but I couldn't convince Eric that a spreadsheet was a valid database.

In another class from Eric I learned how to draw pictures, but it wasn't an art class. It was a system analysis class. System analysis is the process of deciding what a computer system should do. It entails drawing system blueprints and making models of how the system will be used.

Eric suggested we should make a REAL business process model, a type of blueprint. After I graduated, Eric updated the REA acronym that McCarthy had coined to be REAL, which stands for Resource, Events, Agents, and Locations. Similar to any blueprint, the paper version can be easily changed before the real thing is constructed.

If the basic component of a building blueprint is a room, with walls, a door, and windows, the following would be the basic blueprint component of McCarthy's business process model.

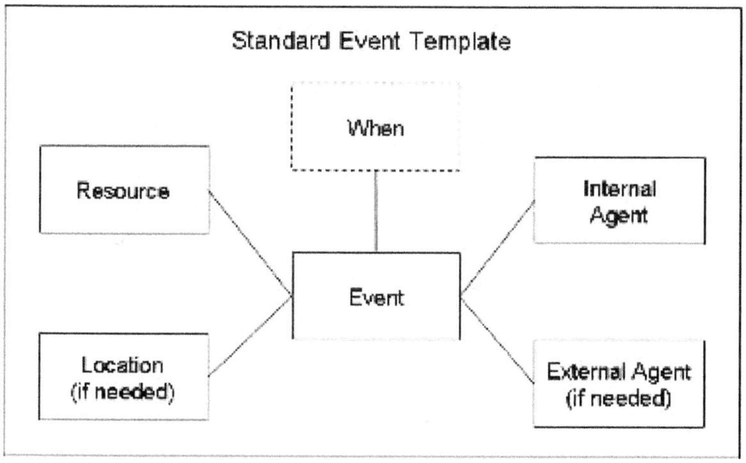

Figure 23. Standard Event Template

The following picture shows the basic blueprint for the financial transactions we talked about in the prior chapter.

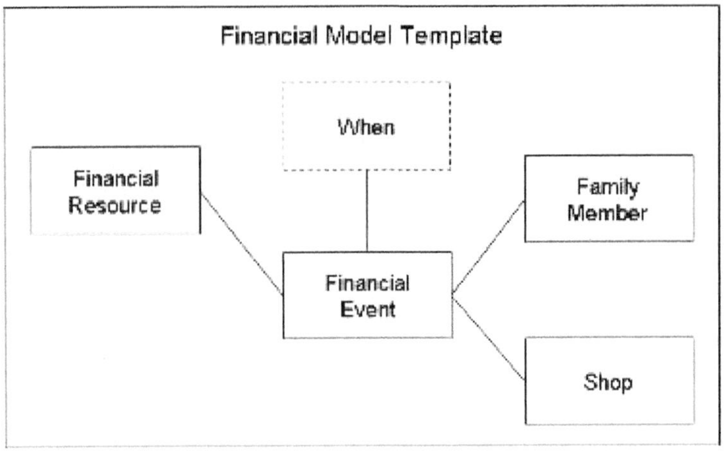

Figure 24. Financial Event Model

Expanding on the example in the prior chapter, financial resources are our Balance Sheet accounts and financial events are the Income Statement accounts, as well as the transfers between Balance Sheet accounts. Agents define the family members in our example system, in addition to the store or shop. The "when" is shown in dashed lines because if we simply record the date on the financial events we will have the "when" recorded.

To begin creating our blueprints, Eric suggested we start by identifying "strategically significant business activities" or events.[31]

Step 1: Understand the Organization's Environment and Objectives

This step throws the scope of what our system might do wide open. It assumes that the purpose of accounting is to provide information, and not just financial information. It goes back to the premise of Pacioli's system: accounting was the information provider for the organization. So we start by deciding what information is worth the time and cost to capture and maintain. The type of information we could gather is almost unlimited. Keeping with our family example, most every family records birth, graduation, marriage, and death dates, but we probably don't require a sophisticated system for one family's events. On the other hand, no one I know reports on washing dishes, vacuuming, doing the laundry, or mowing the lawn.

Let's assume we need financial information, so all our journals are events. So our new system has to at least do what the personal accounting system above does. From there, what other type of information do we want to capture?

Looking at our family journal entries, we have a few transactions dealing with cars. Let's assume that we really like cars, and we buy fairly expensive cars. Perhaps we also pride ourselves on maintaining our cars very well, but if we had better information about what had been done when, we could do even better.

---

31. Although not taught in my classes in school, Eric, working with Anita Sawyer and Owen Cherrington, developed these six steps later and documented them. Anita Sawyer Hollander, Eric L. Denna, J. Owen Cherrington, *Accounting, Information Technology, and Business Solutions*, 2nd ed. (© McGraw-Hill Companies Inc.: 2000) 46 -64.

Journal Entry ID	Date	Account Number	Account Title	Debit/ Credit	Amount	Description
JE0	01 Apr. 2008	121	Automobile	Debit	23,985.00	Opening Balance
JE1	08 Apr. 2008	534	Gas Expense	Debit	34.93	Purchased gas
JE5	20 Apr. 2008	532	Auto Insurance Expense	Debit	425.00	Auto insurance
JE6	22 Apr. 2008	533	Auto Repair Expense	Debit	198.78	Purchased new tires
JE7	22 Apr. 2008	533	Auto Repair Expense	Debit	278.95	Replaced alternator
JE9	27 Apr. 2008	534	Gas Expense	Debit	28.58	Purchased gas

Figure 25. Car Related Journal Entries

So our new system is a Personal Finances and Car Maintenance Information System.

Step 2: Identify Strategically Significant Operating Events

Do we need to record every event that deals with the car, such as when we wash it? Probably not. As we look at our car related journal entries, we can see that not every act of maintaining the car results in a journal entry. Suppose we know that we checked the oil and tire pressure during the month. But neither of those had any financial impact, so we don't have a journal entry about them. Yet, to maintain the car better, we need to know about them as well. Let's assume that we really like cars, and we buy fairly expensive cars. Perhaps we also pride ourselves on maintaining our cars very well. But if we had better information about what had been done when, we could do even better. Additionally, let's record the following events related to the car.

- Gas purchases, to track gas mileage
- Tire maintenance, including purchase and rotation
- Additional details about other maintenance

Step 3: Analyze Each Event and Identify Resources, Agents, and Locations

So what about those events do we want to know? Eric suggested we think like a reporter.

- What happened?
- When did it occur?
- Who was involved and what roles did they play?
- What resources were involved and how much?
- Where did the event occur?
- What can go wrong during the execution of the event?

Looking at the car journal entries above, we can see that there really isn't much information about the car in the entries themselves. We know when something happened, at least the payment date. We know we used the credit card, a financial resource, and the amount. Our financial system has external and internal agents. The company name might also tell us the where—the location—at least imprecisely.

So elements of what we need to know are on the financial events. But the main thing that is missing is the car maintenance event. The journal entry documents the paying for maintenance, not maintaining the car. The only thing that gives some sense of the maintenance done is the description. And how complete is that?

Think about the receipt from the auto mechanic. The journal entry and financial event is what is at the bottom of it: the total amount. But think of all the lines on the receipt. They checked oil, filled wiper fluid, checked brake pads, rotated tires, and perhaps a host of other things. Each one of those rows might have a price on it, but we didn't record that. The events our financial system recorded were a summary of the details of maintaining the car. That is the point of what Eric was trying to teach us: the accounting view of the data precludes other uses. It leaves out information that doesn't affect the financial statements, but may be critical to the organization.

So for each car maintenance event, we are going to record:

- The mileage (a form of time) at the time of maintenance
- The vehicle (resource)
- Each service (resource) we are paying for
- The family member who was responsible for getting it done (internal agent)
- The shop that did the work (external agent and location)
- The date and time of the payment.

The next steps start to move us from the accounting world into the technology world; but don't take that to mean it doesn't need to be understood by the business. Similar to building a home, the homeowner still has a lot to say about what kinds of lighting will be used, and how big the shower is after the basic rooms have been designed.

Step 4: Identify Direct Relationships Among Resources, Events, Agents, and Locations

We now move into the world of database design. To keep our explanation simple, we'll use the concept of spreadsheets to explain the next steps. Many of the basic functions of a database can be understood by someone familiar with a spreadsheet.

Similar to spreadsheets, databases are made up of tables, which usually have a set number of columns, that are "populated" with, or contain, rows of data. In our spreadsheet world, let's assume that each tab of the spreadsheet is a table. Each Resource, Event, Agent, or Location and perhaps Time would be a separate tab on the spreadsheet. We next specify the relationship between each of the tabs: Each row on one tab relates to one (1) or many (m) rows on the other tab. We end up with a picture that might look like Figure 26 on page 47:

This is an entity-relationship diagram, a very common type of 'blueprint' for information systems. Small letters are used to indicate the relationship of the rows in the tables to the rows in other tables. For example, each car (a row in the car table) has maintenance done to it (a row in the maintenance event table), but each maintenance event only services one car. We don't record on one service event the lube for one car and check tire pressure for the other car. We represent this on the diagram as a 1 on the side of car, and an 'm" on the side of Maintain Car events: one car is involved in many maintenance events. These numbers are called the cardinality.

Think of each box on the diagram as a tab of a spreadsheet. Each maintenance event adds a new row to the maintenance tab of the spreadsheet. But as we add new maintenance events, we don't add new cars to the cars tab of the spreadsheet. We simply have one column in the maintenance event tab that records which car (using its identifier like a car number or name) is involved in the maintenance.[32]

32. Linking the REA business modeling approach to an Entity Relationship Diagram is discussed in Armitage, Howard M., *Linking Management Accounting Systems with Computer Technology*, published by The Society of Management Accountants of Canada, Hamilton, Ont. [September 1985].

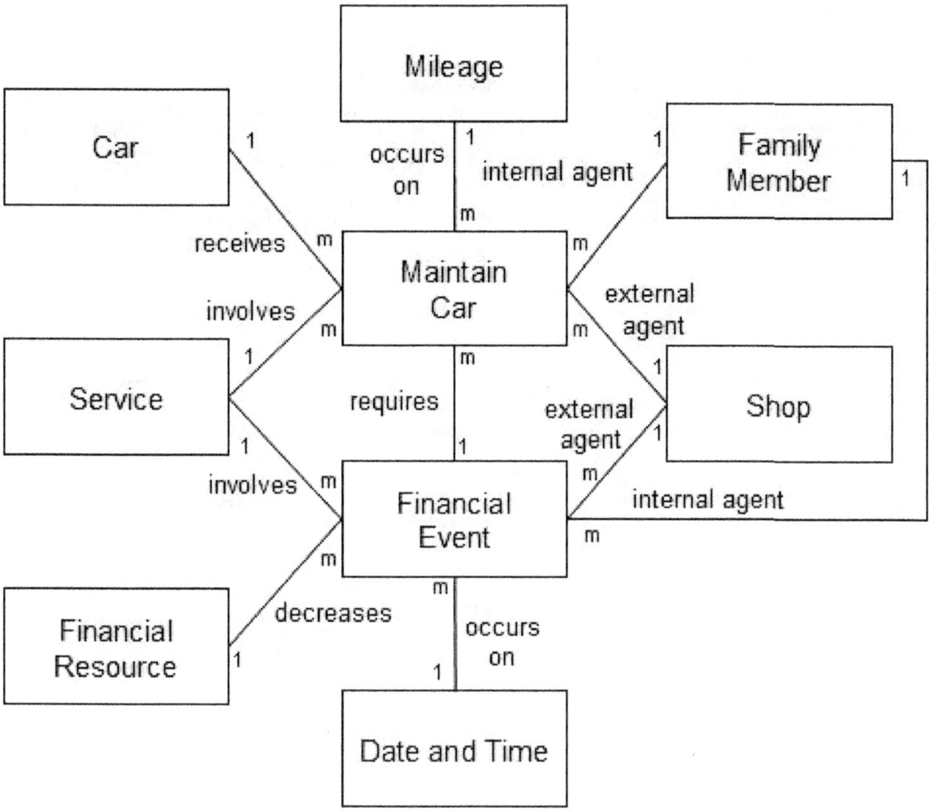

Figure 26. Process Model with Relationships

Step 5: Identify the REAL Relevant Behaviors, Characteristics, and Attributes

The next step in the process is to define what we want to know about each one of the boxes. This is identifying the attributes of our tables in the database, or more simply the column headings for each tab of our spreadsheet.

Suppose that below are the things we want to know about each of our Resources, Events, Agents, Location, or Time, the columns of our tables.[33] We'll underline the key or unique identifier for each row.

Entity (Table)	**Attributes (Columns)**
Financial Resource	Financial Resource ID Name, Bank or Credit Card Account Number, Institution Name, Contact Name
Car	Car ID Car Name, Car Make, Car Model, Year Made, Year Purchased
Family Members	Family Member ID Family Member Name, Birth Date, Drivers License Number
Shop	Shop ID Shop Name, Address, Phone, Contact Name, Hours
Mileage	Mileage

33. Mileage and Date and Time, you can see, don't have many things to describe them. We only want to keep track of one attribute on each one of them. For this reason, we will likely simply put the mileage and the timestamp on the events themselves. Thus, in the last version of our plans, we'll make these boxes dashed boxes, meaning we are recording these things, but not in separate tables.

Entity (Table)	Attributes (Columns)
Date and Time	Timestamp
Maintain Cars	Maintain Event ID ID's from other tables: Car ID, Family Member ID, Shop ID, Other Attributes: Amount, Mileage and Date and Time (the actual mileage and date and time, rather than an ID, are placed right in the table)
Service	Service ID Service Name (change oil, replace alternator, etc.), Maintenance Event ID

Defining the columns takes longer than defining the tables because there are more of them. Populating the rows takes even longer. Imagine how long it would take to type in all the values for a spreadsheet that has 10 columns, each one is about 10 characters in length, and which contains 1000 rows: That is 100,000 characters that would need to be typed. That is perhaps 10 hours of typing for an average typist.[34] The rows of data are really what we need to get to; they are the point of reporting.

Results

We now have a simplified set of plans for our new information system[35]. This set of steps, and the resulting plans, are not that foreign to anyone who has constructed business information systems. A very similar set of diagrams, and the system built from them, could be used to build systems for manufacturing, banking, sales, and a host of others.[36]

Now imagine we have actually constructed the system, in a very simple way. Imagine a spreadsheet with a tab for each of the boxes, with the above column headings for each tab. Having created the spreadsheet, we have diligently captured each business event we outlined, our car maintenance events and all financial transactions for some period of time. Having captured this data, we can now query against the tables, combining them in myriad ways to produce reports.

This single system can not only generate the financial statements, it also can generate car maintenance reports. These car maintenance reports will always reconcile to the financial statements. The two types of reports can be integrated, showing costs of car maintenance, cost by car, cost by shop, and financial responsibility by family member.

The rows of data in our "spreadsheet" database are very different from the simple little financial system our accountant set up. Eric taught us, and McCarthy's paper exposed that, really there is no need for a finance system at all. In modern corporations, with modern information systems, the amount of data actually created by finance is very small compared with the data that comes from these other systems. It is, therefore, theoretically possible to gather the finance data needed from all these other systems and combine it together to produce the financial reports. The amount of data duplication is reduced; finance becomes a more relevant function as it drives a broader view of information needs in the organization; and the overall IT architecture becomes more flexible.

Having gained this understanding, my time in school was coming to a close. Such changes naturally cause reflection upon what one has learned and what one still doesn't seem to understand.

34. Assuming 33 words per minute and each word contains on average five characters.

35. Of course, many more plans are necessary to determine how data is put into these table and taken out of them to produce reports. But the premise of the theory is that capturing the appropriate data for each business event will make the these tasks much easier.

36. Kevin W. Young and Terry Magee took these concepts further in the PwC methodology Ascendant Section R0615 Event-Driven Business Modelling. See"Appendix 2: Event Driven Business Modelling" on page 335 for more information.

Chapter 9. The Ivory Tower

We have reviewed what I learned in school about the basics of computers and bookkeeping and financial reporting. We have explored whether an alternative to the standard general ledger and journal entries could provide the financial statements. We reflected on what else might be considered the book of record besides the general ledger. We considered using just the journal entries which meant we didn't have to store balances because the computer can add them up quite efficiently. This system could generate the financial statements at any point in time. We no longer have to close the books in order to have the Income Statement.

We then considered a different set of "journal entries" as the book of record, something close to single sided accounting. This reduced the number of rows we had to record to get to the same answer. But both of these approaches are still pretty focused on the accounting process; the information we captured wasn't expanded to other attributes very easily.

We then analyzed the system in terms of all information needs, not just the accounting needs. This last approach, in a certain sense, placed the accounting function for automobile related transactions right in the middle of a car maintenance system. We could, therefore, from the same data, produce not only car maintenance reports, like cost per mile driven, but also the data needed for financial reports as well. We could do this without having duplicated the data in a car maintenance system and a separate financial system, or having tried to put that data back together to show the reports after it had been captured and stored separately.

We've shown that the financial information in our personal financial system can be stored in different forms, and yet produce the basic financial information needed. Neither of the last two systems have much resemblance to Pacioli's system, or something that would immediately qualify for most accountants as the book of record. But all the information needed is there.

However, moving from the ivory towers of academia to the real world teaches there are a lot of reasons why things have developed the way they have; and changing all that is not easy or inexpensive.

As noted, one reason is that accounting is tradition bound. The other though, is that although computers are much more efficient at math than humans, they still have limited capacities: The space on the white board is limited, the speed of the data transfer from disk is slow, and the verboseness of the language or meeting procedures dictates processing speed.

The pure unadulterated academic theory could require massive amounts of storage and processing power, and experience shows is impractical to implement at scale. This is because the volume of data needed to recreate the ledger if no summarization process were performed at all is very large.

This need to balance computing and storage costs with the broader use of data was recognized by McCarthy in his original 1982 paper: "To this point in the paper, events accounting has been viewed in terms of maximum temporal generality with all transaction data being maintained indefinitely. During design of an actual system, quite obviously, consideration of both decision usefulness and storage costs would temper these requirements somewhat and identify places where temporal summation of event data might be appropriate. An important point to remember about REA accounting model in this respect is that modifications to the ideal (complete events system) are made knowingly and only after an exhaustive cost-benefit analysis of *all* (not just accounting) data usage has indicated that the adjustments make economic sense. Imperfections are the result of deliberate choice. Such a process is in sharp contrast where traditional summations are routinely directed by reporting cycles. In REA terms, closing summations are usually derived data or viewed data, and they should be treated as such."[37]

Both accounting tradition and computer scalability have resulted in few practical implementations of the theory over the years.[38]

I remember meeting with Eric in his office after the last class I took from him. Eric asked me how I had felt about the final exam. I don't remember doing poorly on it, but not acing it either. I sensed he wanted to understand what I had learned from the class, and how to improve his explanation of the topics; I don't think I provided much insight. Yet I do remember feeling as if the material all made sense to me, but I just wasn't sure why it all mattered. If what he explained was possible, what was all the fuss about? We should just do it. With more practical experience, I would come to understand why it wasn't that easy.

I also remember another time in Eric's class. It seems he had returned from a consulting trip and had learned more about how the theory was being advanced on a project. I vaguely remember him handing out a picture that looked something like the following, and saying the technology feasibility of the approach was much more possible than he had previously thought.

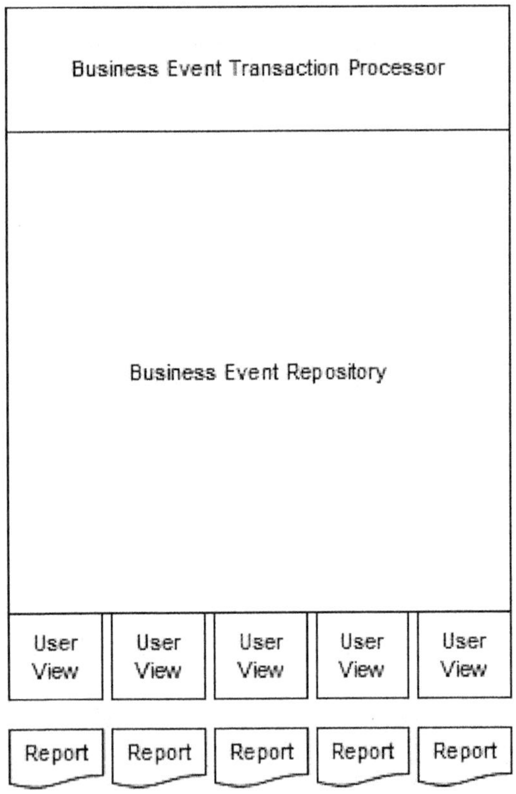

Figure 27. Event Repository Architecture

To take my understanding further, I needed to study with the person who had drawn that picture.

---

37. William E. McCarthy, *The REA Accounting Model* p. 572.

38. As McCarthy concluded in 1999, "Completely customized implementation of a new enterprise information system is not a common occurrence..." William E. McCarthy, *Semantic Modeling...*, 6 of 11.

Part 3. The Partner

The number of potential home configurations is possibly unlimited. However, not every configuration one might imagine is possible. A roof cannot be made to levitate without support. Yet innovations in home building have occurred, at times with dramatic effect. Those innovations are built upon understanding the principles of the engineering involved.

Likewise, computers can be applied to problems in perhaps unlimited ways. And yet, certain things are not possible; others could be possible if the engineering principles involved were understood and applied. We aren't talking about inventing new molecular structures. It's about using computing principles that we discarded when the price of computer capacity dropped: we thought we no longer needed them.

The cost of abandoning these principles is never presented on a single bill to an organization. Rather, they are hidden and agreed to in small decisions, which accumulate later into very large numbers.

If we think about how the machine works, and we dust off these long dormant principles, we find incredible power in today's computers, power which makes some things possible. Rick has often said "How you solve a problem can be more important than what problem you solve." If we use these principles, a host of other problems never appear.

Chapter 10. Reality

In my final years in college I had more classes in traditional accounting, including the two broad categories of accounting: financial and management accounting. After that I graduated and went to work for Price Waterhouse in Salt Lake City as a staff accountant in the auditing department. I worked there for 2 ½ years and gained an appreciation for why things are the way they are.

Financial Standards

Financial accounting is concerned with external reporting, or releasing financial information outside the organization. The annual statement for a company is produced by financial accounting. These financial statements are built upon financial reporting standards. The free-market economy is built upon the premise that financial results in different companies can be compared because objective standards were used to measure the results.

Financial accounting standards in the US started to be codified in 1930 in response to the US stock market crash. As they became codified, they were called GAAP, Generally Accepted Accounting Principles. Because of this long development process, they are very advanced, perhaps the most comprehensive and advanced reporting standards that exist. Initial standards were developed locally in many countries, but with globalization new standards have been developed and are taking hold. The latest set of standards is called IFRS, International Financial Reporting Standards. Standardization continues.

Accounting standards are meant to increase consistency, reliability, relevance, and comparability.[39] The process of creating and selling an airplane is much different from making and selling potato chips, and making the financial results comparable is challenging. Suppose an airplane manufacturer could only recognize revenue (record on the income statement) when they actually shipped a plane. They would have huge losses for many years to be followed by a period with huge revenues. Comparing their financial results to a potato chip manufacturer could only be done with income statements that cover a decade or so when the airplane manufacturer's financial results leveled out. Measuring the financial results of an airline manufacturer against a consulting services company means even more differences. But the standards form agreement about what those differences are, and how to compare the results of the two organizations.

Although they aren't expressed this way too often, effectively, the standards are a set of definitions of business events we are all familiar with: Sale, shipment, withdrawal, payment, etc. They help define when these events occur, and what basis should be used to measure them. For example, if one system recorded the salary expense business event when one receives an offer for employment, and another system when paid, obviously the financial reports will not be consistent. Effectively, people know what a sale means because the accounting standards define it.

I left some of Eric's classes feeling the accounting model could be thrown out. However, I came to understand that these definitions must be applied consistently in the business systems. For example, some systems which "sell" materials to another part of the business just treat the other division as if it were a separate company. The system doesn't care if it is a real customer or not. The source system applies "system GAAP" which is whatever the programmer understood. The financial system might be responsible to identify these internal customers and eliminate these "sales" from showing up on the income statement. So although over the course of all the systems within a company the financial reporting standards might be applied, at any one point in the process, they might not be met.

39. Financial Accounting Standards Board (FASB) *Statements of Financial Accounting Concepts: Accounting Standards* 1997/98 Edition Statement No. 2 (John Wiley & Sons, Inc. © 1997) 27-29.

Although the standards can't be thrown out, they also shouldn't be mistaken for dictating how the financial systems should work. At times people believe they do, and they confuse the process for the results. The importance of these standards, and the authority and responsibility of the accountants to "sign-off" or certify their accuracy (with the all-important caveat of "in all material respects") means at times those who have come to understand technology little have an inordinate say in how it must be applied.

Management Accounting

Management accounting is concerned with internal reporting, or producing information for use inside the organization. Historically it was concerned with determining cost of products. For example, the accountants would add up the costs for a factory for some period of time, divide that by the number of units produced to arrive at a cost per unit. This process isn't as straightforward as the example seems. How much of the cost of building the factory should be included in the cost of each unit? The cost of the first item manufactured is very high. So accountants develop assumptions about how long the factory will be used to determine how much should be allocated to each product.

If the company only has one factory and makes one type of product, then perhaps the life of the factory is the only assumption that has to be developed. This is unlikely for most companies, and thus the process of allocating costs can become very complex. For example, how much of the lowly accountant's salary for developing these estimates should be allocated to each product produced in different factories? And how much of the payroll clerk's cost for paying the accountant should be charged? The list of estimates and assumptions can get very, very long.

Rick Roth, my future partner in business, told me one time that as he was teaching these courses in college before joining the accounting firm of Price Waterhouse, he realized that the financial reporting and management reporting systems were simply parallel systems that recorded the same events from the source systems through two supply chains to produce similar types of outputs, just with different attributes.

Auditing

During an internship I had as an internal auditor, and then at Price Waterhouse, I learned that audits gather two types of evidence to support the accuracy of financial statements. First is evidence that internal controls are properly functioning. Internal controls are business processes such as authorizing invoices prior to payment, and depositing cash the day of receipt. I gained practical experience in this type of evidence. I sampled records from various subsystems processes, A/R, A/P, etc., and saw that proper authorization had been performed, data was entered correctly into systems, and that those transactions were properly posted. I also learned the basics of audit documentation (and I learned that I was not very good at audit documentation). In my experience, I have not found a case where the event based concepts damaged internal controls. In fact, additional attributes may be recorded on each business event which increases internal controls. Also, each business event can be seen within the context of all reports, increasing visibility and auditability.

The second type of evidence auditors gather is that the numbers are actually correct. These tests are called substantive tests. A substantive test would be to have the bank confirm that the amount of cash on deposit actually matches the cash on the balance sheet. Auditing begins with the balance sheet because balances as of a point in time can be confirmed and counted. Financial reporting begins with the balance sheet. After establishing that the balance sheet at both ends of the income statement is correct, auditing then looks to explain changes in balances, thus moving to the income statement and explaining activity over time. Audit work papers have a section to explain each significant balance on the balance sheet, and a much smaller set that examines the changes in those balances.

Event based concepts can actually enhance the types of substantive evidence auditors can gather. The ability to see what transactions at a more detailed level created which balances increases confidence that the balances are correct. It may provide more direct evidence for the income statement. As I have watched auditors interact and test event based financial systems, they have endorsed them without reservations.[40]

Auditing is a kind of "quality control" function for reporting. This quality control process is what brings people back to the financial systems over and over and over again. For all its complexity, it is by and large reliable. If it provided greater information to more people, better decisions would likely be made because it is reconciled and controlled.

After a few years, I had gained an appreciation for how things really are, and how they differed from how they could theoretically be. But, I also learned that I wasn't cut out to be an auditor. It wasn't standards, and comparability, and reliability that I was interested in. I did my most admired work by automating auditing working papers when the process was mostly manual—a self-serving achievement because my handwriting was still so bad. I also had some success assisting one organization understand the relationships between the reports produced by their new computer systems. It whetted my appetite to understand large computer systems, and the reports and information they produced.

I came to the conclusion that I should change careers. I was coached by a kind manager and an understanding partner to look for something that fired my interest. The audit partner said to keep him informed as I looked for a new job. After walking out of his office, I returned to my office and called Eric Denna for advice about what I should do next.

40. O'Reilly, Vincent, et al. *Montgomery's Auditing: Continuing Professional Education Version*, Twelfth Edition (John Wiley & Sons © 1999), Chapter 6 – The Audit Process.

Chapter 11. Consulting

It seems my conversation with Eric was short. He asked who I was working for, and then suggested I call Richard K. "Rick" Roth. He didn't tell me anything about him, so I immediately called. He wasn't in, but his voice mail picked up and said, "This is Rick Roth with Price Waterhouse ...". I left a message. As I reflected on the lead the next morning in the shower, I remember looking at the faucet and saying to myself, "It is 1 to 1 million odds I would ever work for that guy." I felt like my attitude and abilities in auditing had burned all my bridges in the firm.

Rick called a few days later. I told him Eric had suggested I call. We talked about my background. Rick was a consulting partner, building accounting and reporting systems for state governments and others. I guess I must have said I was interested in doing consulting, although I don't remember when I made that decision. Rick said that some things were happening in his work and perhaps a position would be opening up. He didn't give me a lot of specifics but told me to call him back the next week.

I was sent to Phoenix on audit assignments while I waited to find a new job. Even though I thought it was very unlikely I would work for Rick, I rarely felt the need to look for additional job opportunities. I had consulted with my wife Kari about it; she felt quite peaceful as well. I remember discussing consulting and travel and the potential we might have to move one day and her saying to me, "Kip, we aren't going to look back and wonder where we would be if we had taken that route." I agreed. So I would call Rick up every week or two, and ask if things had changed. He would say they were still making progress, but nothing yet. This went on for nearly three months.

Then one weekend I received word that my audit partner was quitting to go to work for a client. Also, my audit assignments in Phoenix were ending, perhaps more because I just couldn't stand to do the work any more and they could tell. I left Rick a voice mail on a Thursday in the middle of June and told him the status and went home for the weekend.

When I returned to Phoenix on Monday, I received a voicemail from Rick saying he wasn't going to be able to hire me for his new group, but that perhaps the Chicago office would be interested. This struck me with a bit of fear, and I think Rick must have sensed the urgency in my next voice mail to him. He called me at the hotel just a few minutes later.

He said something like, "So, are you really serious about this?" I explained that I definitely was; I hadn't pursued any other option. He said, "OK then, we need to meet and talk about this. I live in Santa Fe, New Mexico." I said I had a brother in Albuquerque that I could stay with. So I flew there on Friday night to talk to Rick on Saturday morning.

Rick called and said he was a pilot, and that he would fly his private plane and meet me at the commuter airport in Albuquerque. I stood waiting and as each plane landed I would ask the attendant if that was a Cessna something or other until the right plane landed. I walked out on the tarmac and shook Rick's hand.

We went to a local coffee shop. Rick had a cup of coffee, and I had a glass of water. I don't remember much of what we talked about, but I remember at the end him saying, "OK, we're going to go do this." I took that to mean I had a new job. When I called my wife to tell her I said, "But I don't know where I will be working, what I will be doing, when I will start, or how much I will be paid." She said it didn't sound much different than the day before.

I thought the process was near its end, but was surprised a couple weeks later to hear Rick tell me I needed to fly to Cheyenne, Wyoming for an interview the next day. He apologized, saying it was a fire drill to fly up there for an interview and then back home that night, but he needed me to do it. I wondered, "Do I have a job or not?" But I got on the very small plane with the six other people the next day.

I was the only one in a suit. Someone was waiting who I don't think even knew my name. He simply asked if I worked for Price Waterhouse. He took me to this 1940's craftsman style home. He was working on a report of some kind at the dining room table. I sat down in the living room. The TV in the corner was turned to the weather channel, but the volume was turned clear down. It showed the radar image over and over and over. As I sat there, I thought this whole thing was a little surreal.

Finally a guy showed up in Levis. He introduced himself as Dale Gentsch, a partner like Rick in consulting. He had been asked to chat with me. He invited me out to the backyard. We sat opposite each other at a picnic table. Dale put on his sunglasses because it was bright. Dale sort of reminded me of a tough army sergeant, and I was the new recruit.

He proceeded to grill me on what it would mean to be a consultant. I think he had been asked to confirm that I really was willing to undertake the travel week in and week out. I remember thinking to myself, "Hey, I can do this job. I have been traveling weekly for a few months now, and I think I can do it—besides, I have no other jobs lined up if this doesn't work."

A few minutes later Rick drove up. He walked over and asked Dale what he thought. Dale looked up and said something like, "Well, yea. I think it is OK." Rick took me inside the house and put me on the phone with a recruiter in Chicago. She said, "Kip, I heard your name yesterday. I understand you might be coming to join us for training." I said yes, and that I wanted to bring my family along with me for the three months in Tampa Florida. We agreed the only way to make it happen was if I brought them to Chicago for the first part of the training, to begin the following Monday morning.

It was Tuesday afternoon by this time. The recruiter said she would call back in a few minutes and let me know if there was some place for my family to stay. Only a few minutes later she did and said there would be a corporate apartment for me Sunday night at Lake and Dearborn streets in Chicago. I told her to "wish me luck!". I had to call my wife and ask if we could pack up the trunk of the car and leave the next day with our two children and not return home for months.

I called Kari and asked if she was sitting down; she asked why. I asked if it was possible for us to pack up the kids, and what we'd need to live in furnished apartments for three months, and leave the next evening for Chicago. She replied, "You have to be kidding. You have to be kidding. You have to be kidding." I said I wasn't. There was a pause. And then in a determined voice she said, "OK. We're going to do this".

Thus I began my consulting career. It should have been very clear from this beginning that my consulting was going to be anything but boring, and my career path anything but traditional. It would become very challenging. But for the next few months I left behind the worry about my job and the world of accounting and finance, and went back to school to learn about information systems development.

Chapter 12. Types of Computers and Processes

After three years of in depth study and application of accounting and financial reporting, I was immersed back into the world of computers. My training picked up where my college training had ended. The training began in Chicago for three weeks and then continuing for nearly 3 months in Tampa, Florida.

Mainframes and Batch Processes

My study in Chicago began by reviewing the concept we discussed back in Chapter 4, "Computers," on page 15. Remember we likened a computer to a meeting, with the data written in a binder being like the data written on the hard disk; the white board similar to the computer's memory, and the people in the meeting being the CPUs or processors using the data on the white board. We suggested the meeting language and procedures determined what had to be done and how fast that gets done. We suggested there is consistent pace at which the meeting works. In my training, I reviewed all these basic concepts by reading manuals.

We didn't touch a computer in any way while in Chicago. Reading about large computers called mainframes in Chicago didn't make them any more real to me than when I had read about them in college. Unlike personal computers, I couldn't touch, see or feel one. Perhaps if a PC is a "personal computer" then anything else must be an "impersonal computer". Although said in jest, a person could work on these machines for years and never actually see one. Over the years, they have become much less impressive to see. Whereas they used to fill up rooms, they now look more like a 6 foot tall, black, double door modern styled refrigerator. In some cases, they're half that size.

As I learned about these machines, I have gained a sense of connection with those heroic stories about the advent of computing I learned in my first computer class. I gained a sense of why certain programs are still written in 80 character strings: because in 1928, IBM patented 80 character punch cards.[41] It isn't too much to imagine these same size files being used 100 years after their invention. Thinking of each journal entry line as being written on an individual card so that a computer can read it might help to envision the earliest computer programs.

Data input for the earliest business systems was not done using a keyboard attached to a terminal; it was more like a typewriter that punched holes in cards. The first programs written read these cards in "batches"; thus the programs were called batch programs.

Because there are few such processes on a personal computer, most people today have little experience with batch programs. An antivirus or malware scan or hard disk defrag are perhaps the closest things. When an antivirus scan starts, it reads the first file from the hard disk and checks the file for computer viruses. It then reads the next file and repeats the check until all the files have been read.

The early batch programs read all the journal entries for a day in one stack of cards, all the ledger balances produced yesterday in another stack, and it created a new stack of cards with today's updated ledger balances. Although the stacks of cards were replaced long ago by files on disk, the basic processing paradigm exists in tens of thousands if not more processes in businesses around the world. Mainframe computers were designed from the ground up and have a great many tools to support these types of processes. Batch programs, by and larger, consume computing resources based upon the number of records read and written.

---

41. Interview with Paul C. Lasewicz, IBM corporate archivist.

Servers and Online Processes

The opposite of a batch program is an "on-line" program. These programs were developed as punch card machines were replaced with computer terminals. Typist couldn't correct an incorrectly punched card; but on a computer terminal they could do that and much more; previously entered information could be recalled and shown to the data entry clerk; tests could be applied against entered data to make sure they were correct; and confirmation of actions performed could be given. The mainframe on-line terminals functioned something like a PC loaded only with an internet browser; all the computing is done on the machine on the internet and might support hundreds if not thousands of users. But the screens were always character based. In other words rather than all the graphics that can be shown on a web page they looked like this:

```
VIEW DEFINITION NUMBER: 08332  SUB-DEFINITION NUMBER: 00              STATUS: A
VIEW DESCRIPTION       : HARDCOPY DEMONSTRATION VIEW SUBTOTALS


SUBTOTAL LABEL: STORE SUBTOTAL


SORT FIELD     : STI STORE LOCATION                         SORT SEQUENCE (A,D)  : A
OVERRIDE FIELD LABEL: ______________________________        SORT BREAK COL       : 000
SORT FIELD LENGTH    : 020     LOOKUP PATH          : 001   HIER STRUCTURE :
MASK: ____________________     NUMBER OF DECIMALS: 0        HIER LEVEL     :
SORT LABEL LENGTH    : 014     ROUNDING FACTOR      : 0     FORMAT         : X
USE LOOKUP FILL? (Y,N) : N     LOOKUP FILL VALUE :  ________________________
TITLE FIELD LENGTH   : 000     LOOKUP PATH          : ___    FORMAT        : _
```

Figure 28. Character Based Screen

Mainframe computers[42] didn't adapt very quickly to the advent of graphical user interfaces we have on personal computers. This allowed another type of computer called servers to develop and ultimately to dominate the Internet. They often run an operating system called UNIX.

These computers were developed to serve on-line computing. On-line programs are very different in structure from batch programs. In my training class I coded programs in CICS, another sixties era technology, but the structure still holds true for today's Internet enabled programs. Every time the program is invoked, it is executed from top to bottom. In other words, there is very little looping or repeating of steps in this type of program. Each time the user hits the enter key or clicks the mouse, the program starts at the top, determines where the user clicked, and then does those things the user asked for. It can potentially use all the data entered on the screen, and performs all the functions against that data. It might store the data in the file if it is valid, or sends it back to the screen with an error message if it is not. If in error, the program then stops, and waits for the users to press enter or click the mouse again. If the input was OK, the data is stored to disk somewhere, a new program—and thus a new screen—is likely invoked and shown to the user.

So although the program could do quite a bit of work each time a user hits enter, it is unlikely to run as long as a batch program. Resource consumption—in other words computer usage—for this type of computing is driven more by the number of users hitting enter or clicking a mouse than by the number of records.

42. And their smaller cousins mini-computers which were closer in size to an industrial copier.

Online systems are more about data entry and creating journals; batch systems are more about processes and posting them to the ledger. But what of reporting? Financial systems need to produce reports. How has this changed over time? To understand this, we need to attend one of Rick's lectures on business system IT architecture.

Chapter 13. Business System Architecture

In November 1996, a number of years after my training, I was with Rick at a presentation to an automobile manufacturer. I had worked with Rick for a few years by that time. After explaining the importance of not ignoring batch reporting processes, he went on to explain something I have never heard anyone describe: the subsystem architecture. I remember thinking at the time that the people sitting around the table must be much smarter than I am because I could barely understand what Rick was talking about, and why it was important. But having pondered it now for nearly a decade and a half, I see how critical it is to understand the impediments to wider adoption of the event based reporting theory.[43]

Subsystem Architecture

Rick began by describing this picture to them:

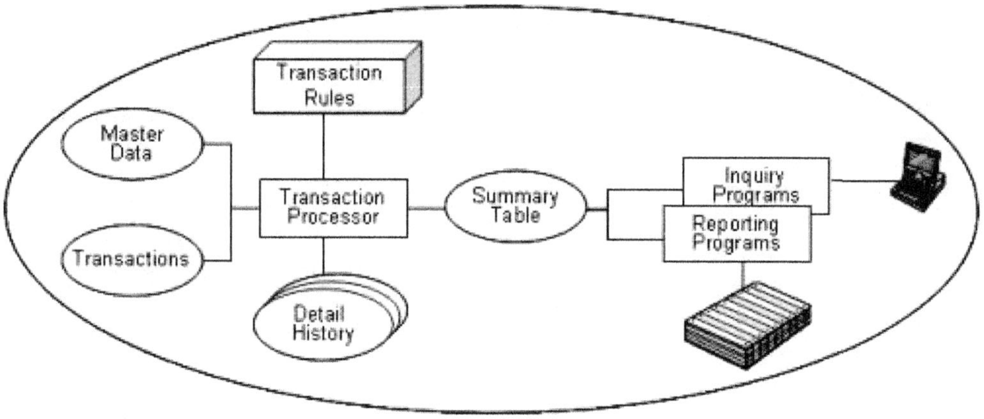

Figure 29. Subsystem Architecture

Rick described that this is the basic architecture for almost all business systems. Almost all systems begin with transactions being entered in some way—usually through on-line screens. There is almost always a set of data that describes those transactions called master data. These are things like the values in drop down boxes such as credit cards types or "M/F" for male or female.

The transactions are taken into a transaction processing program, sometimes called a posting program. This program uses rules of some sort to determine how the transactions should be processed. In earlier days, it was a batch program that worked once a night against all the transactions input during the day. More and more they are on-line programs that operate against one record at a time as the user clicks the mouse.

The detailed transactions are written to a history file that is only used if there is a problem of some sort. Because of their volume, the detailed records are quickly archived. The records are also used to update the summary table. This summary table is used in either inquiry programs, or reporting programs. Inquiry programs tend to be on-line programs that find a particular record in the summary table to display to a particular user. For example, this program might be used to find someone's checking account balance from the checking account summary table. Report programs tend to be batch programs that read

43. These concepts are stated in Roth, Richard K., Denna, Eric L., Ph.D., *A Summary of Event-Driven Systems Concepts*, Price Waterhouse White Paper, undated.

the summary table and produce a report from it, for example perhaps showing the total deposited within the bank branch for that day.

The Accounting Subsystem

A few years later, I modified Rick's slide again to give an example of a system.

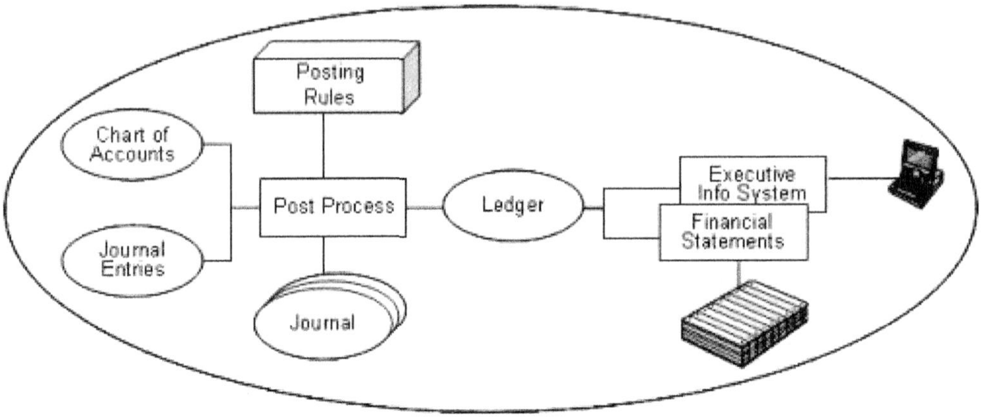

Figure 30. The Accounting Subsystem

As you can see, the general subsystem architecture Rick described fits the accounting system to a T. Accounting was one of the first business systems to be automated.[44]

I suspect system development in the 1950's and early 1960's was no different than today: when a new system needs to be built, programmers start with a program they have already written. Because the accounting system was one of the first to be automated, other business systems followed a similar pattern.

Suppose a company in the early days of business computing has automated their basic accounting system by writing custom programs, and now needs a payroll system. The easiest thing to do would be to (1) copy the accounting system programs; (2) change the structure of the journal entry to have the values needed for time cards; (3) change general ledger account to be employee ID, (4) change the chart of accounts to be employee reference data containing items like pay rate, (5) change the ledger to be the payroll master file, with a record summarizing each employee's overtime hours and year to date pay; and (6) write a reporting program that prints payroll statements.

The same thing likely happened with accounts receivable systems, where the journal entries became billings and cash receipts, GL account becoming customer account, the ledger became the customer master file and customer statements became the report programs. Accounts payable underwent a similar process, where invoice line items replaced journal entries, vendor ID replaced GL account, the vendor master file replaced the ledger and checks where the output of the report programs.

44. "At the risk of over-generalizing, it is useful to understand some patterns of adoption and, equally, broad types of applications. At the birth of the computer in the 1940's, there were two types of applications: military and scientific... A second category of users, which appeared in the early 1950's, has come to be referred to as business applications... At first—in the 1950's and early 1960's—pre-existing accounting practices were automated, often being moved from tabulating and billing equipment to computers because they could be performed quicker and with less human labor, thereby lowering operating costs. If one were to write a history of accounting applications, the story would be about the ever-increasing migration of accounting to computers, the speeding up their turnaround of reports from quarterly to monthly to weekly or daily and from only large companies to the private individuals, sitting at the PC. As with computers in scientific research, by the 1970's one could see the technology beginning to affect accounting practices, initially providing increasing amounts of and variety of data more and more frequently and putting stress on long-established accounting practices." James W. Cortada, *The Digital Hand: How Computers Changed the Work of American Manufacturing, Transportation, and Retail Industries* (Oxford University Press: © 2004) 49.

ERP Systems

The large accounting firms were some of the first to help companies automate processes. "The first use of computers in a commercial setting, at GE, was made possible by bringing in Arthur Andersen's technical personnel to assist in designing processes, writing software, and getting them launched."[45] In the years immediately following my training, Price Waterhouse, another national accounting and consultancy firm, was on the verge of a transformation from a lot of engagements doing large-scale custom software development to implementing package software.

Package software dealt with configuring and implementing software built by large software vendors like SAP or Oracle. In a couple of years, the majority of the firm's revenues would come from implementing Enterprise Resource Planning or ERP packages. "Planning" is somewhat a misnomer; these systems do much more than "plan." They are operational systems. They integrate all of the above functions and many more. But peel back the covers of all of these packages and functions, and you will find each of the functions more or less uses the subsystem architecture.

Layering

As companies grew, or divisions were created, this architecture facilitated the growth. An inventory system in one part of the company could be copied, modified, and implemented in another division. They could have duplicate part numbers for different parts as long as the master files were never shared. They could customize the system to have different functions for different divisions, one for retail bank customer and another for commercial.

The need for combined summaries for various segments of the business was facilitated by having another system (general ledger or another type of reporting system) accept summary results from these more detailed systems comprising a division for example. Thus an additional program was created that read the lower level master file during every cycle and created a set of journal entries that were sent as input to the general ledger. It was a "reporting" program, except the "report" was a file used to input to the GL. Visibility at higher levels of the organization is accomplished in the same way. Each of these subsystems sent a summary of the activity for the day or month to the higher level reporting system.

Rick's point was that this process of layering can go on nearly indefinitely—if the objective is to report on higher and higher levels of summaries of the same sets of attributes posted in the first system. It is a bit like using masonry construction. Each of these subsystems can be "picked up" and "put down" by a small team of people focused on a specific problem for a limited set of business events and limited set of reports.

The fundamental problem with this approach can be understood by anyone who has reconciled a checking account or analyzed a credit card statement. What if the statement came and all it presented was the change in the balance each month? As long as the change in the balance was as expected, for example because one didn't write any checks or make any purchases, there may be no problem. But if the balance at the end of the month is not what was expected, then the first thing that is needed is the detailed transactions to understand the activity in the month.

So if the statement doesn't provide the detailed activity, does that negate its need? No, it just means non-automated approaches must be used. Those might be going back to the check register or personal financial system if it was kept up, going to the receipts themselves, or calling the bank or credit card company to ask someone to research and provide the answer.

Suppose one has all the transactions in an electronic format in a personal financial system like Quicken. Just having the data in an electronic format does not mean these steps are automated. One might need to dump the check registers to a spreadsheet, sort the columns by date, and account, then having selected a

45. Cortada, 47.

set of rows, add formulas to see if the rows selected matched the balance on the report. If the balance can be recreated from the detail, then the analysis of the detail can finally begin.

Now, imagine the confusion that would come if instead of receiving one bank or credit card statement, two, three or more for the same account came in the mail. The first might be the statement as of the last day of the month; the next might be after the "closing" process has occurred over the first few days of the month; the next could be listing the balance in foreign currency if the bank is not a home town bank. If each had some piece of information that is important, it would be impossible to ignore it completely.

And yet this is exactly what our reporting systems do. The need to understand what happened and why it happened drives people in every organization to go back to the details—the same business events—in non-automated ways.

This need, similar to the business needs that demanded creation of skyscrapers, demands new approaches for reporting problems.

In the late 1800's business leaders needed better access to lawyers, bankers and other downtown services. Soaring land prices created the need for taller buildings. The weight of the masonry prevented architects from constructing taller buildings; as they added stories to a building, the lower level walls had to become thicker and thicker and rooms became darker and darker. Skyscraper can't be built using bricks. Thus metal framing was invented, and the skyscraper was born.[46]

The cost of maintaining all these subsystems—all having similar architectures but each one being slightly different and thus requiring individual attention and supporting IT people—and the need for better, more accurate, more timely information is driving organizations to build modern reporting skyscrapers. The subsystem approach is reaching its practical limits.

---

46. Alice Sinkevitch, Editor, American Institute of Architects, *AIA Guide to Chicago: Second Edition* (Harcourt, Inc. © 2004) 8 –10.

Chapter 14. Reporting

In my training I learned how to write a batch reporting program in COBOL, a ubiquitous language for such processes. I believe we may have even printed the report on something called green bar paper. The paper contained shaded light green bars to help trace information across the rows. The principles behind these reports are still valid today.

Classifying Attributes

Reporting is a process of classifying attributes. Some of the earliest arithmetic children are taught is how to classify objects. Very young children begin by making piles, even though those piles may not be intuitive to an adult. One pile might include "things that have some shiny part to them" and thus a toy car with a shiny plastic window and a mirror are combined in the same pile. Over time and with maturity, commonly understood and measured characteristics are used, such as size, shape and color.

Making piles reduces the number of objects the child has to perceive at any one time. If asked what colored objects exist—a request for a report—the child can name the piles. To the question of how many big objects exist, the count of objects in one pile is the response. The child understands the nature of the objects more easily by classifying them.

Later, we use more complex schemes by making enough piles for the combinations of all of the possible values for all of the possible groups. For example, if we wanted to classify objects by shape (round, long, or flat), size (large, medium, or small), and color (red, yellow, or blue), we would make 27 piles; objects that are flat, red, and large in one pile, and objects that are yellow, medium sized, and round in another.

The different characteristics of physical objects, color, size, shape, might be called attributes by IT. In business systems, IT assigns attributes to many things, including customers, employees, even IT systems. Common accounting attributes include business unit, cost or profit center, and account. We use these groups to decide what the business events mean, what action should be taken because of them, or what relationship they should have to other events.

Because business events aren't "real" objects, they don't have a natural set of characteristics. What are legal entities, accounts and cost centers? They aren't some naturally occurring thing, but something we make up and assign to business events to "plan, execute, control, or evaluate" them.[47] A "legal entity" might be a corporation—a made up person that can own property, sue, and do other things real people can do before the law. A "cost center" is a group of people, often with someone in charge and accountable for a budget. And perhaps account means what everyone agrees the business event means as interpreted by the accounting standards. Our example financial and car maintenance system had planned about 25 different things—attributes—we wanted to track.

Of course, comprehending nine piles of things is possible but nine hundred thousands piles is not. Because the piles are the product of possible values, the numbers grow quickly. Quickly finding three piles containing yellow objects (large, medium and small) and adding the numbers together to determine the number of yellow objects is possible, although more tedious than having all the yellow in one place. Dealing with larger numbers of piles becomes impractical.

Today's businesses of course have millions, and in some cases billions of events daily. Understanding the events themselves has long been impossible. Major businesses are run today by keeping track of various piles.

---

47. See "Events" on page 33 in the Business Events chapter.

And every new question someone asks—the need for a report—has the potential to require a new pile.

Answers in a Single Row

The reports I created in my training class, and most of those still produced today, are usually composed of rows of information with numbers on the right hand side, and the descriptions of those numbers to the left. Most spreadsheets still look much like this. Here is something that looks much like the reports I would have created in my class.

Program ID: STGMR88 Company Name: Family Finances Date: 09 May 2009
Report ID: View 13456 Report Name: Trial Balance Time: 10:40 AM

Legal Entity 522349999: K & N Jones Family	**Debit**	**Credit**	**Grand Total**
Cost Centre CC110: Dad			
Account Number 111: Checking Account	6,039.70	2,787.44	3,252.26
Account Number 121: Automobile	23,985.00	0.00	23,985.00
Account Number 122: Home	185,000.00	0.00	185,000.00
Account Number 211: Credit Card payable	200.00	124.24	75.76
Account Number 222: Mortgage payable	309.25	155,377.03	(155,067.78)
Account Number 411: Salary Revenue	0.00	4,487.30	(4,487.30)
Subtotal CC110: Dad	215,533.95	162,776.01	52,757.94
Cost Centre CC120: Mum			
Account Number 111: Checking Account	(432.32)	6,821.16	(7,253.48)
Account Number 121: Automobile	18,285.00	0.00	18,285.00
Account Number 122: Home	0.00	0.00	0.00
Account Number 122: Personal Property	15,245.00	0.00	15,245.00
Account Number 211: Credit Card payable	600.00	4,024.24	(3,424.24)
Account Number 222: Mortgage payable	567.00	0.00	567.00
Account Number 411: Salary Revenue	543.00	6,893.00	(6,350.00)
Subtotal CC120: Mum	34,807.68	17,738.40	17,069.28
Subtotal K & N Jones Family Total	250,341.63	180,514.41	69,827.22
Legal Entity 522349314: C Wheeler			
Cost Centre CC218: Charles			
Account Number 111: Investment 401 (k)	58,655.43	0.00	58,655.43
Account Number 121: Automobile	15,567.00	0.00	15,567.00
Account Number 123: Home	387,000.00	0.00	387,000.00
Account Number 211: Credit Card payable	1,000.00	8,065.77	(7,065.77)
Account Number 411: Salary Revenue	0.00	12,638.00	(12,638.00)
Subtotal CC218: Charles	462,222.43	20,703.77	441,518.66
Subtotal C Wheeler Total	462,222.43	20,703.77	441,518.66
Grand Total	712,564.06	201,218.18	511,345.88

Figure 31. Sample Hardcopy Report

Reports are useful when they contain answers to questions. Sometimes the answers come from a single row on a report; how many flat red large objects there are, or how much were expenses for the sales department of XYZ Company for last year.

These hard copy reports contained a great deal of information. Because the sort keys, those values on the left of the report, were in sorted order, one can search through them in order and quickly find the legal entity, cost center, or account total they are interested in. The report, in a certain sense, contains a number of different reports within it: account total by cost center and legal entity, cost center totals by legal entity, and legal entity totals. For each of these it contains the debits, the credits, and the grand total. In more recent IT trends, these three things may have ended up being three or even nine different reports or database tables.

But the end of the reporting process might still result in the need for one row of information.

This need to find one row of information is sort of ironic since the beginning of the subsystem architecture begins with data, captured as business events, often being recorded on one row as data. Thus the beginning of the basic business system starts with a single row, and it ends with a single row as well.

Although single rows of data are needed at both ends of the process, the two rows are very different things. There is work that must be performed in the middle to create the reporting record. This is because the row at the beginning most often represents a single business event; a deposit, a sale, a receipt of inventory, a payroll payment. But the row at the back of the system represents an accumulation of many business events; total deposits, total revenue, total inventory received, total payroll expense. Somewhere between the beginning and the end of the system, these business events must be accumulated before the row that answers the question can be displayed.

And note there is, by definition, a passage of time between the business event and the reporting record, because the reporting record is an accumulation of business events. This accumulation can be done one record at a time, as each business event occurs, or it can be done after batches of business events have occurred.

The Posting Process

Of course this accumulation is what the posting process does. Historically, it did this at the end of the day, after the batch of business events had been received. The structure of these programs has probably changed very little since standardized in structured programming not long after the first ones were written. The program reads two files, and writes one file. The basic structure is

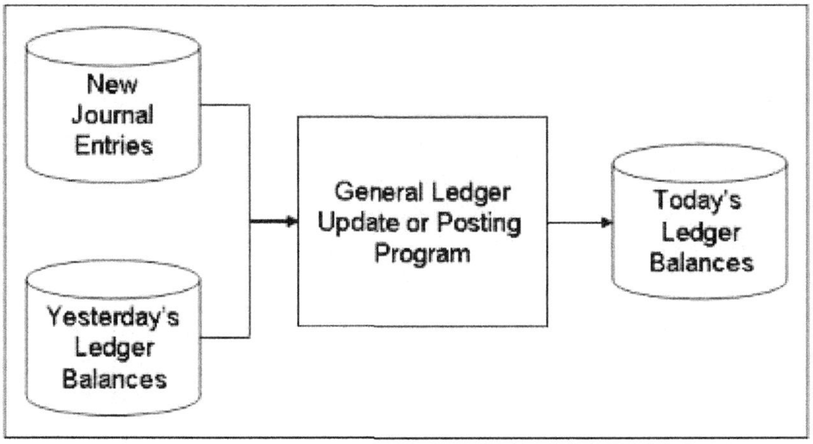

Figure 32. Basic Batch Program

The parts of the program are as follows:

1. Perform initialization. This section starts the program and gets ready for processing. It also usually reads the first record from the journal entry file, and the first record from the ledger file.
2. Process records. This process compares the account number on the journal entry with the ledger record. Obviously a comparison has three possible results, less than, equal, or greater than.
   a. If the ledger account is lower, then updates to the ledger account are complete. The program writes the ledger balance for this account to Today's Ledger Balance file. The program then reads the next ledger record from Yesterday's Ledger Balance file and goes back to step 2.
   b. If they match, the program updates the Ledger Balance record with the amount from the journal entry. It does not write the new record to Today's Ledger Balances file yet, but rather reads a new journal entry record, and returns to step 2.
   c. If the ledger account is high, then the journal entry is for a brand new account that we don't have on yesterday's file. So the program creates a new Ledger Balance record and adds the Journal entry amount to it. Again, it does not write the new record, but rather reads a new journal entry record and returns to step 2.

Logic has to be added to force the program to continue until the end of each file is reached. In other words, it has to continue to copy all the ledger balances out to the new file even after it reaches the end of Journal File, or ensure that all new accounts created in the Journal File are created on Today's Ledger file.

3. Perform termination. Having read the last input record from both files, this section prints out a control report and the program cleans up after itself and stops processing.[48]

After the update program, a report using the updated balances was produced by another program. It simply read the new Ledger Balances, and created a report of the new balances. Because it only read the ledger balances, only the attributes that were part of that record were available for reporting; balances by other attributes on the journal entries could not be reported.

Summarization

This posting process of the subsystem architecture defines what answers can be provided at the time it is created; whatever attributes are assigned to the summary file (effectively the ledger in our accounting example) are the only things that can be used in reporting. Other attributes are immediately dropped and thus unavailable for use in answering any other questions. In effect the piles are predefined at the time the system is started and the system can create no others.

So alternatively, what if the posting process was defined to not drop any attributes? This could be done, usually with significant performance implications because almost no summarization would happen. Each business event is almost unique simply because it has recorded on it the date and time the business event happened. This would also result in the posting processes answering almost no questions; it simply delays the problem of accumulating the rows to get to the answer to another place in the system. Ultimately these rows have to be accumulated to present the single row answer to a question.[49]

So the fundamental question is where in the system architecture to do the accumulation of business events to reporting answers? That depends on which approach is taken to the reporting problem.

---

48. As noted earlier, most people today have little experience with batch programs. An antivirus scan or a hard disk defragmentation process might be the closest. Many people from experience can tell how long it takes for a virus scan to happen, and how slow the machine can be when they are running. Although there are not too many of these types of processes on PC, in the business world there are still millions of such processes, and they can consume large amounts of computing time. Perhaps because these processes are so rare on PCs contributes to the lack of general understanding of the process involved.

49. See discussion of adding the cost center to the simple accounting model in "Additional Attributes" on page 34 in the Business Events chapter.

Chapter 15. Operational Versus Informational

The last step in my training class was a class project. I remember I was assigned the task of working with the database to produce the final outputs of the system. Although I didn't know it, I was using a technology developed to solve both ends of the subsystem architecture, the data capture and reporting. Over the years IT recognized the limits of the traditional reporting model, as implemented in the subsystem architecture. There were a number of initiatives to overcome them. They go by names of data management, decisions support systems, executive information systems, business intelligence and data warehousing, and started with the advent of data bases; the same technology that spurred McCarthy's initial paper.[50]

Operational versus Informational

In data warehousing, one of the latest approaches to overcoming reporting problems, the reports supported by the posting processes are called *operational* reports; the systems which do the posting are operational systems. Data warehousing says that reports which are needed beyond the posting attributes are *informational*. By some definitions, data warehousing is intended to support the informational reports, not the operational.

Bill Inmon, often referred to as the father of data warehousing, in his preface to his very influential book *Building the Data Warehouse*, noted:

> "Databases and database theory have been around for a long time. Early renditions of databases centered around a single database serving every purpose known to the information processing community—from transaction to batch processing to analytical processing. In most cases, the primary focus of the early database systems was operational—usually transactional—processing. In recent years, a more sophisticated notion of database has emerged—one that serves operational needs and another that serves informational or analytical needs ..."
>
> "The split of operational and informational databases occurs for many reasons:
>
> - The data serving operational needs is physically different data from that serving informational or analytical needs.
> - The supporting technology for operational processing is fundamentally different from the technology used to support informational or analytical needs.
> - The user community for operational data is different from the one served by informational or analytical data.
> - The processing characteristics for the operational environment and the informational environment are fundamentally different."[51]

I wouldn't disagree with any of these points as they related to the state of system development at the time. However, I would argue the next evolution in reporting is recognizing that the informational systems must take on more operational characteristics. The finance systems provide the example of why that needs to be done, and how to accomplish it.

- The finance systems cannot completely separate the informational from the operational. The finance system is an informational system. In fact, it was the original enterprise data warehouse. The finance system has to deal with history, whereas the operational systems do not. Yet, with the required timing and critical nature of it, and because it does generate some original data, the finance system is an

50. Frank Hayes, "The Story So Far" *Computerworld*, April 15, 2002 or at http://www.computerworld.com/databasetopics/data/story/0,10801,70102,00.html, Accessed May 2009.

51. W.H. Inmon, *Building the Data Warehouse: Second Edition*, (John Wiley & Sons, Inc. © 1996) vii – viii.

operational system. In fact, because it was the first to be automated, it is perhaps the original operational system. Thus it is both informational and operational. There is constant demand for higher integration of this finance data with additional attributes held in other originating operational systems.

- Because of the blended operational and informational need, the technology has to support both. The missing piece of technology is not the database. Data warehousing has driven innovations in the database that were needed to support better reporting. The missing technology is a high performance posting and report generation engine. We have not advanced the posting processes at the same rate as the database, exacerbating the distinction.
- The differentiation between types of users is not as distinct as it once was because operational reporting at times involves summaries and informational at times involves details; Demands for better information and tighter integration will cause this distinction to become less and less over time.
- Focusing on system performance—a near single minded focus on performance—can significantly reduce the differences in processing characteristics of the two environments and thus enable greater reporting, greater system flexibility, and lower IT maintenance cost by not having to support two different environments and processes.

To highlight the overlap further, consider certain finance processes which generate large amounts of data, and those which require access to detail business events.

Allocation Processes

A number of years later I was the architect for an allocation process for a large insurance company. An allocation process, as we noted in "Management Accounting" on page 54, assigns costs or overhead to individual production items, like the salary of the CEO to each bank loan. More often it is for costs such as the HR, finance, IT, and other support functions whose output is not measured by what the company sells.

The input to these processes could be composed of thousands to millions of business events, such as a listing of loans. The outputs could be millions more transactions as each one is assigned a portion of the cost. Are these types of processes operational or informational? I think it is difficult to say. Do these types of processes fit in a business event based model. I think they do.

Imagine if you will the desire of someone to know how much of the CEO's salary is attributable to a single insurance policy. If there were a need to manage such a low level of detail, then the outputs from the allocation process would be the product of the number of rows to be allocated to (the count of the number of specifically produced items) times the count of the items to be allocated. That could be a very large number indeed.

However, that fact that no one manages these detailed events does not mean these types of processes have no value. A well formulated set of allocation rules can inform and motivate some important behaviors. And we shouldn't doubt the fact that they are business events just because these processes produce millions of outputs. Business events are anything we want to plan, control, execute or evaluate. Each resulting row of data from an allocation process is an event and could be created in isolation from all others. We simply have millions of business events occurring in a relatively short period of time as the allocation process is executed. And what triggers the event is the fact that another event has happened; if not generated in batch from a time trigger, it might simply be based upon capturing the original transaction record.

Funds Transfer Pricing

A similar type of process is called Funds Transfer Pricing. This process assigns a cost to funds provided to various parts of a financial services company. For example, the commercial loan department might have an opportunity to invest for a short time in a particular high risk real estate fund. Other opportunities exist in other areas of the organization. The financial institution needs to assess what is the best use of its funds, something the market uses interest rates to decide. Funds transfer pricing is a type of internal interest rate calculation.

The outputs from this process are intended to motivate appropriate behaviors—to inform specific actions if you will—choosing the best use of funds available. If risk is not assessed correctly, the appropriate returns may not be obtained. The end result can be very damaging.

Determining interest rates requires understanding risk, which means dealing with the details of loans or deposits. The greater the number of parameters that can be used in the formulas, the greater the assessment of risk, and the better the motivation. Having the ability to do funding at the detail level increases its accuracy. Again, this is about generating business events, not reporting on them.

Balance Versus Transaction Based Processes

Other processes reflect the passage of time, often called temporal events. Accrual entries are a reflection of this; others are like allocations and funds transfer pricing, and revaluing balances in foreign currencies to reflect the impact of exchange rate fluctuations. These types of processes often depend upon balances as of a point in time.

For example, currency revaluation is the process of making journal entries to reflect a change in exchange rates. Suppose you live in the US and keep most of your finances in US dollars, but you have one account in the UK where you keep 100 pounds. If you want to produce a balance sheet, you can't add a 100 pound row in the midst of the dollar rows on the report; the report would be meaningless. So you have to convert the 100 pounds into dollars using the exchange rate as of the date of the balance sheet. You need a journal entry affecting an income statement account that reflects the difference in the exchange rate multiplied by the 100 pounds.

The event that causes creation of this entry could be the change in exchange rates, but they can change minute by minute depending on which rate is chosen. Mathematically creating journal entries every second and then summarizing them will result in the same answer as waiting until the balance sheet date to create a single entry with the accumulated exchange rate changes. It is much more efficient to create the entries at some predetermined time—like closing the books. Thus processing the record containing the 100 pound balance during the close process can become the triggering event. This first can be used to perform processes against detailed balances covering history during the night, and then processing in the same way the remaining transactions that come later.

Note this point: Just because a process is a point-in-time process does not mean it must use a balance record as input. Because all balances are the result of accumulating individual movements, mathematically the results are the same if the amount is calculated from the movements or from the balance.

And remember, all these processes become more accurate or capable of informing more specific actions if they are informed by the details of preceding business events. I have often heard experts, with tools that struggle with volume, question why anyone would need all the details from these types of processes. Who has the time or need to go look at an individual product, be it a loan or deposit or policy or something else? Doesn't leverage require managers to find ways of not having to do everything manually at the detailed level?

This argument moves from the subject of generating business events to reporting on them. It misses the point that the number of summaries required from these processes are quite expansive. The principles involved in reporting on the results of processes, including these newly generated business events, are exactly the same as for any other business event. Business events are anything the business wants to plan, execute, control or evaluate. By and large, reporting is the process of accumulating business events, and reporting from the detail provides more flexibility than any other approach.

In the end, the line where operational processes stop and informational processes start is at the back end of the finance processes, just before report production — when data creation stops and only summarizing to produce the report remains. The implications on reporting processes from any finance generated data are no different from business events which are sent to the finance system.

Let's consider the reporting piece of IT architecture in more detail.

Chapter 16. Data Warehousing

In June of 1996 a few years after my training I was asked to staff a Price Waterhouse (PW) booth at a data warehousing conference. There I think I met Mike Schroeck, a PW partner, for the first time. Mike was head of PW's Data Warehousing (DW) practice, a mentor and respected expert on reporting. Over a number of years Rick and I worked closely with Mike as the firm attacked reporting problems. Let's set aside the operational aspects of the system, and focus on report production assuming all the data we need to produce the reports has been created, focusing on how data warehousing architecture attacks these problems.

ETL, Databases, and Report Package

Perhaps the simplest architecture layout of a data warehouse would be this:

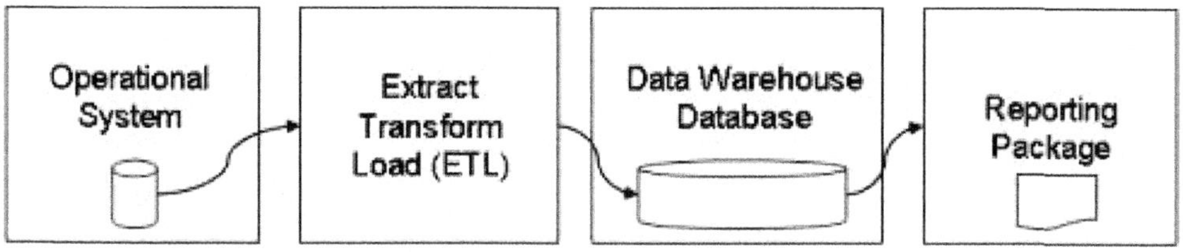

Figure 33. Simplified Data Warehouse Architecture

The Extract Transform and Load process (ETL) accesses either the detailed data or the master file in the operational system, and loads it into the data warehouse database. The users interact with the reporting tool to request a report. The reporting tool accesses the data warehouse to retrieve and create the report.

The ETL tool tends to be more closely associated with the business event capture and operational system posting process. In other words, it most often is a batch process that occurs at a scheduled time after the business events have been captured and recorded in the operational system. The reporting package tends to be more closely associated with the user report demands; its work is performed as users request reports. The database works in both worlds, accepting, loading, reorganizing data as it is presented by the ETL tool, and responding to requests for reports from the reporting tool.

We'll discuss these components more in later chapters.

Report Inventory

Let's get back to the question of where in this architecture to perform summarization.

In the DW model, summarization occurs any number of places. For example, if the master file is used in the source system, then the posting process in the operational system is still doing the summarization. The ETL process may either summarize the master data file further, or using the detailed transactional files may load the data warehouse with summaries, detailed data or both. All modern databases have the ability to summarize data, either as requested by the reporting package (a sum function in SQL for example), or internally through other means.[52]

52. Materialized views would be an example where the database creates and stores summaries.

Each of these approaches, though, really relies on the principles of the subsystem architecture to facilitate reporting processes. Each step of the process summarizes data for specific database target tables ultimately attempting to provide what may be single records in an efficient manner for the end users reporting needs.[53]

Perhaps a useful way of thinking about this problem is to liken it to the traditional approach to inventory management in the PC business compared to Dell's just-in-time manufacturing process which was developing in the 1990's.

The traditional manufacturing process was to guess what type and how many items the buyers might demand, produce that many items, store them until needed, and then ship them to the user when ordered. What Dell realized was that assembled PCs are a lot like groceries; the longer they sit on the shelf the less valuable they become. Instead of making machines and then hoping to sell them, Dell changed the manufacturing process to assemble the machines quickly, in some cases in just four hours after a customer orders the machine. To do this, Dell worked to organize the factory floor to keep all the materials in the most efficient manner for manufacturing.[54]

Instead of a PC, let's think of the answer a user wants as the thing the system needs to produce. The traditional reporting architecture demanded that answers be defined up front, and thus create a master file or database table to answer that question. These master files, whether in the operational system or later in the data warehouse, are updated so answers are always ready when the user asks the question.

Dell realized that giving customers tremendous choices in their PC configurations would drive greater sales. In the world of reporting, consider what proliferates faster, the number of source systems or the number of reports? The answer is always the number of reports. The business events are relatively stable, and thus the source systems are too. But the number and types and permutations of those attributes gathered in each of those systems in reporting processes are almost limitless. The demand for reports will always exceed the capacity to produce them if we continue to demand that all questions be anticipated.

Another problem is that the demand for non-financial summaries gets the short shrift. The traditional accounting answers tend to take precedence over other views of the data; this is similar to allowing the assembly line to be set up to favor word processing configurations precluding gaming, multimedia, laptop and other possible needs. The accounting answer manufacturing process destroys the data it should be providing.

Supply and Demand

And it isn't simply demand for reports exceeding capacity: ultimately using summarization as a means to overcome volume results in overwhelming the system with the number of summaries that must be maintained. This is because as the number of summaries that must be maintained grows, the overall workload of the system experiences diseconomies of scale, as shown here:

---

53. "Once the data ages [note passage of time], it passes from current detail to older detail. As the data is summarized, it passes from current detail to lightly summarized data, then from lightly summarized data to highly summarized data." Inmon, p. 37.

54. "Dell is able to achieve a four-hour production cycle time using an Internet-based supply-chain management system, Figueroa says. After getting an order, Dell notifies its suppliers about what components are needed, and they're delivered within an hour and a half.
"With our pull-to-order system, we've been able to eliminate warehouses in our factories and have improved factory output by double by adding production lines where warehouses used to be; says Figueroa....
"The just-in-time method demands a very disciplined assembly-line process, says David Dobrin, an analyst at Surgency Inc. in Cambridge, Mass." Marc L. Songini, "Just-in-Time Manufacturing" *Computerworld*, November 20, 2000, or at http://www.computerworld.com/action/article.do?command=viewArticleBasic&taxonomyName=Manufacturing&articleId=54131&taxonomyId=136&pageNumber=2, Accessed May 2009.

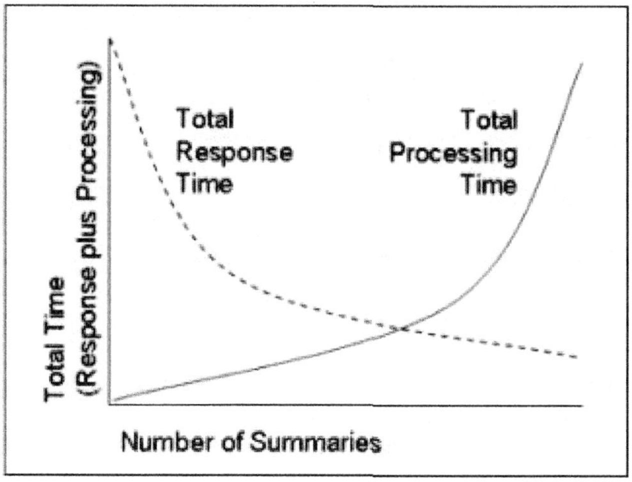

Figure 34. Posting Process Diseconomies of Scale

This shows that each summary structure updated to answer a specific question reduces the response time of the entire system to provide that answer, because the single record to provide the answer is readily available from the database to be displayed to the user. This reduction in user response time continues as more and more summaries are created to answer more and more questions.

Correspondingly, the system has to perform a posting process for each transaction received against each of these summary structures. As volumes increase, this is normally done as part of transaction processing, not at report time. At some point, the reduction in response time for a user is less than the additional update time for posting. Not all answers in the summaries are used; people don't need answers to some questions. However, having established the summaries, the update cycle is constant for each transaction record received.

Thus there is a computer cost to maintaining the reporting inventory, and at a certain scale the computer cannot support all possible predefined answers. And because the summarization process, whether in the operational system, the ETL layer, or the database is tied more closely to the daily end of business event processing, the problem shows up in elongated batch processing times.

Working within the constraints of the traditional report inventory system, the IT community only supplies a limited set of summaries to answer a limited set of questions that can be updated by the batch processing time and still provide end users with an adequate response time. In other words the users can choose from the configurations the manufacturing line can produce when the line was established.

The Alternative

The alternative is to organize the manufacturing of answers such that the answer needed is produced as close to the time the question is asked as possible. Certainly people ask questions that need to be answered by reports much more often than they buy PCs; thus four hours for each report would not be acceptable for most reporting problems. But if it were possible to reduce it to four seconds instead of a usual on-line response time for a limited set of report inventory of two seconds, people might be willing to buy that solution.

Manufacturing PCs to custom specifications for each individual user requires organizing the buyer's configurable components in the proper order so they can be assembled rapidly. What would a just-in-time manufacturing line for reports look like? The answer from McCarthy is quite clear: all reports are made from detailed business events. The record of business events is the stuff of which reports are made.

Dell used suppliers for many of its components; it did not try to start with silicone and make the actual CPU processor in its assembly line. That would have taken too long to do. In the same way, as we'll see later, it would take too long to accumulate raw detailed business events for the prior 2 years into a common format and then summarize them to produce a financial statement in any time acceptable for a user.

But every time we build a component part, we build inventory we must manage. If at every choice we come to, we compare the cost of maintaining the inventory to the cost of engineering the fabrication process we can continually drive down cost of inventory, and increase the flexibility of the reporting environment.

There is another reason why the detail in reporting processes is needed. Dell would like the PCs' design to be consistent to drive down maintenance cost when they have to repair them. Similarly, report answers have a relationship to each other. Reconciliation is the maintenance process of proving the relationship between each answer is correct. Reconciliation, a common finance function, requires finding a common set of attributes between two summaries and showing that the accumulated amounts in both summaries are the same. Any difference is an indication one or the other summary and the corresponding answers are wrong.

This process of reconciliation, the process of finding a common set of attributes between different summaries, is facilitated by having ready access to the detail transactions—the business events—that were used to make the summaries. The shorter the distance between the business events and the answers, the easier the reconciliation and subsequent correction is if problems are identified. Reconciliation in finance is so pervasive in some cases, elimination of the cost of reconciliation in the finance process alone can pay for the construction of the new system.

Thus, if we are to attempt to streamline the answer production process, it will require nearly manic focus on a single goal: efficiency of report production. The assembly line must be as efficient as possible in delivering the answers.

Chapter 17. Programming Tools

After my training class in October 1992, Rick sent me to Minneapolis, Minnesota for a project. The project was building a software product, sponsored jointly by my company and a client to do activity based costing, a type of cost accounting. A new type of IT tool was in vogue called CASE tools. CASE tools were designed to make programmers more productive. CASE allowed the programmer to write one statement that would tell the computer to do many things.

The key issue for performance is the processing patterns generalized by the tool. A hammer and a screw driver both insert a long, thin object with a flat head into materials to hold them together. Although a screw driver might make driving a nail easier in the absence of any other tool, and a hammer might successfully insert a screw enough to hold things together, they were designed for different patterns of work.

Computer Instructions

At the bottom of all computer languages and procedures used by the processors are a series of ones and zeros. Each one or zero is called a bit. A grouping of usually eight bits makes a byte. For example, on an IBM mainframe the letters "Y E S" would be represented as "11101000 11000101 11100010". The eight digits of either zeros or ones—a byte—can be combined in 256 possible ways. Only 26 of those combinations are used for capital letters, another 26 for lower case letters, and 10 more for numbers. The others are used for punctuation, and other characters.[55] In a sense, extending our people in a meeting analogy, these combinations of ones and zeros are the alphabet of languages used in every computer "meeting", even though the language itself might be different.[56]

Considering our analogy further, take note that language is used in two different ways in our meeting: (1) It records the information we write in the notebook and on the white board; (2) it is also used by people as they think and communicate. These are very different things. If the processors—people—are determining how much to pay employees, the whiteboard might be filled with numbers like hours worked and pay rate, and then ultimately the pay for the current period. All these items would be written in the notebook when the meeting is over. This is generally referred to as data.

The second category of communication, telling a person in the meeting to multiply the hours worked by the pay rate, is called the program. It is written in a different binder, in this case the binder of payroll procedures, only when the program is created. These programs change must less frequently than the data changes, and are much more time consuming to develop. For the most part creating these procedures is the work of IT projects.

Although both categories of language used in our meeting are composed of zeros and ones they aren't really the same language. It is a bit like the fact that Hawaiian and Japanese are both composed of very similar sounds, but the combinations of those sounds means completely different things. The language of a computer program is almost always not the same as the language of the data.

For example, the 11101000 that represents a "Y" in the data means something different in a program. That set of zeros and ones means a Move Character Inverse (MVCIN) instruction. When the processors see that instruction, it tells them to copy data on the white board to another part of the white board, but

55. Other types of computers, like PCs, use a slightly different representation called ASCII, rather than the Mainframe named coding structure of EBCDIC. For example, instead of EBCIDIC "11101000" in ASCII it is "10101001". But the principles involved are the same for almost all types of computers.

56. *IBM System/370 Reference Summary, Eighth Edition,* (February 1989) 34 – 37.

reverse the order of the letters. Thus when the computer executes an instruction a person would read as "Y", it might make a copy of the white board word "Hello" as "olleH".[57]

Computer Languages

Almost no one writes computer programs by typing in ones and zeros. That is far too time-consuming. Instead, people instruct computers to do things through various computer languages. In a simplified way, they write "MVCIN" and a computer program called a complier[58] translates it into the instructions 11101000. There are compilers for each computer language which do this function.

Over the course of computer development, there have been more and more languages created—each one a slightly different tool. Each language has its particular strengths, similar to the way vocabulary is developed in specialized fields (like accounting and computers) to describe different concepts. Some computer languages are better suited to expression of scientific functions, others for graphics and others for a host of other types of computer problems.

Languages have also been developed to work at different levels of specificity. The most specific language is called "assembler." Assembler is specific to a particular computer, and translates directly into the ones and zeros that computer recognizes. The MVCIN instruction above is an assembler instruction for an IBM mainframe. Because someone has to specify every specific action the computer should take in assembler, it is called a low level language.

Higher level languages don't require programmers to specify every single action. For example, COBOL is considered a third generation computer language—a higher level language. Binary, the ones and zeros, is the first generation; assembler is the second. In COBOL someone can write the following phase:

```
IF HOURS-WORKED GREATER THAN STANDARD-HOURS (EMPLOYEE-GRADE)
```

And the COBOL compiler will translate this into the following assembler instructions:

```
LH 2,240(0,10)
L 3,16(0,12)
MH 2,96(0,3)
L 4,308(0,9)
PACK 568(2,13),8(2,4)
OI 569(13),X'0F'
AR 2,10
PACK 576(2,13),174(2,2)
OI 577(13),X'0F'
CLC 568(2,13),576(13)
BC 13,2348(0,11)
```

One COBOL phrase translates into 11 assembler instructions; 11 assembler instructions translate into 11 machine instructions of ones and zeros.[59]

Patterns

Using higher level languages makes programmers more efficient; it takes less time to write the COBOL statement above than the assembler instructions. Because programmer time is a significant element of

57. IBM Enterprise Systems Architecture/390, *Principles of Operation* Seventh Edition (July 1999), 7-53, A-24.

58. Technically "assembler" when the language is assembler.

59. The following is a more detailed description of these assembler instructions: Load half word (LH) puts the value EMPLOYEE-GRADE into register 2. The next three instructions, load (L), multiply half word (MH) and load (L) adjust register 2 to point at HOURS-WORKED. The Pack and Or Immediate (OI) instructions format the HOURS-WORKED to be in a comparable format. Add Register (AR) instruction finds the STANDARD-HOURS in memory, and its format is made comparable through the Pack and Or Immediate (OI) instructions. The Compare Logical Character (CLC) instruction compares the STANDARD-HOURS and HOURS-WORKED. The Branch on Condition (BC) instruction then branches based upon which value is greater.

automating functions, this is a reasonable approach; making programmers more efficient means automation takes less time. But this efficiency can come at a cost if the language and compiler used—the tool—doesn't automate the correct pattern.

The person that designed the COBOL language and wrote the COBOL complier had certain processing patterns in mind. He or she designed templates of assembler code for each COBOL statement. If that pattern matches the work that needs to be done then that code will be efficient. If not, it will not be. It may be as inefficient as using a screwdriver to pound in a nail.

For example, if in our example above the person designing the compiler knew that for some reason the HOURS-WORKED and the STANDARD-HOURS for the specific EMPLOYEE-GRADE are already loaded into computer registers—something like the eyes of those in the meeting reading information from the white board—they could have designed the pattern of assembler instructions to be different. The first ten rows of assembler instruct meeting participants where on the white board to look for the data, and how to get the data into a format that can be compared; if the values were the words "twenty-two" in one case and "25" in the other, the comparison won't work. But perhaps the way the language is structured, the person designing the compiler knows that the eyes of processor will be looking at the right data to be compared when they come to this point and the data is in the right format. If that were the case, then instead of the 11 instructions above, the program would only need the following two:

```
CR 2,10[60]
BC 13,2348(0,11)
```

The COBOL complier doesn't have this pattern; it chose the pattern shown above. For the most part, when it sees an IF statement that compares two numbers, it will assume the computer will need to find the data, and change the format of the data to be comparable. One experienced assembler programmer has found he can remove 1/3rd of the computer instructions generated by COBOL if he writes the program in assembler.

Efficiency Matters

But of course, writing compilers is very time consuming; very labor intensive. At times it may be more efficient to use an existing compiler and have the program perform the 11 functions rather than taking the time to build a compiler or for the programmer to write it in assembler. This is often the case because of what is called Moore's law which states that since the mid 1960's computers double in speeds about every two years. Thus as computers become faster, the cost of the more efficient programmer (and less efficient program) is made up for by the faster computer.

However, in the case of producing answers as close to the time when someone asks the question, 11 machine instructions might matter, particularly if it is 11 machine instructions per business event record summarized. Remember, some questions require accumulation of millions of business events.

Computer processors run at constant speeds. In a CPU "cycle" a processor can basically execute one machine instruction. If our computer runs at 1 gigahertz, or 1 billion machine instructions a second, and our answer requires summarizing 1 billion business events,[61] then if we use an inefficient tool which uses 13 machine instructions, we will get our results in 13 seconds. If we use a different language or compiler which uses two machine instructions, we'll get our answer in 2 seconds.

---

60. If the values for HOURS-WORKED and STANDARD-HOURS were loaded into registers already, their formats would have already been located (obviating the need for the L, MH or AR instructions) and adjusted to be comparable before they could have been loaded (obviating the need for the PACK and OI instructions). So the Compare Register (CR) can be used instead of the CLC instruction. These values might have been loaded into the registers to perform some other function, such as testing for reasonable limits or some other test. At a minimum, the PACK and OI instructions could be eliminated as the formats of the fields are actually comparable.

61. The example assumes all the records fit into memory—the white board in our analogy. Time to read the data from disk (the binder) is thousands of times slower than the CPU clock speed of 1 gigahertz.

Meetings that use very flowery language like congressional debates take more time to communicate affirmation than someone saying, "Yep."

Now remember, if the existing system today is providing the answer to this question, and that answer really takes summarizing 1 billion business events, the existing system today must be doing that work. It might be doing that work in pieces; a portion in the operational system in posting the transactions, a portion in the ETL layer loading the data warehouse, and a portion in the database as it does a sum function for the last level of summarization for the actual report request, but the work is being done today. It is simply that the work is done all along the supply chain, a portion of which is hidden during nightly or transaction system processing. Doing this existing work more efficiently will either (1) reduce the time to produce the reports if 13 seconds is unacceptable, or (2) reduce the compute cost if 13 seconds is acceptable.

SQL

CASE tools were considered a "higher level language," a fourth generation language, meaning they are even less detailed than COBOL. CASE tools were viewed as another step up in evolution of computer programming. In the same way a few COBOL lines generates many assembler instructions, a few lines of a CASE tool language could generate a lot of either COBOL or C, another third generation computer language.

The tool that spurred McCarthy's paper was not CASE tools, but rather the database. Inmon's first word in his book on data warehousing is "Databases". Databases and database technology are very important. They make most of the functions needed at both ends of the subsystem architecture possible: they capture the initial business events, and they present the rows of data the users need to find answers to reporting problems. Because of this fact, the database has become the generalized tool for reporting processes.

SQL has become the most widely used language to interact with databases, although it is only for a specific type of database called a relational database. SQL is not a procedural but rather a declarative language, something that specifies what has to be done not how it should be done. Thus the patterns chosen by the developers of the databases—the functions that turn SQL into machine code—are even less under the control of the programmer than in other languages where the programmer can specify how the program should solve the problem, like COBOL.

The patterns SQL is focused on automating are data access; particularly at both ends of the subsystem architecture. These patterns are not the same as the functions for accumulating business events for reporting. SQL was not designed to perform this function.

As I approached the end of the project, Rick's fiancée, Julia gave me some good counsel: "Kip, remember, tools are just that; they are tools. Don't confuse them with the results." Matching the tool to the work to be performed will end in better results. Over the next few years, I would see lots of cases where the wrong approach was taken to solving a reporting problem, with terrible results.

Chapter 18. Input/Output

My time in training and on this first project had taken about a year. In July of 1993, Rick asked that I now join the Geneva team in Sacramento, California. This team was building a software product called Geneva, which was an amalgamation of the letters from the phrase Generalized Event-based Architecture. I believe Rick drew the picture Eric had shown, and this tool was the embodiment of that picture. The tool is now IBM Scalable Architecture for Financial Reporting (SAFR). One of my first assignments for Rick was to help upgrade Alaska to the latest version of the software.

Alaska

Rick was one of the principle architects on the Price Waterhouse team designing the state-wide accounting system for the Alaska Division of Finance in the 1980s. In 1978, Rick was writing a program which needed to solve a particular problem that couldn't be done with the ledger balances. He realized that reading all the required journal entries would make the problem trivial. He did that and wondered why more systems didn't work that way.

In designing the system in Alaska, he again came to a similar conclusion to McCarthy, that end user access to the detailed event data would provide the greatest flexibility in reporting. State governments were some of the first to undertake "enterprise" wide systems, and Alaska, with oil revenues and resulting tax revenue at a peak, undertook a very extensive system for the time.

The system processes and posts detail transaction line items. The technology of the day could handle posting one day's worth of journals. However, the financial reports require history, amounting to 53 million transactions in 48 gigabytes of data for two-year period, and 300 users and 400 different reports in various formats (download, hardcopy on-line tape, microfiche and file format output.) They also needed access up to 5 years worth of data on weekends upon request.[62]

The problem with the volume of data wasn't the processor's ability to add it up; it was the ability to get the data into memory for the processor to access; the reading of the data from the binder to white board. Reading data from disk is thousands of times slower than reading it from memory. Because we hear very large numbers today, such as the US Federal deficit, we sometimes are unfazed by them. But a multiplier of a thousand is a very large number.

Consider a thousand times difference in travel speeds. Large commercial airliners travel at about 500 miles per hour. Consider that the difference with the speed of a car at 50 miles per hour is only a factor of 10 times. An experienced hiker can walk at 5 miles an hour if pressed. So the difference between a commercial airplane and someone walking is a factor of 100 times—the difference between being able to cross half the world in 15 hours, and attempting to walk 24 hours a day seven days a week for two straight months. A factor of 1000 is the difference between flying halfway around the world and the more practical Marco Polo paced trip.

Our 13 second response time above becomes 3 ½ hours when multiplied by 1000.

Input/Output or IO is often the slowest part of computing.

62. Price Waterhouse Data Warehouse Reporting Solution brochure, *State of Alaska benefits from data warehouse high-performance solution*, May 1996. Copyright IBM Corporation.

Single Pass

The Alaska team came up with a fairly simple answer to get around the IO problem: a single pass architecture. As the data, the business events, are read from the disk into memory, every report is allowed to see and use the data in any way it would like. Thus instead of transferring the 53 million records into memory 400 times to solve each report individually, the 53 million records are brought into memory once, and all 400 reports get to see each record. A marketing brochure from a few years later stated:

> In a typical run, Geneva [SAFR] reads 69 million records, performs 1.6 billion foreign key lookups to hierarchical account structure and vendor tables and produces more than 400 separate reports in about 90 minutes of both wall clock and CPU time. A major feature that makes this possible is [SAFR]'s hyper-performance in processing external table joins. [SAFR] performs look-ups at an average rate of approximately 500,000 table joins per CPU second.
>
> "By using [SAFR], we reduced data processing costs and reallocated the funds to absorb budgetary cuts without making cuts in financial services", states Don Wanie, Director of the Division of Finance. The Division has also found opportunities to replace subsystems made redundant by [SAFR]. The money saved in annual processing costs now translates to additional funds for staff and technology resources to focus on client inquiry and audit as the number of constituents and federal reporting requirements grow.
>
> Beyond providing the savings to employ additional resources, [SAFR] also allows the existing personnel to work more effectively. Several agencies have reduced federal reporting processes that took 2-3 weeks down to one day. This was accomplished by producing data directly from [SAFR] according to the specific needs of the respective reporting requirements.
>
> According to Cheryl Crawford, Division of Legislative Audit, "[SAFR] opens up new reporting possibilities that make our jobs more efficient." The faster and cheaper report/view production and tailored report formats support more thorough and efficient audits and superior client service. The state estimates the total cost for each report is only 50 cents.[63]

These are the benefits of a business event based reporting architecture.

Database Size

There is a lot of talk about database sizes: the larger the database, the more impressive must be the system. However there are a myriad of examples of systems where data is put into the system but can never be gotten out. Loading data isn't usually the issue; reporting on it is.

Very large sizes can also be an indicator of a poor system or data design. As Steve Mongulla, a long time friend, told Rick one day, "If you denormalize a data structure with enough attributes to stretch from here to China, you can avoid data design all together."

An aspect of database design that the Alaska team hit upon is the difference between balances and movements, much of which has been explained in Part 2 - The Professor. The impact of this difference became clear in 2006 when designing the reporting database for a very large financial services customer. The team responsible created tables to store balances for all the reports the system was supposed to support. The resulting database size for just the North American installation was 46 terabytes. That is 46 followed by twelve zeros. That was more than all the other data the entire company used in North America, just for the finance system.

---

63. Ibid.

Movements

When a movement based approach was applied to the problem, the system that was actually implemented required about 250 gigabytes to store data needed to produce the vast majority of the reports. That is 250 followed by only nine zeros—nearly a factor of 1000 smaller.

How is that possible? It is possible by properly balancing summarization with the need for detail; balancing the desire to make intermediate inventories of answers—balances—with keeping all the data in its raw format from the beginning of time—transactions—to assemble when a report is needed.

The following graph shows this relationship.

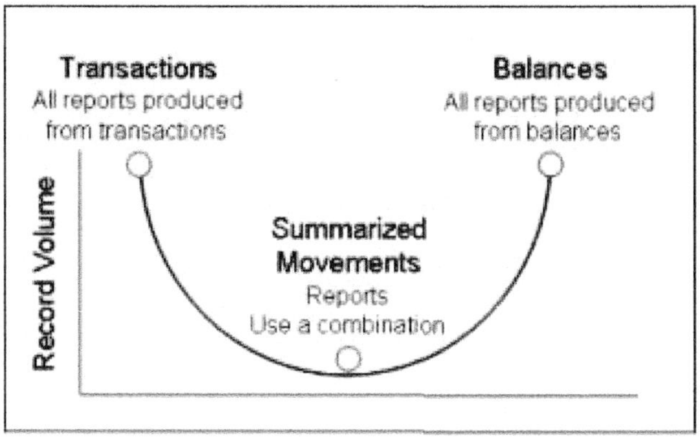

Figure 35. Relationship of Transactions, Balances, and Movements

Any report can be produced from the business events. If all the business events for any organization were kept from the beginning of that organization, any report using them can be reproduced. But the data volumes to do so may be enormous.

If every row on every report that was ever needed inside an organization—effectively every balance—were kept, the data volumes would be equally large. This is particularly true if the date of the reported balance is stored with the balance, thus causing balances to be replicated every day even though they may never have changed.

The value of the transactions diminishes quickly; no one produces reports as of 15 years ago. All the richness of the data from distant periods provides no benefits.

Not all balances are needed every day, and not all balances have transactions affecting them each day; in other words the number of transactions for a given day is lower than the number of balances on that day.

Transactions				**Balances**			
Ref	Date	Customer	Amount	Ref	Date	Customer	Balance
	Jan 1920	XYZ	$12	1	Aug 2006	ABC	$54,765
	Jan 1920	ABC	$12	2	Aug 2006	XYZ	$20,064
	Feb 1923	ABC	$234		Sep 2006	ABC	$55,518
	Mar 1934	XYZ	$8		Sep 2006	XYZ	$20,064
	Oct 1934	ABC	$2,334		Oct 2006	ABC	$55,518
	Aug 1940	ABC	$234		Oct 2006	XYZ	$20,064
	Jun 1945	XYZ	$2		Nov 2006	ABC	$55,518
	Sep 1956	ABC	$943		Nov 2006	XYZ	$20,064
	Oct 1960	XYZ	$972		Dec 2006	ABC	$55,518
	Dec 1961	ABC	$8,439		Dec 2006	XYZ	$20,064
	Mar 1968	ABC	$394		Jan 2007	ABC	$55,518
	Jan 1972	XYZ	$3,943		Jan 2007	XYZ	$20,064
	Feb 1975	XYZ	$2,903		Feb 2007	ABC	$61,853
	Jun 1977	XYZ	$23		Feb 2007	XYZ	$20,064
	Jul 1984	ABC	$40,923		Mar 2007	ABC	$61,853
	Feb 1989	ABC	$934		Mar 2007	XYZ	$20,741
	Jan 1993	ABC	$4		Apr 2007	ABC	$61,853
	Apr 2001	XYZ	$4,223		Apr 2007	XYZ	$20,741
	Jun 2002	ABC	$234		May 2007	ABC	$61,853
	Jul 2002	ABC	$80		May 2007	XYZ	$20,741
	Aug 2003	XYZ	$7,978		Jun 2007	ABC	$85,285
3	Sep 2006	ABC	$753		Jun 2007	XYZ	$20,741
4	Feb 2007	ABC	$6,335		Jul 2007	ABC	$85,285
5	Mar 2007	XYZ	$677		Jul 2007	XYZ	$20,741
6	Jun 2007	ABC	$23,432		Aug 2007	ABC	$85,285
					Aug 2007	XYZ	$20,741

Figure 36. Sample Transactions and Balances

On the left of the Sample Transactions and Balances figure are all the transactions for a company since its inception. On the right are the balances that could be created from those transactions for every month since the beginning of August 2006.

If the system were designed to keep only the following records, any of the balances shown on the right hand side of the table could be calculated. The reduction in the number of rows needed is visually apparent.

Movements			
Ref	Date	Customer	Movement
1	Aug 2006	ABC	$54,765
2	Aug 2006	XYZ	$20,064
3	Sep 2006	ABC	$753
4	Feb 2007	ABC	$6,335
5	Mar 2007	XYZ	$677
6	Jun 2007	ABC	$23,432

Figure 37. Sample Movements

The first balance records represent the opening movements; the change in the value from the beginning of the company history to the date of the record. The other records represent the movements for the particular month. In this manner the size of the database can be reduced to a manageable level. This same technique can be applied to maintaining summaries of transactions within a day.

The impact of this will be to allow faster data access, and less time in producing reports, a highly efficient report production system. In the Alaska system, the historical transactions were collapsed by all the relevant attributes and carried forward into the new file for the new years. Then, the transactions for the period were appended to this file, thus keeping the information-rich current data available for reporting, but not burdening the system with all of the history.

Balancing the Use of Movements and Balances

This point of movements, transactions, and balances, is focused on only one part of the data in the database: the numbers. These different approaches mostly change the numbers on the ends of all the attributes of interest (the business unit, ledger account, etc.). The single pass architecture also addresses another problem with reporting: how to let users select, sort and summarize the data of interest to them. These are key steps in the reporting pattern that must also be automated efficiently.

Chapter 19. Select, Sort, Summarize

The Alaska team recognized a processing pattern, and built the system to automate that pattern. The pattern is selection of business events, sorting those events by the attributes of interest, and then summarizing the numbers by those attributes. While these things were happening in Alaska, database reporting systems were focused on using the database capabilities to solve similar problems. One of the major features of databases that allow for selection of records is the index.

Indexes

In Chapter 4, "Computers," on page 15, we reviewed two approaches to getting data from a book; one was reading the book from beginning to end, and the other was to use an index at the end of the book. For the most part, databases provide direct access to the data that is needed. Rather than having to read all records to find the one of interest, databases allow programs to nearly immediately retrieve the exact information that is needed. This is important for processes at both ends of the subsystem architecture, input and ultimate output.

Indexes, though, are focused on answering one type of question. Questions about business units use the business unit index; questions around account use the account index. Thus within databases, there isn't just one index like in a book, there are many indices. And using each one takes computing (CPU) and IO time.

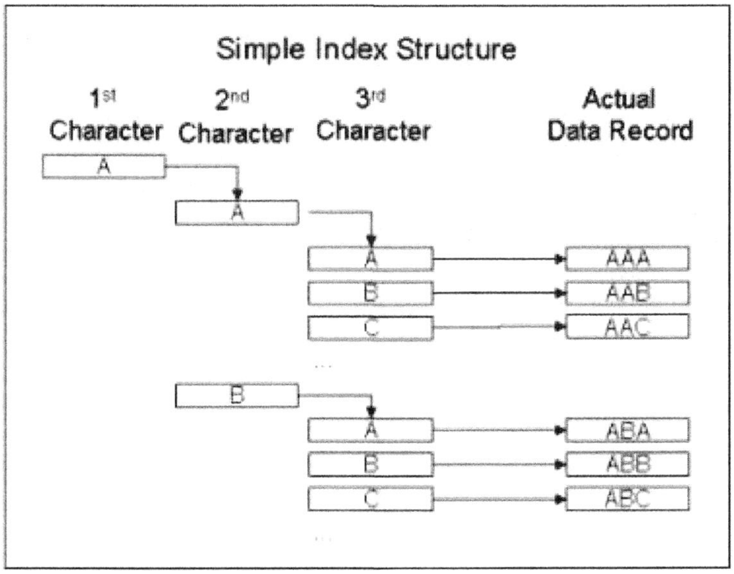

Figure 38. Account ID Index Structure

Although for databases (and books) of any size, indexed access is much faster than scanning the data, the process of finding the right information does require processing time. There are many types of indexes, but for our example, let's assume that we have an attribute named account ID, made up only of letters, and that it is 3 characters long like ABC. This would mean we could have a total of 17,576 accounts (26 x 26 x 26). The first level of the index might have the 26 entries representing the first letter of the account in it, A through Z. Each row of this level of the index points to another level in the index. These second level, 26 of them, could have 26 entries in each of them, representing the second character of the account ID, the "B" in "ABC". Each of these entries could point to the third level of indexes, 676 in total (26 for the first character x26 for the second character), and again, each of these would contain 26 rows for the third letter of the account ID, the "C" in our example. These rows would point to the position (page number, paragraph, and even page line and column if it were a book index) of individual accounts in the actual data.[64]

This scheme allows a program to find the record needed at worst after searching 78 rows for account ID ZZZ, and at best 3 rows for account ID AAA; on average searching 42 rows of the index. Even for the worst case of searching 78 rows to find the location of account ZZZ, the search is much more efficient than a sequential search of over 17,000 rows in the data file. But take note that indexed access does not mean instantaneous access; the process requires a varying number of searches in the index to find the correct account. And the index must be transferred into memory to be searched (the people in our meeting can't read from the index in the binder, they only can read from the whiteboard). So searching an index requires IO.

Block Sizes

Data isn't transferred into memory by record; it is transferred by something called a block. An easy way to think of this is to say that although the sizes of records can change for each system, the record size used to transfer data from disk to memory is fixed, and it is called a block. It is usually fairly large, on mainframes it is 32,768 bytes. If the records for our system are less than half that size, a block can contain multiple "logical" records. At times a block can contain a lot of records.

If our index of 17,567 records has three bytes for the letters of the index, and one additional byte for an address that specifies where the data exists in the file, then it is in total 70,268 bytes. It will be stored in three different blocks on a mainframe disk: the first block might contain entries from AAA to LCZ, the second block may contain LDA to YEZ, and the last block may contain entries YFA to ZZZ. If our search is for AAA then we only need the first block read into memory. If the data we are searching for is LDA, then we'll need the first block (to find where the L entries are), and the second block. If we are searching for YFA, then we'll need the first and last blocks.

The time to transfer data into memory is not the same as the time taken to search the index to find the specific index entries. Once we find a pointer from the index to the actual data—the actual page in the book, we also need to transfer the actual block containing the data or page into memory to find the record itself.

Multiple Indexes

Now this index scheme works when we search for one attribute. But searching on two attributes requires that we build a single index that combines the two values. In others words, if the ABC value used above were actually three different one character attributes, the process of finding the appropriate record which contains the values ABC would be the same, but searching for each of those characters independently would have required three additional indexes.

What happens if I want to search by the first and last characters, the A and the C, and find all possible combinations of the center character? The index above won't help with this, because the first set of indexes must point to the second set of values. We need another index to be able to do that. In order to search all the permutations of ABC, six indexes would be needed.[65]

So now, the database needs nine indexes, one for each of the permutations of ABC, and one for each of the individual attributes themselves. The more attributes that are indexed, and the more values in each of those attributes, the greater the data volume maintained in the indexes. Indexes can add substantially to the total amount of data maintained in data base.

---

64. Each of these last entries would point to a single row in the actual data file unless the keys could be non-unique; in other words, there can be two rows of data with the same "ABC" characters.

65. Factorial of 3. Combinations include ABC, ACB, BCA, BAC, CAB, CBA.

Knowing what indexes to add requires deciding how we are going to use the information, just like the choices an editor of a book makes as to what words are important to include in the index and what are not. Indexed access is important for on-line applications: getting to the right record as fast as possible is critical. People will not, for the most part, wait for a program to read all the records in a file to get to the right record. Indexed access is critical for both ends of the subsystem architecture; the on-line components.

If an index hasn't been planned or is not available to answer a specific question, then the only way to answer the question is to scan the primary data—a process called a table scan, similar to reading the book from beginning to end in a sequential fashion. It doesn't matter if the user is unhappy waiting; it is the only way to get the answer. In producing 400 reports, if one—just one—report needed to select data based upon an attribute or combination of attributes that were not indexed, the database has to scan all the business events to produce the report. If the disk system was bringing the primary data into memory, it would be more efficient to resolve all the queries from the primary data than to also transfer the indexes into memory. The total IO would be lower if the indexes are not used at all. The more reports that are produced, the greater the chances one will require a table scan. One of Rick's white papers stated:

> In general, indexed access works at about 200,000 bytes per second (about an hour and a half per billion). So, as long as the transaction processing or reporting involved only requires that single billions of bytes be touched in the process once a processing cycle, indexed access is sufficiently fast for the purpose ...
>
> Sequential access methods are the basic alternative to indexed access methods. The advantage of sequential access is that it is very fast (1 – 20 million bytes/second depending on hardware and software configuration) compared to indexed access.[66]

Sort

This discussion about indexes can miss the bigger point. The people requesting those reports are not looking for a listing of all the transactions that have applicability to the question they were trying to answer; they want the answer. In most instances, the answer is an accumulation of transactions. And in financial reporting, because financial reporting deals with history, it is an accumulation of lots of transactions or business events.

Accumulating transactions in an efficient manner—turning business events into balances as of a point in time—requires the records to be sorted. Sorting doesn't have to happen after the records have been selected. If we use an index to select which records we want, no sort is necessary after the selection. But building the index required the data to be sorted: to search an index to find the values we wanted, the index has to be in a sorted order and so the data has to be put in proper order to build the correct pointers. Sorting the data by the necessary attributes is needed somewhere between data capture and report production.

Although perhaps many questions can be answered by one row of information on a report, the questions asked aren't always that specific. At times users want a report, like a trial balance, that has many different rows, each of which requires accumulating business events for different attributes. Answering this question from an indexed search is even more difficult because it requires selecting blocks of values[67].

Sorting data can be a very slow process—a very slow process. This is because all of the data to be sorted must be understood within the context of a single process. Effectively every record in the file up to and including the last record has to be read and analyzed before the computer can decide which record

66. Roth, Richard K., *A Practical S/390 Parallel Processing Option for Data Warehouses* Price Waterhouse White Paper, undated (c. mid 1990s) p. 2.

67. Unless the table were loaded with just the information that was needed at the level of detail it was needed which means we anticipated the need and already did the work of producing the report and just stored the results in the table

should be the first record output. If the memory is too small for all the data to fit into—the white board can't contain everything in the binder—then sections have to be brought into memory, sorted, and then written out to a temporary disk—a temporary binder. The last step, after the last record from the file has been read, is to bring one record[68] from each of the temporary files into memory, compare which is lowest or highest (depending on the sort order), and then write it out to the permanent file. This means the data may be passed onto and out of disk multiple times within a single process. For sizable files, because of all the IO involved, it can feel as long as walking half way around the world.

There are many computer books written about sorting data alone. The details of how to sort data are outside the scope of this work (at this point in the book, I am sure you are relieved).

What is important to note here is that building a system to assemble reports from business events as close as possible to the time the report is needed requires sorting in the midst of the assembly line process. And if we are producing hundreds of reports, we may well have hundreds of sorts occurring simultaneously. An experiment to replicate this reporting architecture with a well known ETL tool in the fall of 2006 proves the point.

ETL Approach

ETL tools can do many of the functions in the general reporting pattern we have talked about. They have the ability to scan the data to select events that are relevant for a particular report. They can either sort, or can call sort utilities to perform sorting operations; and they can accumulate or summarize values into rows. Because ETL tools are not concerned with actually delivering reports to the end user, but rather leave that to the database as request by the reporting tool, they tend to be implemented as point to point solutions, taking data from one location and loading into one other location. I have yet to see an instance where an ETL has been configured to scan a repository of business events based upon users' specifications of the reports they need, and in one pass through the data produce all the outputs needed.

In the fall of 2006, Rick thought in fairness to a customer we should see if a lower cost, more commonly used technology would be adequate. He asked experts with the tool to do the following: The team was to take 36,425,958 business events with various attributes on them and produce 33 different summaries from them. Because the summaries were financial summaries, there was little selection logic that needed to be applied. The summaries included hierarchies, because users need to know what the subtotals are for various levels in an organization, product or account hierarchies.

The results of the prototype were that the initial process of selecting records to go into the sort processes worked fine. However, that process ended up turning 36 million records into 47,996,555,264 — nearly 48 billion records! Again, perhaps the size of that number won't mean anything to you, but no one I know of in business ever sorts 1 billion records without really thinking about how to do it, let alone sorting 48 billion records.[69]

Ultimately, the machine failed not because the data was too large, but because the number of concurrent tasks to be managed by the operating system overwhelmed the UNIX operating system. This issue is discussed in greater detail in the next chapter[70].

Summarize

Another very common "old school" processing paradigm is a program doing control break logic. A control break program reads a file with multiple attributes in sorted order. It accumulates the rows into totals. As it detects a change in one of the attributes, it prints an extra line with the subtotal for that level.

68. Actually, entire blocks are brought in but the eyes of the computer only focus on one record at a time.

69. Report to client, unpublished, in author's possession.

70. Techniques that can be used to reduce the records that must be sorted are discussed in Chapter 44, "Sort," on page 227.

This is the process by which the figure Sample Hardcopy Report was made. Creating these subtotals when the data is available and in sorted order is a very efficient way of being prepared to answer the next question that will be asked[71].

So using a scan as opposed to an index, with selection, sort and summarize is a different processing pattern for resolving reporting problems. But can it be done within the timeframes required of reporting? The next step in the process would prove that scan processes could be accomplished very rapidly when focus is maintained on performance.

71. This process is explained further in Chapter 44, "Sort," on page 227, Chapter 45, "Sort User Exits," on page 233, and Chapter 46, "Format Phase," on page 237.

Chapter 20. Parallelism and Platform

A few months after I joined the SAFR project, Rick allowed a major US retailer to challenge the system to solve the most difficult problem of their choosing. The results of these benchmarks showed that a scan process, the heart of organizing the report production process to produce the results at the last possible minute, could be performed very rapidly.

Major Retailer

A major US retailer had a customer marketing database containing all of this retailer's point of sale credit transactions during the last two years, organized by household. A series of COBOL programs, the standard tool for this type of work in 1993, would scan this data, and score each household's buying activity according to various criteria as to attractiveness for marketing mailings. The output of this weekly process is used to drive mailing list applications.

The following are the results from the runs from November 1993. The data was stored on 80 tapes.[72]

	NUMBER OF RECORDS		WALL	CPU	CPU
	READ	EXTRACT	TIME (hours)	TIME (minutes)	COST ($)
PRODUCTION	720,789,844	62,627,442	28.3700	22.44	18,878.04
GENEVA	776,966,927	62,627,448	1.0022	0.78	752.95
	Actual GENEVA Improvement:		**96.47%**	**96.52%**	**96.01%**

Figure 39. Major Retailer CMDB Benchmark Results

The results[73] were astounding to everyone involved: A 96% reduction in wall time from 28 hours to just over one hour, CPU time from 22 minutes to less than a minute, and CPU (computing) costs from US $18 thousand to less than US $1000.

The reduction in wall or elapsed time is due to parallelism. Parallelism is designing a computer system to use more than one CPU at a time. Think of it as using multiple computers at the same time, although in large computers each computer actually contains multiple CPUs. Suppose instead of doing road construction from one end of the project to the other, a city deployed multiple work crews along the road to work on segments of the road at the same time. The total length of the project might be as low as dividing the estimated time for the project by the number of work crews deployed.

CPU time is the accumulation of time used by all processors or computers. In our road work example, the total work time spent on the road project is the accumulation of each of the work crews' time. One would have to pay each work crew for the time spent on the project, even though they are working all at the same time. So although using parallelism takes less time to complete the project, the total time worked and cost may not be reduced at all. In fact, if the plan for parallelism is poor, it may actually be slower and cost more: having one crew responsible for paving and the other responsible for grading means they would be working over the top of each other and saving no time or money.

The reduction in cost and CPU time for this application is purely because the machine code used by SAFR to solve the problem has many less instructions in it than the machine code of the COBOL program. Rick called this instruction path length. If the number of instructions for the COBOL program

72. Data for the major US retailer benchmarks from interview with Jay Poulos on May 18, 2009. As part of the project, the retailer's IT personnel review system outputs to verify results.

73. The differences in the records read were because SAFR didn't ignore voided records or households with more than 1,000 purchases. Thus SAFR did more work than the production system.

to accomplish the task were 100, SAFR accomplished the same work in less than four. There is no way around this. Not all of this reduction may be attributable to poor patterns in the COBOL compiler; some portion may attributable to a poorly written program that performed tasks that were not essential to solving the problem that needed to be solved. But consistent tests like this have shown that SAFR was 30% to 60% more efficient than COBOL for particular types of computing patterns. And those patterns exist in thousands, perhaps millions of business processes.[74]

Being able to scan 1 billion records in one hour was an unheard of level of performance at the time, and is still impressive today. It proved that organizing the report manufacturing process to use a great deal more detail than is used in the subsystem architecture is technically feasible.

The retailer couldn't believe the results. So they asked to have SAFR applied to another problem of their choosing. They selected a system called Delinquent Account Collector Assignment. This nightly process evaluated all accounts that are one or more days past due and determined the follow up action to be taken and the collector assigned to follow up. Approximately 80,000 unique criteria were used in making the determination. Wall or elapsed time was a critical issue in this application as the results had to be available for the collectors each morning, and the production system ran multiple hours nightly. Here are the results:

	NUMBER OF RECORDS		WALL	CPU	CPU
	READ	EXTRACT	TIME	TIME	COST ($)
PRODUCTION	5,477,663	5,477,663	3.4 (hours)	2.5 (hours)	2100.00
GENEVA	5,477,663	5,477,663	9.96 (minutes)	2.76 (minutes)	38.64
	Actual GENEVA Improvement:		**95.12%**	**98.16%**	**98.16%**

Figure 40. Major Retailer Delinquent Account Collector Benchmark Results

Again, the reduction in wall, CPU, and cost was similar to the prior application. Over the years, these types of results were repeated again and again and again.

Death of the Mainframe

Around this time, the IT industry was embracing a new processing model called client-server. Client-server used a combination of PCs with larger servers to perform much of the computing. Many in the industry proclaimed the death of the mainframe.[75]

One of the drives for this was the cost of mainframe computing. I remember joking with Rick at this time that one of the problems with the mainframe was its ability to track its own costs; because it showed up as a line item on the IT financial report, people knew how much it costs, whereas PCs and servers tended to be buried amid other numbers in the report. Thus to reduce cost, the mainframe was attacked because it was visible.

Yet in truth at the time the machines were very expensive compared to getting similar computing capacities from PCs and servers. These less expensive machines used less expensive operating systems as

74. A 2009 program translated from COBOL to assembler results in a reduction in the load module size from 13,808 bytes, to 5,416 bytes, a 60% reduction in the load modules size. Load module size is not exactly the same as the machine instructions contained in the program, but it is indicative. One of the major efficiencies in the retail benchmark likely came from the use of BSAM access method rather than COBOL's default QSAM access method. The access method is a function of the operating system, not COBOL.

75. "It was around that same time that some industry observers were declaring the impending death of the mainframe. One such analyst wrote in the March 1991 issue of *InfoWorld*, for example, 'I predict that the last mainframe will be unplugged on March 15, 1996.'" *IBM Online Archives, Exhibits, Mainframes*, Page 4, or at http://www-03.ibm.com/ibm/history/exhibits/mainframe/mainframe_intro4.html, (Accessed May 2009).

well. One operating system that came to be used extensively was UNIX. You'll remember that UNIX operating system is well suited to on-line processes, and the mainframe operating system tends to emphasize batch processes.[76]

This trend to client server computing tended to emphasize the processing characteristics at both ends of the subsystem architecture—the input and the final output. This trend contributed further to a de-emphasis of the need for the process in the middle, the process of turning business events into report values.

Rick responded to this trend first with a series of papers that pointed out the need for these functions, some coauthored by Eric.[77] At times the discussion led to what some would call a holy war, with those supporting the mainframe allied against those supporting other platform architectures. The high point in this battle was when IBM asked Rick to install SAFR on the IBM Executive Briefing Center machine in Poughkeepsie, NY and show what it could do. The IBM engineers that monitored the system said they had never seen a system more fully utilize all aspects of a mainframe, from the disk processing system getting the data into and out of memory to the CPU processes. Not even IBM's own software exploited the hardware more effectively to solving a business problem.

But our product had just come to market at a time when the market was being declared dead. At times the team felt like we were lone voices in the wilderness. With time and the maturing of the UNIX operating system, Rick proved that the concepts were not platform dependent while he was engaged at a global investment bank.

Global Investment Bank

Beginning in 1998 Rick was engaged on a project for a worldwide investment bank, to manage its Detail Repository, a central component of the Global General Ledger ERP implementation. The constructed repository provided trade-level detail analysis for internal and external global reporting. The project ported SAFR to UNIX to build the detailed financial reporting environment.

Approximately 1.3 million detailed transaction data records from twenty-two different feeder systems were loaded into the Detail Repository nightly. These transactions were trade level detail records from Europe, Asia Pacific, and North America. The UNIX version of SAFR scanned the repositories' 51 million records in 22 entities and 269 physical partitions. It extracted 20 million records that were aggregated into approximately 480,000 summary balances. These summary records were sent to the GL for balance sheet and summary profit and loss reporting. This process ran in approximately 3 hours of elapsed time and 5 and ½ hours of CPU time and produced 30 different outputs.

A second Detail Repository process used the UNIX version of SAFR and custom programs to satisfy the intricate regulatory requirements. This system was executed 19 times with each execution handling a subset of the core business requirements. During this nightly process SAFR read 71 million records in 40 gigabytes, extracted 59 million records in 30 gigabytes, and performed 229 million table joins. The output was created in 12 CPU hours and 8 wall clock hours. In comparison, legacy applications required 24 hours to complete a limited number of these processes.

Outputs from these processes were used for US tax and regulatory, Asia-specific regulatory management, and Swiss regulatory reporting. They included information on:

- Capital Allocations
- Average Balancing and Multi-Currency Revaluation

---

76. See "Servers and Online Processes" on page 60 in the Types of Computers and Processes chapter.

77. Richard K Roth, Denna, Eric L. Ph.D. *Making Good on a Promise: Platform Assignment is the Key to Leveraging Data Warehouses Manufacturing Systems*, February 1996 (© Chilton Publications).
Richard K. Roth, Denna, Eric L., Ph.D., *Platform Assignment Principles For Decision Support Systems And Data Warehouses*, Price Waterhouse White Paper, Nov. 1995.

- Syndicated Loan Netting
- Federal and Swiss Regulatory Collateral Allocation
- Residual Maturity
- Interest Rate Selection
- Product Risk Weighting
- Specific Reserve Allocation
- Un-utilized Facility Calculation.

The process outputs included files used in additional processing or to feed other systems, delimited files, tabular reports, and inputs to a cube-based reporting system.

The following slide depicts the system architecture for this implementation:

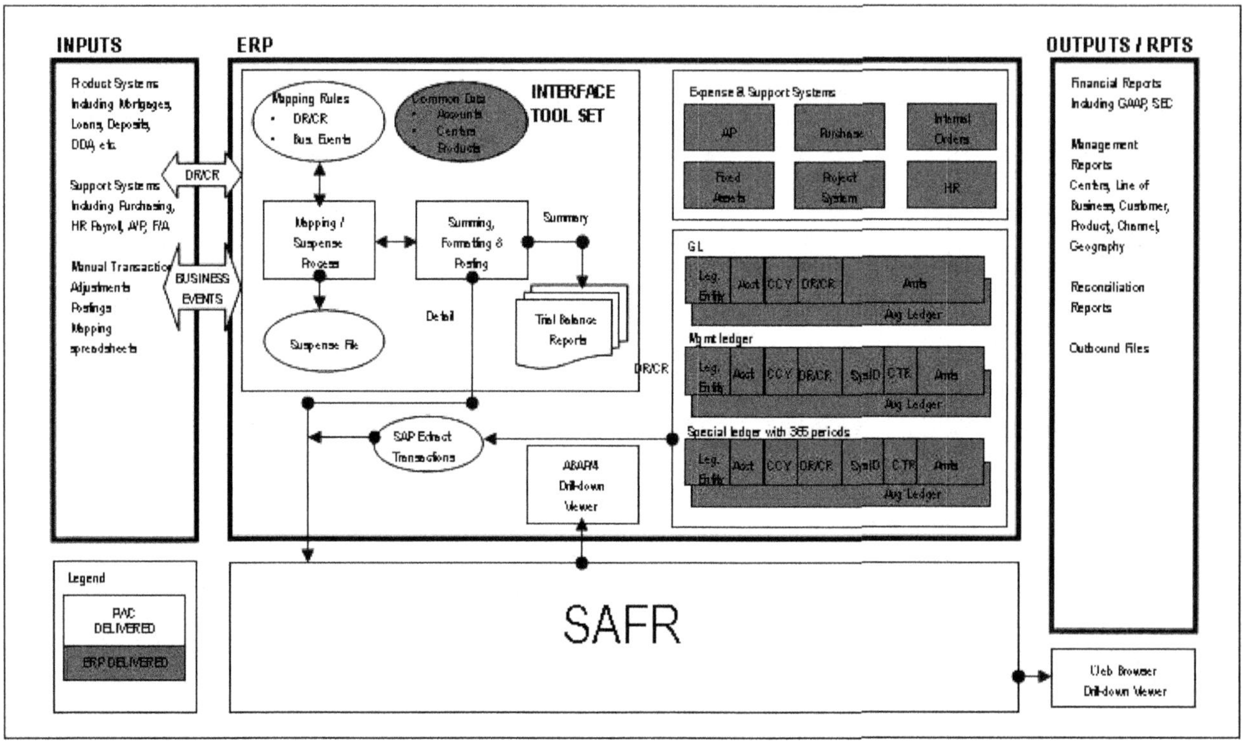

Figure 41. Global Investment Bank Solution Architecture Diagram

UNIX Benchmark

In the spring of 2002 the team conducted a head-to-head benchmark of the UNIX version of SAFR against the mainframe version. The test consisted of running 10 concurrent SAFR extract processes (in parallel) writing to 10 extract files. Each thread read 1 million rows, 100 megabyte source file and wrote 1 million rows, 300 megabyte output file.

Each output row contained 6 sort key columns, 10 columns with fields from the source file, and 16 columns with derived fields from joins. The results show that the UNIX and mainframe versions of the software were similar, and performance increased roughly in a linear fashion with platform power.[78]

78. Mainframe power is measured in Millions of Instructions per Second, (MIPS) rather than in mega or gigahertz.

Platform	Computer Model	Operating System	CPUs	CPU Power (MIPS/MHz)	Elapsed Time	CPU Time
	IBM 9672-RA5	OS/390 V2R10	1	49 MIPS	1hr 14 min	31min 41 sec
Mainframe						
Mainframe	IBM 2064-110	z/OS V1R2	10	1934 MIPS	5 min 19 sec	6 min 02 sec
UNIX	Sun Ultra 450	Solaris 8	2	400 MHz	16 min	Not available
UNIX	Sun Fire 4800	Solaris 8	16	833 MIPS 750MHz	1 min 54 sec	9 min 31 sec

Figure 42. UNIX vs. Mainframe Platform Benchmark Results

The test showed that the UNIX platform actually could perform the functions faster than the mainframe, although the mainframe CPU time was less.

In 1999 Doug, Jay and Al Sung, who performed the z/OS to UNIX port, investigated porting SAFR to a new generation Intel processor called Itanium. They worked with Intel on the potential for having a much smaller computer perform data analysis like no other small machine.[79]

Batch

The issue isn't really the platform; it's the need for a process between event capture and reporting. My experience is that people who work with mainframes understand batch processes, particularly long running batch processes, better than those that work with UNIX.

It seems to me that writing a batch program is a dying art, or science, or craft, or whatever you care to call it; fewer and fewer people can write these programs. One reason is the overwhelming emphasis on on-line systems, and the desire to reduce latency in processes, the lag between the time the transactions are created and when the reports are produced.

Does this mean that batch processing will someday go away? Over my career, I have heard a lot of opinions saying yes; but I don't believe it. Innovation, by and large, usually does not eliminate earlier classes of technology, but rather adds to them. Batch processes are not in danger of being eliminated soon for a number of reasons.

As we have noted, reporting processes by their nature deal with history, they deal with business events that happened hours, days, weeks, months or even years ago. They also require accumulation of those events. Also, financial reporting processes in particular include cutoff points. Year end reports, a whole raft of them, are produced including business events up to 12:00 midnight December 31. All reports are using this data, and should be produced consistently. The use of a batch program facilitates these requirements nicely.

It seems to me they are unlikely to go away for a more fundamental reason: The most advanced information processing mechanism on the planet, the human brain, sleeps every night. The earth turns on an axis as it revolves around the Sun, and half the world is dark at any one time. Sleep and dreaming are a type of batch processing. If evolutionary biology hasn't eliminated batch processes, they are unlikely to go away in my lifetime.

So although initial data capture of business events and the ultimate display of accumulated business events will likely always entail some type of on-line processing, the reporting processes in the middle will likely continue to have a batch component. ETL processes are by and large batch. What many people are saying when they argue batch should be done away with is the length of time batch processes take is too long. Because on-line systems are driven by clicks with people sitting in front of the screens, their processing cycles from start to end of each transaction must be short.

79. Notes from interview with Jay Poulos and Doug Kunkel, June 11, 2009.

Yet if the report production process was driven down to an acceptable level, the number of new "configurations" if reports that may be available may dramatically change the nature and structure of the reporting solution.

Chapter 21. ERP Reporting

As part of the trend towards client server applications, Price Waterhouse caught the wave of ERP system implementations. These, like most major systems projects tend to focus first on getting the data into the system—the operational systems that do data capture. All of the project time gets eaten by defining and capturing business events. Then, when it comes time to produce reports the system has performance problems.

Through the mid 90's, many SAFR projects were started by following a common trend:

- Get a call from a project that now had accumulated a lot of data but can't report on it
- Do a benchmark with SAFR to show that using a different approach works
- Build the reporting solution around SAFR.

We have already noted the Global Investment Bank example above which followed this trend. Before talking more about the solutions to these problems, let's highlight other examples of the tell-tale signs of analytic challenges.

Cookie Manufacturer

In the fall of 1995 a major US cookie manufacturer installed an ERP system to manage all aspects of its manufacturing, HR and financial operations. The system captured data and provided adequate information for managing most operational aspects of the business. But it could not deliver the detailed sales analysis necessary to support the highly detailed, store-specific sales process.

The reporting requirements were substantial. The company required detailed information at the customer/line item level over various time slices from daily to year-to-date, for over 60,000 customer stores and 2,000 items, selecting and summarizing by over 100 fields. The company sold over a million items per week, and they needed comparative information for each time period for at least the last two years. They also needed comparative data to be reorganized to reflect changes in organizational structure over time.

The team attempted to write a query—one query—against the main reporting table. The query ran for more than 24 hours without completing. This would have solved only one of the hundreds or thousands of permutations that ultimately would be needed. They canceled the query and called Rick.

Rick analyzed the reporting requirements. After the fact he wrote a white paper that summarized the results of the project.

> Implementation experience is demonstrating that current [ERP] reporting and data warehousing facilities effectively support most information delivery requirements. In some cases, primarily where substantial data volumes are involved, a reporting architecture that includes additional components is required to meet needs that are outside the scalability bound of baseline [ERP] facilities.

In other words, operational reporting, mostly satisfied by indexed access, works well within the framework of the ERP tool set.

> Although the number of high data-basis operational reports tends to be dramatically smaller than the number of low data-basis reports, the data basis and size for these reports tends to be dramatically larger. The experience at A-REAL-Co. clearly bears this out: in the original analysis of high data-basis operational reporting requirements, only 45 sales analysis reports were identified,

but the data basis for these reports turned out to be approximately 23 gigabytes per week on average[80] (peak loads at end of period are much higher than the average indicates). Examples of these reports are included below:

- FS Sales Force Ranking
- FS Item Customer Pch: SIUs
- FS Item Customer Pch: Cases
- Food Service Ranking - ITEM
- Food Service Ranking - Customer
- Food Service Comparison CASES
- Food Service Comparison $$$
- Food Service Budget - PTD to HYTD
- Item Sales to Budget (Div.)
- Diversified Retail Sales - Final
- SBU Item Sales for Period: (by Sales Org)
- SBU Item Sales for Period: (SBU-Brand-Item) Corp Type
- Item Sales to Budget (Store Door)
- Budget Buster RANKED
- Final Sales BT
- Budget Buster
- Military Account Item
- Account Item - Trend & YTD
- Customer Purchase (Store Detail)
- Gain & Loss, w/ Allow.
- FS Cat. Grouping

As should be evident from the titles, these do not represent "nice to have" reporting requirements, but are blocking and tackling period-to-period comparisons of key volume statistics needed to run the company. The 23 gigabytes also does not include A-REAL-Co.-specific requirements for data reorganization due to material, sales and other account hierarchy changes, legacy systems data integration, replacement of reporting currently outsourced and substantial ad hoc requirements that are anticipated. Unless a detailed analysis of the high data-basis operational reporting requirements is done, it is easy to dismiss these kinds of basic reporting requirements as something that will be handled in background processes when time is available.

Note that Rick isn't talking about optional reporting, reports that don't matter if they don't get done today. These are operational reports that have to be done to run the business every day, and yet they require summarization of a large number of business events—the definition of data basis.

In order to understand whether a given reporting load could be handled in background when time is available, it is necessary to have some basic metrics about how fast this kind of processing can be done in a given environment. Assuming an HP T-500 8-Way world with EMC disk (the A-REAL-Co. configuration), extract processing can be done at a rate of about 6 megabytes/minute (if table joins are required, calculations need to be adjusted to reflect processing at a rate of about 3,000 joins/minute). These numbers are consistent with information from [the ERP vendor] on performance in reporting and general Price Waterhouse experience with UNIX SMP machines running third-party relational data bases. In the A-REAL-Co. case, this would mean approximately 65 hours per week of continuous processing just to complete the initial extract, assuming no table joins were required. Taking into account table joins would mean the basic extract processing would take about 260 hours of continuous single-threaded processing. Further, a general rule of thumb is that reports with a data basis of several hundred thousand records will require several hours to process. Considering that the 23 weekly A-REAL-Co. gigabytes represent about 210 million extract records, something on the order of 2,000 processing hours per week would be a reasonable estimate (albeit a practical impossibility to implement) of the end-to-end processing load, given the A-REAL-Co. environment.[81]

80. Footnoted in original white paper: "The weekly data basis would have been over 20 times the 23 gigabytes if all processing had been done using transaction level data (basic transaction volume is 120,000 order lines per day @ 1,608 bytes per line). Based on the reporting requirements identified, summary file structures were defined that would reduce total data manipulation load necessary to produce the reports. As new reporting requirements emerged during development, summary files were repeatedly modified and regenerated from the transaction detail as necessary to support efficient production processing. It is expected that the summary file structures will continue to be modified and regenerated over time as new reporting requirements evolve."

81. Roth, Richard K., *[ERP] High-volume Operational Reporting/Data Warehousing Summary of Sizing Concepts and Architectural Alternatives*, Price Waterhouse White Paper, September, 1996 p. 1, 4, 5. Copyright IBM Corporation. Used by permission.

In other words the work involved in producing these reports would completely consume the servers purchased to do the operational tasks; there was no additional capacity to accumulate the needed business events and produce the reports.

This paper was one of the key elements for following engagements. The methodology and approach it outlined to analyze data basis are discussed in depth in Part 4. The results of the project are described in Chapter 32, "Define Summary Structures," on page 165.

In March of 1996, I was asked to go help warn a Fortune 100 PC chip manufacturer about the experience of the cookie maker. They said they didn't have significant volumes, and so they wouldn't have a problem. We'll talk more about this example in Chapter 37, "Maintain Focus," on page 187.

US Insurance Provider

After assisting the chip manufacture for a couple of months to solve their problem I was at the front of convincing a Fortune 100 Insurance Company that their data volumes for reporting and allocation processes would likely overwhelm the ERP financial implementation. After two years of work by scores of people trying to get the ERP allocation engine to work, the team constructed a SAFR process that generated all the outputs but at much greater speeds. Programs were developed which generate over 6,000 SAFR processes based upon over 7,000 ERP rules. SAFR executes these views to scan the financial repository selecting records eligible for allocation. It then allocates these costs through four allocation layers, such as products, and geographical units. At 1999 year-end, this process read over 50 million records selecting nearly 3 million that were eligible for allocation. These 3 million records were exploded into over 290 million virtual allocation records, of which 186 million summarized records were written to physical files. The process ran in 7½ hours wall clock time and 28½ hours of CPU time.

Global Bank

In 2009, after 5 years of work and tens of millions of US dollars (if not a hundred million), a major global bank determined that neither they, nor the ERP vendor, could make the ERP GL posting and other financial functions to process much more than 6,000 records a minute. This was substantially below the 140,000 rows a minute published by the vendor in a benchmark for a similar hardware configuration. A major difference is the functionality performed in each test. The customer had chosen to use almost all features of the product simultaneously, including daily accounting periods, large numbers of key values, multi-currency processing, etc. This was in comparison to the SAFR performing the same functions at, on average, a million records a minute.

SQL Benchmark

People find it difficult to believe that major software products produced by the largest software vendors in the world are only capable of these types of results in spite of spending millions of dollars by those implementing them. The root cause is the automation pattern of the tools does not match what the actual computers have to do, and these tools are added layer upon layer resulting in greater and greater inefficiencies. Let's analyze some of these layers.

In the fall of 1994, I was surprised to learn one day that Doug Kunkel, the key SAFR developer, had added the ability for SAFR to read data base tables instead of just reading sequential files, and he had added the ability to do this two different ways. One way was going through the database facilities, in effect presenting the entire database to SAFR within SQL. The other was by actually reading the file the database stores the data in, called a VSAM file. [82]

I was the first to test and use this feature at a benchmark for a large transportation company in November. In that test I saw SAFR using the Direct VSAM method extract 2 million rows from SQL

82. See the introduction of Part 5 Part 5, "The Programmer," on page 191.

tables in about the same CPU and wall time as a BMC load utility, admittedly at the time the fastest way to get data into and out of a SQL table. The BMC utility also accessed the underlying VSAM files. So SAFR was effectively as fast in resolving a single query as the load utility.[83]

In 1999 a SAFR customer wanted to compare the difference in accessing data using these methods and the standard approach accessing through SQL. They devised a test, and here are the results:[84]

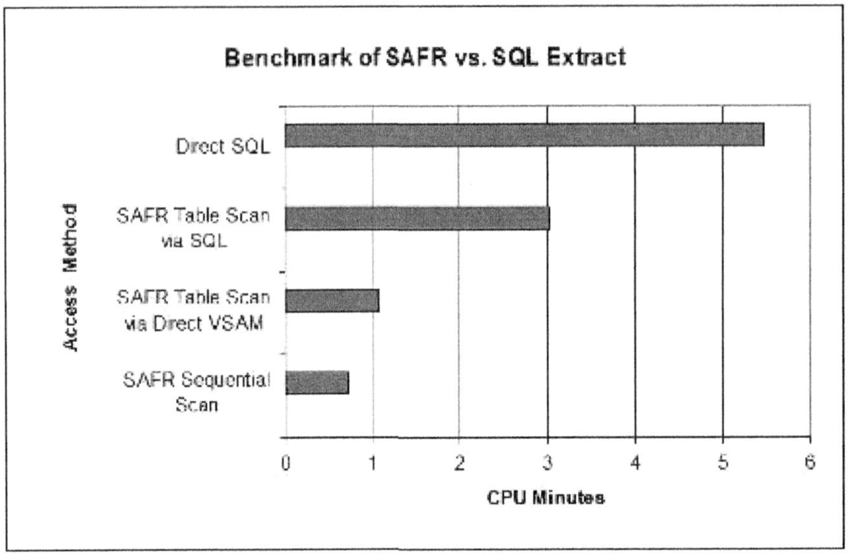

Figure 43. SAFR vs. SQL Extract Benchmark Results

Using SQL, the only way anyone every really goes at data in the database, is seven times slower than it could be. So to begin with, the first layer of software, SQL has longer instruction path lengths than other approaches. The lowest level technology is not all that efficient.

ERP Approach

Commercialized software is built upon the premise that software does not need to be created from scratch for each customer. However, unlike the PC with the ubiquitous Windows operating system, the server market was not dominated by any one operating system. Software vendors require a large enough

83. SAFR (module STGMR95) extracted 2,047,630 from 32 physical partitions in the following time.

IEF373I STEP /STEP65 / START 94314.0706
IEF374I STEP /STEP65 / STOP 94314.0717 CPU 4MIN 49.51SEC SRB 0MIN
17.16SEC VIRT 4036K SYS 664K EXT 22272K SYS 9792K

The BMC Load utility (ADUUMAIN) extracted 2,036,921 rows from the same 32 partitions:

IEF373I STEP /UNLDSTEP/ START 94303.0632
IEF374I STEP /UNLDSTEP/ STOP 94303.0738 CPU 4MIN 12.45SEC SRB 0MIN
14.53SEC VIRT 236K SYS 472K EXT 7420K SYS 8964K

The difference in the records extracted is unexplained, but may be attributable to activity in the database between the runs. Earlier test with small test files showed no differences in the outputs when compared byte for byte. Copies of control reports from November 10, 1994 in possession of author.

Note that the single pass architecture of SAFR means that the incremental time for the second extract of the same data for different criteria performed at the same time is minimal.

84. Report to client, unpublished, in author's possession. Again, note that the single pass architecture of SAFR means that the incremental time for the second extract of the same data for different criteria performed at the same time is minimal, while the time for a second similar report doubles the total CPU time required.

potential market to justify the investment in building the software. Thus they need a way to make their product work across the various operating systems used by large businesses. Many hit upon the idea to use SQL[85].

SQL was standardized well enough that they could have their packages generate and issue SQL, and then the database vendors had the responsibility for working with the various operating systems. Thus the software vendors did not need to manage small differences between the operating systems.

The result, though, was that another level of abstraction was introduced into the system. The ERP package generated SQL, which the database then used to generate machine code. This approach works just fine for indexed access—those processes at either ends of the architecture.

In other cases—most notably batch processes—the work pattern that is automated by the ERP package has little to do with the work the machine will actually have to do; in fact I suspect in some cases it may be geared towards reducing the work effort of programmers at the software vendors; an easy to read and debug form of language might be used, even though its form has little to do with what the computer actually does.

Certainly there is value to be gained by purchasing the investment in software made by others, even if the investment requires additional computing capacity and larger machines. I remember Rick saying to a customer about this time that on many projects the ERP aspects of the program were critical, particularly for transaction processing. Certainly data that is not captured cannot be used in reporting, and as we'll see in the next part of this book, consistency in the coding structures used in that data is critical to exposing connections and patterns in reporting. It is, however, critical to recognize the scale limitations of the tools for reporting. The scale, even for the largest organizations in the world, for payroll analysis typically does not exceed the capacity of the tools, or make them too expensive. But for analysis of higher volume transaction processing areas, there are times when choosing a more efficient method, but with more up front costs in development time, will be more appropriate.

85. Others have chosen to use a virtualized operating system like Java--a program that runs on top of one operating system and allows other programs to run on top of it, giving the appearance to the program that the virtual operating system was actually interacting with the hardware. The additional CPU instructions required by the virtual operating system have the same impact as SQL can have if they do not reflect the underlying compute patterns.

Chapter 22. Order of Operations

When I went to Sacramento, the development center for SAFR, I started on the system test team. I remember finding a problem with the system not many days or perhaps a couple weeks after starting. I went into the on-site project manager Bill Bengston, and described what I had found. I was surprised when he asked what I would suggest to fix it: I was the newest guy. I thought for a moment, and suggested some course of action. Bill considered it, and said, "That sounds good. Why don't we do that." I think I then was responsible to communicate to the programmer how to fix the bug. I have thought for years that that inclusive style of leadership demonstrated by Bill was nurtured from the top by Rick.

Consulting

Our heritage was slightly different than many later start-ups of the internet age. It was based upon consulting work. The way the problem was solved cut across traditional lines of the reporting architecture and the standard commercial software products that had grown up to support it. It was an incredibly ambitious scope.

Because of its development in the consulting world, it didn't have to appeal to a large number of potential buyers to be commercially viable. By focusing on solving problems for the largest organizations, performance was always kept top of mind. It also had the freedom to pursue whatever technology or processing options needed to solve the problems. Over years and years, the patterns have emerged and been refined based upon the principles McCarthy outlined.

Effectively, the result is a highly tuned compiler, processing language and flow that automates report production processes from the detail, minimizing the intermediate inventories that must be developed.

One other aspect of being successful in the rapid development of reports is, as Rick often says, doing things in the right order. A more technical term for that is controlling the order of operations.

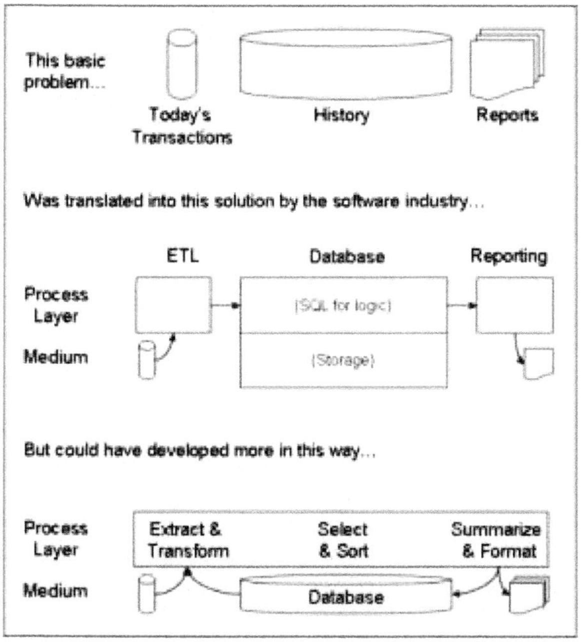

Figure 44. Cross Component Development

The Right Order

To understand what "order of operations means" think of the order in which a building is built. If the simplified steps were (1) design building, (2) procure materials, (3) ship to site, and (4) assemble building almost any building can be built. Consider the implications on the possible size of the building if just the last two steps are reversed. Instead of shipping materials to the site and assembling, we assemble the building and then ship to the site. The scale of possible building is now a mobile home, not a skyscraper.

The same thing would be true of Dell's manufacturing line. Imagine they first dumped all the raw materials inside the computer case before connecting any of them. The manufacturing process would be very expensive if not impossible.

In a similar way in reporting, the entire input file could be sorted for each particular report before selection of what records are needed for the report is performed. This would be very inefficient as records and attributes would be processed (with potentially significant IO) which then would not be used in the report. Sorting after selection is more efficient.

Another example: In banking, a particularly useful type of balance is an average daily balance. Use of this type of balance eliminates temporary spikes from large but short-lived transactions. The creation of an average daily balance, though, can mean an entire new supply chain of data to balances for specific answers, with a tremendous amount of intermediate report inventory.

However, use of a movement based architecture with control over the order of operations enables average daily balance calculations from the movements at almost the very last step in report production. Doing this simple divide at the appropriate time is the critical difference between being able to produce a greater number of reports to answer more questions from the same data in a timely manner, or not. SQL as a tool does not provide adequate control over the order of operations to enable use of a movement based architecture.

The Next Wave

Most companies have established the ability to produce enterprise level summaries of financial results. Most have taken this further to implement processes such as funds transfer pricing, allocations, and at times multi-currency processing in a patchwork way into that environment. The deadline for implementing IFRS is looming, and will cause additional changes to the environment. But I am convinced that the next wave progression in financial reporting must come by removing layers of accumulated processes to the financial report supply chain. Each additional layer of processing adds to the diseconomies of scale the environment already has. Only by doing the hard work of removing layers, getting back down to and then carrying forward the details—the business events, can the needs for financial reporting be supported in a cost effective manner.

Fortunately, the SAFR projects over the years, and the way the tool has developed, have established a pattern, a method if you will, for doing just that. To understand that method let me describe those projects, the broader team, and the next key mentor in implementation, Jay Poulos.

Part 4. The Projects

Jay is nothing if not practical; incredibly practical, in fact frustratingly practical at times. But without a dedication to being practical, to really making the theory work, and consistently testing the tenets of the theory through large, complex projects, the benefits of it would never have become clear.

In Chapter 8, "REAL Analysis Method," on page 43, Eric taught me an approach about how to build a system that would capture business events. This implies a soup to nuts approach to the problem: "Let's build a system that captures all the business events and their associated attributes needed for reporting, and then we'll worry about the reporting problem." As we just noted, reporting problems often appear because of data volume issues, and event based systems have even more volume than a normal system. Thus although a nice idea, this theoretical approach from my experience isn't currently practical.

Even if it was, as noted by McCarthy, the business world, particularly the financial systems world, doesn't work in that wholesale change sort of way. The risks of reporting errors from too radical a shift in systems can be catastrophic: It could cause the demise of the entire enterprise. So incremental—or perhaps in Jay's language, practical—approaches are needed.

So what are the steps in these practical approaches? The best way to understand them might be through descriptions of the various projects SAFR has been involved with through the years and the parts of SAFR that support those projects. These projects affected not only the companies for which they were implemented, but were the basis for features being added to the software, architectural choices in those solutions, and the steps taken to solve specific problems.

Rick always emphasized that people capable in multiple domains created the best results. The practical approaches may be listed as a set of sequential steps, but what Rick said is true when applying the steps. If one does not think about performance until the end, the system will not perform. Processes generate new business events, some of which will likely be needed when finding more detailed events. Performing the steps effectively is a bit like solving simultaneous equations; one must work up and down the list multiple times in order for each answer to balance and integrate with the others. It requires a real balancing act.

Chapter 23. Development

"Then let's add an edit." That was the inevitable concluding line from discussing any bug in one of Jay Poulos's programs when I first came to the SAFR team in Sacramento. I was on the system testing team, and would report any problems I found to Jay. Jay was the on-site system architect. He also wrote some of the programs. His programs built the logic table. They ran as the second set of programs in the SAFR process. Whenever I discovered something that didn't work in his process, it turned into a new on-line edit to prevent someone from entering that condition. "The system was never intended to do that" might be the reason given. He never referred to any document, so I had no right to appeal except based upon my own instincts of what was right or wrong. After a few months of this, everyone on the project knew that the "us" in "let's add an edit" didn't really include Jay.

In fact, only a few weeks into my assignment on the test team, I had found a number of bugs, and learned that a fairly common end result of an unstable program written in assembler for mainframes is called a System message OC1, or SOC1 - an invalid operation exception. I so thoroughly understood Jay's role as designer and Doug Kunkel's role as writer of the assembler programs, I struck off the following poem one Wednesday afternoon:

ODE TO SOC 1

While performing my testing one day
In the consistent and usual way
I viewed my results, expecting some fun
But instead I found I had a Soc 1

I called up Jay, he said "NOT!"
And then Doug replied "So what?"
I yanked on my hair till the set of the sun
Then said to myself,
"I think the Soc won."

KMT 8/19/1993[86]

In the years following the Teflon president—Ronald Reagan—Jay became known as the Teflon programmer: bugs just wouldn't stick to him, no matter how fast we were going.

And it felt at times we were trying to go very fast. Although a start-up high-tech company, we weren't really working in a "garage." Rather, it was a six story office building in quiet downtown Sacramento, the capital of California. The office was only about five blocks from the capital, yet didn't have much of a view. In my mind's eye, the building is brown, the carpet brown, the walls brown, traditional brown wooden desks in the offices. The sixth floor probably hadn't been redecorated since the early 80's or perhaps even late 70's; a very brown time.

There were a lot of questions about why we were located in Sacramento. SAFR had grown out of the state government practice. The state and local government arm was consolidated in Sacramento from a lot of smaller regional offices in the West. Rick explained one time that state governments were the first organizations to try to do enterprise type systems. They had legal mandates from the federal government that required them to do so. The federal government was too large to tackle an enterprise system, and the subsystem architecture was working well enough for businesses.

86. The date was contained in the electronic version of the poem in the author's possession.

However, we weren't really part of the office all that much. Just a few months later we were transferred to the Midwest region, I think because of Rick's ties to Chicago. Our little group in Sacramento was definitely the far western edge of the Midwest, by about a thousand miles. Geographically, the firm's audit and tax divisions on the fifth floor were much closer. Their office manager and staff were kind to us; they invited us to all the office functions like the Christmas party and such, but we really didn't work closely with any of them. I remember the office HR partner, Sean Barry, one day saying to Randall Ness, "Oh, you Geneva guys, you're like a bunch of cowboys out on the range." He was right.

Most of the people that had worked with Rick on the early SAFR projects, in Oregon, Washington, and Wyoming, didn't move to Sacramento. Randall Ness did; and Renae Bell, who joined the firm after the Washington project, did too. Bill Bengsten was there for a few months, but decided to move his family back to Minnesota a few months later. Mostly people flew in when they needed to be on site. Jay flew down from Oregon. Brandy Smith welcomed me to the office the first morning, but she lived in Texas. Sometimes Doug drove up from the Bay area, I only remember a couple of visits by Mike Tabb, Dave "Murph" Murphy, Tony Talarico, and Jeff Gibbs from the Wyoming project.

Probably like many a successful start-up, demand exceeded supply. The software wasn't really finished when Jay led the retailer benchmark in November of 1993. It was buggy. The problem given us fit the software exactly, but they thought—and we hoped—that perhaps there were a thousand other possible uses for it in their company. So there was a massive effort to find all those other uses and then apply them to the software to cut the cost of computing. Each of these uses demanded new features or exposed problems in the software. Rick pulled all the prior projects' team members on site in Chicago for those projects in 1994, including Mukesh Patel from the Oregon project, and Renae from Sacramento.

That left Randall in charge of the development center in Sacramento, composed of the three remaining local contract programmers Bill had hired to build the system before I arrived, and me. We were supposed to fix the bugs found on the project, test them, find more bugs to prevent them from showing up on the project, and independently install the new software as upgrades for Alaska, Oregon, and Wyoming. Oh, and then we also had to actually finish the last components of the software.

The first all-nighter I worked was with Randall; the retailer expected a product-like set of scripts to run the system. The benchmark efforts used cobbled together scripts from the test JCL, a primitive mainframe scripting language. I remember being a little surprised as I explained to Randall how I thought the system flow should work. I hadn't worked much with Randall; he was developing another part of the system, and hadn't been involved at all in testing. That had kept him from learning the overall perspective of the latest system. He listened to me as I told him which programs had to execute in which order, and through the night he constructed the first set of product scripts. Over the next week or so I wrote the operations manual that explained that flow.

We were overwhelmed. The excitement caused by it all allowed Rick to add new people. At first we had new people fly into Sacramento. Mona Breed, one of my instructors in Tampa, came. Julia Braun Roth, recently married to Rick and my project manager on the CASE tool project, came and brought Cheryl Gentsch, wife of Dale from my Wyoming interview. They managed things for a few weeks through the crisis as we brought on more team members.

We then added more permanent team members who moved to Sacramento. Clyde Simmons, one of the contractors, joined the company. I took Rob Clark, another State of Washington employee, and his wife to lunch as part of their recruiting visit. Monica Logan and Chris Stallman joined the firm the same day, were in the same training class in Tampa, and both came directly from training to be part of the team. Later Barry Arabi and Mark Ashton joined the team as well.

Sean the HR partner was scheduled to interview for the firm at Sacramento State University; but, no students signed up. To avoid embarrassment, some school official grabbed Spiros Velianitis, a teaching assistant, and said he needed to sign up. Spiros protested that he was in jeans and wasn't looking for a job, but dutifully did it. Pat noted his attire and Spiros simply responded, "I didn't think I would be doing this today, but decided I should." Spiros impressed Pat, who suggested Rick make him an offer.

Spiros knew nothing about the firm or the job. But, looking at the offer letter, he said, "I don't want to wonder what would have happened if I had taken the job." Immediately, this passionate Greek, a waiter on weekends because he loved to be with his friends, was whisked off to Tampa for three months training. He was so homesick he almost quit, yet he survived to come join us in the office.[87]

By the spring of 1995, we actually had a pretty good system. The Retailer projects had provided testing in ways we never could have imagined. And with the additional resources all working in one location towards the goal of being a software product, we developed documentation, installation and source code maintenance procedures, obtained pagers and set up a help line with a call tickets data base Randall and I built using Lotus Notes.

We only had one problem: new sales didn't come piling in. Besides, being a mainframe product, it was also because there was no part of the system that really could be demonstrated. The on-line functions were only character based screens just as graphical user interfaces were all the rage. The outputs from the system were files and hard copy reports. There was nothing exciting about watching a batch program run on a mainframe. Software sales are driven by features. Our product didn't neatly fit into any software category to allow it to be compared. So, it came up short in each category because it didn't have all the features of any one category. The theoretical underpinnings of the event based reporting architecture probably overwhelmed a lot more people than we knew.

Performance issues are very difficult to anticipate. People choose products based upon features, and then in most cases scale the data volume presented to those products by summarizing the input to avoid performance problems. Only people who have been through performance problems, who haven't followed the manufacturer's recommendations on safe volumes, know how painful performance can be. They become conversant with the parameters of performance and are able to assess if something is really fast or not. Others can almost literally be convinced by the uninitiated who proclaim that their bicycle traveling at 10,000 units an hour is so much faster than a car that only averages 60 units an hour, when one is measured in feet and the other is in miles. Many projects buy bikes, and set their project goal in feet, and proclaim success when they reach it.

In the spring of 1996 I remember commenting to Doug that we had the world's hottest engine, but it was in a really ugly body. Only people who know engines would find it cool. By 1997 we had a dozen customers who knew engines. It was clear we weren't going to have a list of hundreds of customers.

But the customers we had allowed Randall to refine and establish enough software company processes to have critical mass to keep going. He developed source code management techniques from scratch, and bug tracking processes. We worked with clients on testing fixes and new features. We had perhaps a hundred thousand lines of COBOL, Assembler, and JCL, and kept it all working with a very small maintenance and development staff. Randall used who ever wasn't on a project at the time to help do maintenance, and he himself did this along with his full-time job on projects as well. When everyone was on projects, people helped with maintenance after hours. They did this because we all had a sense of mission.

I remember when I was on the top of the support call list and received a call one night. I had flown home from a project and hadn't gotten home until perhaps 8 PM or so. When the phone rang at 1:00 AM I found my way to the desk, picked up the phone but couldn't hold on to it. It dropped in the metal trash can and banged around as I tried to pull it out but fumbled. The person on the other end was very

---

87. Spiros was very good at the work. However, after two and a half years, at an intense time on the Pharmaceutical Litigation project, Spiros was again homesick, having to be in New York weekly. He looked to me as his boss although he didn't functionally report to me, and wrote me a letter saying he was resigning. I called Rick; we couldn't afford to lose him. Rick didn't have any suggestions what to do. I thought for a few minutes after I hung up and then found Spiros and said, "You can't resign to me; I'm not your boss. You have to do that to Rick, so this letter isn't any good. Now, before you send something to Rick let me tell you what I think. I think you should stick this out, should learn how to push through something like this when it is difficult. You aren't at the end of what you should know from this job." He pondered for a moment, and then said he thought I was right. He stayed through the project and finished up some important assignments before going back to teach at Sacramento State a year and a half later.

concerned I was seriously hurt. I know Randall had probably scores and perhaps even hundreds of those experiences. But he kept the system going for all the clients.

Finally in 1998 there was no pull for anyone to stay in Sacramento. And as consulting projects opened up in different parts of the country using the software, team members moved to be near them or where they wanted to live and commuted to the project. We had an interesting business model; not wholly services, yet not wholly a software product. Most software products must appeal to potential customer bases of hundreds if not thousands. Most services businesses take few things into the next project but the people and what is in their heads. Our model allowed us to innovate for a customer base of one if needed. Instead of building tract housing for the masses, we could concentrate on those organizations for which standard approaches would not work—those customers that needed skyscrapers.

Chapter 24. Skyscrapers

One day in May 2006 I worked at the IBM office in downtown Chicago. As I left the building that day, I stopped and watched construction workers preparing the foundation for the new 92-story Trump Tower Chicago. After a few mesmerizing minutes of watching all the complexity and activity, and pondering upon the investment taking place in that new building, I thought of the similarities between building a skyscraper and my experience in constructing new systems over the years.

Because software systems are for the most part virtual and not tangible, they can veer off course and move from reality to fantasy much too easily. But there is a way of keeping reporting systems grounded in reality. Understanding this analogy can help.

Data Sources

That afternoon I surveyed the foundations of surrounding buildings, roads, and bridges, which were exposed for the first time in years. The messiness of it all struck me, a mismatch of walls made of differing materials from bricks to concrete at varying angles misaligned in some cases with overhanging structures above. The brick portions by the bridge buttresses appeared more than 75 years old. As I left and walked to my car, I marveled at the thought that all that messiness must undergird all major cities, years and years of accumulated, layered building in the same location.

The same is true of large business systems. As we have noted, the operational systems, the front end of the subsystem architecture, have existed for years. They are misaligned, constructed on various platforms using various technologies of various ages. They have been constructed the same as any major city, piecemeal, over years, with varying degrees of overlap and integration. There are huge investments in these systems, in people, processes, and technologies that support them.

The finance systems have grown up in like manner, adding layer and layer of processing on top of each other, after each acquisition or as each reporting problem was tackled. The mass of code and data flows is almost overwhelming to anyone trying to understand it all.

If our system is a building, how could we build it on such a foundation? Alternatively, do we really need to rip everything out and start over again? A few people, including enterprise data stewards, may dream of doing just that. Like their counterparts in the public works departments, they may wish they could clean it all up, start with a fresh set of plans, straighten out the inconsistencies and permanently fix the problem-prone locations. Yet even they recognize the impracticability of doing so. The cost of replacing this foundation likely outweighs the potential benefits, even if the capital could be found to do so.

The operational systems are the "factory" that produces the materials from which the finance system is constructed. The material produced is data. The data has varying degrees of quality and suitability for use in finance. The reporting data needs are different from the transaction processing systems data requirements. For example, completing the transaction in the operation system may not require all the fields captured as input. Some fields are captured for analysis after the transactions are complete, sometimes long after the transactions are complete. Thus, the focus of operational system maintenance, including on-line edits and validations on these reporting fields, is often low. Operational systems can tolerate inconsistent data that reporting systems cannot.

Skyscrapers—multi-purpose skyscrapers—are built within the existing city infrastructure, within all the messiness. And the existing finance systems accept and tolerate the data imperfection of the operational systems. The data produced by the operational systems may have problems, but it is certainly not worthless. Yet understanding the messiness is a critical guide to the development of a new finance system.

Plans

While watching the construction, I spotted a few engineers, building plans in-hand, marking points and inspecting progress. Developing the building plans is certainly a critical step in the process. However, it is not done in isolation I am sure. It includes inspecting the existing site, investigating below the street surface and taking core samples. That day I envisioned engineers crawling through manhole covers and touring basements with flashlights before the land purchase even occurred.

This interaction between creating plans and inspecting the real world is sometimes lost in IT projects. Inspecting the data is a critical, often ignored step in building the finance systems. It is important not just to inspect the data but also understand its potential uses. When the need for inspections is ignored, many projects shift focus completely to developing plans.

This approach often centers on creating a cosmic global data model, the plan of all plans. Such a plan would solve all the data problems because then all data would be neatly categorized and filed. And the approach seems reasonable. If we are going to construct an enterprise financial system, then obviously we need some portion of an enterprise data model. Yet to focus exclusively on the data model is approaching the problem as if we are constructing a new city out of farm land in the middle of the prairie. It is no more practical than tearing down an entire city to start over again.

Don't get me wrong; data models are important, and an enterprise data model can be a good idea. But the enterprise data models and similar types of documents should be thought of more like a zoning plan. Zoning plans develop over time with the city. They change. They have limited details about each building and simply give an overall perspective. Build an enterprise data model to determine the kinds of data the organization has, where it is located and how it is organized. But don't confuse the plan for the data. The plan is not the building. The data model is not the data.

Structure

Using our understanding of the basic structure of the building can balance the need for planning at too low level of detail. If all the subdivisions of each floor had to be worked out prior to making progress on the skyscraper, again the planning cycle would be interminable. When building the basic structure, it isn't necessary to know what rooms will be the copy rooms, or the conference rooms, or the offices. Much of that can be decided later.

Skyscrapers are composed of basic components. The building that will rise will have a foundation, lobby, shops, and elevators on the main floors, and then general office areas above. Similarly, most reporting environments contain certain standardized components. In buildings, the concept of open floors that are configured later provides the flexibility to make progress without knowing all the details.

The finance system, as the original enterprise data warehouse, also has a basic structure to it, with ETL, repository, and reports. Yet at times it feels as if to configure any one of those things, all the details about what reports are needed must be known. This drives projects to plans at inappropriate levels. We need some grounding principles upon which to start, that guide us away from wanting all the details defined up front.

Alternatively, understanding the business events provides a structure for us to begin. Looking back at the operational systems can help. Data in the operational systems are normally organized into business events. These are the individual transactions so familiar to business people. These transactions provide the basis for an enormous amount of reporting within an organization. They are counted, added, sorted, summarized, selected, and categorized. Focusing on these business events—thinking of them as the basic building block for any reporting system—can help guide both the mock-up phase of the project, and the proper repository structure later on. Focusing on business events from the source systems eliminates some of the variability that can side track progress.

Data Tests

Inspecting the site and suitability of the materials should involve much more than it does in most reporting projects. Certainly all good data modelers obtain samples of data from the various systems to develop an accurate data model. But the inspections I am talking about take this idea much further.

Consider for a moment that, although a skyscraper is enormous, most people only interact with a small piece of the building at any one time: they experience the entrance, the elevator, the office, and the conference room. Few people interact with it in much more holistic ways, such as the window washers and HVAC maintenance workers.

Most people only interact with small parts of the finance systems at any time as well. When it comes to data analysis, people interact with a report or a few lines of a report at a time. The mind can only comprehend a few data points at any one moment. Admittedly, the number of interactions can be significant; as data is absorbed, new points of investigation emerge. Sometimes these points are near the previous points and are contained within the same report. Often they are lower levels of detail.

It is possible to take data samples and allow some level of interaction for people. In most cases, the data provided from the operational systems can be used to produce reports or cubes. People can react to these, similar to walking into an office mock-up. There are key attributes contained in the source systems that can be of enormous interest to the business, that are used in reports they already know, and can give a sense of the immediate value of the data. Yes, these "mock-ups" have limitations; for the skyscrapers, they do not have the real window views; for the reports, they may not have the time dimensions, and some operational systems attributes may be inconsistent or completely unusable.

Yet exposing limitations early is critical to accurately determining what type of system can be built. These "core samples" if you will, are at the heart of inspecting the site, testing the materials, and stepping into mock-ups of the completed structure.

Tools

Some aspects of the standard technology stack used in reporting processes present impediments to taking core data samples. The nature of most reporting tools does not allow turning real data into some useful reports without going through many layers of development.

ETL tools can read data from the operational systems, but they focus on obtaining data, not delivering reports. They contain limited reporting capabilities. Most repositories have the database at the middle of them. By and large, databases have very low tolerance for the messiness of operational data. They can enforce data types and relationships that the operational system built on different technology may violate. Data typing, saying whether the value in a field is numeric or character as a simple example, is effective when data is being created. But in reporting systems, the data has already been created; it is too late to enforce rules that data already breaks. Reporting tools, by and large, leave most of the work of generating the reports up to the database. They also expect the rows to be in nearly displayable format in some cases. Thus the data sample reports have to be defined in the database and populated by the ETL tools.

What is needed for this mock-up stage of the project is the ability to combine the ETL and reporting layers; data needs to be read, perhaps even directly from the operational systems, and turned into reports, without worrying about laying it down in the ultimately structured repository. A tool with this capability would significantly enhance the ability to guide construction of the finance system. If this tool also focused on reporting on business events, so much the better.

Keep this analogy in mind as we explore how SAFR has been implemented through the years. Theses steps have developed into something that might be called The SAFR Method. The steps are:

1. Find the Event File
2. Balance the Event File

3. Find More Detailed Events
4. Define Reference Data
5. Iteratively View Results
6. Assess Reporting Needs
7. Estimate the Data Basis
8. Define Summary Structures
9. Define Processes
10. Consider Complex Joins
11. Model the Repository
12. Optimize for Performance

We'll examine each of these steps in the following chapters.

Chapter 25. Find the Event File

The subsystem architecture theory says that operational systems usually capture and process business events. In Rick's lectures about the system, he would point out that the transaction files, which are archived off as soon as they are created, could be used instead of the posted balances. In July of 1995 I was asked to help build a pharmaceutical company litigation support database. A number of pharmaceutical companies were being sued for antitrust practices. They had agreed to join up and provide data that could be analyzed to show that their pricing practices were not anti-competitive.

Find the Event File

The first step to apply SAFR to any problem is to identify the event file. The event file contains business events; or more simply, transactions. Most systems have them stored somewhere. It is normally made up of a series of fields that simply have codes in them like 8456, QRM, etc., and have at least one amount somewhere in the record. They aren't very meaningful in and of themselves, but they contain the raw data from business events.

The pharmaceutical companies created computer tapes of their sales files for the prior 5 years. These were pretty raw dumps of data; there was very little programmer time involved in making them. However, the records were identifiable, and representatives from each company could tell us what each field meant. In some cases the source system had changed during those five years, or sales were recorded in more than just one system, so we received multiple record formats for one company.

SAFR Components

SAFR at the time was composed of three major divisions, the Developer Workbench, the Scan Engine which produced multiple outputs called Viewpoints, and the Insight Viewer.

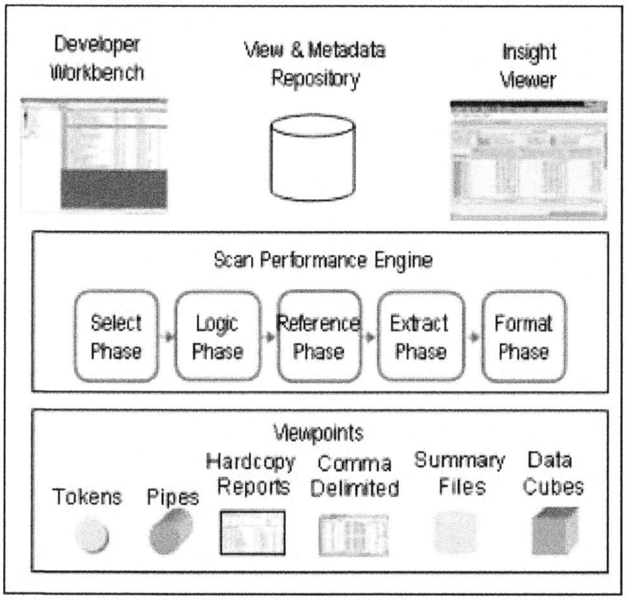

Figure 45. SAFR Components

Our work begins with the Developer Workbench.

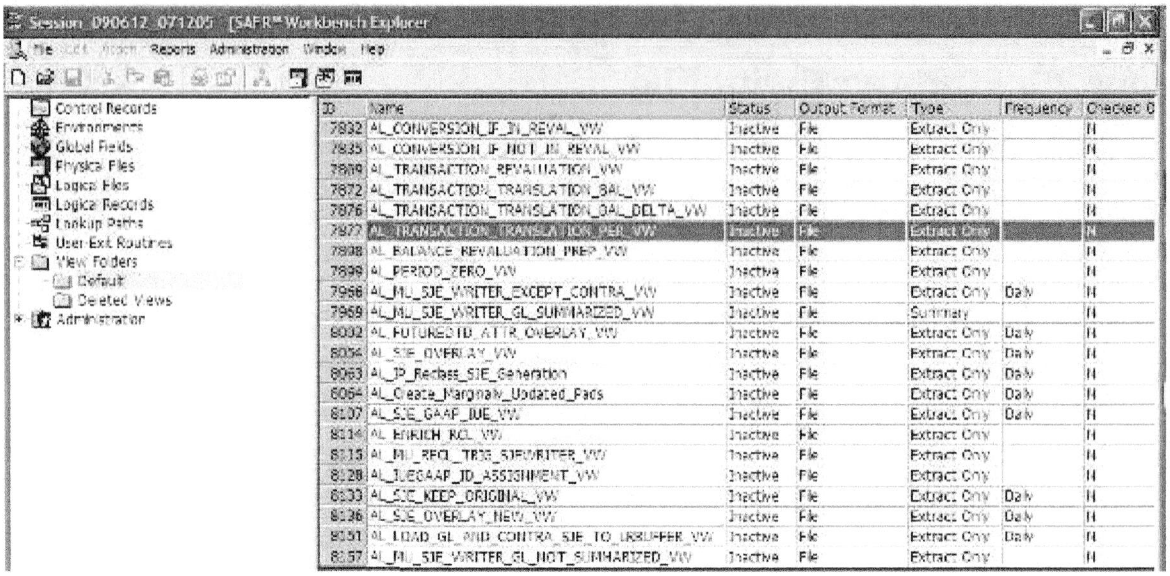

Figure 46. The SAFR Developer Workbench

Define Metadata

SAFR as a tool was designed to be data independent. In other words, it was designed to read different types of files without having to change or write specific programs. The tool's programs adjust to interpret the data in the file. The first thing to do is to define the file to SAFR, and its associated structure or layout. We call these Logical Files and Logical Records (LRs); logical because they may be used to describe records in many different files.

Logical Records are composed of many fields or attributes. SAFR is able to interpret different kinds of field formats. For example, on mainframes numeric data is often stored in a format called "packed." SAFR can make sense of the numbers in these fields if we tell it how to interpret them.

The file definition, the LR, and the fields are part of the SAFR metadata. Metadata is data that describes data. A system administrator creates these once, and they are used over and over and over again.

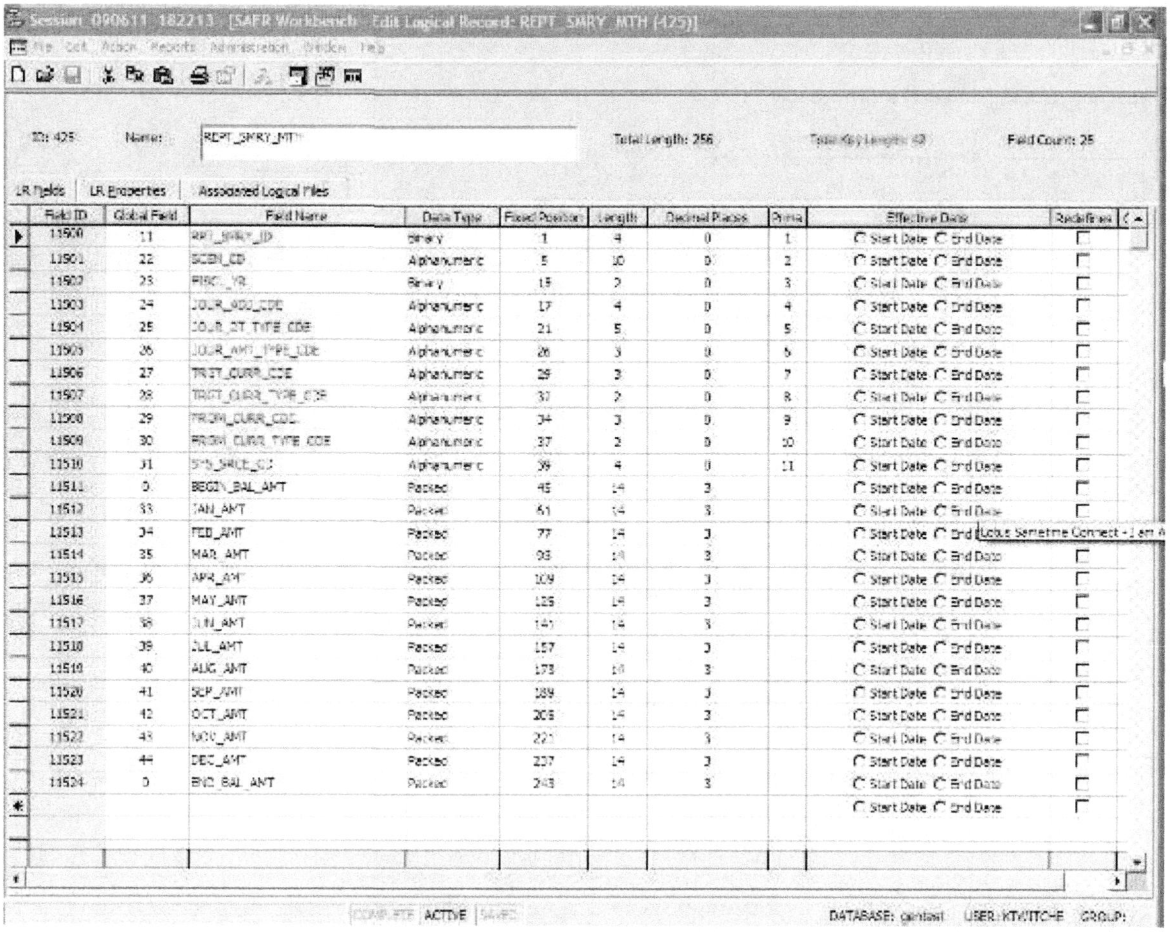

Figure 47. Logical Record Definition

Test Metadata by Creating a View

The next step on the project was to test to make sure the metadata was defined correctly. To do this, we construct a SAFR View. Back in Chapter 9, "The Ivory Tower," on page 49, Eric passed out a piece of paper with a very simple architecture diagram on it. It described SAFR, and it looked somewhat like this:

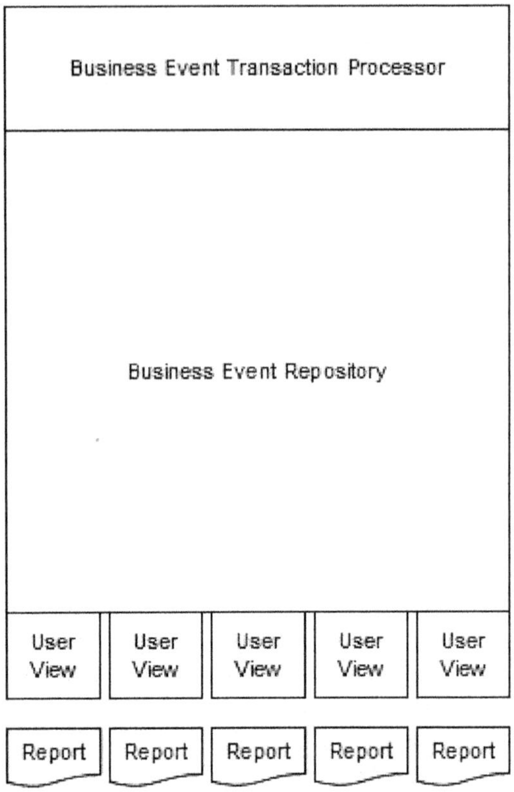

Figure 48. Simplified SAFR Architecture

Eric explained that each report generated is simply that user's view of those business events. The accounting view of the data is independent from other legitimate views. Thus the Views don't change the business events; they simply summarize and report them.

The business event repository isn't necessarily some mysterious structure with hundreds of different database tables all interlinked and updated by a web of processes. Rather as in the case of the litigation support warehouse, it could be thought of containing a single type of record, with all the desired attributes on it. In data warehouses this is often called the fact table. This generalization isn't quite accurate for the pharmaceutical data, in that each company's record format was slightly different, but the concept is not much different.

Creating a view requires the following steps:

Step 1: Specify view format and level

What output do we want SAFR to produce? Do we want a file that can be processed in another system, do we want a report, a file to download? Do we want each record read to be an output record, or do we want to summarize the inputs records creating fewer, accumulated output records? We specify those on the View Properties screen.

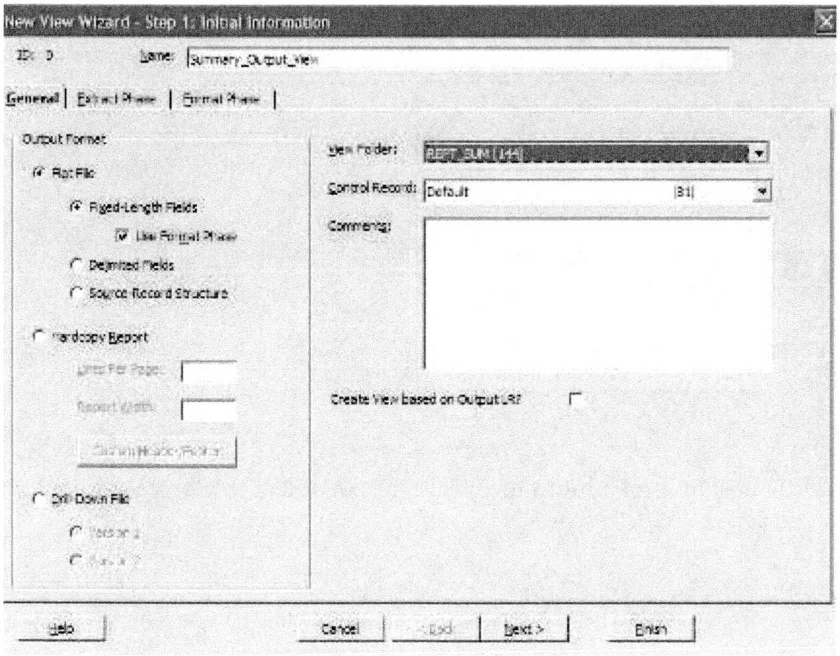

Figure 49. View Properties Wizard

Step 2: Select the event logical record

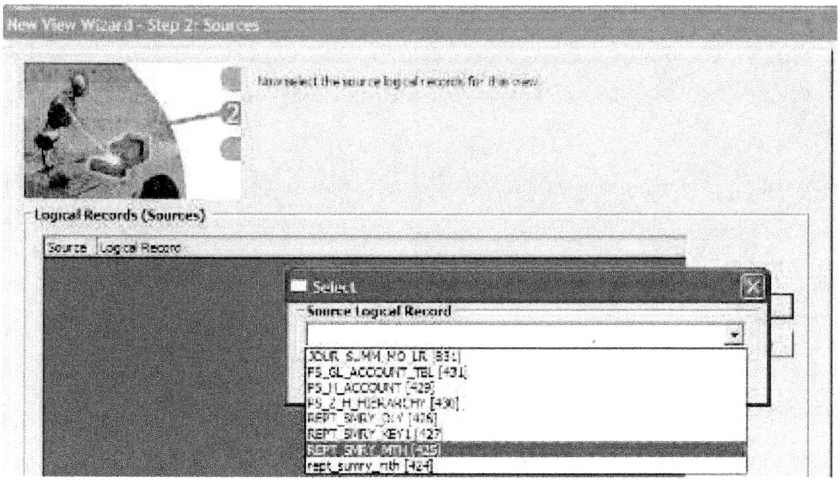

Figure 50. Logical Record Selection Wizard

Which event file in the business event repository has the data we want to report on? For example, let's assume we want a phone list of people on our street, and we have an event file with names and address of all the people in the country.

Step 3: Specify the logical file

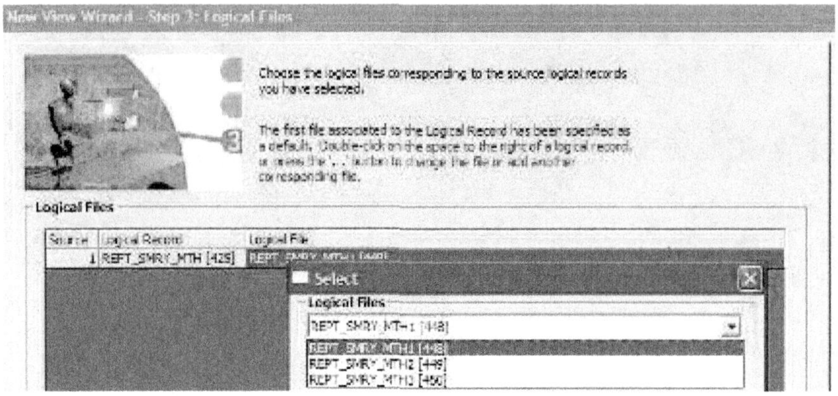

Figure 51. Logical File Selection Wizard

Let's assume the actual names and addresses are broken into files by state. We select the logical file containing our state.

Step 4: Select output fields

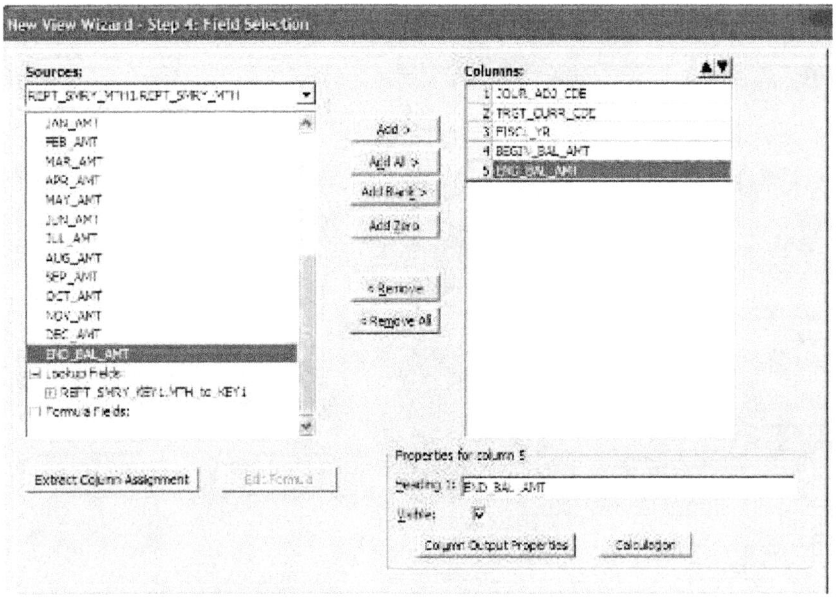

Figure 52. Field Selection Wizard

Next we select which fields from the LR we want on the output report. Let's assume we want name and phone number on our report.

Step 5: Specify sort order

Then we specify in what order we want the fields sorted on the output. For example, a typical name and address report is sorted in ascending order by last name, then first name.

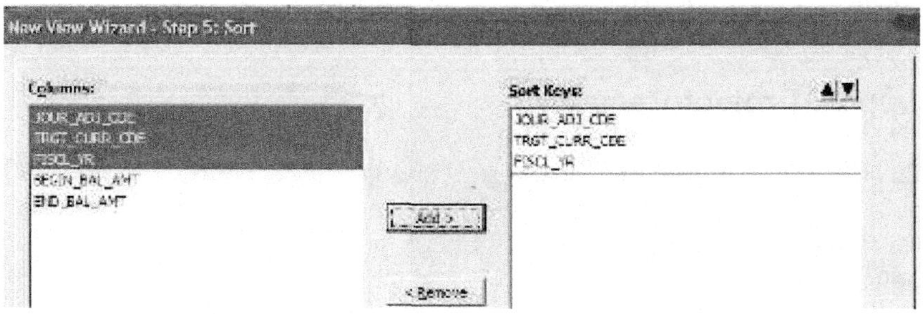

Figure 53. Sort Order Wizard

Step 6: Filter business events

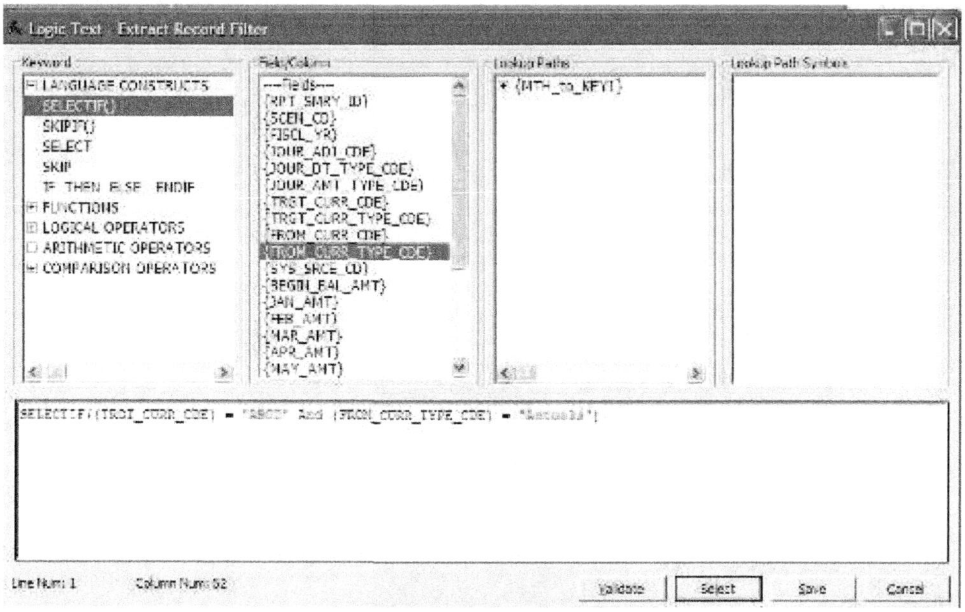

Figure 54. Event Filter Wizard

Last we specify which records to include or exclude. Let's assume we only want people who live on our street; so we'll specify that the address field should contain the value "Maple Ave.". Note that this field doesn't have to be shown on our report, but is in the event file.

The next step in the process is to run the SAFR Scan Engine. This set of programs translates the metadata and view into a program. The program then reads the event file from top to bottom and produces the desired output.

Test Metadata

On the project, the first view we created after defining the metadata was to test if it had been created correctly. These views were very simple. We selected every field on the event file, in the order defined on the LR, and output them to another file. We ran the Scan Engine, and inspected the output file. If the output records looked like the input records, then the metadata (and the documentation provided from the pharmaceutical companies) was correct.

Finding the event file is the first step, even if not working with legacy transaction systems. Even in a database world, at the bottom of the database there are tables, and those tables are files. By examining the database structure and the SQL one can determine what the event file must be to start the process; it's often in the "from" clause.

Pharmaceutical Litigation Support Project Results

This was the first step in the pharmaceutical litigation support project. Having established the ability to read and produce reports from the raw data, the team continued over four and a half months to process data for 17 different companies, reading 10 billion and extracting 5.9 billion records, performing 8.5 billion joins, and processing 6,000 views.[88]

The starting step in building a business event based insight system is locating the event file. This often starts with the journal entries for an existing ledger, defining that to SAFR, and then testing that the metadata has been created correctly. Now, the next step is to balance the event file to a known report.

88. Billing documentation from project in author's possession. The 6000 views do not translate into 6000 reports. Views are processed against individual file partitions, but reports can combine many files. Created a simple billing process that used the Billing File from MR95 to accumulate statistics from each run over time.

Chapter 26. Balance the Event File

Two years or so later, in 1997 I was working at a very large US insurer. They had determined to replace their legacy general ledgers, and had independently come to the idea of an event-based architecture simply by considering how accounting works. I worked with Lloyd Jackson, an IT employee at the insurance company, for three or four months determining how might be the best way to go about the financial data warehouse project.

I remember being surprised when I learned I was to participate in the formal oral proposal from Price Waterhouse to implement an ERP GL there; I had never before seen the ERP software. In our discussions, we were open about that. Rather, I was to be part of the reporting team, and discussed the approach Rick had written in the white paper about offloading the heavy lifting to another reporting tool.

PW didn't win the proposal; another consulting company did. But our previous work at the insurer proved we could find the data needed for reporting. The custom GL team was struggling with how to begin. I suggested the best approach was to find the event file within the legacy general ledger. We named the effort after a line in a recently released movie and called it: "Show me the money!".

Preliminary Analysis

Show me the money means balancing the event file to a known report or source. Transaction files sometimes are not complete; special processes may generate certain partial information, or additional transaction files may be processed periodically.

This insurance company had a ledger system that was imbedded as part of what might be called a home grown thirty-year old ERP system. The system flowed policy and loss level data from policy administration systems into the legacy ledger in a series of files and a network of programs. The system was so integrated, and had required so few changes that real in-depth knowledge of how the system worked was mostly lost. The best system diagrams were large printed paper copies.

Trying to recreate the system knowledge could have required hundreds of hours of tracing through listings of programs. The event based approach, and having a tool capable of some level of ETL like functions, meant this wasn't needed.

The business users still knew the key reports to look at, and the IT team could trace those reports to the program that generated them. Those reports showed, on a daily basis, the dollars processed in summary by a few key attributes. The IT team identified from the scripting (JCL in this case) what files were read by the program. They then saved one day's worth of files to use as the event files.

Jim Hladyshewsky, a new project team member, was drafted to define the files to SAFR without having much more than a ten minute introduction to the tool. His willingness to dive into the deep end with only a part-time lifeguard around was remarkable. He created the metadata, and then tested it to make sure it was accurate.

The next step in the process was to create a view that summarized the file. Working with the legacy system program, he looked over the names of the fields on the file and tried to guess which ones were on the report. In a few cases, he had to search the program to confirm if a field ended up on the report.

Using the steps to create views, Jim:

- **Specified view format and level:** Summary hardcopy (printable) report to recreate the data on the control report.
- **Selected the event logical record:** Fire System journal entry.

- **Specified logical file:** All the files collected because we assumed they all went into the legacy process that created the report.
- **Selected output fields:** Fields he thought showed up on the report, or at least some portion of them, starting with the highest level summary field and the dollar value.
- **Specified sort order:** He selected the highest level field he thought corresponded to the first field on the report, and specified the view should summarize the dollar value by that field.
- **Filtered business event** to include or exclude. Jim didn't specify any filter criteria, thinking perhaps all the records were included in the report.

Jim then ran the Scan Engine and looked at the output. We had taken our first sample of the data.

Refining the Sample

As I remember, nothing matched on the two reports from the initial run. I think the dollars on the SAFR report were significantly overstated. Thus, we began the process of guessing at what might be wrong.

I don't remember the exact steps Jim did; but from doing this multiple times I can describe his approach. I think Jim and I looked at the output and identified a row with the lowest dollar value. Perhaps we modified the view, adding a column with a constant of 1, sub-totaled to give us a count of the number of records from the event file that made up the dollar value we were seeing. We ran that view and saw that the row with the lowest dollar value also had the lowest record count. Perhaps the output might have looked like the following:

Legal Entity	Cost Center	Account	Record Count	Amount
522339999	CC110	111	88	6,039.70
522339999	CC110	121	7,994	23,985.00
522339999	CC110	123	10	185,000.00
522339999	CC110	211	28,004	200.00
522339999	CC110	222	87	309.25
522339999	CC110	411	41	0.00
522339999	CC111	111	603	(432.32)
522339999	CC111	121	172	18,285.00
522339999	CC111	123	1	1.00
522339999	CC111	122	70	15,245.00
522339999	CC111	211	500	600.00
522339999	CC111	222	32	567.00
522339999	CC111	411	61	543.00
522349731	CC218	111	91	58,655.43
522349731	CC218	121	76	15,567.00
522349731	CC218	123	44,803	387,000.00
522349731	CC218	211	2	1,000.00
522349731	CC218	411	10	0.00

Figure 55. Event File Analysis Sample Output

From this report, if all amounts don't match the values on the legacy system, Jim might have chosen to analyze the one record for the value 522339999, CC111, 123, since it is only one record to look up. He might then have created another view, this one with the following characteristics:

- **Specify view format and level:** a detailed view of the input records read by SAFR. This means that SAFR doesn't actually change the records it reads. It only applies filter criteria to the event records.
- **Select the event logical record:** Fire System journal entry.
- **Specify logical file:** All the files collected because we assumed they all went into the legacy process that created the report.

- **Filter business events** to include or exclude. Whereas the prior view Jim hadn't specified any selection or filtering criteria, this time Jim told SAFR that it should only select records with the value we saw on the report for the lowest dollar summary row.

The selection criteria might have looked like this:

Figure 56. Sample Filter Logic Text

Jim then ran the Scan Engine, with both views, producing two outputs but having only passed through the file once; (1) the control report view which we hadn't changed so the results were exactly the same, and (2) the new view which selected only detailed records for one particular type of journal entry.

Jim then looked at the output file. He might have noted something about that record that told him why it was different than the number on the report. Perhaps a different amount field needed to be used, or two fields needed to be combined in some way.

Another test for another set of records might have selected a score of records. As he scanned the actual amount field, perhaps one record had the correct amount on it that matched the legacy system report. He then compared that record to the other records and noted one field was different on this one record. He then modified the control report view so instead of selecting every record in the file, it only included these records with the value he had just noted. He would have run the view again, and noted this time that one row matched exactly, and other rows in the report were closer in value.

Another useful approach, if faced with dead-ends, is to build a new view with permutations of the sort keys. In other words, instead of sorting by business unit, cost center, account, sort by business unit, account, cost center. These permutations give something similar to a 3D perspective on the data, and can help identify how to reduce the data down to a manageable set to investigate.

And thus began the process of determining what events produced the report. Working with two other team members, who knew no more about the system than he did, in about three weeks he was able to reproduce the report for one day's data.

Note carefully that this process took about three weeks. If the control report chosen is a trial balance for a business unit, a critical set of business event records will have been identified.

The next step in the process was to collect the files for a month, and run them through the same refined view, refine it a bit more by identifying a special file that was received only at the end of the month, and prove that all the financial events were accounted for. In this way, one piece of the balanced based system—the control reports—were replaced with a very simple event-based system.

Insurance Financial Warehouse Project Results

Proving our ability to understand legacy code demonstrated our ability to do the integration work for the new financial system. These steps, these techniques, were taught to me by Jay. I watched him do these same steps over and over again as we did various benchmarks. Those benchmarks required understanding quickly what an existing process produced, and reproducing it in a more efficient way. It is amazing how consistent these legacy processes are, because processing patterns don't change all that much. Having learned from Jay, I passed that knowledge onto Jim.

Other feeds had to be discovered for the Auto Company; Wendy Lucas, Fred Horwitz, and a team led the charge on this effort. A similar process had to be followed in reverse to make files for downstream feeds. Scott Penland, Andrea Orth, Michael Shapiro, and others led the charge here. In each case, determining what story the data told was critical to a consistent plot. Lynn Groves Zuccala and Laurie Lesniak helped manage the overall effort.

So having discovered and balanced event files, the next step is to expand the elements available to report, by searching for more detailed files and repeating the balancing process.

Chapter 27. Find More Detailed Events

Starting work at the insurance company had happened a year earlier than the financial warehouse effort. Rick received an e-mail from Mike Schroeck about an opportunity at this insurance company. Rick never liked to commit his people full-time to other partners for projects; he was very careful about that. I don't know why I responded the way I did when he told me about the e-mail. I said, "Rick I want to go do this." Little did I know what a journey I had started. It lasted on and off for nearly seven years.

I was met on the project by Lynn Groves Zuccala and Anthony Boles, and later by Peter Corbett. They had worked with the insurance company for a number of months helping them craft a vision for the reporting environment. The company had concluded "...to build a single, consistent source of financially balanced data to be used by multiple business users for decision support, data mining, and internal/external reporting."[89] They determined that keeping event level data would provide the most flexible reporting framework possible.

The project needed to find an event file, at the policy and loss level, for statistical (rather than financial) reporting. Mark Kimmell, another project team member, worked on this with Doug Kunkel. They were both guided by Vanessa Menke from the client who really understood the data. Mark had started looking for the detailed events in this same Fire Divisional Processing system that Jim ended up using later for the financial warehouse "Show me the money" effort. The file they had to work with was anything but typical.

Lower Level Detail

The file at the heart of their home grown "ERP" system had the flavor of a home grown database system. The data was stored in a unique format in the file called Stacked Data Elements (SDE), and a set of utilities created by the company had to be used to interpret the file. This required Doug to write a program, called a user or a read exit, that SAFR Scan Engine called to read the file before the data was presented to the views. This program exposed the richness of the information contained in this file.

Mark and Doug found that this file had the policy and loss level transactions in it. It recorded changes to policies, the structure and parameters of the policy and each individual loss, policy renewals and payments, loss estimates and payments - all the business events at the core of the fire and casualty insurance business. This work required a number of months because of its more detailed nature and expansive scope. But the results were remarkable.

Jim later took this same file and found the additional records which were summary journal entries for the financial warehouse project. Whereas on Jim's report the entries were summarized to something like the business unit, cost center, account level, Mark's set of views could add policy number as well, where applicable.

Through this means, the company could produce policy level trial balances. The attributes on these trial balances weren't limited to the small set of items on the journal entries; they could be by term, or risk, or policy, any of the elements that were captured by the policy and loss admin systems.

Insurance Statistical Warehouse Project Results

The insurance company created detailed Operations Data Stores (ODSs) which maintained significant descriptions of the property and casualty policies along with their premium and loss transactions and balances for 7 years of data. It isn't just the ability to put the data into these systems that is significant, but the ability to also get it out, nightly for a variety of reporting purposes including regulatory

89. Client data warehouse strategy, 1997.

reporting. The environment also balances and feeds the financial reporting environment; thus regulatory reporting at the most detailed levels is consistent and balanced with all financial reporting.

The following are statistics complied by Kevin Bly, the system architect for the Fire ODS, and Lyn Kilhoffer, the system architect for the Auto ODSs, on August 8th, 2001, about five years after having started the project on the first Fire system.[90]

Fire	**Auto**
Scenario:	
The Daily process on 10 CPU machine capable of 1,934 MIPS but limited to 80% of capacity by workload governor	The Daily process on 10 CPU machine capable of 1,934 MIPS but limited to 80% of capacity by workload governor
Extract started at 03:15 AM	Extract started at 02:08 AM
Extract completed at 03:45 AM	Extract completed at 02:37 AM
30 minutes of elapsed time	Approximately 30 minutes of elapsed time
21 parallel threads were processed	38 parallel threads were processed at any given time (169 total threads processed)
CPU Time:	
00:28:54 minutes of clock time elapsed	00:29:15 minutes of clock time elapsed
02:55:02 hours of CPU time elapsed	01:11:08 hours of CPU time elapsed
Equates to 6.05 CPU engines running at full capacity during those 30 minutes of elapsed time.	Equates to 2.43 CPU engines running at full capacity during those 30 minutes of elapsed time.
Records Processed:	
906 input files were allocated	1,029 input files were allocated
493 output files were allocated	529 output files were allocated
Totaling 1,399 files allocated for I/O	Totaling 1,558 files allocated for I/O
Bytes Processed:	
2.4 billion records read (190 Gigabytes)	258 million records read (67 Gigabytes)
72 million records written (10 Gigabytes)	264 million records written (72 Gigabytes)
Totaling 1.4 million records (118.35 Megabytes) processed	Totaling 297,333 records (81.21 Megabytes) processed
Joins:	
873 million ODS Joins were performed	293 million ODS Joins were performed
105 million non-ODS Joins were performed	310 million non-ODS Joins were performed
Totaling 978 million joins (563,624 joins per second)	Totaling 603 million joins (343,255 joins per second)

I am not aware of any batch process performing a larger workload in a shorter amount of time anywhere.[91]

90. Statistics from presentation by Kevin Bly to Decision Support and Technical Leadership Group, Oct. 1, 2001.

91. The company found that the one pass architecture of SAFR meant that actually making the back-up copies during the daily process was more efficient than having a separate process read and write the data again through a backup utility at a different time of the day. So the daily critical path process includes the back-up process as well.

The following diagram depicts the architecture components of the financial and statistical ODSs.

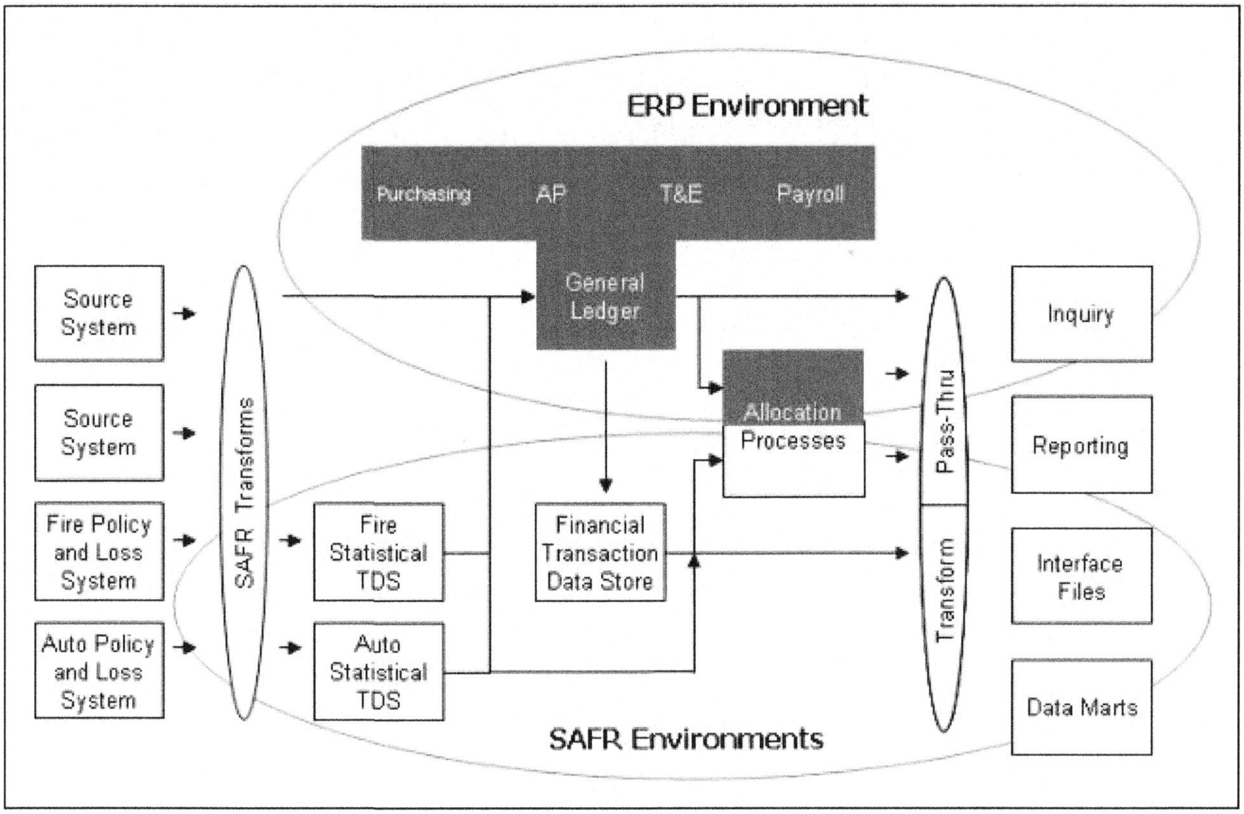

Figure 57. Insurance Company Financial & Statistical Architecture Diagram

Sort/Merge

Efficiently comparing values from two different events files—the summary and the detailed event file—requires slightly different views than Jim's sub-totaled values from one file. Jim had to swap between two different reports and see if the subtotals match. A more efficient approach is to have a column in the report show any difference. To do this requires building something that looks like two different views reading the two different LRs, the summary and detailed LRs, but the results get combined into one output.

This is called a multiple source view, but we'll describe it as if it were two views. Here are the common elements of both of them:

- **Specify view format and level:** Summary hardcopy (printable) report.
- **Select the event logical record:** Source 1: Summary event file and Source 2: Detailed event file.
- **Select output fields:** Select the common fields, such as business unit or ledger account and the amount from each logical record.
- **Specify sort order:** Select business unit, cost center, account.
- **Filter business event** to include or exclude. None if all the records were included in the report.

To build this view, it is important to understand the difference between two key phases of the Scan Engine: the Extract and the Format phases.

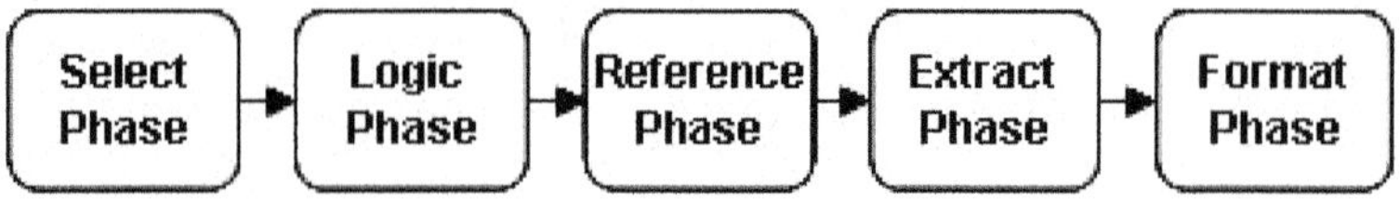

Figure 58. Performance Engine Phases

The following table summarizes some of the key differences between the extract phase processes and the format phase.

Function	Extract Phase	Format Phase
In general output record counts with no filtering:		
Summary Views	One event record out for every record read	One record out for every sort key combination
Detailed Views	One event record out for every record read	One event record out for every record read
Filter Logic	Against input event file fields	Against view columns
Calculating and subtotaling:		
Logic	Against input event file fields	Against view columns
Level	Detailed event file record level	Detail or summary level
Record order	Random, as sequenced in event files and through parallelism	In sorted order by view sort fields
Joins	Detailed, multi level joins, used in filter and calculation logic and column assignment	Only at summary level for sort titles on limited view output types. Not used in filtering or calcs

Figure 59. Extract and Format Phase Differences

So the extract phase works on event file records, and the format phase works on extracted records. Because the Format phase works on extracted outputs, common fields in different files can be combined into a single output. This is a different kind of "join" processing that is very efficient called a sort/merge.

The following figures show the view definitions and results of processing from the Extract and Format phases.

Legal Entity Field	Cost Center Field	Acct. Field	Constant of 1	Constant of 0	To be calced after sum	Amount Field	Constant of 0	To be calced after sum

Legal Entity	Cost Center	Acct.	File 1 Record Count	File 2 Record Count	Record Count Dif.	Event File 1 Amount	Event File 2 Amount	Amount Diff.
522339999	CC110	111	1	0		33.21	0.00	
522339999	CC110	111	1	0		68.32	0.00	
522339999	CC110	111	1	0		12.60	0.00	
522339999	CC110	111	1	0		4.52	0.00	

Figure 60. View Definition and Extract Phase output from Summary file

Legal Entity Field	Cost Center Field	Acct. Field	Constant of 0	Constant of 1	To be calced after sum	Constant of 0	Amount Field	To be calced after sum

Legal Entity	Cost Center	Acct.	File 1 Record Count	File 2 Record Count	Record Count Dif.	Event File 1 Amount	Event File 2 Amount	Amount Diff.
522339999	CC110	111	0	1		0.00	2.31	
522339999	CC110	111	0	1		0.00	45.32	
522339999	CC110	111	0	1		0.00	7.86	
522339999	CC110	111	0	1		0.00	10.21	
522339999	CC110	111	0	1		0.00	2.32	
522339999	CC110	111	0	1		0.00	50.63	

Figure 61. View Definition and Extract Phase output from Detail file

Legal Entity	Cost Center	Acct.	File 1 Record Count	File 2 Record Count	Record Count Dif.	Event File 1 Amount	Event File 2 Amount	Amount Diff.
522339999	CC110	111	4	6	(2)	118.65	118.65	0.00

Figure 62. Format Phase output after summarization and calculation

This approach to processing isn't strange to anyone who has written many batch programs. In fact, the type of program described in the Figure 32 on page 69 figure performed this same function. It read two different types of records, and combined them into a single output based upon common keys and summarization.

These same approaches, using multi-sourced SAFR views, can be used to do union, full outer, and right outer joins in many cases.

Tranching

At a later client, the team working with the client developed a formal method for transitioning from higher level summaries to lower level sources. This process was called tranching, since subsets of the full set of lower level sources, or feeds, can be brought in in "tranches" or groups (there is no need to convert all the sources at once, nor do they each need to be done individually one at a time). The process was really fairly simple in concept, but very powerful. It was used not just in the analysis phase of the project, but actually in production to change the level of detail available within the financial reporting environment—effectively a new GL but at a very detailed level. It looked something like the following:

1. Identify the more detailed source to substitute for a source already provided to a legacy general ledger environment.
2. Turn the detailed source into journal entries at the detailed level, with effectively the same information as the summary level but more attributes. Test if the detail has the same results as the summaries did.
3. Capture the summary balances in the General Ledger for the source on a specified day and create reversal entries of all the balances, with the offset going to a due to/from account.
4. Capture the balances from the source system on the same specified day, and create opening entries for all the balances with the offset going to the opposite side of the due to/from account.
5. Load both sets of journal entries created from point in time balances onto the reporting environment, effectively removing the summary balances, and initializing the detailed balances.
6. Stop the daily summary level feed to the legacy general ledger.
7. Start the daily feed of the detailed data into the new reporting environment.

In this way, more detailed feeds can be substituted for existing summary feeds, without disrupting the reporting environment. These more detailed feeds can then be used to provide a richer reporting environment. Because this is a controlled process, it can go on, tranche by tranche, for years, as the organization tackles improving their financial reporting environment. In this way ultimately all summary feeds can be replaced with more detailed equivalents.

So after finding the event file, then balancing that file to a known source, we expanded the elements available to report on by searching for more detailed files and repeating the balancing process. The next step is to begin to define reference data to describe and classify those business events.

Chapter 28. Define Reference Data

In the year 2000, Jim assisted me with a prototype of SAFR to detect ticketing fraud for a large US air carrier. Again, the data we were to read was not in a very simple format, so Doug wrote a read exit that would read the IDMS database and present the records to the views. Jay made enhancements to SAFR so it would automatically detect the number of database partitions that existed and create that many parallel threads.

Jim and I worked to define views that, as we scanned the production database, detected when ticketing fraud had occurred. Unlike transaction system tests which audit each individual transaction, these tests could only be done after the ticketing process and travel was complete, and all the data from all the independent ticketing systems were brought together.

Airline Project Results

SAFR scanned the production database containing over a year worth of airline tickets, 587 million records, in 2 hours and 46 minutes, 6 1/3 hours CPU time. It extracted 23.5 million records, composing about 100,000 tickets that potentially were fraudulent. The data wouldn't tell us if fraud had actually occurred; that required people looking at the data and making judgment calls. But the potential for savings were more than enough to pay for the project itself.

Reference Data Keys

You'll remember, from Chapter 14, "Reporting," on page 67, that reporting is a process of classifying. We said that we assigned attributes to business events to describe them. Also looking at the tables defined in Chapter 8, "REAL Analysis Method," on page 43, you'll note we did not store the descriptions or titles of each of these values on every row. This not only saves space because duplicated values aren't stored on every row, but allows the descriptions to change with time if needed. These descriptions of business units, cost centers, and accounts can generically be referred to as reference data.

One day during this airline project the project manager brought someone to my desk who was on another project attempting to use some data from the production database. He said they had created programs to deal with the documented values in a particular field. But as they were testing, things were not working right and they weren't sure why. He asked if it would be possible for us to scan the database to tell them all the values in a particular field. I said that would be pretty easy.

I created a summary view sorting by the single field he was interested in, and accumulating a constant of one in the column for a counter of the number of occurrences. I ran it and printed the small file. His reaction was interesting. It was something like, "Well I knew about these fifteen values, but what are these other four values no one told us about?" We found a support person who had long experience with the database. She looked at them and said, "Oh, yea, I remember now, there was a conversion done on the database four or five years ago and we used that value to mean ..." She went on and could name a few others. She didn't know what one was for.

This is a common tale in IT. And there are a couple of lessons to be learned here. First, the moment documentation is finished it is out of date because something on the system has changed; documentation is no substitute for using the data. Second, understanding the keys, the identifiers in the data, is fundamental to developing reference data to describe those keys. Getting a complete list of the descriptions of business events as captured by the source system is critical to understanding the data.

Remember also, in Chapter 8, "REAL Analysis Method," on page 43, we noted that the longest process is understanding the rows of data. Determining the event file is relatively short. Defining the fields on those on the event logical record takes a bit more time. Determining the values for each field takes even more time.

But the real value in reporting comes only as the rows of data are understood. There is no purpose to all of the work if the rows of data don't provide answers to questions that inform specific actions. We can make this point again without overemphasizing it: Real value comes from understanding the rows of data. For example, with people, it isn't the list of possible hair colors or potential heights that makes a difference. The actual people are what matters, their names, sizes and shapes and colors. Until we get to the rows of data we have nothing really to report.

Joins or Lookups

SAFR supports joining data together to combine the results on a view output. For example, if we built views against our sample event file for Legal Entity, Cost Center, and Account, the outputs would have given a list of all values in those fields, shown on the left column in each of the three areas below.

Cost Center Descriptions

Cost Center	Cost Center Title
CC110	Dad
CC111	Mum
CC218	Charles

Legal Entity Descriptions

Legal Entity	Legal Entity Title
522349999	K & N Jones Family
522349731	C Wheeler

Account Titles

Account	Account Title
111	Checking Account
121	Automobile
122	Personal Property
123	Home
211	Credit Card payable
222	Mortgage payable
411	Salary Revenue

Figure 63. Sample Reference Data Tables

Once armed with all of these possible key values, names or descriptions can be assigned to all of them by making simple editable files that describe them.

The following screen shows how in SAFR to build a join. Let's suppose this Event LR would have been used in doing our reports thus far.

ID: 1264 Name: EVENT JOURNAL

R Fields | LR Properties | Associated Logical Files

Field ID	Global Field	Field Name	Data Type	Fixed Position	Length	De
63311	0	LEGAL_ENTITY	Zoned Decimal	1	9	
63312	0	COST_CENTRE	Alphanumeric	10	5	
63313	0	ACCOUNT	Zoned Decimal	15	3	
63314	0	RECORD_COUNT	Zoned Decimal	18	8	
63315	0	AMOUNT	Zoned Decimal	26	10	

Figure 64. Event Logical Record

The LR below describes the file that contains the Account Titles, the file shown in the Sample Reference Data Tables figure.

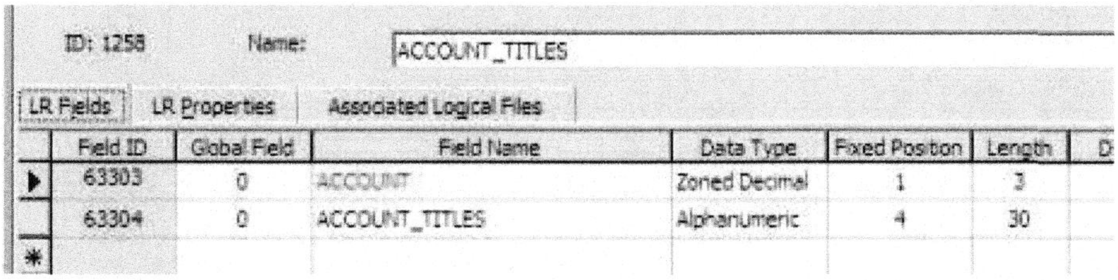

Figure 65. Account Titles Reference Table LR

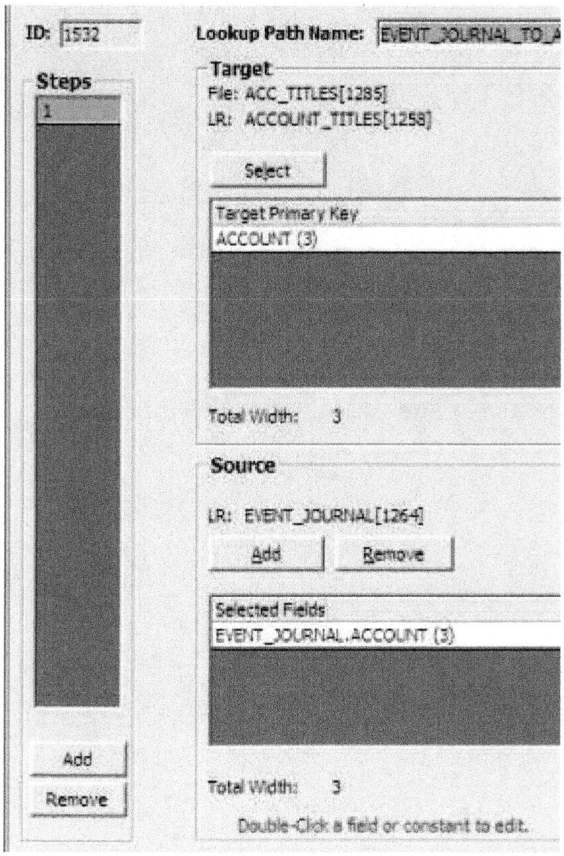

Figure 66. Look up or Join Path Creation

The next step is to define the actual join. Joins are considered part of the metadata, set up by an administrator, someone who understands how to connect SAFR Scan Engine to the files that contain the data, and how to interpret the data in the files.

To build the join, we select the source event file and the target table we want to join to. We then select those fields from the source that will be used to populate the key to the target table, the account field. When the length of the fields provided from the source matches the length of the key in the target, the join is valid. Having defined the join, we can now use any of the fields on the join table in our view.

This join only has one step to it, i.e. we go directly from the source to the target. Although if needed, we could have repeatedly selected targets and sources to go through interim tables and find additional values; those are called multistep joins.

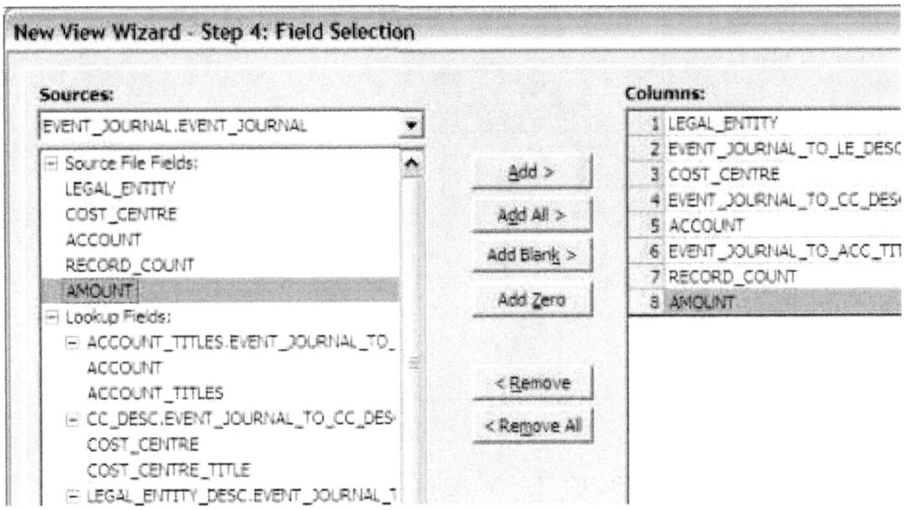

Figure 67. New View Wizard Join Field Selection

As we build our view, we can see all the fields on the account table, our event LR. Note that this screen shows that joins have also been defined for cost center descriptions and legal entity titles. Also note that these reference tables aren't simply to display results on the reports; the values in them can be used for filtering and calculation functions.[92]

Sample output from the view is shown below. The reports become more useful because the titles are more informative than the code values by themselves.

92. Note that in a pervious chapter we spoke of creating a view which selected only records for one particular account using the following selection criteria:

```
If  (  {Legal_Entity} = "522339999"  And {Cost_Centre} = "CC111"  And {Account} = "123" )
 Then Select
EndIf
```

With these reference file tables, the selection criteria could have been written as

```
If  ( {Legal_Entity_Desc.Event_Journal_To_Legal_Entity_Title_Join.Legal_Entity_Title} = "K & N Jones Family"
 And {CC_Desc.Event_Journal_To_CC_Desc_Join.Cost_Center_Title} = "Mum"
 And {Account_Titles.Event_Journal_to_Account_Titles_Join.Account_Titles} = "Home" )
 Then Select
EndIf
```

The values tested for are more readable, but the logic text is more verbose. This selection also causes look-ups to be performed on each record—something that requires additional CPU instructions over simply testing values in the event file; so it is less efficient. But there are cases when it is useful to join to perform selection and calculation logic. For example testing to see if the reference data is complete can be done by using the key words FOUND or NOT-FOUND. Records that either have or do not have corresponding reference data can be selected for reporting or more analysis.

Legal Entity	Legal Entity Title	Cost Center	Cost Center Title	Acct.	Account Title	Record Count	Amount
522339999	K & N Jones Family	CC110	Dad	111	Checking Account	88	6,039.70
522339999	K & N Jones Family	CC110	Dad	121	Automobile	7,994	23,985.00
522339999	K & N Jones Family	CC110	Dad	123	Home	10	185,000.00
522339999	K & N Jones Family	CC110	Dad	211	Credit Card payable	28,004	200.00
522339999	K & N Jones Family	CC110	Dad	222	Mortgage payable	87	309.25
522339999	K & N Jones Family	CC110	Dad	411	Salary Revenue	41	0.00
522339999	K & N Jones Family	CC111	Mum	111	Checking Account	603	(432.32)
522339999	K & N Jones Family	CC111	Mum	121	Automobile	172	18,285.00
522339999	K & N Jones Family	CC111	Mum	123	Home	1	1.00
522339999	K & N Jones Family	CC111	Mum	122	Personal Property	70	15,245.00
522339999	K & N Jones Family	CC111	Mum	211	Credit Card payable	500	600.00
522339999	K & N Jones Family	CC111	Mum	222	Mortgage payable	32	567.00
522339999	K & N Jones Family	CC111	Mum	411	Salary Revenue	61	543.00
522349731	C Wheeler	CC218	Charles	111	Investment 401 (k)	91	58,655.43
522349731	C Wheeler	CC218	Charles	121	Automobile	76	15,567.00
522349731	C Wheeler	CC218	Charles	123	Home	44,803	387,000.00
522349731	C Wheeler	CC218	Charles	211	Credit Card payable	2	1,000.00
522349731	C Wheeler	CC218	Charles	411	Salary Revenue	10	0.00

Figure 68. Sample Report with Reference Data Descriptions

A couple of important notes:

- All physical reference files must be presented to the SAFR process in sorted order by the key specified on the LR if the file will be used in a join.
- All reference file keys must be unique; duplicates are not allowed in any case.
- SAFR has to be able to locate one specific reference file record as the result of SAFR join processing.

SAFR join processing then requires a many to one join. Many event file records can look up to one reference file record, or many lower level reference file records can look up to one higher level reference file record on a multistep join[93]. Approaches to performing union, full outer, and right outer joins are discussed in Chapter 34, "Consider Complex Joins," on page 177.

Static Data

Reference data isn't all created by finance users; some very important reference, or static, data comes from the operational systems. For example, it is unlikely finance will update customer names, like the K & N Jones Family on the report above. Static data is data residing in the operational or close to operational systems which describe the business events, like customers, contracts, products, offices, etc. The process of gathering this data is no different than finding the event files in the legacy systems. It is critical to have it available in reporting processes to make sense of the business events, and it is sampled and refined just like reference data.

To do standard SAFR join processing, SAFR loads the reference data structures into memory. At times the volume of this static data may exceed the memory available on the machine. The Common Key Data Buffer feature, discussed in Chapter 35, "Model the Repository," on page 179 and Chapter 52, "Common Key Data Buffering," on page 271, may be necessary. At this stage consider using a limited set of this data in producing the initial reports.

Mapping

Thus far in these chapters, we've had the simple view that attributes of business events are assigned when business events are first captured in the operational systems. However, as noted in Rick's subsystem lecture, in reality there can be layers and layers of classifications established before anyone

93. See also Chapter 41, "Look-ups," on page 211 and Chapter 42, "Reference File Phase," on page 217

attempts to understand the data. Legacy accounts in operational systems may be a couple of decades old, and not used for reporting or analysis any longer. Somewhere within the accumulated systems constructed over the years, those accounts are translated into other accounts that are now used for reporting. That can be true for any reporting attribute.

The translation process is not always one field to another field. At times, multiple fields are used to determine one new value in a new system, or a single field produces multiple attributes in the new system. For example, accounting systems from 30 to 40 years ago had only the three fields of legal entity, account, and perhaps cost center. Newer systems usually have numerous other fields, like product, customer type, and intercompany affiliate. So when the legacy account, which sometimes also meant the product for that customer type, is translated into the new ledger, it may result in three field values, account, product, and customer type.

The insurance company had a company code structure that had grown up over 30 or more years. When they decided to break down all the embedded meaning in it, like mail stop and cost center, legal entity, and HR department, they found it took over thirty tables, each with many fields, to describe the one ten character field they had used for so many years. This field is likely still used 10 years after starting the process of replacing it in a host of systems, and will likely be used in some way for years to come.

Mapping tables don't describe the values in one system, as much as translate them to the values for another system. The keys to the tables are those from the source system, and the targets or answers are those for the new system. Mapping tables are simply reference data files to SAFR.

How To Begin

Making up reference data, categorization schemes from scratch if you will, takes a long time. A faster way is to leverage the thought already put into legacy reporting systems. New accounts are never added to the chart of accounts because someone hoped someone else would want them. Most are added as some piece of information is needed to address some specific action. So start with and modify the existing reference data. If two ledgers are to be combined into a single chart of accounts, then start by either identifying the one to keep, or building the new chart by referencing both.

In addition to using the legacy chart of accounts, reference data in other systems should be leveraged when working with lower levels of data. For example, reference data is used to classify arrangement level attributes in financial data warehouses for regulatory purposes. These types of classifications can be used when exploring the event files from lower level data in other systems.

Reference data can't fix lack of detail. There is no way to translate from a summarized record and create a lower level detailed record for a receiving system. Summarization destroys visibility to the details. Translation processes are made easier when working with the details, as long as the details are preserved out of the translation process. A single value in a source system can be translated into a single value in the target system. Again, keeping the detail provides greater flexibility.

If we look at all the summarized results of financial data for all financial reporting systems, in other words if the set of reference data for all finance systems is combined into one set, we will find the lowest common denominator is pretty close to the customer contract level. Maintaining the detail will provide economies of scale in the long run.

There is really no short cut for this work of creating reference data. It will take longer than anyone wants it to, and thus it must be started early, perhaps even before finding the event files. Finding and balancing the events files is a way IT can help. Perhaps every project I have been on has missed nearly every deadline for when the reference data would be known. In some cases it was missed by nine months or 50% of the time. In others it was missed by 2 years or 90% of the estimate. That's because it is an iterative process of adding values to reference descriptions or mapping tables, and looking at the outputs to see if they properly characterize the results of the business events and inform potential actions.

The more iterations of viewing the results, the better the results will be. The system can't be built until the reference data is understood, but the reference data can't be built without looking at the results of the system. Thus, again, a tool that supports a prototyping approach to the problem, including going clear to producing usable outputs, is nearly mandatory.

Chapter 29. Iteratively View Results

The cookie manufacturer in the fall of 1995 needed a solution to their reporting problems. Doug developed a solution called the Executive Information File, or XIF. In later years a similar capability in other tools would be termed a cube. The structure of this file had the most summarized information at the top, and lower and lower levels of detail farther down.

For example, from our sample hardcopy report, below:

Program ID: STGMD88	Company Name: Family Finances	Date: 09 May 2009
Report ID: View 13456	Report Name: Trial Balance	Time: 10:40 AM

Legal Entity 522349999: K & N Jones Family	**Debit**	**Credit**	**Grand Total**
Cost Centre CC110: Dad			
Account Number 111: Checking Account	6,039.70	2,787.44	3,252.26
Account Number 121: Automobile	23,985.00	0.00	23,985.00
Account Number 122: Home	185,000.00	0.00	185,000.00
Account Number 211: Credit Card payable	200.00	124.24	75.76
Account Number 222: Mortgage payable	309.25	155,377.03	(155,067.78)
Account Number 411: Salary Revenue	0.00	4,487.30	(4,487.30)
Subtotal CC110: Dad	215,533.95	162,776.01	52,757.94
Cost Centre CC120: Mum			
Account Number 111: Checking Account	(432.32)	6,821.16	(7,253.48)
Account Number 121: Automobile	18,285.00	0.00	18,285.00
Account Number 122: Home	0.00	0.00	0.00
Account Number 122: Personal Property	15,245.00	0.00	15,245.00
Account Number 211: Credit Card payable	600.00	4,024.24	(3,424.24)
Account Number 222: Mortgage payable	567.00	0.00	567.00
Account Number 411: Salary Revenue	543.00	6,893.00	(6,350.00)
Subtotal CC120: Mum	34,807.68	17,738.40	17,069.28
Subtotal K & N Jones Family Total	250,341.63	180,514.41	69,827.22
Legal Entity 5223497314: C Wheeler			
Cost Centre CC218: Charles			
Account Number 111: Investment 401 (k)	58,655.43	0.00	58,655.43
Account Number 121: Automobile	15,567.00	0.00	15,567.00
Account Number 123: Home	387,000.00	0.00	387,000.00
Account Number 211: Credit Card payable	1,000.00	8,065.77	(7,065.77)
Account Number 411: Salary Revenue	0.00	12,638.00	(12,638.00)
Subtotal CC218: Charles	462,222.43	20.703.77	441,518.66
Subtotal C Wheeler Total	462,222.43	20.703.77	441,518.66
Grand Total	712,564.06	201,218.18	511,345.88

Figure 69. Sample Hardcopy Report

The XIF file would have the subtotals for the two families listed at the top of the file, as shown on the top portion of the next figure.

Program ID: STGMR88	Company Name: Family Finances		Date: 09 May 2009
Report ID: View 13456	Report Name: Trial Balance		Time: 10:40 AM

	Debit	Credit	Grand Total
Subtotal K & N Jones Family Total	250,341.63	180,514.41	69,827.22
Subtotal C Wheeler Total	462,222.43	20.703.77	441,518.66
Grand Total	712,564.06	201,218.18	511,345.88

Program ID: STGMR88	Company Name: Family Finances		Date: 09 May 2009
Report ID: View 13456	Report Name: Trial Balance		Time: 10:40 AM

Legal Entity 522349999: K & N Jones Family	Debit	Credit	Grand Total
Subtotal CC110: Dad	215,533.95	162,776.01	52,757.94
Subtotal CC120: Mum	34,807.68	17,738.40	17,069.28
Legal Entity 5223497314: C Wheeler			
Subtotal CC218: Charles	462,222.43	20.703.77	441,518.66

Figure 70. Drill-down Views

When the user double clicked on one of the families, the subtotals for the next level down would appear, as shown in the bottom portion. The process could then be repeated, showing the individual account subtotals if the user selected Dad, Mom, or Charles.

This approach simply automated the manual process of searching sort fields on a hardcopy report to find the desired information at lower and lower levels.

There were a couple of unusual aspects to this file. One was that instead of using SQL to find the next level down, it used a very simple addressing scheme called relative byte addressing. Because SAFR had built the report, and then turned it upside down, it knew how big the report was, and where the subtotal records for the next level down would be. It could simply add on to the front of each record an address of where in the file the next records would be. Computers have the ability to open and read a file at a particular point, rather than starting at the top. It would be similar to opening a binder or book to a particular page and beginning to read. This approach required that no unnecessary data be transferred into memory for each click by a user. It made the access of the file very, very efficient.

The other unique aspect of the file was that the entire definition of the report was contained in one place: the view. In many systems, portions of what a report needs to contain are in the ETL definition, portions in the database, and portions in the reporting tool. Changes to a report might mean changes to each of these layers. The Executive Information File, though, contained the definition of the view in the top records. Thus the Scan Performance Engine changed the report however requested by the user as it read the data, and the web page that displayed the results to the user could simply adjust what it displayed based upon this data in the file. No heavy duty programmer needed to be involved to make report changes.

This characteristic is important for the work we have been describing. Our process has involved many changes - defining and reading new files, adding new columns for record counts, changing selection criteria, adding new views and outputs which investigate areas in more detail, adding new reference data to describe fields, and changing the sort criteria to identify a subset of records of interest.

Output Types

Of course the same flexibility exists for all the different types of SAFR outputs. SAFR has the ability to produce the following outputs: Insight Viewer, Hardcopy reports, delimited files, and sequential files.

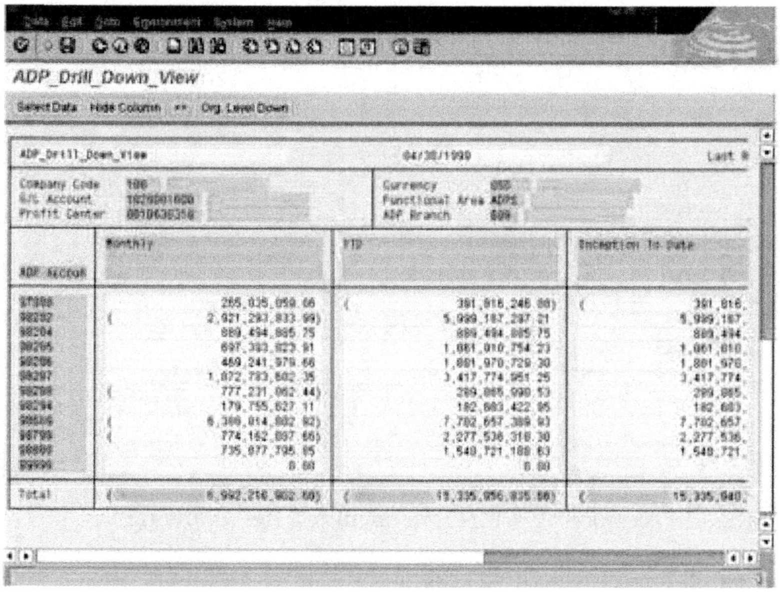

Figure 71. SAFR Insight Viewer

The Insight Viewer output from the Scan Performance Engine provides the summary totals first, allowing a user to select additional detail they wish to see by drilling down on the file. The output is a simple sequential file; no database is involved.

The limitation of this format is that it creates a copy of the lowest level detail included in the view in each output file. It is an effective format for investigating summary results, or results of samples of data from very large systems, but is not a mechanism to maintain access to all the detail needed for enterprise reporting.[94]

The SAFR Hardcopy reports are traditional print ready, character based reports. Sort data can be presented as columns or more elegantly as indented values based upon the sort order. The view builder can control report headings, column headings, subtotal descriptions, sort titles, masking or display format for numbers. Additional formatting can be done via user exits for more specific shop standards.

The limitation is the basic format is fixed, as columnar character based reports for up to 255 characters in width. Tools for on-line investigation of these reports tend to be mainframe based products, which are not very glamorous in today's reporting world.

SAFR has the ability to put out two different types of files, delimited files which can be used to download into common tools such as spreadsheets, or sequential files which can be used either as interface files or loaded into databases and other reporting structures.

The limitation on these outputs is they aren't immediately easily viewable, but rather have to be placed in other tools to see the results.

94. See Chapter 46, "Format Phase," on page 237 for more details on the file structure.

ETL Functions

SAFR's heritage was as a reporting tool. But it transitioned from the early years of being a reporting product to being more ETL focused. This occurred because SAFR was a mainframe tool and the mainframe batch characteristics were so critical to its performance, and it was influenced by the advent of graphical user interfaces and the "death of the mainframe". Thus, while retaining certain reporting capabilities, it grew in the ability to transform data from raw structures into those reports. This happened to such an extent that for a number of years in the late 90's we described it in marketing literature as an ETL tool.

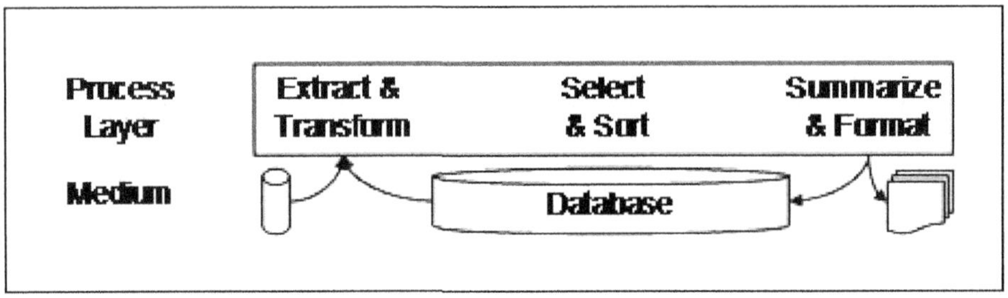

Figure 72. SAFR ETL Process

Some of the ETL like features that were added to the tool over this time included the following.

SAFR can read, write, or convert any of the following numeric data types, a number of which are not even supported by COBOL

- Binary Coded Decimal
- Binary, 2, 4 or 8 byte
- Sortable Binary
- Edited Numeric
- Masked Numeric
- Zoned Decimal
- Packed
- Sortable Packed

It can convert and interpret data in more than two score different date formats; it can convert numeric data into four score masks, comma and decimal format combinations; ASCII or EBCIDIC code sets. The UNIX version can translate between big and little endian structures.

These functions allow it to do many things an ETL tool can do. But real ETL tools are defined by the types of file formats they can read. The UNIX version of SAFR only reads sequential files. The mainframe version can read data in the following formats and ways:

- Sequential access of sequential files using high performance BSAM access method
- Sequential access using SAFR channel programs
- VSAM files in sequential access
- DB2 data by reading and interpreting the underlying VSAM data structures
- DB2 data via SQL

These relatively limited set of data types I don't think qualify as it as an ETL tool. It breaks the boundary between traditional tools.

SAFR also has a host of key words including testing field values for SPACES, NUMERIC, HIGH-VALUES, LOW-VALUES and others, as well as testing join results for FOUND, and NOT-FOUND.

These key words allow it to help in an inevitable, but unenviable reporting system task called data cleansing.

Extensibility

One of the first things recognized immediately after the retailer benchmark was the need to be able to extend SAFR for non-native functions. On mainframes this capability was termed the ability to call an exit, a custom program at a specific point in the process. A more common term now is an application program interface or API. SAFR has multiple points where a custom program can be called to perform logic that SAFR itself cannot do. This extensibility has been used to add new features to SAFR over time, as most new features are first written as APIs and then folded into the base product as they prove durable for other implementations. The following are the common API points in the Scan Engine.

- VDP XML API. Although not traditionally called an exit, this API allows a completely different way of defining SAFR metadata and views. It is discussed more in Chapter 33, "Define Processes," on page 171.
- Read Exit. This API point emulates an access method, allowing for custom code before a SAFR thread sees data from the event file. It can be used to manipulate an event file, combine multiple physical files into one event file for the SAFR views or even completely generate an event file. From a SAFR perspective, the views read the output from the exit rather than a physical file.
- Lookup or Join Exit. This API point is called whenever a join to a reference file table is to be performed. The parameters of the join are passed to the program, and a pointer to a resulting record is returned. From a SAFR perspective the result of the join is the output from the called program. This feature is often used to create function calls which accept parameters and return results.
- Write Exit. This function is called when a view is to write a detailed record to the extract file. It can be used to manipulate the output, evaluate if the record should be written at all, or write multiple records if desired.
- Sort Exits. The standard sort utilities used to sort extract files have the ability to call exits. A commonly used SAFR sort exit creates permutations of extract records to simulate the creation of multiple views from a single SAFR extract file. This reduces the total data extracted and sorted. This is used to create SAFR cubes which are composed of multiple executive information or XIF files.
- Format Exit. This function is called at the end of the format program after summarization has occurred. Similar to write exits, it can change the record, determine not to write it at all, or write multiple records if desired. See Chapter 51, "Exits," on page 267 for more details on Exits.

Data Cleansing

Data cleansing is a process of making data conform to a standard, like the values in the airline database. Data cleansing can be a very long process on some projects. In some approaches to reporting problems, data has to be clean before any reporting can be done on it. Therefore, it must be cleaned in ETL processes before it can be loaded into the database.

The approach we have suggested can find value in the data immediately, without first having to make sure all values are consistent. It is much like any type of cleaning: whatever is visible is what gets cleaned up. The first step to cleaning is understanding the data. Think back to the airline example above, when I handed the guy the list of values that actually existed in the data. Until you know what's in the data, you can't clean it up. Visibility will drive more data cleansing than any other activity could.

Having a tool that facilitates both ETL and reporting functions allows us to work closely with the operational systems data, and assess the quality of the information of that data. The next step in our process is to assess the reporting needs and how they measure up against the data samples we have taken.

For the first time in our method we are going to look at what we need to build, what the new systems must do. Consider this carefully; all the steps we have performed thus far have been focused on the data that exists in the organization today. When undertaking reporting projects so many organizations become distracted by what needs to be built; the structure of the new skyscraper. They spend years working on them, when the hardest part of the project is dealing with the data they already have.

So care must be taken as we begin to focus forward. To help keep from losing focus, our analysis of the reporting needs of the new system is best informed by the reporting already being done in the organization. These help uncover the real reporting needs.

Chapter 30. Assess Reporting Needs

It should be clear that most of the steps of the SAFR method we have discussed are embedded as part of the tool. In other words, the way the tool is constructed enforces them in some measure. The next step in the process uses information gathered through these steps, but requires a level of analysis outside of SAFR itself.

As mentioned in Chapter 21, "ERP Reporting," on page 101, Rick wrote a white paper at the conclusion of the Cookie Manufacturer project summarizing the analysis performed entitled *[ERP] High-Volume Operational Reporting/Data Warehousing: Summary of Sizing Concepts and Architectural Alternatives*. Following the steps Rick outlined is the next step in the process regardless of what the source system is, whether an ERP package or a legacy system of some kind. This chapter summarizes many of the points made in Part 3, "The Partner," on page 51. Assessing the reporting requirements is important to getting the right set of numbers to estimate the data load, discussed in the next chapter. The following are excerpts from that white paper.[95]

Reporting Problem in General

Reporting problems come in varying sizes depending on the data basis and size of the reports in the mix. The data basis for a report means the number and size of data records that must be manipulated in order to produce the report. Report size means the number and length of the lines that constitute the final report output.[96] By far the largest single factor in determining overall reporting load is data basis.

The most important aspect of data basis usually relates to the number and size of records that must be extracted then further manipulated to produce the report output. However, in cases where the extract data basis is small, but large sequential table scans must be executed in order to identify the extract records, input table size becomes the relevant data basis for projecting reporting load.[97]

In general, the size of an overall reporting load can be determined by aggregating the data basis and report sizes across the number of reports and the frequency with which they will be executed in a given period of time. By stratifying reporting requirements in categories of on-demand, daily, weekly, monthly, quarterly, and annual, an accurate picture of report processing load over time can be projected.[98] It generally is a good practice to project detail reporting load separately from the summary reporting load.

---

95. Roth, Richard K., *[ERP] High-volume Operational Reporting*, 2, 3, 5 - 11. Copyright IBM Corporation. Used by permission. Footnotes below, except as noted, are also from the paper.

96. For example, a data basis of all invoices for the last year would be a large data basis when compared to only invoices for yesterday, which would constitute a relatively smaller data basis. Last year's invoices or yesterday's invoices could be summarized at a high organizational level such as division, which would result in a small report size, or either data basis could be summarized by customer, item and week, which would result in a relatively larger report size. Footnote in original.

97. Detail (audit trail) reporting is a class of analytical reports that fits this profile. The general problem is to enumerate the detail transactions that support summary numbers accumulated as part of transaction processing, or summary numbers generated on other operational and analytical reports. Unless an index is available that permits going directly to the small subset of transactions required, sequential table scans are required to pick out the transactions that qualify for a given set of selection criteria. If the criteria require that table joins be executed as part of the processing, this needs to be accounted for accordingly. While the extract data basis and consequent report sizes are small for the bulk of detail reporting requirements, the number of detail report requests can be substantial and the primary selection criteria can be based on any field in the data base, not just those with indices. The more robust the summary analytical reporting framework, the more demand there will be for detail reporting to substantiate the summary numbers. And the more likely it is that the robust summary numbers will be based on dimensions of the data base that do not have indices to facilitate selection processing. Footnote in original.

98. The nature of the processing necessary to produce reports also is an important factor. To the extent that the source data structures for a report are denormalized, or a report requires only a single table for input, data basis and size provide a good surrogate for describing reporting loads. To the extent that normalized structures are involved that force numerous table joins to be performed as part of extraction, calculation and formatting processes, projections of overall reporting load must be adjusted accordingly. Footnote in original.

Until an attempt is made to project the reporting load in this way, it almost certainly will be under scoped. Fortunately, most reports (largest number of reports) are low data-basis operational reports that typically are small in terms of data basis and report size. As a class, these reporting requirements do not contribute greatly to overall reporting load and do not need to be evaluated in detail. However, high data-basis reports tend to be comparatively few in number but account for the bulk of the overall reporting load. The under scoping risk primarily comes from high data-basis operational reporting requirements.

Low data-basis operational reports tend to deal with business problems involving small subsets of data constrained to a limited period of time, like open orders or transactions for individual customers. Very often the indices that support ERP transaction processing also support the access requirements of operational reporting. Consequently, only limited table scans are required to access the few records in the data basis for these kinds of reports. In general, the majority of low data-basis operational reporting requirements can be satisfied with a data basis under a hundred records and most with under a thousand; they are good candidates for on-demand processing. Even a large number of people executing these kinds of reports frequently will not create an unmanageable reporting load. High data-basis operational reports tend to include requirements for retrospective analyses of transaction processing over time.

High data-basis operational reporting requirements come from all major aspects of a business - marketing, sales, product development, financial, production, human resources, procurement or legal, to name some major constituencies. And all of these constituencies are interested in the basic transactions captured and processed by the ERP modules for analytical purposes.[99]

Projecting Data Basis

Data basis is a function of:

- Transaction volume;
- Data structure complexity; and
- Number of reports, level of detail, and content requirements.

Transaction volume

Transaction detail represents the richest source of information about financial and other events captured by a system. As part of transaction processing, information entered about individual events is augmented with data from master tables according to business rules that constitute the accounting model in place at that point in time. Depending on the ERP module and configuration options implemented, detail transaction files are posted in addition to various summary balances in the ERP data model.[100]

In principle, a cumulative inception-to-date transaction file plus the related effective-dated reference tables could be the source data for all types of operational reporting. Projecting data basis for this reporting architecture would be relatively easy: total gigabytes of transaction files that would have to be scanned for each report, taking into account the number of reference table joins that would have to be performed as part of processing, extended by the frequency for reports over a period of time.

Taking the A-REAL-Co. case as an example [As described inChapter 21, "ERP Reporting," on page 101], 120,000 1,608 byte transaction records per day comes out to about 4.5 gigabytes per month or 111 gigabytes for the two years of history. The 45 basic reports actually represent an average of about 5 alternate sequences per report. So taking into account the repetitive aspects of daily, weekly, and monthly cycles, there are about 700 elemental reports that have to be produced to accomplish the basic high

99. Rick then discussed the specific company problem as discussed in the Cookie Manufacturer section of Chapter 21, "ERP Reporting," on page 101.

100. In some cases, obtaining detail transaction records from the ERP is difficult for a variety of reasons. Since this is the richest source of information, as well as the basis for auditability of numbers generated by the ERP, it is important that this issue be explicitly addressed in the reporting architecture. Footnote in original.

data-basis monthly reporting requirement. Producing one set of all reports directly off the detail would mean a data basis of something like 2.8 terabytes; this is clearly an impractical load to process at a rate of several hours per gigabyte, or even at a rate of several gigabytes per hour.

For audit trail or archive reporting purposes, there is no way to avoid facing up to the volumes associated with cumulative transaction files, unless these requirements simply are ignored.[101] However, for most summary reporting purposes, effectively designed summary files can dramatically reduce the data basis required to accomplish these requirements. The degree to which data basis reductions can be realized through use of summary file schemes depends primarily on data structure complexity.

Data Structure Complexity

The driver behind development of the manual accounting cycle was the simple physics of routinely reprocessing raw transaction data as the method for producing reports. By determining the important summary totals required in advance, then classifying all transactions as they were journalized, detail could be archived period-by-period, leaving a practical size data basis for report processing over time. In the manual world, this required maintaining a separate set of account structures and subsidiary ledgers for each summarization structure. General ledger accounting, cost accounting, revenue accounting, tax accounting, fixed asset accounting, inventory accounting, regulatory accounting, receivable accounting, payable accounting, and so on, all had needs for different sets of summary totals derived from various subsets and supersets of the same basic transactions. As automation of these reporting processes advanced through the 60's and 70's, the basic subsidiary ledger structure of the manual world was preserved in the subsystem architecture of computer-based applications.

As computers became faster at re-sequencing the same basic transaction set in different ways, more granular account structures started to emerge in subsystem implementations. Product, organizational, and project dimensions started to be included in general ledger account structures by the early 80s, simply because it became practical to extract, sort, and summarize a few hundred thousand to a million or so fully qualified summary accounts in several different ways; that had been strictly impractical in a manual world. As a result, separate subsystems were no longer needed for each business function that required a different rollup of transaction detail. But, the determination of what could be consolidated and what had to be broken out in a separate subsystem continued to be arbitrated primarily based on the volume of fully qualified accounts implied by the dimensions in the account classification structure.

The ERP presents a highly integrated profile for transaction processing[102], leaving the impression that highly integrated cross-dimensional views of the data captured also should be available. However, there are virtually an unlimited number of ways transaction-level data from the ERP could be summarized when taking into account all the possible cross-structural and time-delimited combinations. Fortunately for a given implementation, patterns in the use of cross-structural combinations usually emerge; they permit reporting data basis to be minimized by taking advantage of "locality" in the transactions when maintaining summary files. Locality means that a large number of transactions create a much smaller set of combinations when summarized by a set of cross-structural dimensions, e.g. customer / product /

---

101. Fortunately, audit trail reporting tends to involve large table scans but small extract sets, which means that processing subsequent to extraction is minimal. Footnote in original.

102. The ERP highly integrates the interrelated aspects of transaction processing that traditionally have been disconnected by subsystem architectures. As transaction detail is captured in the ERP, a very rich set of attributes about each business event is recorded. On a go-forward basis, business rules can be modified to accommodate new requirements or other changes over time. And the ERP provides for posting a wide variety of summary records at transaction processing time to facilitate inquiry and operational reporting requirements.
But, the determination of what summary totals will be required for each aspect of managing the business remains part of the up front configuration exercise. The ability to adapt to retrospective information requirements that were not foreseen up front, or new requirements that emerge over time, is very limited in the ERP world.
The ERP will post only those summary totals that it is configured to post at the time a transaction is processed. No systematic facilities are provided for accessing or analyzing the rich detail that gets captured. There is no framework for mass regeneration of summary totals that are posted in error due to configuration problems. There is no general method for reorganizing data to reflect retrospective changes in account hierarchy relationships. The ERP effectively addresses problems with transaction processing integration. But the ERP does not effectively address integration problems related to high data-basis operational reporting. Footnote in original.

organization. How substantial the locality effect is depends on transaction coding patterns, the cross-structural dimensions that are required given the patterns of report usage, and the number, breadth, and depth of the structures — data structure complexity.

The benefits of locality are usually substantial. But summary files are often assumed to be the "big" answer that makes the high data-basis operational reporting problem go away. The truth is that summary files quickly get larger than the detail files if a new summary file is created for each new use of the data that requires a different slice; the summary files become a significant volume and maintenance problem unto themselves. In practice, summary files should be maintained to the point where the data basis reduction related to report production is greater than the data basis created by the need for summary file maintenance functions. In addition, summary files should be employed as sparingly as possible due to the substantial system administration requirements that attend their maintenance and use. In the A-REAL-Co. case, only three (3) different cross-dimensional summary files maintained in multiple partitions by time-slice were required to satisfy these conditions, which is typical for data models of this type.

Modeling the degree of locality can be done fairly easily by using data from existing systems to calculate the collapse rate across structures. Simply sorting the transaction files and calculating the average number of unique cross-structural key combinations by week, month and quarter will give a reasonably good picture of what kinds of collapse rates can be expected. It's usually sufficient to work with three-to-six months of the two-to-four highest volume transaction types related to the structures in question. The result usually is far less dramatic than is assumed in the absence of a detailed analysis.

Frequently, special reporting requirements will emerge that have not been (or cannot be) anticipated and are not supported by summary files. If the requirements relate to summary reports that will be produced with some frequency, the summary files can be modified and regenerated, or new summary files can be created, by reprocessing the detail transaction data. If the requirements relate to special requests with no pattern of usage, or if they are audit trail or archive requirements, or if the summary files need to reflect the current account structure hierarchies, processing the transaction detail will be unavoidable, unless these reporting requirements are ignored. Summary files are not the "big" answer. They are just an important part of the solution.

Number of Reports, Level of Detail, and Content Requirements

Easily the biggest driver of data basis is the requirement to report at low levels of hierarchies in cross-structural combinations. In subsystem reporting, data typically is summarized one structure at a time. As a result, the number of fully qualified accounts that get created by even large volumes of transactions is limited to the number of accounts in the given structure. By avoiding the need to report by customer / product / organization, vendor / SKU / location, employee ID / general ledger account, and so on, subsystem architectures limit their reporting data basis exposure — and consequently their usefulness.

Reporting at low levels of cross-structural detail usually is important because that is the level at which day-to-day resource allocation decisions are made. Inventory replenishment, sales force management and compensation, promotional campaigns, and crew scheduling are examples of large dollar investments managed in atomized quantities of resources, location-by-location, vendor-by-vendor, days at a time. High-level performance measures, that show out of whack inventory turnover rates or sales per employee, do not help identify the out-of-stock problems that need to be fixed or the particular sales calls not getting made. The thousands of reports in legacy systems got created because figuring out what was going wrong required a specific cross-structural slice of the data to illuminate the drivers about which something could be done.

It is unlikely that thousands of reports are needed to run any business at a given point in time. But, over time, the number of problems that need to be solved certainly accumulate into the thousands. In the world of subsystem architectures, a new problem meant building a new reporting subsystem (that mostly never gets retired). In the integrated ERP world, the underlying assumption is that any needed slice will be available because the transactions were captured by an integrated process. But, as we have seen, availability of any slice means access to detail or maintenance of every summary total (a clearly impractical alternative).

Two basic approaches to defining reporting level of detail and content requirements can be taken:

- Produce a predefined set of reports in case they are needed;
- Provide a framework that can generate almost anything, but produce only what people ask for.

The first approach is easiest to manage from a project standpoint. But, limiting the set of reports to a practical number is difficult. And it results in an enormous amount of processing for generating numbers nobody looks at. Also, it is not what most clients have in mind when they embark on implementing a new integrated information system. The second approach is preferable, but more difficult to achieve. Something that takes both into account is required.

Chapter 31. Estimate the Data Basis

As part of the Cookie manufacturer project, I analyzed the existing reports that were being used to run the business from the legacy environment. After compiling that list, I analyzed the data from the new system that would be needed to produce those legacy reports. At Rick's request, I generalized my work into a sizing tool and created instructions for others to follow the same steps. But sizing a reporting environment won't necessarily be done the same way for all companies; we will need to accommodate variations in circumstances. So, let's first discuss how to think about the sizing method before we look closer at how to construct a sizing spreadsheet.

Overview

The primary purpose of the method is to assist in sizing the reporting environment- providing number of bytes per report, files used by each report, and performance requirements for hardware and software. But, additional benefits accrue by being able to track each significant report, its use and creation.

Assessing the reporting requirements is important for getting the right set of numbers to estimate the data load for report processing over time; and by far the largest single factor in determining overall reporting load is data basis. The approach seeks to create an accurate picture by aggregating the data basis and report sizes across the number of reports and the frequency with which they will be executed in a given period of time, stratifying by frequency like on-demand, daily, weekly, monthly, quarterly, and annually. Then analysis can determine if processing can be performed within software and hardware constraints.

This step of the method consists of several smaller steps, shown in the following high level flow diagram.

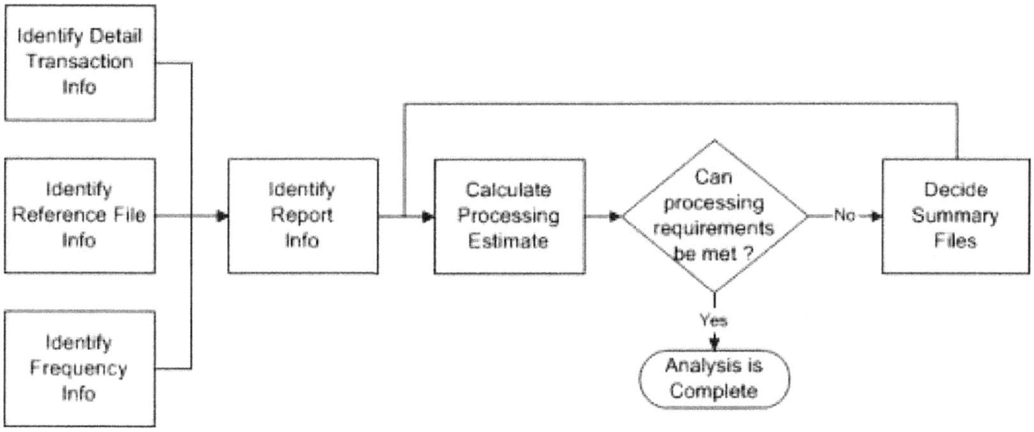

Figure 73. High Level Process Flow of Reporting Environment Estimation Method

Our process starts by first gathering information or estimating the data that will be used to process all the reports in the new system.

- Estimate the size of the detail source transactions or event file (called a fact table in data warehousing).
- Define the reference files (called dimension tables in data warehousing).
- Identify how often reports will be produced. And choose a base frequency so all our data for analysis are "apples to apples".

Then we need to analyze all the reports expected to be generated by the new system, and their impact on processing.

- Identify what reports will be produced, what reports will use which files to determine the number of records read to produce the reports, and the number of foreign/primary key joins each report requires with the reference files.
- Then, calculate the amount of processing required to produce the reports, and analyze if the processing requirements can be met within the project hardware and software constraints. If yes, no additional work is necessary.

If our analysis reveals that processing requirements cannot be met, we proceed with decisions about summarization to improve processing.

- Determine what summary files to create to reduce the reporting load. And then, recalculate the processing estimates to determine if processing can now be performed within the software and hardware constraints.

The basic point here is we first see if we can produce all the reports from the business events themselves. If our business required ten transactions a year, sales reporting can probably be accomplished without performing any intermediate summaries.

Now, let's begin to explore the steps of our sizing method in greater detail.

Detail Transaction Files

We need to estimate the number and size of the business events the system will generate to produce the report covering the greatest amount of history. For example, if we want to produce the balance sheet for the last five years and all income statements in between, we start with the assumption that doing so from the business events is the most flexible approach. So we estimate the business events that might be generated which will have an impact on the balance sheet and income statement for those five years.

The largest single factor in determining overall reporting load is data basis. The most important aspect of data basis usually relates to the number and size of records that must be extracted then further manipulated to produce the report output.

Retrieve daily volume estimates from current transaction posting systems. Use the information gathered by finding the event file and then finding more detailed events. If only an estimate is available, use known statistics about the company to estimate the number of detail records. For example, current invoice line items may be an appropriate estimate for a sales system, the number of customers and their average transactions per day for a retail banking system.

This isn't a completely theoretical step either; be practical as well. Although it is possible to calculate payroll costs from individual timesheet records from the HR system, for many businesses there is little benefit to having that level of detail in a financial reporting repository. High value customer details have a great deal more value in a financial reporting repository.

Reference Files

As described above, reference tables supplement information when reports are built, for example, account descriptions, cost center names and have a notable impact on processing. Later in the method when we identify all report information, we will list the number of table joins per report, reflecting the number of times the report will require a foreign to primary key join (lookup) to a reference or summary table for use as constraints (selection parameters) or descriptive titles. Table joins can have a significant impact on processing time and are another aspect of data load.

Use the reference data tables created as part of the Define Reference Data step already performed. For the reference data, the number of keys and answers is more important than the size of the files which are usually relatively small. However estimating the size of the static data—things like customers and arrangements—is akin to estimating the transaction files. Size of these files can be significant.

Frequency

Identify each of the frequency types for which reports are produced, e.g. daily, monthly, quarterly, annually.

Choose a base frequency that will allow you to 'normalize' all report data for a consistent analysis. Typically this is daily or monthly depending on the frequency of the majority of the reports to be produced.

Report Information

We need to project the reports or queries that are expected to be processed. For each report, we need to know frequency produced, report name, report description, width of the report (# bytes), estimated extract percent, and number of table joins. The impact from all table joins, whether to reference files or static data, needs to be included in the calculations for report processing load.

If the information about all the reports is not available from recent project efforts, then this data may also have to be gathered from current system documentation, soliciting assistance from the business, or even potentially reading the report programs. Most systems projects are expected to improve the situation which means, at a minimum, old reports which are still used will need to be produced by the new system. I refer to this as the do no harm principle.

Knowledge of the business process and reporting requirements will be necessary to provide an approximate extract percent - the number of records extracted from the event file(s). For example, if a report of customers from Nebraska is produced from a file containing all customers in the United States, the report might extract on 1/50 of the total records in the file. Because a balance sheet is to summarize all financial transactions, it typically will require a very high percentage of event records.

Ad hoc queries should be identified as a report.

Some reports are produced with permutations of the sort keys. This will commonly be done where a report needs to be sorted and presented in various ways but all reports select the same data and are essentially the same columns. It may be easier to multiply one of the reports by the permutations than to track each individually.

Calculate Processing Estimates

We need to calculate the total number of detail and summary records being processed to meet the reporting requirements.

The information we have identified so far - about the detail transaction file, the reference files, the frequencies, and reports - must all come together through calculations to create a picture of the anticipated report processing load. We need to aggregate the data basis and report sizes across the number of reports and the normalized frequency with which they will be executed in a given period of time, and take into account the processing load from table joins.

Compare the required number of table joins, records read and the number of records and megabytes extracted with the standards for your hardware and software platforms. If the processing requirements can be met within the project hardware and software constraints, no additional work is necessary. If not, we need to proceed to determine what summary files to create to reduce the reporting load.

Here's where the use of the sizing spreadsheet can help with the calculations of processing estimates.

Using the Sizing Spreadsheet

I created a template spreadsheet that was distributed with Rick's white paper. There is nothing magical about it or the formulas it contained. Mostly the principles I learned in my first Information Systems class were all that was needed in order to construct it. The following descriptions and screen shots may be adequate to perform similar steps on your project.

The specific steps I took are not the most important point. The most important step to take is one that I have heard Jay, and Doug and Rick say multiple times over the years: "DO THE MATH!" There is no excuse for not doing the math to calculate what is and what is not possible. Computers are very predictable when the principles upon which they operate are understood. If the principles are not understood, the results will appear random.

You may not have all the data I had available to me, and you may have other data I didn't have available. Adjust your approach to make the best use of the data you have and to analyze problems that may be unique to your situation.

I made spreadsheets to ask as few questions as possible and use the input in calculations and sizing methods - the spreadsheet did all calculations and roll-ups.

My spreadsheet had the following tabs:

- Detail Temp—Detail Source File Data Template (fact table)
- Sum Temp—Summary File Data Template (aggregate fact table)
- Ref Temp—Reference File Template (dimension table)
- Freq—Reporting Frequency Listing
- Report—Listing of Reports to be produced
- Sum Norm—Summary Adjusted to a Common Frequency (i.e., records read and extracted daily)
- Sum Not Norm—Summary Not Adjusted to a Common Frequency

All the worksheets were required, except Sum Temp if summary tables are not needed. In the next chapter we'll review the detail file findings before deciding if we must build summary file structures. If the detail can be adequately processed, creation of summary files may be unnecessary.

Step 1 - Complete the Detail Temp Worksheet Area 1

In the top portion of the Detail Template worksheet, I estimated the number and size of the detail records which would be needed to produce all reports. This is estimating basic characteristics about the primary event file. The required input items include File Name, File Abbreviation, Number of records estimated per day and Bytes per record.

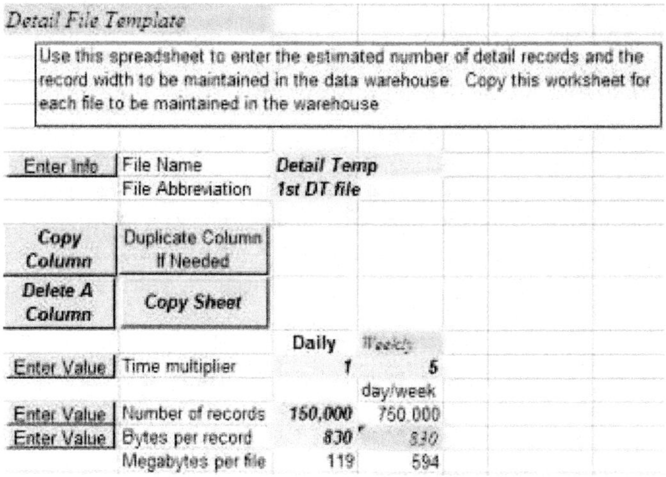

Figure 74. Detail Temp Worksheet Area 1

Step 2 - Complete the Frequency Worksheet

I entered each frequency for which reports needed to be produced.[103]

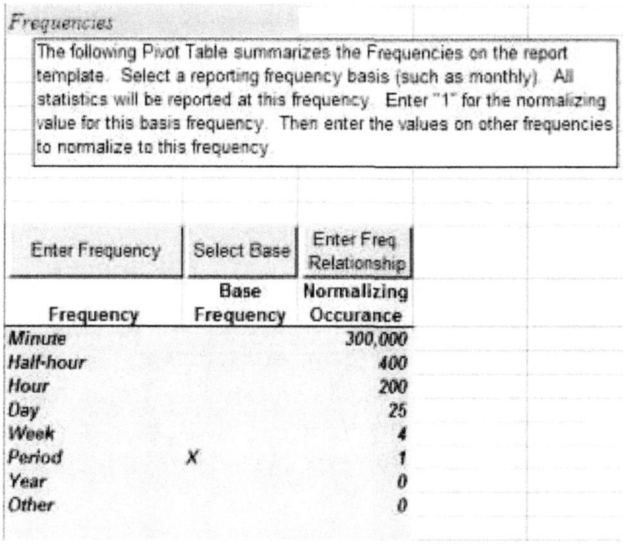

Figure 75. Frequency Worksheet

Step 3 - Complete the Reports Worksheet

Using the Reports worksheet, I projected the reports or queries to be executed. I entered each report to be produced as a separate line with the columns to record information such as Frequency Produced, Report Count, Report Name, Report Description, Number of Table Joins, Width of the Report (# bytes), and Estimated Extract Percent.

---

103. The tool allows selecting a base frequency to 'normalize' the data. The required input items include Frequency, Base Frequency Indicator (X), and Normalizing Occurrence for each Frequency.
For example, to see all data reported by year (megabytes and records per year), "year" will be the base frequency and you should place a '1' in the Normalizing Occurrence on that line. You would then report 12 and 52 in the Normalizing Occurrence for Period and Week respectively (e.g., 12 months in a year and 52 weeks in a year). This information is used to create a summary that is normalized to a yearly reporting period. You may change the frequency at any time during the completion of the workbook but it will change the numbers reported in the summary normalized worksheet.

When I had completed all the worksheets, this sheet provided a list of each report, the megabytes estimated to read and extract for each and the number of table joins. These listings of reports were also shown in the lower section of the detail and summary file worksheets so I could decide the number of records to be read and extracted from that particular file based on extract percent and report file usage retrieved from the other worksheets.

You might complain you don't have a listing of the reports the new system needs to produce. I didn't either. But I knew the new system would need to produce equivalent information to the old system, so my report listings were from the old system. The business events hadn't changed, they just came from a new system. New reports were possible, but I knew without the old reports the company couldn't continue to operate so they were required.

Report Template

The worksheet summarizes the reports or queries to be processed by the data warehouse. Complete all editable columns. If more than one detail and summary file is used as input, duplicate the "Records to be read" column, and change references in the formula to the correct worksheet. **Do not sort this section. Do not change the column headings.**

Enter Frequency	Calcu-lated	Enter Count	Enter Name	Enter Report Description	Enter Bytes	Enter Percent	Duplicate If Necessary	Duplicate If Necessary	Calculated	Duplicate If Necessary	Duplicate If Necessary	Calculated	Duplicate If Necessary
							Records Read From:			**Megabytes Read From:**			**Table Joins From:**
Frequency Produced	**Occur-ance**	**Report Count**	**Report Name**	**Report Description**	**Extract Width**	**Extract Percent**	**Recs from 1st DT file**	**Recs from 1st SM File**	**Recs Read - Total**	**MBs from 1st DT file**	**MBs from 1st SM File**	**MB Read - Total**	**Joins from 1st RF File**
Day	25	*1*	*Sample 1*	*Sample Report*	*90*	*50%*	150,000		150,000	119		119	
Period	1	*1*	*Sample 2*	*Sample Report*	*200*	*100%*	3,750,000		3,750,000	2,968		2,968	750,000
Year	0.08333	*1*	*Sample 3*	*Sample Report*	*100*	*5%*	39,000,000		39,000,000	30,870		30,870	78,000,000
Week	4	*1*	*Sample 4*	*Sample Report*	*500*	*20%*	750,000		750,000	594		594	375,000
Hour	200	*1*	*Sample 5*	*Sample Report*	*10*	*10%*	150,000		150,000	119		119	
Half-hour	400	*1*	*Sample 6*	*Sample Report*	*30*	*1%*	150,000		150,000	119		119	
Minute	300000	*1*	*Sample 7*	*Sample Report*	*60*	*2%*	150,000		150,000	119		119	
Week	4	*1*	*Sample 8*	*Sample Report*	*20*	*30%*	750,000		750,000	594		594	
Day	25	*1*	*Sample 9*	*Sample Report*	*500*	*10%*	150,000		150,000	119		119	
Period	1	*1*	*Sample 10*	*Sample Customer Rpt*	*50*	*100%*							

Figure 76. Reports Worksheet

Step 4 - Complete the Detail Temp Worksheet

As I noted above, after completing the Reports Worksheet, each report and its frequency was displayed by reference in the lower section of the Detail Worksheet. I inserted columns for each file frequencies. I then went down the list of each report and specified how many files of each frequency that report will use. For example, a daily report might show data in columns for the last 3 business days plus a month-to-date column. This report would use a maximum of 4 daily files and 4 weekly files. I recorded the maximum numbers of records needed. Because this report has a month-to-date column, assume it is being produced on the last day of the month, not the first when the volume would be the lowest. In this example, record 4 under daily and 4 under weekly.

Records Read Per Report

Complete Table

After completing the Report worksheet, return to the section below. Enter the number of files to be read under each heading to produce the report. For example, if a weekly report also contains period-to-date values, it might read a weekly and period file. Do not delete rows from this section. Simply leave the files read section blank.

Frequency Produced	Report Name	Daily	Weekly	Daily Records	Weekly Records	Total Read	Daily MB	Weekly MB	Total MB
Day	Sample 1	*1*		150,000		150,000	119		119
Period	Sample 2		*5*		3,750,000	3,750,000		2,968	2,968
Year	Sample 3		*52*		39,000,000	39,000,000		30,870	30,870
Week	Sample 4		*1*		750,000	750,000		594	594
Hour	Sample 5	*1*		150,000		150,000	119		119
Half-hour	Sample 6	*1*		150,000		150,000	119		119
Minute	Sample 7	*1*		150,000		150,000	119		119
Week	Sample 8		*1*		750,000	750,000		594	594
Day	Sample 9	*1*		150,000		150,000	119		119

Figure 77. Detail Temp Worksheet Area 2

Step 5 - Complete Reference File Worksheet

I created a Reference File Worksheet for significant known reference files (dimension table). The purpose of this tab is to estimate join processes, which can be a significant consumption of processing time. The required input items include Reference File Name, File Name Abbreviation, Key Fields, Number of Occurrences of Key Fields, and Number of Table Joins to This File. This will approximate the number of records expected in the completed file.

Reference File Template

Use this spreadsheet for all reference files or table data files to be mantained in the data warehouse. A reference file may also be a summary file. All reports which read the summary file should be listed on the summary file worksheet. This worksheet only includes table joins to the reference file.

Enter Info	Ref. file name	***Ref Temp***
	File Abbreviation	***1st RF File***

Copy Sheet

		Reference	Enter Value
Frequency Produced	**Report Name**	**Total Recs. Read from "Reports"**	**Table Joins To This File**
Day	Sample 1	150,000	
Period	Sample 2	3,750,000	***750,000***
Year	Sample 3	39,000,000	***78,000,000***
Week	Sample 4	750,000	***375,000***
Hour	Sample 5	150,000	
Half-hour	Sample 6	150,000	
Minute	Sample 7	150,000	
Week	Sample 8	750,000	
Day	Sample 9	150,000	
Period	Sample 10		

Figure 78. Reference File Worksheet

On the lower section of this worksheet I again showed by reference each report, allowing the entry of number of table joins per report. I entered the number of table joins required for a foreign to primary key join (lookup) for use as constraints (selection parameters) or descriptive titles.

Step 6 - Analyze Summary Worksheets

Next I created a Summary Worksheet containing a pivot table. It showed the number of detail or summary records being processed to produce the reports.

Reporting Summary - Not Normalized

The following Pivot Table summarizes the results of the detail file analysis. Press the button to summarize the amount of processing for the frequency. These values are not multiplied by the Normalizing Occurrence value listed on the Frequency Table

Update Table

Frequency	Not Normalized	Total
Day	Sum of Report Count	17
	Sum of Table Joins - Total	124,818,052
	Sum of Recs Read - Total	42,960,000
	Sum of MB Read - Total	34,005
	Sum of Records Extracted	22,774,204
	Sum of MB Extracted	2,004
Week	Sum of Report Count	54
	Sum of Table Joins - Total	873,863,473
	Sum of Recs Read - Total	182,064,000
	Sum of MB Read - Total	173,751
	Sum of Records Extracted	57,880,800
	Sum of MB Extracted	5,708
Period	Sum of Report Count	75
	Sum of Table Joins - Total	507,524,187
	Sum of Recs Read - Total	506,832,000
	Sum of MB Read - Total	337,157
	Sum of Records Extracted	56,289,420
	Sum of MB Extracted	21,670
Quarter	Sum of Report Count	2
	Sum of Table Joins - Total	1,514,661,174
	Sum of Recs Read - Total	16,584,000
	Sum of MB Read - Total	7,500
	Sum of Records Extracted	10,209,000
	Sum of MB Extracted	876
Half year	Sum of Report Count	9
	Sum of Table Joins - Total	-
	Sum of Recs Read - Total	105,300,000
	Sum of MB Read - Total	89,771
	Sum of Records Extracted	19,908,000
	Sum of MB Extracted	6,993

Figure 79. Summary Worksheet

This summary sheet[104] reported the processing requirements by all the frequencies of reports and computed the totals. I compared the required number of table joins, records read and the number of records and megabytes extracted to what others knew were the standard processing capabilities for the hardware and software platforms.

If the processing requirements could have been met within the project hardware and purchased software constraints, then no additional work would have been necessary. However, it couldn't, which meant I had to proceed with step 7 to determine what summary files to create to reduce the reporting load.

104. This summary is actually after estimating the summary files which were constructed for the customer as outlined in the next chapter. The version prior to creation of summary files is no longer available but would have shown "the weekly data basis would have been over 20 times the 23 gigabytes if all processing had been done using transaction level data..." as noted in Rick's original paper.

Chapter 32. Define Summary Structures

The results of the above analysis led Rick to the conclusion in the white paper that "approximately 65 hours per week of continuous processing" would be needed " just to complete the initial extract" with no table joins. Adding table joins took the processing time to "about 260 hours of continuous single-threaded processing." Thinking about summarizing the required 210 million extracted records for the 23 reports meant, "...something on the order of 2,000 processing hours per week would be a reasonable estimate ...of the end-to-end processing load, given the [customer] environment."[105] Remember, there are only 168 hours in a week. Two thousand hours is a lot of parallel processing.

Even with the SAFR software, the processing requirements were formidable. Thus after review of the detail file findings from our first calculations and comparison of the findings against the processing performance standards of the hardware and software environment, we found we needed summary file structures to reduce the reporting load.

And thus we have a balancing act to perform. The event based principles say that the most flexible environment is to work from the business events, and yet we find that the needed reports cannot be reasonably processed with the given resources. Creating summary files means we will be adding processing layers between the business events and the reports, but it is necessary. The approach we have taken with the method, though, has been to estimate based upon no summarization, and then add only those summaries necessary to support specific reporting requirements. We still maintain access to the details in order to regenerate summaries, or to use with reports requiring that detail.

We must estimate the impact of adding a summary file, then reassess if the processing requirements can be met within the project hardware and software constraints. More summary files are designed until the processing requirements can be met.

The process of defining summary structures includes determining criteria fields, locality, and time impact.

Criteria Fields

In determining how to create summary files, first determine which fields to summarize. Any criteria fields used in the report, fields used to select which events to include, must be included in the summarization. If multiple reports use the same criteria fields, a summary file collapsing to these criteria fields may reduce the amount of data processed.

If possible, perform a test summarization to verify the expected collapse using different combinations of criteria fields.

Locality

Next determine the locality. "Locality means that a large number of transactions create a much smaller set of combinations when summarized by a set of cross-structural dimensions"[106] e.g. customer / product / organization. For example, assume that the company has two customers and three products. The summary file could theoretically contain six records (2 x 3). However, assume that Company 2 for some reason will never purchase Product Y, and Company 1 will never purchase Product Z. The number of summary records now is four (2 x 3 - 2). Locality can occur because of the definition of data elements.

105. Richard K. Roth, *[ERP] High-volume Operational Reporting/Data Warehousing Summary of Sizing Concepts and Architectural Alternatives* Price Waterhouse White Paper, September, 1996, 1, 4, 5. Copyright IBM Corporation. Used by permission.

106. Ibid., 7.

For example, a hierarchical structure will result in very high locality. If there are 25 sales districts contained within 3 sales regions, the theoretical limit is 75 (3 x 25). However, if all sales districts are unique across regions, the limit is 25.

Modeling the degree of locality can be done fairly easily by using data from existing systems or from prior steps in the SAFR method to calculate the collapse rate across structures. Simply sorting and summarizing the transaction files and calculating the average number of unique cross-structural key combinations by week, month and quarter will give a reasonably good picture of what kinds of collapse rates can be expected. It's usually sufficient to work with three-to-six months of the two-to-four highest volume transaction types related to the structures in question.

Time Impact

We need to understand the reporting periods of time to appropriately incorporate the effects on the expected collapse of number of records.

The greater the number of records due to passage of time, the greater the potential collapse when summarizing. For example, assume that within a single day a customer will probably not buy the same product twice. Thus summarizing the day's transactions to the customer product level will result in very little collapse. However, assume that over the course of a year the customer purchases the same product at least once a month. The estimated collapse will then be 12 times higher for a yearly file.

Using the Sizing Spreadsheet

Step 7 - Complete the Summary Temp Worksheet

Once I had determined that the reports could not be produced from the detail transactions, I copied the Detailed Template and made a new summary spreadsheet. In this I named the summary file, and guessed at what fields might summarize it, I estimated the number of occurrences/locality of those fields, and then estimated by report the number of records which would be used from it.

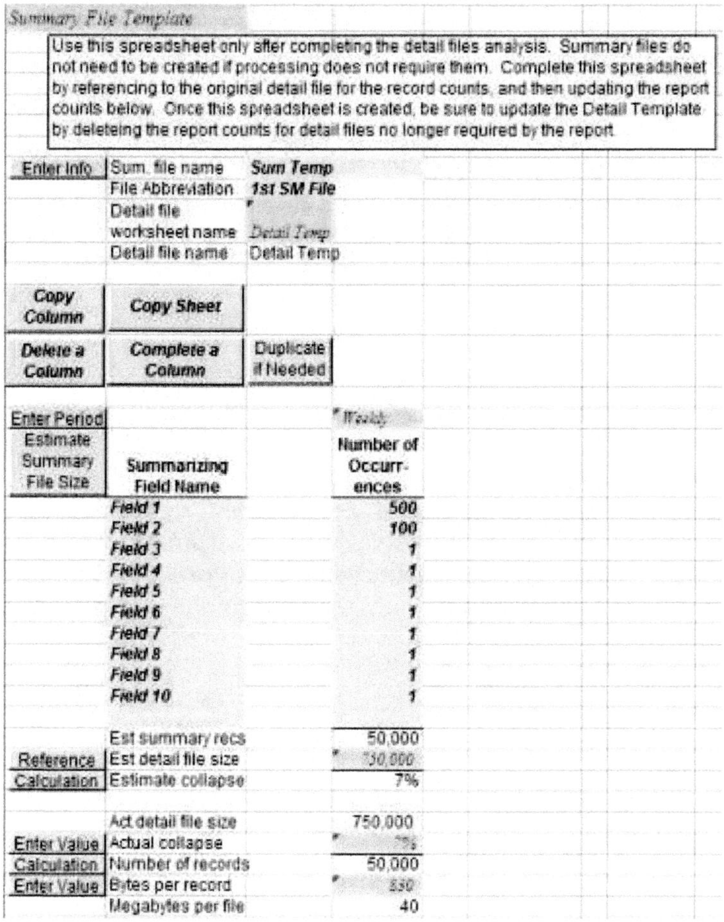

Figure 80. Summary Temp Worksheet

Step 7.1. Determine Criteria Fields (Summarizing Field Name)

Summary files are created by summarizing criteria fields and accumulating the value fields. Consider the following example:

Criteria Field 1	Criteria Field 2	Value Field 1
Customer	**Product**	**Sales Price**
Company 1	Product X	1.00
Company 2	Product X	2.00
Company 1	Product Y	2.00
Company 1	Product Y	1.00
Company 2	Product Z	3.00

Figure 81. Detail File Example

If the above table were summarized by Customer, the following summary file would result:

Criteria Field 1	Criteria Field 2	Value Field 1
Customer	**Product**	**Sales Price**
Company 1	?	4.00
Company 2	?	6.00

Figure 82. Summary File Example

Because the table was summarized at a level greater than Product, the product field is no longer meaningful. It could be removed from the file, because we no longer know how much was paid for each product. This file would not be useful to produce a product report.

At the Cookie Manufacturer, I first tried to create a single summary structure collapsing on all three hierarchies, the Material, Sales, and Customers. I found that even summarizing these, because customer is such a low level of detail, the resulting files were still very large. I then noted from analyzing the detailed reports that a lot of the reports used the Material, and the Sales hierarchies, but not the Customer hierarchy. When I tested the summarization, I found the records reduce to about 5% of the original records but this file could be used in 60% of the reports.

Step 7.2. Determine Locality

In the Sum Temp worksheet, enter the number of unique occurrences adjusted for locality in the Number of Occurrences cells. Locality makes the summary structures smaller.

In my spreadsheet I multiplied the possible combinations of values in each field to guess at what the summary structure might be. When I actually ran tests, I found that the files were much smaller because some combinations never happen. Analyzing the results of my tests I found that all but one combination of customers and salespersons were not valid because customers were only assigned to one salesperson.

Step 7.3. Determine Time Impact

In the Sum Temp worksheet, adjust the Number of Occurrences for the effect of time.

I noted that the number of reports that needed only daily and weekly values was relatively low. Most of the reports, although run on a daily basis, showed month-to-date numbers. Also, in analyzing the data I determined that there was almost no collapse on daily files, and very little on weekly. I determined that I needed to only make summary files for the monthly records.

Step 8 – Create New "Reports"

After creating summary files, I updated the report page to reflect what source should be used for which report using the summary structures whenever possible. I also added a new row to the report page to reflect the need to create each one of the summary files. To SAFR, production of a file or production of a report requires the same steps. These rows read the detail files on the periodic basis.

I then analyzed the pivot table based upon this new information and determined if processing could be completed cost effectively.

Balancing Summary Structures

One significant difference between this approach and the standard summary file creation approach is that in the SAFR approach the summary files are recreated from the detail periodically. On a daily basis the new transactions are added to the file. But when the hierarchies change, which affects the rows in the summary files, the files would be rebuilt from scratch.

This means the summaries are temporary files, not posted permanent files. This approach allows us to maintain as much of the flexibility the business event based reporting approach allows while accommodating processing and cost constraints.

Cookie Manufacturer Project Results

A few years after the project, I wrote the following description of its results:

The Problem

In 1996 a major US cookie manufacturer installed an ERP to manage all aspects of the manufacturing, HR and financial operations. The system captured data and provided adequate information for managing most operational aspects of the business. But the ERP could not deliver the detailed sales analysis necessary to support the highly detailed, store-specific sales process. They chose SAFR to solve the problem in an integrated ERP environment.

The reporting requirements were substantial. The company required detailed information at the customer/line item level over various time slices from daily to year-to-date, for over 60,000 customer stores and 2,000 items, selecting and summarizing by over 100 fields. The company sells over a million items per week, and they needed comparative information for each time period for at least the last two years. They also needed comparative data be reorganized to reflect changes in organizational structure over time!

The Solution

A SAFR application was developed to deliver the full benefit of the ERP implementation, without burdening users with another tool. The ERP's profitability analysis module was configured to capture the required data. Programs were written to extract the sales items from the ERP on a nightly basis. A series of SAFR processes were developed to manage the data warehouse, including creation of various summary file structures. The completed data warehouse contains over 250 gigabytes of data in 15 entities, containing over 300 million records.

SAFR was configured to produce executive information files, commonly called "information cubes." The company defined SAFR "Views" to create over 150 cubes, and 75 interface files. SAFR's effective date lookup processing allowed for recasting the historical detail to reflect the current management structures.

The ERP Executive Report Viewer was also developed. Constructed within the ERP environment and fully integrated with the profitability analysis reporting environment, this analysis tool gives users a single source of information. Through this tool, users are able to select a time period, and then the respective cube. Users can specify selection criteria, drill down into reports to lower and lower levels of detail. They can export to Excel, view the data in a graphical format, format the report, and save a profile of the report.

The Results

Users have commented that the sales reporting system has been one of the most successful components of the ERP implementation. It has allowed the company to capitalize on its national sales force that makes personal contact with stores nearly 3 times each week. The sales representatives are armed with needed information. They can analyze customer and product information for daily, weekly, monthly, year to date, and spot trends from over 3 years of data. The system has helped fuel their growth in net income nearly 10 times from 1996 to 1999, and has scaled as the company has purchased and integrated three additional companies.

Indeed, the system scaled so effectively it was selected as the surviving application when the Cookie Manufacturer was purchased by a much larger company. The following is the architecture diagram depicting the implementation.

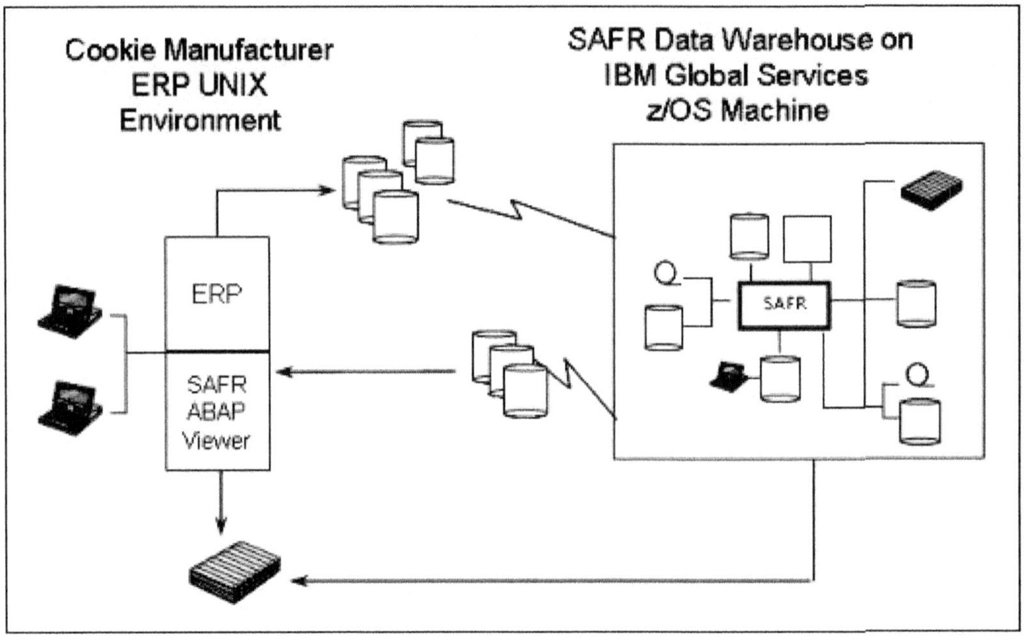

Figure 83. Cookie Manufacturer Solution System Architecture

Our steps to this point have assumed all business events are presented to the system. For the Cookie Manufacturer this was true, and based upon these steps Monica Logan helped me build the SAFR processes necessary to produce the required outputs. Additional steps are necessary if not all the business events are presented to the reporting environment.

Chapter 33. Define Processes

In the fall of 1993 after being on the test team for a number of months and learning the system, Rick asked if I would go up to Oregon to help them understand the upgraded software that could be applied to their existing application. This was one of my first solo consulting assignments, although I remember Jay, who lived nearby, sitting in on my sessions. Jay was the fatherly figure who helped make sure I didn't drive the car off the road on my first trip.

I remember their reaction when they learned that in addition to creating reports, the latest version had the ability to write out files as well. This turned the product from a reporting tool to a potential ETL or processing tool.

Event Generation

To this point in the SAFR method we have assumed all business events needed for producing reports have been generated by other systems and presented to the reporting environment. As noted in Chapter 15, "Operational Versus Informational," on page 71, that may not be the case. Certain SAFR projects have had those characteristics. The Cookie Manufacturer which resulted in the steps outlined in the prior three chapters did. All data needed for reporting was generated inside the ERP environment. The extracted business events were used purely in a reporting process managed by SAFR.

Other projects require additional business events be generated. Most often these business events are generated through the use of rules or parameters; with the exception of adjustments discussed below, they do not require a person capturing the business event in any way. The work we have done thus far helps to determine what events need to be generated.

This work really doesn't wait until all the prior steps have been completed. In fact, the first deficiencies in the business events available for reporting likely showed up when we attempted to find more detailed events. Turning detailed transactions into journal entries often includes processes that happen after the transactions from the operational systems have been summarized. Thus in attempting to balance the detailed events to the journal entries, we would have found that only portions of the file could be balanced: business events for some accounts would likely be completely missing.

So the work of generating additional business events begins by determining what events trigger additional events. In the case of the detailed operational file missing particular offsetting entries, the triggering event is probably one of the transactions in the source system.

SAFR could be used to generate these events by defining a file format output view, filtering for the specific transactions, and then using column filtering and column constants or lookups to form a new output record. When these new records are combined with the input records into one file, fully formed journal entries might be created.

Balance Based Processes

Remember that some processes, such as currency revaluation, are dependent upon some event that may happen so frequently that using an arbitrary cut off for generating the events may be more appropriate. These types of processes require greater attention to issues of volume and scale because they demand a balance as of a point in time and that requires accessing history. This is in contrast to generating offsets for journal entries which only requires reading the set of dependent business events.

Requiring balances as of a point in time is dependent upon the same decisions and analysis we performed in assessing reporting needs, estimating the data basis and defining summary structures. Instead of reporting needs, we concentrate on processing needs. All the same rules apply, plus few additional rules. In addition to analysis of transaction volumes, data structure complexity, and number of reports and level of detail, we have to be cognizant of (1) the dependencies between processes, and (2) the outputs from these processes.

Process Dependencies

The order of operations must be understood for processes to work effectively. These processes generate new business events, which may be the input or triggers for other business events. For example currency translation, the process of converting a balance or transaction into another currency for reporting, must be done before that balance can be revalued. In other words going back to our example in Chapter 15, "Operational Versus Informational," on page 71 where we had a UK bank account we needed to include in our US dollar denominated balance sheet, we have to convert the pounds into dollars before we can include it in our balance sheet. Reflecting the changes in exchange rates on the income statement happens when we produce the next balance sheet. So in analyzing processes which need to generate new business events, determine what the triggering event, often called the driver file in batch programming, is for each.

Remember that all balances are composed of individual movements; this can open up processing opportunities. For example, supposed early in the morning the daily process could start with the summary file of the balance from the last day, but the balances will be incomplete. They have not yet been updated with yesterday's transactions. There may be little reason to summarize all of the transactions from the source system into the summary file before generating the new events based upon those balances. Mathematically, generating two business events, one based upon the balance as of yesterday and another based upon only that portion of the balance that was updated yesterday (yesterday's transaction or movement) the results are the same. This allows that all of the business events, both those received from the source system and those generated in the finance system processes can be applied or posted to the summary structure at the same time. We'll show how this is done in Chapter 52, "Common Key Data Buffering," on page 271.

Outputs

The standard SAFR View process puts out one record for each record selected in record filtering. This is adequate for producing reports from fully formed business events in an event repository. However, this may or may not be adequate for business event creation processes. At times a single input record may need to generate multiple output records.

For example, originating a loan may result in a single transaction from the loan origination system. This record may reflect simply the increase in bank assets from making the loan. However, to make a fully formed journal entry an offset may need to be created to reflect the disbursement of funds for the loan typically recorded in a different system.

This may not be all. Let's assume that these amounts and entries comply with US generally accepted accounting principles. Perhaps there is a difference in the amounts that should be recognized for International Financial Reporting Standards (IFRS). Meeting the contradictory objectives of both standards isn't mutually exclusive. What is required is a field on the records which identifies which book the transaction is for similar to the below.

Business Unit	Cost Center	Account	Book Code	Amount
BU 1	CC 1	Asset 1	IFRS	10,000
BU 1	CC 1	Contra Asset 1	IFRS	(1,000)
BU 1	CC 1	Asset 2	IFRS	(9,000)
BU 1	CC 1	Asset 1	USGAAP	(10,000)
BU 1	CC 1	Contra Asset 1	USGAAP	1,000
BU 1	CC 1	Asset 2	USGAAP	9,000
BU 1	CC 1	Asset 1	USGAAP	10,000
BU 1	CC 1	Asset 2	USGAAP	(10,000)

The original entry, the first row above, came from the source system. The second and third records are offsets. These are the amounts required for IFRS standards. These three rows are then reversed for the USGAAP view of the data, and the USGAAP entries are made. At report time, if someone wants an IFRS view of the data, they only select the IFRS rows of data. If they want a USGAAP view, they select both the IFRS and USGAAP view of the data.

Using SAFR to accomplish this could be accomplished by making a view for each type of output record that needs to be created. In other words, there could be a view to reformat the original input transaction from the source system to make IFRS Asset 1 entry, another for reading that same event file and creating IFRS Contra Asset 1 record, another for IFRS Asset 2 entry and so on. In total there would be eight views, thus one record into the extract engine becomes eight records out.

The downside of this approach is that a great deal of logic may be replicated in each view. For example, the logic to populate the business unit and cost center in each of the views would likely be the same. This becomes a maintenance problem.

To overcome this, SAFR has a special logic text construct called the WRITE verb described in Chapter 50, "Piping, Tokens, and the Write Verb," on page 259. This instructs the Scan Engine to write the record formed so far by the view to a specified file. Each view can contain many write statements. Thus with this verb, a single input record to a view can become multiple output records.

SAFR has been used in other ways to solve these types of problems. To understand those approaches, we should first discuss the structure of the rules.

Rules

The word rule in this sense means "A determinate method for performing a mathematical operation and obtaining a certain result".[107] In my mind, it is difficult to distinguish between any program logic and rules or parameters those programs use; they all are determinate methods of obtaining a certain result. However, there are some generalizations that can be made about what is called processing rules.

Rules tend to change more frequently than programs do. They also tend to be maintained by non-IT people. In a sense, they are those parts of programs that the end users want to control without having the entire burden of being programmers.

As SAFR has been used as a processing engine, various means have been constructed to allow end users to control their rules. For simple processes users can change values in the views themselves. However, for more complex processes where the views become something closer to programs, users want control without all the programming responsibilities.

Using reference files updated by users is a very common way of accomplishing this. Another more sophisticated approach is to build screens for the user to define their rules, and then create a custom SAFR process which generates SAFR views. For example, if a screen were created that allowed the user

---

107. Merriam-Webster 11th Collegiate Dictionary sv. Rule.

to maintain the list of journal entries that must be generated above, the eight required views could be created by a program that runs prior to the SAFR Scan Engine. The Scan Engine Select Phase API accepts XML in a SAFR defined schema allowing custom workbenches to create the eight required views.

Errors and Adjustments

Reporting systems which require the highest degree of accuracy require that errors can be corrected and adjustments made. Adjustments might be made to correct errors but also to capture business events which are not automated. This portion of the system is a transaction processing application, and typically requires all that implies. The outputs from it, however, should be architected to the system as if they are simply another type of source system; the business events should be captured and processed as if they came from a completely independent system.

Insurance Company Allocation Engine Project Results

The following is a sample of a process created using SAFR as the processing engine to emulate ERP financial cost allocations. I was on a call with the ERP vendor when the client asked them if their system was capable of generating 10 million output transactions in the space of a couple of hours. There were quite a few caveats attached to the answer. The client projected that their volumes could actually be 10 times that size. So they agreed to build a SAFR process that produced the results in a much shorter time.

The team created custom programs which generate over 6,000 SAFR views based upon over 7,000 allocation rules maintained in the ERP package. SAFR executes these views to scan the Financial ODS selecting records eligible for allocation. It then allocates these costs through four allocation layers, such as products and geographical units.

The following chart depicts the steps of this process.

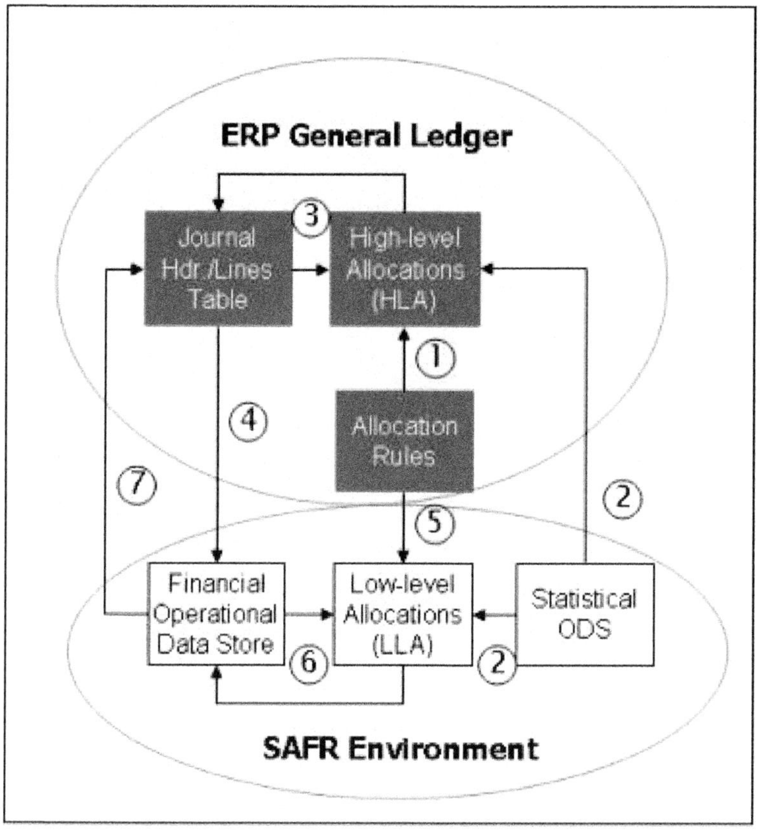

Figure 84. Insurance Company Allocation Process Architecture Diagram

1. Standard ERP rules define all allocation processes
2. Basis for High and Low-level provided by SAFR Statistical ODSs
3. Standard ERP allocations retrieves data from and returns results to journal tables
4. High-level results are extracted to SAFR Financial ODS
5. ERP allocation rules are used to generate SAFR processes
6. Low-level allocates high-level results and returns detailed low level results
7. Summarized results are returned to ERP journal tables

During the first year of implementation, the year end allocation process read over 50 million records selecting nearly 3 million that were eligible for allocation. These 3 million records were exploded into 186 million allocation results. The process ran in 7½ hours wall clock time and 28 hours of CPU time. SAFR generates approximately 210,000 records per minute, compared to the 13,500 per minute for the ERP package. The solution satisfies every business requirement in an acceptable timeframe and the business users were able to have their data represented exactly as they wanted[108].

I have outlined only the basic considerations for defining processes. Doing these steps requires a significant amount of time. However, care should be taken that this prospective work of looking to what the new system should do does not overshadow the more daunting, difficult but critical step of finding business events and building reference data. If those steps continue apace, definition of the processes will be better informed.

108. For additional details about this process, see Chapter 36, "Optimize For Performance," on page 183 and Chapter 50, "Piping, Tokens, and the Write Verb," on page 259.

Similarly, data modeling of the repository, as opposed to the summary structures, is necessary. That is the next step in our process, first considering the joins that might be involved.

Chapter 34. Consider Complex Joins

Over the years, join processing in SAFR has been enhanced to perform more and more functions. Understanding these capabilities is important to creating a SAFR solution.

Although the primary focus of our reporting is business event, the reference files used in reporting have to be maintained as well; and these changes to reference data are business events. For example, employees are promoted, addresses change, departments are reorganized, and customer accounts are closed.

Date Effective Joins

These changes in reference files do have tremendous impact on how the business events are reported. Since its earliest days SAFR has had a unique capability to perform date effective joins.

Sometimes when this term is used it means having a date be part of a key that is matched byte for byte against another record which has the exact same date in it. This means that business events can be combined that occur on the date of the reference data change, but business events on other days cannot without updating either the business event or the reference data. Alternatively, the requirement is sometimes met by having an additional field that marks which reference file record is currently "active", and a constant is used to force the join to that particular record. SAFR can use either of these approaches, but its native date effective join capabilities are more sophisticated.

To trigger SAFR date effective joins, one needs to mark the target reference file LR—the LR being looked up to—as a date effective LR. To do so, one field on the reference file can be selected as a start date. This field is technically not part of the key in defining a join in the SAFR metadata; no value has to be passed to this field in the join.

However, this field must be present on the reference file and must be the last field in the sort order of the reference file. The value in the effective date field can be used to make reference file records unique. In other words, duplicates may exist in the file for all other fields if the start date field is different. This is the only exception to the SAFR rule of no duplicates in join processing.

Which effective date to use in a join—what specific value to search for in that last position—can be passed to a join in a number of ways. The syntax for the join statement used in Logic Text allows for specifying what effective date the report is as of. A value in a date field on the event record can be passed, a hard coded date inside quotation marks in the Join statement can be used, or if nothing is specified, the `RUNDATE`, a parameter passed to the Scan Engine as the effective date of that run can be used[109].

SAFR does not require an exact match for effective date. As it performs its search, the last step in the process is to test if the value passed as the effective date is less than the date on the record to be returned. If so, it returns that record. If not, it tests the record before that to ensure the key is the same. If it is not, it returns a not found condition.

The reference file can also contain an End Date field. If two records have the same key except for the start date and no end date field is specified, the start date of the later record is effectively the end date of the earlier record. If an end date is specified, SAFR tests to ensure that the effective date supplied is between the start and end date of the record located. If it is not, then a not found condition is returned to

109. Note that RUNDATE is not the same as system date. It is important to be able to set the date for which the reports should be produced as of in cases of reruns on a different day than when they should have been produced.

the view. This creates the ability to make gaps between when rows are effective.

Date Effective Reporting

These types of date effective joins allow very sophisticated reports. The cookie manufacturer maintained the sales, material, and customer hierarchies as date effective files whereby any changes were captured as new rows with an effective start date. They would test potential reorganizations by adding contemplated changes as rows to the table, and run reports with future effective dates at the same time other reports were being run for the current date. They could then see the impact of the reorganizations before deciding to make them permanent.

This ability presents two different reporting options:

- Recast: Joined attribute changes result in the entire historical events being associated with the latest attributes. Report totals are not able to provide views of the data in different attributes. This option would typically use either the current (RUNDATE) or hard coded date option. Thus if the reference data contains my home state and I move to a new state, using current date option all of my amounts for all time are shown under the new state. Alternatively, the view could use a hard coded effective date of when I was in the prior state, and all balances, including today's would be shown as if I were in the prior state.
- Switch: Business events are joined to the attributes which were applicable at the time the business event occurred. This option would typically use a field containing a date on the event record as the effective date, typically the date when the business event occurred or balance was created. Using this option a portion of my balance would be shown in two places, under both states depending on the date of the business event field. One would need to add the two categories together to equal the amounts shown under one of the states in the recast method.

Another approach that allows generation of both switch and recast type reports requires that events be generated when attributes in reference files change. This is called reclass processing. Join attribute changes result in explicit events being generated by the system to move the sum of the business events (historically) from older set of attributes to the latest set of attributes. Thus report totals can provide historical views of data in different attributes (like switch) and in addition the summation of the events at any point in time will include the events that moved the sum of business events from one attribute to another. This approach tends to be more complete and accurate from an accounting perspective. See Chapter 60, "Reclassification," on page 301 for additional details.

Reference File Reports

Reports against standard types of reference files themselves are possible, but not tremendously common. Reference files tend to be less voluminous than event files, and the number of reports produced is significantly less. Typical reference files also usually do not contain amounts which can be meaningfully summarized. The one exception is that counts of records of a particular type are sometimes produced, like how many employees are at grade 5. Although there aren't many reports of such a size and consistent frequency that demand a solution like SAFR, there is nothing about SAFR which prevents it from reading reference files to produce reports. However, SAFR will read the data twice if the file is used as an event file and as a reference file.

At times the simple idea, of reference files loaded into memory to do lookups with event files having all the volume, breaks down. In these cases the reference files, usually filled with the static data describing customers and arrangements, etc., become very large, just slightly smaller than the event files. Because of their size, SAFR is an effective means to report against them. However, having to read the file twice, once for use as a reference file and once as an event file is anathema to SAFR performance principles. Building an efficient solution requires careful modeling of the repository.

Chapter 35. Model the Repository

When Eric showed us the simple picture of a business event based system, it gave the impression that the repository of business events contains a single record type where all the attributes to describe the event were recorded along with any amounts. SAFR views are typically created against a single logical record, a single record structure. All views reading that LR and file process see the same kinds of records.

Of course, the repository also contains reference data. But for the most part these files are relatively small, with keys and answers measured in the tens of thousands to hundreds of thousands of rows. Because the summary structures in the same format as the transaction records, The Cookie Manufacturer's repository was no more complex than this.

As we approached new problems, we found some did not fit into the simple view of a single record structure. For example, we used SAFR against the stacked data element file that had multiple record structures in it. The views Jim and Mark created had to first test a common field in each record to select only records that were appropriate for that view. Some records could be interpreted by one LR, other records by another. This use of SAFR is a typical ETL process to get around the complexities of the data to be extracted.

At the insurance company we found a problem with the size of the reference files. Normalization of data elements is more efficient for storage since attributes of a customer account only exist in one place on the customer account record. An account number from the event record can be used to access it. Modern businesses have millions of accounts. The size of these types of "reference" files starts to approach the same size as the event files.

Data Modeling

I remember Greg Forsythe, the most practical data modeler I have ever met in my life (a truly rare breed), working with Doug at the Insurance Company to devise an approach whereby SAFR could process these files effectively. Greg modeled the attributes needed for the reports in 3rd normal form. In other words, he placed the policy attributes on the policy table and only represented one row for each policy. Because policies are renewed over multiple terms, he made a different table for the term attributes with a term key to describe it.

He continued to add tables with additional attributes until he got down to the policy and loss transactions, those that Mark Kimmell had discovered from the Stacked Data Elements. All these other attributes were also in the Stacked Data Elements as separate records. It is likely the source system stored them in a similar manner. On the transactions—the true business events containing monetary amounts—he placed the keys for all the higher level entities: the policy, term, etc.

Having modeled the data in this way, the tables he designed could have been loaded into any relational database. SQL could have been used to join the tables together to produce the outputs as long as the amount of data in them was sufficiently small. The computer would have used indexed access methods explained in Chapter 19, "Select, Sort, Summarize," on page 89 to locate the appropriate records and combine them into the outputs desired.

However, with the issues of scale, a better processing pattern needed to be adopted to more realistically reflect what the machine had to do to combine the data together, and get more out of each stage in that process.

The team chose to use sequential files to exploit the Scan Engine's power and to eliminate the CPU time involved in decoding relational data structures. They chose to maintain the files as zO/S Generation Data Groups, a simple mechanism to manage access to different versions of the sequential files. The files would be maintained in sorted order by their keys.

For example:

Policy File

Policy ID	Policy Type	Policy Holder State	Policy Holder Name
1	Auto	Illinois	Fred Smed
2	Home	Utah	Nnyl Nner Nosnibor

Term File

Policy ID	Term ID	Term Length	Start Date
1	1	6 months	11 Months ago
1	2	6 months	5 Months ago
2	1	1 year	13 Months ago
2	2	1 year	1 Month ago

Policy Event File

Policy ID	Term ID	Policy Event ID	Policy Event Type	Amount
1	1	1	Prem. Payment	100.00
1	1	2	Service Fee	2.50
1	2	1	Prem. Payment	100.00
1	2	2	Service Fee	2.50
2	1	1	Prem. Payment	300.00
2	1	2	Special Endorse	100.00
2	2	1	Prem. Payment	300.00

Loss File

Policy ID	Term ID	Loss ID	Loss Type	Loss Date
1	2	1	Wreck	2 Weeks ago
2	1	1	Fire	14 Months ago

Loss Event File

Policy ID	Term ID	Loss ID	Loss Event ID	Loss Event Type	Amount
1	2	1	1	Rental Car	50.00
1	2	1	2	Medical Costs	75.00
2	1	1	1	Cleaning	1,000.00
2	1	1	2	Materials	700.00
2	1	1	3	Installation	700.00

Figure 85. Sample Insurance Repository

The five files above—Policy, Term, Policy Event, Loss, and Loss Event—are maintained in the order shown in separate files. The Policy, Term, and Loss files are reference or static data files. The Policy Event and Loss Event files are event files. Doug added a new feature to the Scan Engine: the Common Key Data Buffer feature.[110]

Common Key Data Buffer Event Files

This feature is a little like a prefetch function in some databases, whereby data that is expected to be used in the process is brought into memory before it is needed. The common key buffer technique brings all the records for a particularly key, in our example one policy, into memory. It does this through a merge

110. Technically he simply wrote a read exit. SAFR had the ability to call exits since 1994. The exit he created was subsequently generalized and made part of the SAFR product.

process, whereby multiple partitioned files are brought together. The data buffer from our example for the first policy would appear as follows:

Entity ID	Part-ition	Cat	Policy					
Policy	00	A	1	Auto	Illinois	Fred Smed		
Term	00	A	1	1	6 months	11 Months ago		
Term	00	A	1	2	6 months	5 Months ago		
Policy Event	00	A	1	1	1	Prem. Payment	100.00	
Policy Event	00	A	1	1	2	Service Fee	2.50	
Policy Event	00	M	1	2	1	Prem. Payment	100.00	
Policy Event	00	M	1	2	2	Service Fee	2.50	
Loss	00	W	1	2	1	Wreck	2 Weeks ago	
Loss Event	00	W	1	2	1	1	Rental Car	50.00
Loss Event	00	D	1	2	1	2	Medical Costs	75.00

Figure 86. Sample Insurance Input Buffer

Each of these records, as long as they have unique keys, can be used either as an event file or a reference file. The data for this policy is held in memory until all the records in it are read as event file records. When they have been processed as event files, all the data for the next policy is brought into memory.

SAFR's common key buffering feature appends three fields on the front to indicate from which file the records had come. The first field defines what LR describes the record. The next two fields describe from which partitions of that entity it had come and are discussed in the next chapter.

The Entity ID field is used so that the views can filter which business events they are reporting on. Because each of the records is passed to the views, reference data views can be resolved at the same time event file views can be resolved. Thus a view which counts policies of a particular type can select records with the Policy entity ID. Views which are summarizing premium payments can summarize Policy Events. This is similar to having views read an event file with multiple record types within it.

Common Key Data Buffering Lookups

Lookups to other records are accomplished by building a join with the linkage between these records. For example, if my view is summarizing premium payments from the Policy Event record by Term Length, I would define my view to select records where the Entity ID is Policy Event. The first record chosen will be the following.

Entity ID	Partition	Category	Policy ID	Term ID	Policy Event ID	Policy Event Type	Amount
Policy Event	00	A	1	1	1	Prem. Payment	100.00

I'd define a join which uses the Policy ID and Term ID to find the Term record. The join will return the following record.

Entity ID	Partition	Category	Policy ID	Term ID	Term Length	Start Date
Term	00	A	1	1	6 months	11 Months ago

Note that this record has already been processed as an event file record (it is the second record in the Figure 86 figure, but because of the Common Key Data Buffering it is still in memory and available for lookup. The view can now use any of these fields for any purpose, selection, sort, placing in columns, or used to join to other data. Thus I can produce a view of premium payments by term length if desired. This join technique also supports date effective joins as well[111].

111. See Chapter 52, "Common Key Data Buffering," on page 271 for more details.

Chapter 36. Optimize For Performance

As noted earlier, if you don't pay attention to performance throughout the preceding steps, this step won't save you. It is not possible to turn a jalopy into a race car. Performance can be tuned up, but it can't be created after the fact. Having said this, there are certain aspects of performance that complicate building the initial components. These are better added after the components are functionally working.

Piping

Although SAFR is designed to resolve all processes in a single pass of the event file, if SAFR is used to generate events, second passes of the data can be required to actually produce reports. At lunch one day at the Insurance Company, I think it was, I was thinking about the architecture of the allocation process. As noted, the allocation process generated a great many event records. These records needed to then be allocated in additional processes generating more output records. This happened a few more times and then reporting against all those event records needed to occur.

I mused to Doug that I wish we could have the outputs from one view feed into another view, rather than having to write them to disk and having to read them again in another execution of the Scan Engine. Doug thought for a moment and then smiled and said, "Well, that would be possible." He went on to describe how that feature could be added to SAFR. Over the course of the next few months, Doug added that capability we called piping.

Piping allows the output from a view which would be written to a file to simply be passed in memory between SAFR processes. Remember that the CPUs only work against data on the white board. All data has to go through memory after coming from or before going to disk. Thus to programs, data from a file or being written to a file looks the same; it is just data in memory.

SAFR uses this fact to, in a sense, simply trick itself that the data writing processes create data in memory, and data reading processes look at this data in memory; the data is never actually written to disk. Because the "white board" space is less than what is available in the "binder", the switching back and forth between writing and reading must be repeated hundreds, thousands, or even millions of times. Small sections of data are created and then read. Then the next section of data is created and read.

It could be called a virtual file, portions of which only exist in memory for a very short period of time. Piping is used when the views are able to run asynchronously: in other words they operate without knowledge or dependence upon timing between them. This is discussed in Chapter 50, "Piping, Tokens, and the Write Verb," on page 259.

Debugging or even examining data which exists in memory is difficult to do; the pace of changes on the white board is simply too fast for people to actually work with. Because of this fact, it is usually better to not pipe between views until the views and processes have been adequately tested and the results of each step verified by looking at disk output. Thus designing for piping is important, but actually adding it to the process becomes one of the later stages of the SAFR method.

Common Key Data Buffering Writes

A similar capability is available through the Common Key Data Buffering feature discussed in the prior chapter. A new record can be written into the data buffer as if it had come in from a file. This record can be used as an event record for other views, or it can be looked up by other views. In practice this is a bit like adding records onto the end of the input event file, although actually it is in the middle of the file as only one policy or arrangement is read into memory at a time.

The Common Key Data Buffering Write approach is used when there are relationships between views or records created or with large cardinality reference files. In other words, processing must be synchronous. But, the common key data buffering process requires calls to subroutines. Calling subroutines has overhead associated with it. Piping does not. Thus piping is more efficient, and should be used if there is no relationship between records being created and processes can operate asynchronously.

Care must be taken in analyzing dependencies between the views that read the common key data buffer. If the output from one view can create another input record to that same view, an infinite loop can be created. See Chapter 52, "Common Key Data Buffering," on page 271.

Token Processing

A third approach to eliminating writing and rereading records is to use tokens. Tokens allow views to write records that are immediately used by other views within the same process. They might be thought of as preprocess views. Token writing views are placed at the front of the string of views to be executed within a thread.

Token processing allows views to run synchronously. It also uses generated machine code, so there is no overhead for calling subroutines. Thus it is very efficient. It can allow for some level of relationship between records to be managed, but only at fairly low levels of complexity. If there are significant relationships between records, the common key buffering approach should be used. See Chapter 50, "Piping, Tokens, and the Write Verb," on page 259.

Parallelism

Another aspect of optimizing performance is adding parallelism to processes. Parallelism must be designed into the application from the beginning, but again, parallelism creates complexity in debugging processes. The system should be tested with a single process first, and ensure that the outputs are correct prior to adding parallel processes.

Parallelism comes in a couple of different forms. One form often used is dividing the input event files by some key or portion of a key which has no business purpose. For example, often the event files are segregated by two digits of a key ID. This simply creates more threads to use the CPUs available on the machine. There would never be a business reason for not processing all the partitions.

Another type of parallelism often comes from maintaining time partitions. This is done so that views which create new time partitions of files only have to write a limited number of records, and if perchance a SAFR execution does not require historical data, some time partitions do not need to be read.

Thus our example of the policy repository had this type of a structure to it:

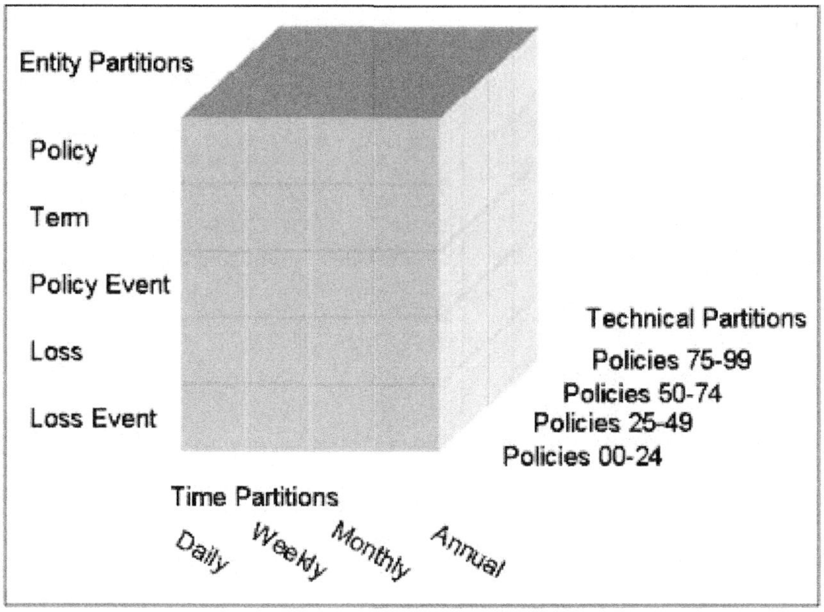

Figure 87. Sample Data Repository Partitioning

Each box in the figure is an individual file. Time partitions may or may not be read, depending upon the views' needs for historical data. However, all Technical Partitions would likely be read. The Entity Partitions contain the differing record types (different LRs).

The partition number added by the Common Key Data Buffering feature says from which technical partition the data was retrieved. The category field indicates from which time partition the data was retrieved. Thus the Common Key Data Buffering processes merge all these files together, one at a time into memory, policy or arrangement or what-have-you.

Views can use these fields to select records from appropriate partitions and to write out selected data. For example, the view might on a daily basis merge a single output file containing both the week's data and the new records for that day. Then once a week the weekly file is copied into a new version of the monthly file.

These steps of the SAFR method are intended to give a sense of the approach to solve reporting problems. Of course nothing compensates for the flexibility and adaptability of the human mind. A fool with a tool is still a fool, and a fool with a method might just mean it takes longer to find out he is a fool.

Following these steps has proven to create very flexible, cost-effective reporting environments.

Chapter 37. Maintain Focus

This last step isn't so much a part of the SAFR method as it seems to be a SAFR team obsession. Sometime in February 1997—I don't know exactly when since the whole month is a blur—I had a particularly memorable meeting with Jay. It wasn't so much what was discussed as when it was discussed. Let me first set the stage.

We've noted in Chapter 21, "ERP Reporting," on page 101 that the high-tech chip manufacturer waited until things got to crisis level before they called Rick. What ensued was the toughest project I think any of the members of that SAFR team on it ever experienced.

It began with the challenge that unless a new processing approach was found, the company wouldn't be able to close their books daily in three month's time. The processes they had constructed functionally worked, they just took too long. And they were taking longer and longer the more the data volumes increased.

The team was charged with translating the programs written in custom ERP language into SAFR processes. Every available SAFR knowledgeable person was flown to the client site. I was pulled off the Insurance Company to go—but I didn't have to fly. The company was a 40 minute drive from my home. Everyone was assigned a multitude of tasks. We didn't start with analysis or specs or even any time at a white board. We were given ERP program listing to start translating.

Oh the pain. Although it was the only project assignment I ever had in that town, and I was no longer required to commute half way across the the country twice a week at eight hours each way, my wife told me she saw me less than at any other time. I didn't make it home a number of nights but stayed in a hotel because I couldn't afford the 40 minute drive. I worked something like 120 of 168 possible hours one week, and something over 200 hours in two weeks.

I worked multiple all-nighters. The whole team ran at a similar pace. Randall called one Monday morning to ask if he should go to the airport to fly down and I said I needed his help right then. So he didn't leave and worked from home in Seattle all week. I put him on speakerphone and we just left the line open hour after hour. We didn't talk constantly, but we didn't want to take the time to dial when we did. Others would walk over to my cube to talk to Randall as if he were working in my cube as well.

One night after midnight I had a very large test file to upload from some server to the mainframe. I started the script to do the file transfer, and from the script messages calculated it would take over an hour to complete. Randall was still on the phone working. The lights in the building were off except for a desk light at my cubicle. I told Randall I was going to lie down on the floor and sleep a bit, and asked if he would wake me up when my transfer job had finished. He said he would.

When I woke up my pager was buzzing at my hip, and I could hear indiscriminate keys being pushed on the phone. Still lying on the hard floor groggy I asked what was going on. Randall said he had yelled into the speakerphone to try to wake me up but he couldn't raise me, so he had to switch over to his other phone line and page me to get me to wake up. He said my job had blown up; I hadn't allocated enough space for the file on the mainframe. Uggggh!

This went on for weeks. Dave Padmos was the associate partner and project manager. He knew the client very well having been there for more than a year. He didn't have any SAFR experience, so he took on the job of protecting the team. I have never seen such an effective job of giving air cover to the troops on the ground. Although the client seemed to be in a panic, he told them that except for one person that could accompany Dave they had no access to any of the team members. They wanted to have daily status meetings, and he said he would be the only one attending. They said they needed more information about what was happening and he said they could ask him any question and he would get the answer.

He ordered food, and kept everything away from interfering so we could meet the deadlines. It was very effective leadership and I learned a great deal from it.

I recall a number of years later I was at lunch with him and we talked about the project. He remembered coming into my cubicle and asking about something. Randall and I would talk about potential ways of solving the problem. Randall was developing a way of generating JCL scripts rather than handwriting them and I was helping. While others were writing views, we knew that the last thing that must be done before the system can be tested was creation of JCL, and the system would come to require hundreds of thousands of lines of scripts to run the Scan Engine. Dave said he would listen to us discuss possible ways of solving a problem, telling him "Well, this way would be more elegant and have these benefits but would take longer..." just like technology people are wont to do. He said, "At times I just wanted to scream, 'Will you guys just make a decision!'"

Jay was the architect of the solution. He was there all the time. He decided how the programs should be translated into views; what the event files would be; how each run of the Scan Engine would interact with the next. Our sleep schedules became so confused we never knew when to sleep. The meeting happened one morning when I woke up at home about 2:00 AM as I remember it. I got out of bed and decided to check and see what needed to be done. I called Monica Logan's cubicle, and Monica picked up. She gave me a short update, and then got interrupted by someone else coming to her cube. I think it was Padmos. She said she would put me on speakerphone. We talked for a moment and then she got another call. It was Jay who had similarly just woken up and was checking in from the hotel. She conferenced him in. We made plans about what needed to be done next. Here it was 2:00 AM and we were having an unscheduled meeting with four professionals all in the same time zone when the deadline was still weeks away!

Over the years when projects have neared deadlines and things were tough, anyone who was on this project would invariably say, "Well, it isn't as bad as the high tech chip manufacturer." I heard that Monica said this on the Investment Bank project and then paused and said, "Well, perhaps it is as bad." But I don't think any of them had quite the same intensity. Work at this pace went on for a number of months.

The team barely completed development in time. The last executions of system testing weren't completely defect-free; there were a couple of small errors, I believe in the JCL scripts. They decided to go forward with the implementation. The first execution without any errors was in production. The team had sprinted to make the first implementation, but it wasn't the last. Additional processes had to be converted as well. So the next phase of the project started, but at a little less intense pace.

A few years after the project, I wrote the following description of the results of the project:

High Tech Chip Manufacturer Project Results

After this Fortune 100 firm implemented multiple ERP modules, they tackled the problem of analyzing all the integrated data captured by the new system. But running the ERP processes 24 hours a day, 7 days a week left very little time for anything but transaction processing. They needed their data warehouses updated three times each day to reflect the close of business in each of its worldwide operations. An innovative solution would be required, and it took a few attempts to find the right one.

One approach might have been to simply analyze the data in the production database. But the potential disruption of transaction processing ruled this out. There was simply no room for analysis in the transaction processing environment.

Another approach involved replicating tables from the transaction database to a separate ERP instance. This was supplemented with third party software to capture changes to specific data. After extracting the data, custom programs were used on other processors to complete the data transformation. The data was then loaded into a variety of EIS and data warehouse applications. While this approach freed up the production server, data volumes were so high that the extract and transform processes were taking 48 hours to complete for each of the three daily processes. They were getting farther behind the harder they worked!

The company turned to SAFR for a solution. To shorten the data extract process, database triggers were used to capture just updates, deletes, and inserts to the database rather than replicating the entire database. To reduce the transform process time, the transformation logic was translated into SAFR "Views" supplemented with custom programs. This approach cut the elapsed time from 48 hours to 45 minutes without impacting the production system.

The company also found some unanticipated benefits as well. The SAFR solution provides a detailed repository of historical data for analysis. This data can be stored in the SAFR environment and archived from the ERP tables, thus improving the transaction system performance. New types of detailed analysis were possible using SAFR and the process has proven itself scaleable as the company continues to grow.

Since the first implementation, the company employed SAFR in several different systems, and used it to replace many data analysis processes originally coded in statistical analysis software. After re-configuring one statistical analysis application with SAFR, the end users were able to slash eight hours off of the delivery time for their reports.

A typical execution of SAFR at this client reads 100 million records, performs 1.2 billion foreign key joins across 2.2 gigabytes of table space. It writes out 100 million records in 70 user extract files. This process takes just under an hour of elapsed time and 73 minutes of CPU time.

The following is the architecture diagram used to describe the project.

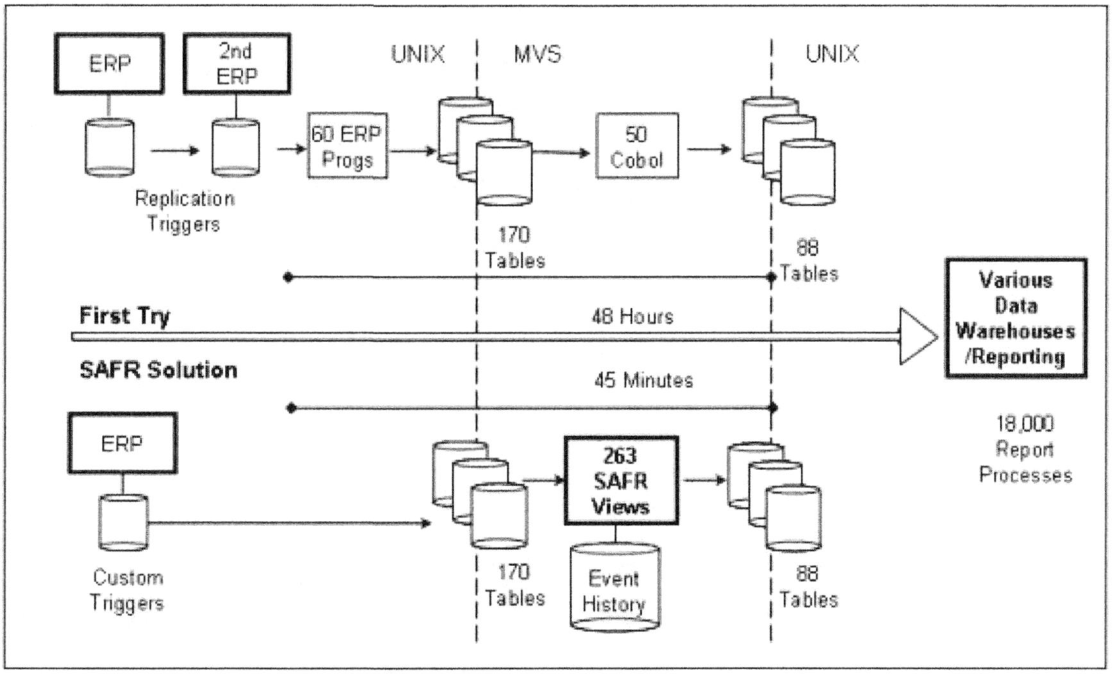

Figure 88. High-tech Chip Manufacturer Project Architecture Diagram

Although the team continued after the initial implementation, my involvement didn't even make it that far. My wife was pregnant with our third child and at her birth, I knew I had to stop calling in to work at 2:00 AM or my wife would kill me. After a week or two, she told me I had better head back to the insurance company. Through experience I had learned to listen when she gave me advice like that. Doing so started a deeper association lasting for five years with my next mentor, Doug.

Part 5. The Programmer

Some have said Doug can code on pure metal; that he almost didn't need an operating system. That isn't quite true, but I have found him to be completely fearless. A year or so after starting system testing, Doug called me up and said he had added a new feature to SAFR, the ability to read DB2 data rather than just sequential files. He asked me to create for him a DB2 table with some data, define an LR and view, and run it against the table. He said it would probably abend the first time it was run; when it did I should call him back.

Consistent with his unassuming manner, I always found Doug willing to take the time to teach anyone that wanted to listen how to do what he did. When I called to say the DB2 test had abended, he asked me where he could locate the system output. As I told him, he found it, and suggested I also follow him into that portion of the output called the system dump or sys dump. This output contained a snapshot of the memory—the white board—at the time the abend happened. The dump can be very large; hundreds of thousands of pages in some cases if it were actually printed. Doug told me once they are only large if you print them, which no one does. Rather they are searched on line, like a large document.

Doug looked at something and told me to find a particular value. I did. He began directing me to other values in the dump, which is composed of only numbers and the characters "A" through "F", and telling me what was in memory at this particular location or another one. I remember something like, "And see that Fox 2 there? That is the first byte of the directory structure for this block of the VSAM dataset. You see, on the mainframe DB2 stores the data in VSAM datasets, and inside each of those datasets it puts in its own directory structures that tell it how to interpret its data. The directory structure says that in this block there are this many data records, see the 34 there? And they are stored in this kind of format, see the 9754 there?"

I realized that Doug was showing me the in-memory version of the VSAM files that sit at the bottom of DB2. I suspect there were a lot of application programmers who used DB2 in programs that didn't know about the VSAM files used underneath it. Only people who really supported the tool would have given those things much thought. I asked, "Doug, have you written SQL?" the basic DB2 language for accessing data. He said something like, "No, not really." I was dumbfounded. Doug didn't go through any of the traditional routes to learning a tool. Instead he went right to the bottom of the tool, to read its underlying data structure picking it apart byte by byte. "Completely fearless", I thought.

This next section begins by examining a system dump, not because I think you will need to do this. But it is important to be fearless, in a sense. It is important to have respect for problems, but not believe that something magical is happening somewhere that ordinary people can't understand. There is nothing too extraordinary in all of this, and analyzing a dump can demonstrate that fact.

The remaining portions of this section explain the SAFR Scan engine at its core, building step upon step in complexity. It begins with a view which copies data, an extract only view, moves through lookups to sorting data and running the format phase. All of this is done without any parallelism. There is a small break in the narrative to allow you to catch your breath; then we examine parallel processing, piping and other advanced topics including exits and common key data buffering which brings together most of the concepts into one process.

By understanding what is at the heart of the Scan Engine, one can see application of these patterns in reporting applications. Automation entails making the machine do what people would have to do to achieve the same results. Understanding these steps, and how they add upon each other to create the desired outputs, this is where the rubber meets the road in creating a business event based reporting system.

Chapter 38. Abends

The first interaction I remember with Doug was soon after meeting Jay when I started as a system tester. I found a problem in one of his programs. Renae Bell, the other system tester with whom I shared an office in Sacramento, told me to call him. I underwent the same initiation many others did through the years when I wondered if it was right to call and tell a partner—in the very real sense an owner of the firm—I had found a bug and he needed to fix it.

Doug was perhaps the most unassuming partner anyone had ever met. I remember him taking assignments to fix problems from people brand new to a project or even the company. His response was even more unexpected for some because of the stories about him they heard before having to call him.

One of the great stories was about Doug finding a bug in the COBOL complier while working in Alaska. I have heard Rick repeat the story a number of times. It seems the system was in construction, but a new version of the compiler was needed to overcome a technical limit of the old compiler. When the new compiler was installed, a new problem showed up. Rick remembers going to the office on the weekend, and seeing Doug surrounded by stacks and stacks of printouts from a computer dump, a listing of all the ones and zeros in computer memory at some particular point in time. Doug showed him he found a series of them that were causing the problem, traced them to the place in the compiler that had put them there, modified the IBM compiler using a utility called Zap that actually allows inserting a different sequences of ones and zeros into any file including the IBM COBOL compiler, and sent a printout of the code in error and his correction to IBM.

In the early days of SAFR most of the defects showed up as system abends, short for abnormal end. If you have experience with the blue screen of death on a Windows platform, you have seen an abend. To many programmers an abend is an extremely bad thing, something that means things went catastrophically wrong.

The truth of the matter is abends in SAFR processes on mainframes rarely affect anything adversely. The blue screen of death is an abend in the operating system, and can mean one has lost data and rebooting can be annoying. That is very different than an abend in a single application, like Excel. I have not seen an abend in the operating system on the mainframe. And because the vast majority of SAFR processes do not perform any updates, the effect of an abend is that Scan Engine simply has to be restarted.

When dealing in the world of high performance computing, the cost of the niceties of controlling all the potential problems becomes simply too expensive. Allowing the operating system to trap certain types of errors is a very efficient approach to the problem. CPU cycles are not spent trying to prevent errors when in fact if an error occurs the process has to be restarted anyway.

Quick Review

But first let's review our computer and business meeting analogy of Chapter 4, "Computers," on page 15. Each execution of a program is like a meeting in a conference room. Memory is like the whiteboard, and disk storage is like a meeting minute binder. The processors or CPUs are like the people in the room. Now, we'll need a bit more detail, so let's enhance this analogy a bit to explain registers and the operating system.

The eyes of the people in the meeting, our processors, need to be looking at the data on the white board before doing something with that data. The "eyes" of the computer are called registers. Just like people have two eyes, computers have multiple registers. In fact, just as some people in the room are better at math than others, some registers have special capabilities for particular types of functions. But in all cases the registers must be "looking" at the data to be acted upon by the computer in order for the computer to work.[112]

There is typically a person responsible for the meeting, the chair. This person follows an agenda or perhaps better, our very detailed set of procedures to conduct the meeting—the computer program. In our example here the procedures are the computer program GVBMR95. The procedures (computer programs) are kept in a separate binder from the minutes of the meeting. Similar to data from the "meeting minutes" binder, the procedures must also be transferred onto the white board in order to be read by the chair of the meeting. The "eyes" of the processor reading this program is a special register called the Program Status Word, or PSW.

Now let's see what happens when something goes wrong in the meeting.

Dumps

Over the course of those few years I got so I could follow the pattern in Doug's analysis of a dump. To give some flavor of what's involved, to demystify the whole thing, let's analyze a dump. A fairly common problem when working with raw data is an OC7 or soc7, a data exception. This occurs when SAFR (or any mainframe program) is asked to perform an arithmetic operation against non-numeric data. The first indication something has gone wrong is the following messages printed in the log file, the top portion of the output containing primary messages from the operating system:

```
14.25.53 JOB00136  -JOBNAME  STEPNAME PROCSTEP     RC    EXCP     CPU     SRB   CLOCK
14.25.53 JOB00136  -TTDEMOE1          PSTEP695     00     226     .00     .00     .00
14.25.53 JOB00136  -TTDEMOE1          PSTEP696 FLUSH        0     .00     .00     .00
14.25.54 JOB00136  -TTDEMOE1          PSTEP700     00      97     .00     .00     .00
14.25.55 JOB00136  + ** GVB002I GVBMR95G - 001 threads started
14.25.55 JOB00136  + ** GVB009U GVBMR95G - Thread 001 abended 0C7, View=00003260
14.25.55 JOB00136  IEC223I 20,IFG0200V,TTDEMOE1,PSTEP705,EVENT,526E,PR2340,GEBT.
14.25.58 JOB00136  IEA995I SYMPTOM DUMP OUTPUT  661
   661             SYSTEM COMPLETION CODE=0C7  REASON CODE=00000000
   661              TIME=14.25.55  SEQ=25847  CPU=0000  ASID=004A
   661              PSW AT TIME OF ERROR  078D2000   920340D6  ILC 6  INTC 07
   661                NO ACTIVE MODULE FOUND
   661                NAME=UNKNOWN
   661                DATA AT PSW  120340D0 - F8B48002  6019F0B5  80020006
   661                AR/GR 0: 90A63EDE/00000000   1: 00000000/FFFC6FE4
   661                      2: 00000000/12034008   3: 00000000/00038F10
   661                      4: 00000000/12064004   5: 00000000/11F056FF
   661                      6: 00000000/11F4805A   7: 00000000/1203A008
   661                      8: 00000000/1203A03B   9: 00000000/120570C0
   661                      A: 00000000/920340D0   B: 00000000/00010000
   661                      C: 00000000/00011000   D: 00000000/00038F10
   661                      E: 00000000/00000000   F: 00000002/00018FA0
   661              END OF SYMPTOM DUMP
```

Figure 89. OC7 Snap System Dump

The printout is chronological, in that new rows show up as the batch process is executed. The first four lines are the results of preprocessing steps. Then there are two rows of messages printed by GVBMR95, the Extract Engine that Doug wrote. The first message says that the program started parallel processing. The next says it detected there was a data exception. GVBMR95 turns the problem back over to the

112. IBM mainframes have 16 "eyes" or general purpose registers. IBM Enterprise Systems Architecture/390, *Principles of Operation* manual (IBM © 1990 – 1999) 2.2 to 2.3.

operating system. The IEC223I message comes from the operating system and says which file the offending record came from. The operating system then prints a snap dump. Doug would begin his analysis here.

```
661              SYSTEM COMPLETION CODE=0C7  REASON CODE=00000000
```

The completion code of OC7 is a data exception, as I have stated. Other common messages are OC4, which means the program tried to use memory that was out of bounds—in other words it tried to read or write data from a white board used in another meeting. Each meeting is considered confidential. An OC1 means that we asked the computer to perform an invalid instruction.

```
661              PSW AT TIME OF ERROR  078D2000   920340D6  ILC 6  INTC 07
661                NO ACTIVE MODULE FOUND
661                NAME=UNKNOWN
```

The next row says where the PSW was looking, the instruction that should have been performed. Then two rows tell what program—which detailed agenda—was at that location. The data here is a bit peculiar to the SAFR extract program, GVBMR95. "No Active Module Found" means that the operating system doesn't recognize what program was at this location. That's because the operating system didn't load a program to that location; it didn't put an agenda there. Rather, the only program/agenda it loaded was GVBMR95. To understand this, we need to discuss code generation and parallel processing.

Our SAFR meeting room actually has more than one meeting happening inside of it. The meeting starts as one meeting, but the first part of the agenda for the meeting is to create other agendas. After those agendas are created, the participants (CPUs) in the meeting are assigned to work on specific agendas for specific periods of time.

The "no active module found" message means that the "meeting" that had a problem was one of these generated agendas, not the main meeting agenda. Because the operating system didn't load this agenda to the white board, it doesn't know as much about this meeting.[113]

Doug had to make sure something else hadn't gone wrong and the OC7 was the symptom, not the cause of the problem. For example, an OC1 can also look similar to the OC7 problem, but can happen in the main meeting, not the sub meeting[114]. To detect between these two different types of problems, and make sure this hadn't happened, Doug would then ask me to tell him a few details in other places in the dump. If those values were in the range of what he would have expected from knowing the program, he would feel comfortable that the problem had occurred in the generated code.

Generated Code

Doug would have me read the series of characters after the dash in the next line.

```
661              DATA AT PSW  120340D0 - F8B48002  6019F0B5  80020006
```

113. A few pages down in the output, after the messages shown above, is another snap dump. In this additional snap dump, the top lines look like this:

```
498              USER COMPLETION CODE=0999
498             PSW AT TIME OF ERROR  078D1000   80010418  ILC 2  INTC 0D
498               ACTIVE LOAD MODULE           ADDRESS=00010000  OFFSET=0000
498               NAME=GVBMR95G
```

This snap dump is from the main program GVBMR95. When the sub-meeting had the OC7, the main meeting - GVBMR95 - called for help by telling the operating system it wanted to stop as well. Thus instead of a system completion code like OC7, we have a user completion code of 999. Note that the memory address, the PSW, for GVBMR95G is at 078D1000 . This is the address of the white board agenda of GVBMR95G, not 078D2000 or submeeting agenda shown in the "No Active Module Found" message.

114. An OC1 can occur if the instructions in the main agenda by mistake say to go over to some other area of the white board and begin to use that data as an agenda. If it pointed the PSW to some part of the white board that had the word "movement" in it, the computer might use the first four characters and think we wanted it to move something. After it had done this, it might then get to "ment" and give us an OC1; it doesn't know what "ment" means any more than it knows what Jones means. Note that the computer program word for "move" is actually the value "D2"

These values F8B48002 6019F0B5 80020006, are the machine instructions. They are contained at memory location 120340D0 where the eyes of the person conducting the sub-meeting are looking; the PSW.

I remember Doug often repeating the actual machine code, the F8B48002 etc., over and over to confirm he had them clearly in his mind, particularly if he was in the car driving and he couldn't write them down. He would then tell me that the "F8" is hexadecimal representation of the machine code for a Zero Add Pack instruction.[115] He knew the hex values of most of the instructions he used in his programs by heart. The Zero Add Pack instruction moves a value from a location to another location, and adds zeros on the left if needed to increase the length.[116] The digits of the F8 instruction have the following meanings:

- F8 = ZAP instruction
- B = The target field length minus 1 is 11, or a B in hexidecimal in the dump
- 4 = The source field length minus 1 is 4
- 8 and 002 = The target memory address is 2 bytes beyond the address in register 8
- 6 and 019 = The source memory address is 19 bytes beyond the address in register 6.

The F0 instruction after the 019 begins the next machine instruction.

The next portion of the snap dump shows the values in the registers.

```
661              AR/GR 0: 90A63EDE/00000000   1: 00000000/FFFC6FE4
661                    2: 00000000/12034008   3: 00000000/00038F10
661                    4: 00000000/12084004   5: 00000000/11F056FF
661                    6: 00000000/11F4805A   7: 00000000/1203A008
661                    8: 00000000/1203A03B   9: 00000000/120570C0
661                    A: 00000000/920340D0   B: 00000000/00010000
661                    C: 00000000/00011000   D: 00000000/00038F10
661                    E: 00000000/00000000   F: 00000002/00018FA0
661             END OF SYMPTOM DUMP
```

The AR/GR says that the first set of numbers is the Access Registers; after the slash is the General Purpose Register values. Doug was only interested in the GR numbers. The registers, the "eyes" of the processors in our meeting, contain the addresses of data on the white board, or at times, numbers. Numbers can be added to registers. Displacements are values that are added to register values without changing the value in the register.

Often based upon what Doug saw in the machine code above he would have me take the value in register 6, the 11FA805A, add the hexadecimal 19 displacement from the machine instruction to get address 11FA8073, and go to a different part of the system output, the sys dump, to find what was at that location.

115. Hexadecimal representation means that four bits of zeros and ones are turned into a number or the characters A – F meaning numbers 10 – 15. Thus "F" in hex is 1111 in binary and 15 in decimal. Hex is a more efficient "language" for expressing binary numbers.

116. IBM Enterprise Systems Architecture/390, *Principles of Operation* manual (IBM © 1990 – 1999) Seventh edition (July 1999) 8-13. Also available on line at http://www-03.ibm.com/systems/z/os/zos/bkserv/.

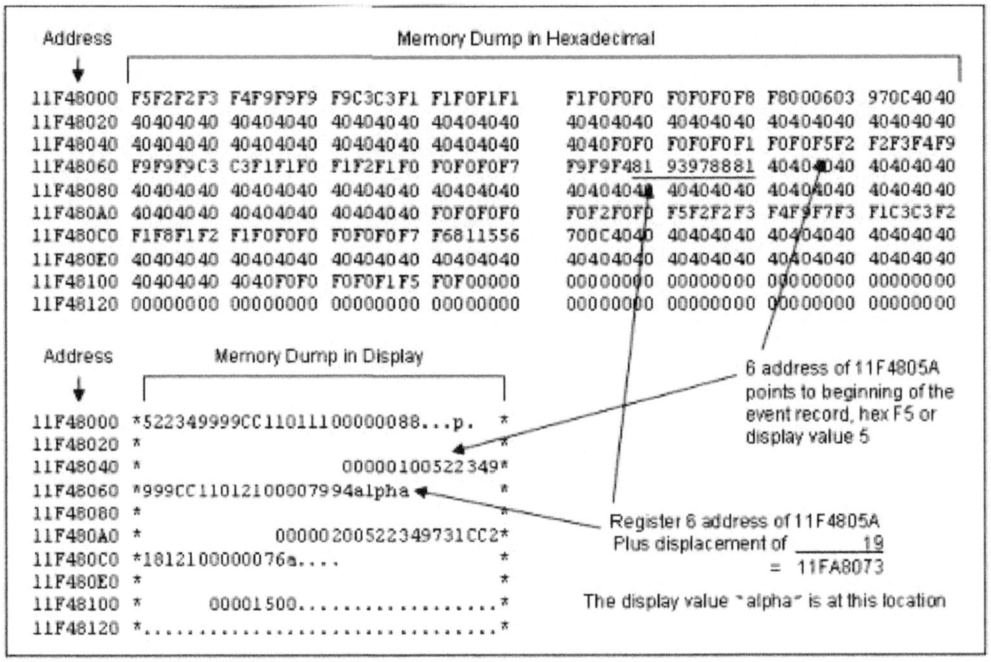

Figure 90. Memory Dump for Address in Register 6

The first column gives the address in memory of the data shown immediately to its right[117]. Doug would have me round down the address in register 6 to the nearest hex 20 to search the dump; not every memory address is labeled in the dump or the dump would be very, very large. So I would search not for 11FA8073 but for 11FA8060. After finding the address at the nearest hex 20, it is necessary to count across the columns to find that address. The second column is exactly the address to its left. Column 2 adds hex 4 to the address, so 11FA8064. The third column is at hex 8, 11FA8068. The fourth column is at hex C, or 11FA806C. The right half columns begin 11FA80570.

We are getting close, so now I start adding hex 1 for every two characters in the display. The value at 11FA8073 begins with 81. I could translate from the hex value into the display value using an EBCIDIC translation card, or I could look at the display portion of the dump. When I look there, I see the word "alpha" which is obviously not numeric. I now know what needed to be fixed for SAFR to complete successfully; either the LR had been defined wrong, or the event data was bad.[118]

Going through these steps I learned that everything that was happening could be understood; that it didn't really take a special mind of some kind to comprehend it; it just took time and attention to details. Building up of these small steps in careful ways results in something quite extraordinary.

A number of years later I remember Doug commented, as we worked on a problem in an area of the code he hadn't been in for quite awhile, that he was going to have to study the program for a bit to remember how it was structured. He then paused and told me a little story.

He said when working towards his master's degree in computer science he was required to write a teleprocessing monitor. He built different parts of the system over time and one day he had to go back to a completed part to either fix or add something else to it. He had the same experience where he had to

117. The Display portion shown in the lower half of this figure actually is to the right of the Hex display in the memory dump.

118. The Extract program, GVBMR95, can be made to print the entire generated program (agenda), which would include the F8...instruction and all the other parts. It accepts a parameter file in the DD Name MR95PARM. A keyword of `SNAP=Y` in this parameter file causes it to print the generated machine code (SNAP data ID 30) and in memory logic table with pointer addresses (SNAP Data ID 20) to the output DD Name SNAPDATA after generation of the machine code.

go remember how the things work. He said, "I realized then that I had created something beyond my ability to keep it all in my head; it was bigger than I was." There are a lot of people who would agree he has constructed something bigger than any one person.

Chapter 39. The Copy Only View

We've discussed in a general sense how the Scan Engine works. Let's make this more specific.

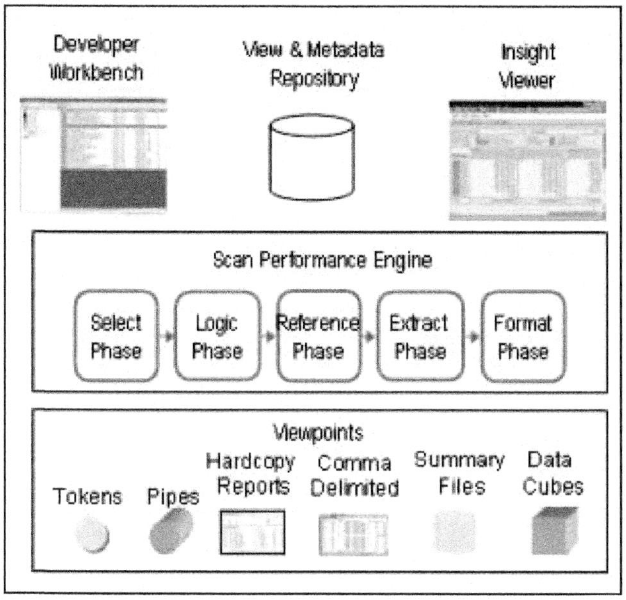

Figure 91. SAFR Scan Engine Overview

We'll start with an example of the simplest kind of view possible, a copy only view. A copy only view only applies record level filtering to copy event file records to the output file.

Select Phase

Users define views in the Developer Workbench, which are stored in the View and Metadata repository. The first step in the SAFR Scan Engine is the VDP Builder. This program accepts parameters that tell it which views to select from the metadata repository.

The output is a file called the VDP, View Definition Parameters, which contains all the needed data from the View and Metadata repository for the Scan Engine to perform the requested process.

The following shows a view in a VDP through a small utility called the VDP Explorer which Al Sung built for debugging processes.

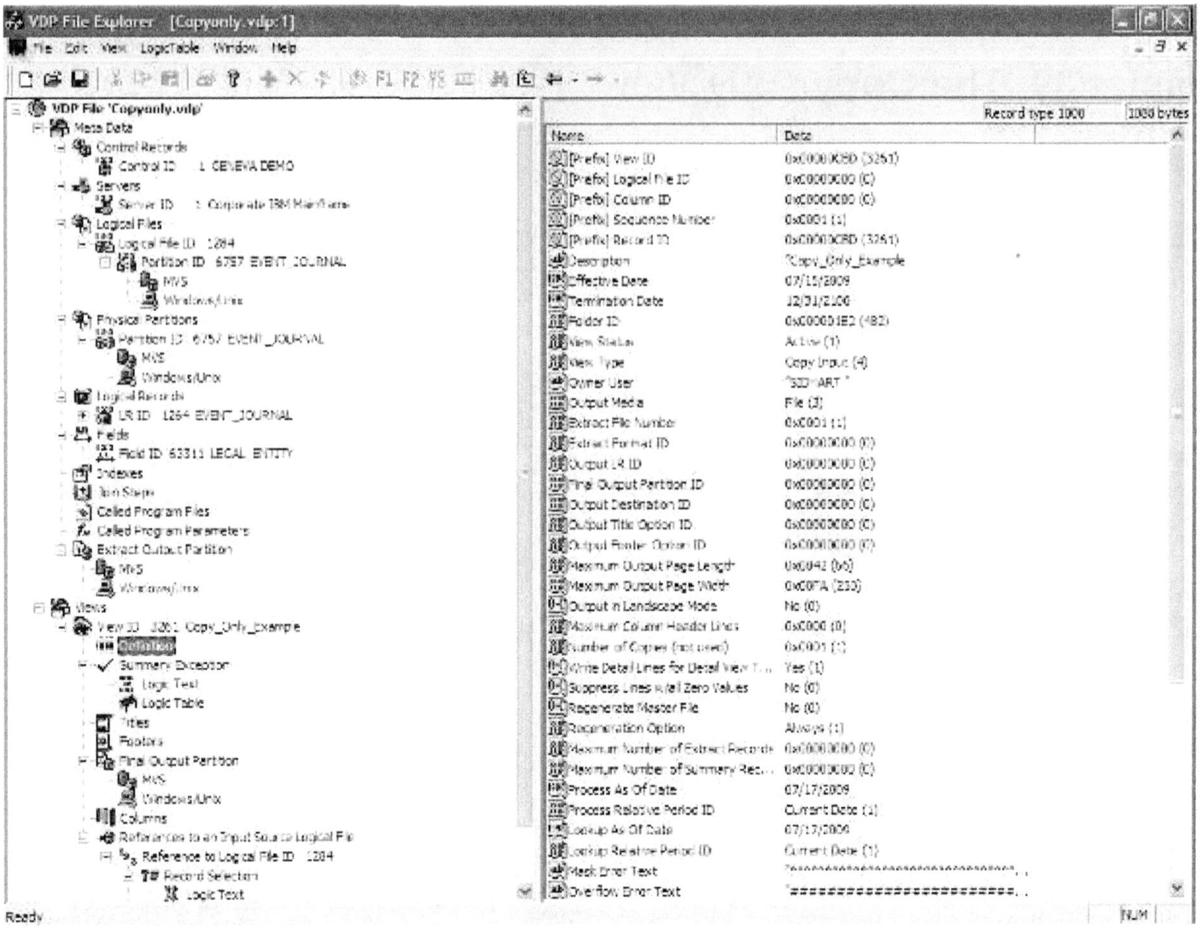

Figure 92. Copy Only View VDP

Logic Phase

The next phase of the process turns the metadata and views contained in the VDP into a logic table. A logic table is a set of detailed commands in a very efficient order to read records from an event file, perform record level filtering, and write selected records to the output file.

The following is a printout of the logic table.

Brackets Logic Table
Brackets Event File
View

```
LOGIC   GOTO  GOTO FUNC SEQ      LR FIELD         SOURCE        OTHER DATA
  ROW   ROW1  ROW2 CODE NUM      ID    ID  POS   LEN FM CN D CMP LEN1 VALUE1
    1              HD
                        FILE ID: 00001284
    2              RENX
VIEW ID: 00003261       FILE ID: 00001284
    3              NV          1264
    4      5     6 CFEC        1264 63311    1     9  3        001  0009 522349999
    5              WRIN    1
                        FILE ID: 00001284
    6              ES
    7              EN
```

Figure 93. Copy Only View Logic Table

The logic table has the following characteristics:

- The Logic Table rows are numbered consecutively from 1 to the last row.
- Each logic table begins with an HD or Header Function and ends with an EN or End Function. SAFR extract engine will perform all of the functions discussed below for each event file to be scanned.
- Each Event File to be read begins with an RENX or Read Next record function and ends with an ES or End of String function. SAFR extract engine performs all of the following functions for every record within an event file.
- Each View begins with an NV or New View function and ends with a WRxx Write function of one type or other. A copy view ends with an WRIN Write Input record function.
- The only real user specified function within this view is a CFEC function, a Compare Field, Event file field to Constant. The Event File field—the field to be tested—is at position 1, for a length of 9, of a format 3 which is zoned numeric.[119] It is to be equal (a 001 comparison) to the constant value of "522349999" of a length of 9
- The CFEC function uses the GOTO ROWx columns to say what should be done based upon the test. If the CFEC comparison with the current event record proves true, execution continues at GOTO Row 5, writing the input record. If the comparison proves false, execution continues at GOTO Row 6 which loops to the RENX function to read the next event record.
- The CFEC row was created because the view contains the following general selection logic text: "SELECTIF({LEGAL_ENTITY}= 522349999)"

Reference Phase

Because the view contains no lookups, the reference phase performs no functions.

Extract Phase

I believe it was during the same month Doug called and asked me to make the DB2 table to test the new SAFR access methods that one day he said he had another feature for me to test out. He showed me how to turn it on, and explained the output. I realized what a powerful debugging tool it was. Doug told me that a few months before when we were debugging a problem, perhaps an OC7 and had to search the dump to find what record caused the problem, I had commented in passing that I would like to be able to see a printout of the logic table against each record of the event file. In that way, I would have known what record and what function I was doing in the view that caused the problem. This feature is known as the Logic Table Trace. We'll use it to explain the Extract Engine.

Suppose our input file looks like the following:

119. Formats can be found in the code table under administration in the Workbench.

```
-------------------------------------------------------------------------------
522349999CC11011100000088...p.
FFFFFFFFFCCFFFFFFFFFFFFFF00090444444444444444444444444444444444444444444444444
522349999331101110000008806 37C000000000000000000000000000000000000000000000000
-------------------------------------------------------------------------------
522349999CC110121000007994alpha
FFFFFFFFFCCFFFFFFFFFFFFFF89988444444444444444444444444444444444444444444444444
5223499993311012100007994137810000000000000000000000000000000000000000000000000
-------------------------------------------------------------------------------
522349731CC21812100000076a.i®.
FFFFFFFFFCCFFFFFFFFFFFFFF81570444444444444444444444444444444444444444444444444
522349731332181210000007615 60C000000000000000000000000000000000000000000000000
-------------------------------------------------------------------------------
\_______/\____/\_/\_______/\____/
  Legal    Cost  Acct. Count Amount
  Entity   Centre
```

Figure 94. Sample Event File

In this display, the hex versions of the displayed values are immediately below the characters. So a display 5 is composed of the hex values F5. This allows viewing the data in packed format—a format that compresses numbers to only use half a byte each—in the amount field.

The logic table trace output from running the extract engine against this input file is as follows:

```
EVENT      EVENT          VIEW        LOGIC
DDNAME     RECORD         NUMBER      ROW          *****VALUE-1**   *****VALUE-2**
EVENT              1 V:    3261 LT:         3 NV
EVENT              1 V:    3261 LT:         4 CFEC  52234999         522349999
EVENT              1 V:    3261 LT:         5 WRIN
EVENT              2 V:    3261 LT:         3 NV
EVENT              2 V:    3261 LT:         4 CFEC  522349999        522349999
EVENT              2 V:    3261 LT:         5 WRIN
EVENT              3 V:    3261 LT:         3 NV
EVENT              3 V:    3261 LT:         4 CFEC  522349731        522349999
```

Figure 95. Copy View Logic Table Trace

It shows that event record 1 from the DD name (a file handle) of "EVENT" was processed against NV, Logic Table Row number 3. The record then went against the CFEC function on logic table row 4. The Value 1 shows the value in the event record—the "E" in CFEC—and Value 2 shows the constant in the logic text. The two values are equal. So the next row to be executed is the true row, or the GOTO 5 row. So execution continues at logic table row 5, the WRIN row which copies the event record to the output file.

The SAFR Scan Engine has just completed the inner most loop of the logic table. It then performs an RENX to obtain the next event record. The RENX is not shown in the logic table trace, but the Event Record count is incremented, and we return to the NV row. This record is processed the same as the previous record.

On the third record, the CEFC comparison shows that the value in the event file record is not equal to the constant. Thus the GOTO 2 row or false row is executed. Since this is the last record in the event file, the program ends.

The output file then contains the following:

```
--------------------------------------------------------------------------------
22349999CC11011100000088    p
FFFFFFFFCCFFFFFFFFFFFFFFF000904444444444444444444444444444444444444444444444444444
2234999933110111000000880637C000000000000000000000000000000000000000000000000000
--------------------------------------------------------------------------------
22349999CC11012100007994alpha
FFFFFFFFCCFFFFFFFFFFFFFFF899884444444444444444444444444444444444444444444444444444
22349999331101210000799413781000000000000000000000000000000000000000000000000000
--------------------------------------------------------------------------------
******************************** BOTTOM OF DATA ********************************
```

Figure 96. Copy View Output File

Format Phase

Because this view was a copy only view, the format phase is not required and performs no work.

Analysis

The function provided by this view is very simple. However, because we have generated machine code, it is even more efficient than is available in COBOL. Similar to what we have shown in Chapter 17, "Programming Tools," on page 79, the CFEC function requires only a CLC Compare Logical Character, and a BC Branch on Condition assembler instruction. This is contrasted with the assembler instructions generated from the COBOL IF statement which uses a much more generalized pattern.

Doug explained one day that because SAFR is designed around an event file and an extract file, his programs dedicated something called base registers, a key register or set of "eyes" to the event file and the extract file. Because COBOL has to be able to solve problems that require opening, reading, and writing to scores of files simultaneously which requires more than the 16 eyes available on the computer, it does not do this. This fact alone can save millions—or even billions—of machine instructions when the event file contains 3 million, 300 million, or 3 billion records.

The copy view is perhaps the simplest type of SAFR process. In the next execution, let's make it a bit more complex. This requires us to understand the extract record, as opposed to the event file.

Chapter 40. Extract Only View

Similar to a copy view, our extract only view will not require the Reference and Format phases. But now, instead of copying the input records to the output files, we will only select those fields we wish to use and write those to the output file. In this example, we'll also still execute the copy view at the same time, demonstrating how the single pass architecture works.

The only change we have to make to the select phase is to ask it to execute two views, so the input parameter to the VDP Builder now includes both 3261 and 3262.

```
****** ************** Top of Data ***************
000001 3261
000002 3262
****** ************** Bottom of Data ************
```

The VDP that is created after running the VDP Builder contains two views, plus all the metadata needed for both.

Logic Table

The following is the logic table created from the VDP which contains both these views.

```
------------------------------------------------------------------------------------------
LOGIC  GOTO  GOTO FUNC SEQ    LR FIELD       SOURCE          TARGET    OTHER DATA
  ROW  ROW1  ROW2 CODE NUM    ID    ID  POS  LEN FM CN D  LEN FM CN D CMP LEN1 VALUE1
------------------------------------------------------------------------------------------
    1             HD
                      FILE ID: 00001284
    2             RENX

VIEW ID: 00003261     FILE ID: 00001284
------------------------------------------------------------------------------------------
LOGIC  GOTO  GOTO FUNC SEQ    LR FIELD       SOURCE          TARGET    OTHER DATA
  ROW  ROW1  ROW2 CODE NUM    ID    ID  POS  LEN FM CN D  LEN FM CN D CMP LEN1 VALUE1
------------------------------------------------------------------------------------------
    3             NV        1264
    4     5     6 CFEC      1264 63311    1    9  3                   001 0009 522349999
    5             WRIN   1

VIEW ID: 00003262     FILE ID: 00001284
------------------------------------------------------------------------------------------
LOGIC  GOTO  GOTO FUNC SEQ    LR FIELD       SOURCE          TARGET    OTHER DATA
  ROW  ROW1  ROW2 CODE NUM    ID    ID  POS  LEN FM CN D  LEN FM CN D CMP LEN1 VALUE1
------------------------------------------------------------------------------------------
    6             NV        1264
    7             DTE    1  1264 63312   10    5  1         5  1      001 0000
    8             DTE    2  1264 63311    1    9  3         9  3      001 0000
    9             DTE    3  1264 63313   15    3  3         3  3      001 0000
   10    13    11 CFEC   4  1264 63313   15    3  3                   001 0003 111
   11    13    12 CFEC   4  1264 63313   15    3  3                   001 0003 121
   12    13    15 CFEC   4  1264 63313   15    3  3                   001 0003 123
   13             DTC    4               13   10  1                   001 0009 AssetAcct
   14    16       GOTO
   15             DTC    4               13   10  1                   001 0009 LiabAcct
   16             DTE    5  1264 63314   18    8  3         8  3      001 0000
   17    18    20 CNE    6  1264 63315   26    5  4    2              001 0000
   18             DTE    6  1264 63315   26    5  4    2    5  4    2 001 0000
   19    21       GOTO
   20             DTC    6               31    5  4    2              001 0001 0
   21             WRDT   1

                        FILE ID: 00001284
   22             ES
   23             EN
```

Figure 97. Extract Only View Logic Table

The HD Header, RENX Read Next, ES End of String and EN End of Logic Table functions are all pretty much the same. The rows for view 3261, logic table rows 3, 4 and 5 area also unchanged.

The Extract Only view, 3262, also is reading file 1284, and so it is placed immediately after view 3261. So when a record is read from that file, it will be passed first to view 3261 and then to 3262. This view is more complex. The Logic Table functions it performs are as follows:

- Output Columns 1, 2, and 3: Rows 7, 8 and 9 are DTE functions, which tell the extract program to perform three "Data Transformations", moving data to the extract file. The view asks that data at position 10, for a length of 5 be moved, next the data at position 1 for a length of 9, then the data at position 15 for a length of 3. The sequence number shows the column of the view requesting these functions.
- If Statement: Rows 10, 11, and 12 are generated based upon the following view logic text in column 4:

  ```
  If ({ACCOUNT} = 111 Or {ACCOUNT} = 121 Or {ACCOUNT} = 123  )
    Then
      COLUMN = "AssetAcct"
    Else
      COLUMN = "LiabAcct"
  EndIf
  ```

  Similar to the copy only view, the row 10 CFEC function tests data in the event file at position 15 for a length of 3 (the same data put in column 3) to see if it is equal to "111". If the value at position 15 is "111" then the next row executed is row 13; the DTE. If it is not, then the next row executed is row 11. Row 11 tests for a value of "121" in a similar way. Then row 12 tests for a value of "123". If the value is not "123" then the next row that executes is row 15. In other words, all "or" conditions failed.
- Output Column 4: Row 13 is a DTC, a Data Transformation Constant. This row, the "then" condition, places a constant of "AssetAcct" into column 4. Row 14 then instructs the program to skip row 15. The DTC in row 15, the "else" condition, places a value of "LiabAcct" in that same column. The only way to get to this row is based upon failing all the "or" conditions on row 12.
- Output Column 5: Another DTE function is executed on row 16 to place the value contained in the event file at position 18 for a length of 8 in the output for column 5.
- Numeric Test: Row 17 is generated based upon this logic text:

  ```
  If ISNUMERIC({AMOUNT})
    Then
     COLUMN = {AMOUNT}
    Else
      COLUMN = 0
  EndIf
  ```

  The CNE is a Class test, Numeric against Event file field. The value in the event file at position 26 for a length of 5 with a format of 4 (which is packed), is tested to see if it contains a numeric value. If the value is numeric, the row 18 is executed. Otherwise, row 20 is executed.
- Output Column 6: The DTE places the Amount field, which is in the event file at position 26 for a length of 5, in the output file. The DTC function places a zero in the same column if the value from the event file is not numeric.
- Write: Instead of the WRIN function used in the copy view which wrote the Input record, this view contains a WRDT function, which writes the results of the Data Transforms, namely any of the data placed in the extract record by DT type functions.

The following table shows how the different areas in memory in GVBMR95 are used by the different function codes.

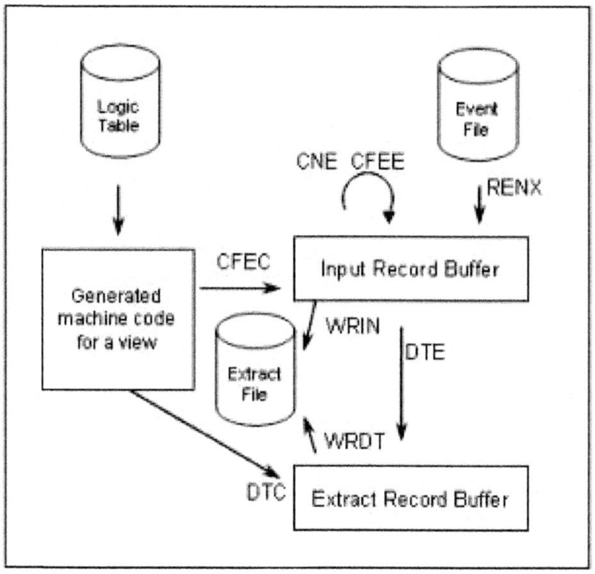

Figure 98. Logic Table Functions and File Buffers

The Logic Table is used to generate the machine code. The RENX brings a record from the event file into the input data buffer. CFEE, Compare Field Event File Field to Event File Field and CNE, Class Numeric Event functions work against only the input record. The DTE Data Transform Event file field moves data from the input buffer to the output record buffer. The constants, in either the CFEC or DTC are in the logic table and in the generated machine code. What record is written to the output file is determined by the Write Functions, either WRIN or WRDT.

Extract Process

The trace from running the same event used in the last chapter is as follows:

```
 EVENT    EVENT       VIEW      LOGIC       SEQ
 DDNAME   RECORD      NUMBER     ROW        NUM *****VALUE-1*******
EVENT           1 V:   3261 LT:      3 NV
EVENT           1 V:   3261 LT:      4 CFEC 000       522349999
EVENT           1 V:   3261 LT:      5 WRIN 007
EVENT           1 V:   3262 LT:      6 NV
EVENT           1 V:   3262 LT:      7 DTE  001       CC110
EVENT           1 V:   3262 LT:      8 DTE  002       522349999
EVENT           1 V:   3262 LT:      9 DTE  003       111
EVENT           1 V:   3262 LT:     10 CFEC 004       111
EVENT           1 V:   3262 LT:     13 DTC  004       AssetAcct
EVENT           1 V:   3262 LT:     14 GOTO
EVENT           1 V:   3262 LT:     16 DTE  005       00000088
EVENT           1 V:   3262 LT:     17 CNE  006          p
EVENT           1 V:   3262 LT:     18 DTE  006          p
EVENT           1 V:   3262 LT:     19 GOTO
EVENT           1 V:   3262 LT:     21 WRDT 008
EVENT           2 V:   3261 LT:      3 NV
EVENT           2 V:   3261 LT:      4 CFEC 000       522349999
EVENT           2 V:   3261 LT:      5 WRIN 007
EVENT           2 V:   3262 LT:      6 NV
EVENT           2 V:   3262 LT:      7 DTE  001       CC110
EVENT           2 V:   3262 LT:      8 DTE  002       522349999
EVENT           2 V:   3262 LT:      9 DTE  003       121
EVENT           2 V:   3262 LT:     10 CFEC 004       121
EVENT           2 V:   3262 LT:     11 CFEC 004       121
EVENT           2 V:   3262 LT:     13 DTC  004       AssetAcct
EVENT           2 V:   3262 LT:     14 GOTO
EVENT           2 V:   3262 LT:     16 DTE  005       00007994
EVENT           2 V:   3262 LT:     17 CNE  006       alpha
EVENT           2 V:   3262 LT:     20 DTC  006
EVENT           2 V:   3262 LT:     21 WRDT 008
EVENT           3 V:   3261 LT:      3 NV
EVENT           3 V:   3261 LT:      4 CFEC 000       522349731
EVENT           3 V:   3262 LT:      6 NV
EVENT           3 V:   3262 LT:      7 DTE  001       CC218
EVENT           3 V:   3262 LT:      8 DTE  002       522349731
EVENT           3 V:   3262 LT:      9 DTE  003       121
EVENT           3 V:   3262 LT:     10 CFEC 004       121
EVENT           3 V:   3262 LT:     11 CFEC 004       121
EVENT           3 V:   3262 LT:     13 DTC  004       AssetAcct
EVENT           3 V:   3262 LT:     14 GOTO
EVENT           3 V:   3262 LT:     16 DTE  005       00000076
EVENT           3 V:   3262 LT:     17 CNE  006       a
EVENT           3 V:   3262 LT:     18 DTE  006       a
EVENT           3 V:   3262 LT:     19 GOTO
EVENT           3 V:   3262 LT:     21 WRDT 008
```

Figure 99. Extract Only Logic Table Trace

Note that event file record 1 is first processed by view 3261, and then serially (not in parallel) processed by view 3262. View 3261 has two WRIN functions, against event record 1 and event record 2. But three records are written for view 3262 by the WRDT function. Here are the records output for view 3262, in hex mode: The record copied by 3261 had the value "alpha" in it, but note that the second record no longer has a value of "alpha" where the number should be because of the numeric test in the view 3262. Instead, logic table row 20 was executed, a DTC function, which placed instead a set of zero's in that location.

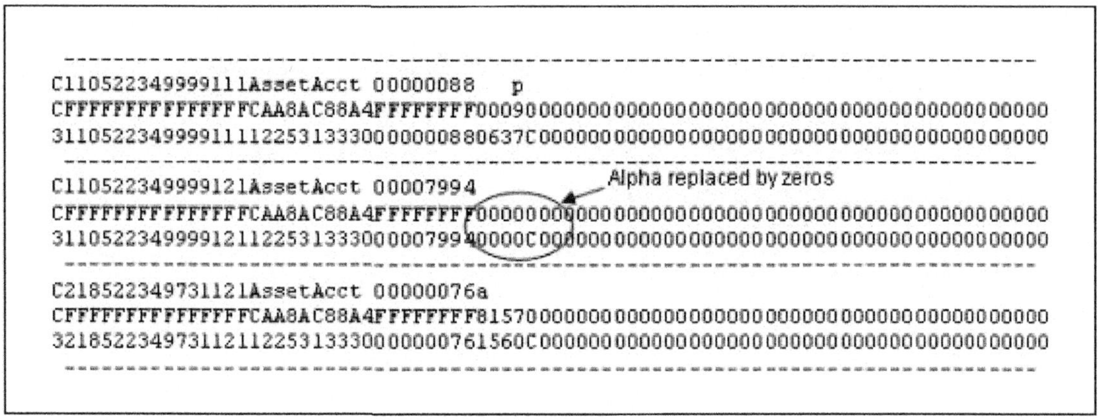

```
------------------------------------------------------------------------------
C110522349999111AssetAcct 00000088   p
CFFFFFFFFFFFFFFFCAA8AC88A4FFFFFFFF00090000000000000000000000000000000000000000000000
3110522349999111122531333000000880637C000000000000000000000000000000000000000000000
------------------------------------------------------------------------------
C110522349999121AssetAcct 00007994
CFFFFFFFFFFFFFFFCAA8AC88A4FFFFFFFF00000000000000000000000000000000000000000000000000
311052234999912112253133300000799400000C00000000000000000000000000000000000000000000
------------------------------------------------------------------------------
C218522349731121AssetAcct 0000076a
CFFFFFFFFFFFFFFFCAA8AC88A4FFFFFFFF81570000000000000000000000000000000000000000000000
3218522349731121122531333000000761560C000000000000000000000000000000000000000000000
------------------------------------------------------------------------------
```


Figure 100. Extract Only View Sample Output

Extract Program Control Report

A key control report in the process is the Extract Engine report, shown below:

```
MR95 - PARALLEL THREADS EXECUTED.............                          1
MR95 - VIEWS PER  FILE PROCESSED.............                          2
MR95 - TOTAL NUMBER OF LOGIC TABLE ROWS.......                        23
MR95 - SIZE  OF GENERATED LOGIC...............                       424
MR95 -       EVENT  FILE  RECORDS  READ.......EVENT                    3
MR95 - TOTAL EVENT RECORDS   READ....................                  3
MR95 - TOTAL PIPE  RECORDS   READ....................                  0
VIEW DEF:    3261/EVENT      F:           0 NF:          0             2(F0003261)
VIEW DEF:    3262/EVENT      F:           0 NF:          0             3(F0003262)
MR95 - TOTAL LOOKUPS PERFORMED.......................                  0
MR95 - TOTAL RECORDS WRITTEN TO FILE..........F0003261                 2
MR95 - TOTAL RECORDS WRITTEN TO FILE..........F0003262                 3
MR95 - TOTAL EXTRACT RECORDS WRITTEN.................                  5
MR95 - TOTAL PIPE    RECORDS WRITTEN.................                  0
MR95 - EXTRACTION  ELAPSED TIME (IN SECONDS).........                  0
```

Figure 101. GVBMR95 Control Report

- Because we only read one event file, only one thread was executed[120].
- There were two views reading this file. If one of these views had been reading another event file as well, the count by "views per file processed" would have been 3, even though there were only two outputs.
- The "logic table rows" is equal to the row number on the EN row, i.e., the total number of rows in the logic table.
- The machine code generated from those logic table rows is 424 bytes. In other words, in the prior chapter we noted the CFEC created a CLC and BC assembler instructions, which required 20 bytes of the 424 generated.
- The record count of the records read from the Event file (with a DD Name of Event) is 3. Because we only read one event file, the total event records read is the same on the next line. Our process used no "pipes" which are virtual event files.
- The next section shows the results of each view against each event file.
  - View 3261 extracted two records, and wrote them to DD Name F0003261.
  - View 3262 extracted three records, and wrote them to DD Name F0003262.

---

120. See Chapter 48, "Multi-Threading," on page 249 for a discussion of reading multiple event files.

  - The zeros next to "F" and "NF" are for lookups "Found" and "Not Found", because these views require no joins.
- Multiple views can write to an extract file. Thus the next set of rows show the total of record written to each extract file, and the total to all extract files, and to all Pipes.
- The Elapsed time is the total wall-clock time for the extract process.

If the outputs are not what was expected, this is perhaps the first places to look.

Analysis

The Extract Engine in this process has significantly increased efficiency over alternative methods of producing these two outputs, because in a single pass of the file, one IO to get the event file into memory for processing has allowed both outputs to be done. Certainly programs can be written to do this same thing, but it demands a programmer writing the program to design it that way. Here, two people independently can create views, and the tool will resolve them efficiently.

Remember, though, that this process does not include any parallelism. View number 2 is executed after view number 1 has seen the event record.

The next step in growing our understanding is to understand how to do lookups.

Chapter 41. Look-ups

The first tests I remember performing on the product were testing look-ups. I remember finding some problem and calling Doug about it; I also remember his comment about the test that I had set up, "Well this is pretty complex."

The look-up process can seem pretty complex, and it will take us two chapters to cover. This one will focus on the logic table and extract process; the next will explain the reference file phase and how it supported those results.

We'll make a change to the input parameters to the VDP Builder to add view 3263 to the other two views we are already executing.

Logic Table

Although we'll execute all three views, we'll only show the logic table for our new view. Thus the rows of the logic table continue from the prior example.

```
VIEW ID: 00003263     FILE ID: 00001284
------------------------------------------------------------------------------------------
 LOGIC  GOTO  GOTO FUNC SEQ   LR FIELD       SOURCE            TARGET     OTHER DATA
   ROW  ROW1  ROW2 CODE NUM   ID    ID  POS  LEN FM CN D  LEN FM CN D CMP LEN1 VALUE1
------------------------------------------------------------------------------------------

    22             NV       1264
    23    26    35 JOIN     1263  2890    1       1                   001 0001
    24             LKE      1264 63311    1    9  3         9  3      001 0000
    25    26    35 LUSM
    26    27    35 CFLC     1263 63316    1   30  1                   001 0018 K & N jone
    27    30    35 JOIN     1262  2889    1       1                   001 0001
    28             LKE      1264 63312   10    5  1         5  1      001 0000
    29    30    35 LUSM
    30    31    35 CFLC     1262 63317    1   30  1                   001 0003 DAD
    31    34    35 JOIN     1258  2888    1       1                   001 0001
    32             LKE      1264 63313   15    3  3         3  3      001 0000
    33    34    35 LUSM
    34    55    35 CFLC     1258 63318    1   30  1                   001 0016 checking a
    35    38    40 JOIN   1 1262  2889    1       1                   001 0001
    36             LKE    1 1264 63312   10    5  1         5  1      001 0000
    37    38    40 LUSM
    38             DTL    1 1262 63317    1   30  1        30  1      001 0000
    39    41       GOTO
    40             DTC    1 1264          1   30  1                   001 0004 NULL
    41    44    46 JOIN   2 1263  2890    1       1                   001 0001
    42             LKE    2 1264 63311    1    9  3         9  3      001 0000
    43    44    46 LUSM
    44             DTL    2 1263 63316    1   30  1        30  1      001 0000
    45    47       GOTO
    46             DTC    2 1264         31   30  1                   001 0004 NULL
    47    50    52 JOIN   3 1258  2888    1       1                   001 0001
    48             LKE    3 1264 63313   15    3  3         3  3      001 0000
    49    50    52 LUSM
    50             DTL    3 1258 63318    1   30  1        30  1      001 0000
    51    53       GOTO
    52             DTC    3 1264         61   30  1                   001 0004 NULL
    53             DTE    4 1264 63314   18    8  3         8  3      001 0000
    54             WRDT   1

FILE ID: 00001284
    55             ES
    56             EN
```

Figure 102. Lookup Logic Table

The logic table contains some new functions.

- The JOIN function specifies that the next few steps are going to prepare the keys for the join.
- The LKE function moves data for a lookup key from each event file record to the lookup key buffer.

- The LUSM uses the values that have been placed in the lookup key buffer to search the in memory table to find a corresponding match. The results from the LUSM can either be that a match was found, or a match was not found, and the GOTO Rows 1 and 2 are next executed for either of those cases respectively.
- If a match was found, the located matching record can be used in a number of ways. It might be used to test to see if additional values on the record are of a particular value for selection. This would use a CFEL function, for Compare Field Event-file value to Looked-up value. A class test against the looked up value could also be executed. Row 26 in this logic table tests to see if the looked-up value at position 1 for a length of 30 on the LR 1262 matches the constant "K & N jone...", thus a CFLC for Compare Field Looked up value to Constant.
- Data from the looked up record can be moved into the extract record through a DTL function, such as row 38.

The following table shows these additional functions.

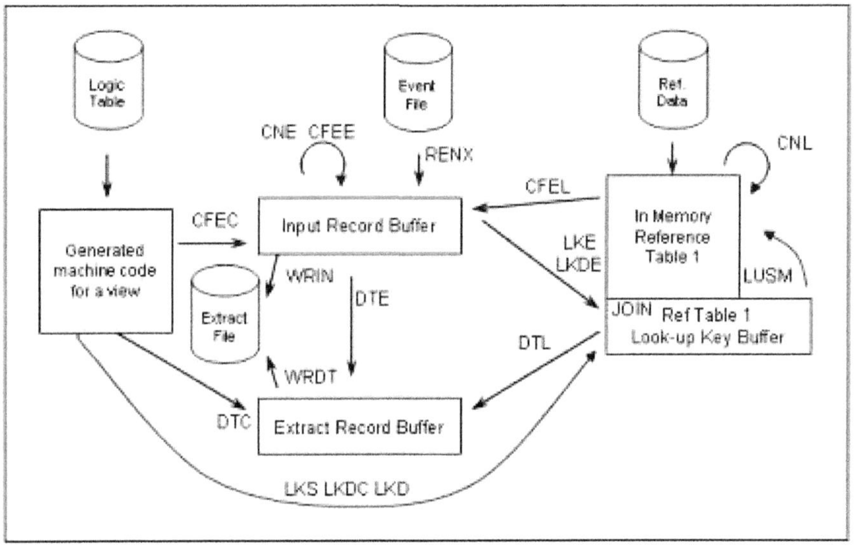

Figure 103. Simple Look-up Functions

The Reference File Phase process prepares the in-memory reference file table, and is discussed in the next chapter.

Extract Phase

The following is the trace output for only those rows applicable to our new view.

```
 EVENT      EVENT          VIEW       LOGIC        SEQ
 DDNAME     RECORD        NUMBER       ROW         NUM *****VALUE-1*******
 Display  Filter  View  Print  Options  Help

EVENT             1 V:    3263 LT:      22 NV
EVENT             1 V:    3263 LT:      23 JOIN
EVENT             1 V:    3263 LT:      24 LKE  000 522349999
EVENT             1 V:    3263 LT:      25 LUSM
EVENT             1 V:    3263 LT:      26 CFLC 000 K & N jones      K & N jones
EVENT             1 V:    3263 LT:      27 JOIN
EVENT             1 V:    3263 LT:      28 LKE  000 CC110
EVENT             1 V:    3263 LT:      29 LUSM
EVENT             1 V:    3263 LT:      30 CFLC 000 DAD                               DAD
EVENT             1 V:    3263 LT:      31 JOIN
EVENT             1 V:    3263 LT:      32 LKE  000 111
EVENT             1 V:    3263 LT:      33 LUSM
EVENT             1 V:    3263 LT:      34 CFLC 000 checking acc      checking acc
EVENT             2 V:    3263 LT:      22 NV
EVENT             2 V:    3263 LT:      23 JOIN
EVENT             2 V:    3263 LT:      24 LKE  000 522349999
EVENT             2 V:    3263 LT:      25 LUSM
EVENT             2 V:    3263 LT:      26 CFLC 000 K & N jones      K & N jones
EVENT             2 V:    3263 LT:      27 JOIN
EVENT             2 V:    3263 LT:      28 LKE  000 CC110
EVENT             2 V:    3263 LT:      29 LUSM
EVENT             2 V:    3263 LT:      30 CFLC 000 DAD                               DAD
EVENT             2 V:    3263 LT:      31 JOIN
EVENT             2 V:    3263 LT:      32 LKE  000 121
EVENT             2 V:    3263 LT:      33 LUSM
EVENT             2 V:    3263 LT:      34 CFLC 000 automobile   checking account
EVENT             2 V:    3263 LT:      35 JOIN
EVENT             2 V:    3263 LT:      38 DTL  001 DAD
EVENT             2 V:    3263 LT:      39 GOTO
EVENT             2 V:    3263 LT:      41 JOIN
EVENT             2 V:    3263 LT:      44 DTL  002 K & N jones family
EVENT             2 V:    3263 LT:      45 GOTO
EVENT             2 V:    3263 LT:      47 JOIN
EVENT             2 V:    3263 LT:      50 DTL  003 automobile
EVENT             2 V:    3263 LT:      51 GOTO
EVENT             2 V:    3263 LT:      53 DTE  004 00007994
EVENT             2 V:    3263 LT:      54 WRDT 009
EVENT             3 V:    3263 LT:      22 NV
EVENT             3 V:    3263 LT:      23 JOIN
EVENT             3 V:    3263 LT:      24 LKE  000 522349731
EVENT             3 V:    3263 LT:      25 LUSM
EVENT             3 V:    3263 LT:      26 CFLC 000 c wheeler   K & N jones family
EVENT             3 V:    3263 LT:      35 JOIN
EVENT             3 V:    3263 LT:      36 LKE  001 CC218
EVENT             3 V:    3263 LT:      37 LUSM
EVENT             3 V:    3263 LT:      38 DTL  001 CHARLES
EVENT             3 V:    3263 LT:      39 GOTO
EVENT             3 V:    3263 LT:      41 JOIN
EVENT             3 V:    3263 LT:      44 DTL  002 c wheeler
EVENT             3 V:    3263 LT:      45 GOTO
EVENT             3 V:    3263 LT:      47 JOIN
EVENT             3 V:    3263 LT:      48 LKE  003 121
EVENT             3 V:    3263 LT:      49 LUSM
EVENT             3 V:    3263 LT:      50 DTL  003 automobile
EVENT             3 V:    3263 LT:      51 GOTO
EVENT             3 V:    3263 LT:      53 DTE  004 00000076
EVENT             3 V:    3263 LT:      54 WRDT 009
```

Figure 104. Lookup Logic Table Trace

Note that we can see that the key values supplied by the event file for the first LKE is "522349999". The LUSM was performed, and because the next executed logic table row is 26, the results of the LUSM were found. In other words, the reference file had a record with the key of 522349999. The CFLC function compares the constant of "K & N jones" to the value on the found looked-up record, which is also "K & N jones".

On this first event record, two other lookups and compares are also performed, until we get to logic table row 34. At this point, the trace for view 3263 against record 1 stops, and we go on to event file record two (we have omitted the trace rows for view 3261 and 3262 in this printout which would have been rows 1-21). This tells us that the view did not meet the general selection criteria.

Here is the selection criteria:

```
If ({EVENT_JOURNAL_TO_LE_DESC.LEGAL_ENTITY_TITLE}= "K & N jones family"
  And {EVENT_JOURNAL_TO_CC_DESC.COST_CENTRE_TITLE} = "DAD"
  And {EVENT_JOURNAL_TO_ACC_TITLES.ACCOUNT_TITLES} = "checking account")Then
    SKIP
EndIf
```

The "Skip" statement is what causes the record to be skipped. The lookups resulted in values of "K & N jones family", "DAD" and "checking account". The skip statement causes the GOTO True and GOTO False rows to be swapped on the CFLC function for the Account Title. Typically the true row is the next logic table row, and the false row is the a few rows later. Because of the skip statement, they are reversed.

The following are the output records for this view. The values in these output records can be seen in the logic table trace for DTL and DTE functions.

```
----------------------------------------------------------------------------------------------------
DAD                       K & N jones family      automobile                       00007994
CCC44444444444444444444444D454D49998A488989A44444444444448AA9998898444444444444444444444444FFFFFFFF
4140000000000000000000000020005016552061493800000000000001436462935000000000000000000000000007994
----------------------------------------------------------------------------------------------------
CHARLES                   c wheeler               automobile                       00000076
CCCDDCE4444444444444444444484A8889894444444444444444444448AA9998898444444444444444444444444FFFFFFFF
3819352000000000000000000003068553590000000000000000000001436462935000000000000000000000000000076
----------------------------------------------------------------------------------------------------
```

Figure 105. Lookup Extract Only View Output

Multi-step Look-up

The test I was performing that day which Doug found fairly complex was a multiple step lookup. That means that the values for a lookup can come from a prior lookup, rather than all having to come from the event file.

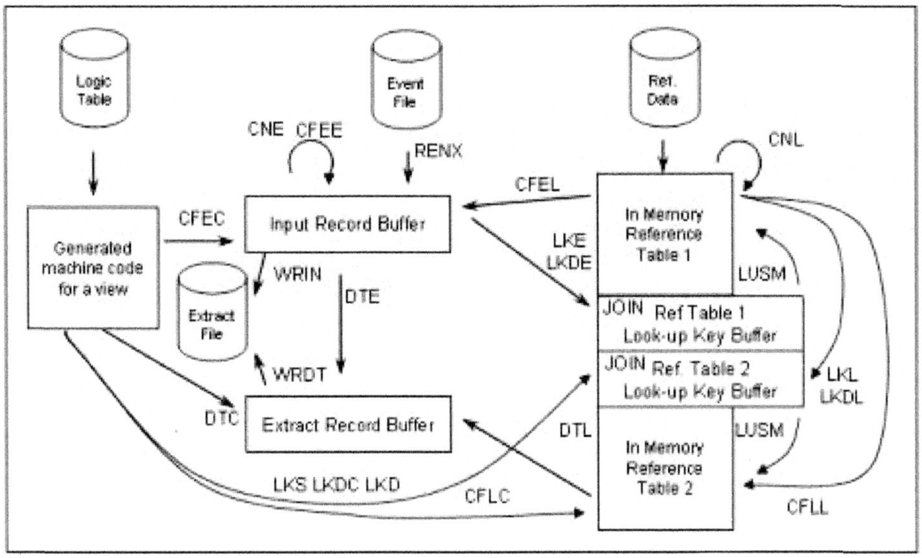

Figure 106. Complex Look-up Functions

LKE function becomes a LKL function: Build Lookup Key from Looked-up value. CFEL functions can similarly become CFLL to compare two looked up values.

Date-effective Joins

You'll remember we considered the needs for date-effective joins when using the SAFR method[121]. Let's examine how date effective joins are implemented in the SAFR process.

The date field on the target reference table is technically not part of the key because the values passed in for the search do not have to be matched byte for byte. So the effective date field on the target logical record could be thought as being between the key and the data areas of the record.

Although technically not part of the key, the logic table contains LK functions, specifically Lookup Key Date or LKD functions, to place the desired effective date in the lookup key buffer. And, predictably, these are the last LK functions for a particular join.[122]

The dates can come from constants, LKDC. The date can come from the event file, LKDE, or from a looked-up value on another reference table, LKDL.

The constant value on the LKDC can come from multiple places. For example, in a view definition someone may place a hard-coded date, like December 31 of some particular year. Alternatively, the developer might also use a keyword in the workbench, such as run-date, when specifying what date to use. This keyword is translated into a specific date constant during the logic table phase of processing. By the time the logic table arrives at the extract process, it is indistinguishable from a hard coded date. The translated constant date value is shown in both the logic table print and the logic table trace. Use of the key words allows for dates to be passed in as part of the batch process; thus the View logic remains the same day after day, but the date used in the view can vary.

When the extract engine performs a search on a date effective table, it will "fall back" to the record with a matching key, whose effective date is less than or equal to the value provided by the LKD function. If

121. See Chapter 34, "Consider Complex Joins," on page 177.

122. Note that if a date is part of a key and should be matched byte for byte, it would typically be moved to the key by an LKE function. Only effective dates use LKD functions. Because date effective joins are not matched byte for byte, placing the date at the end of the keys allows the comparison to be performed after matching the key.

there is no record with an effective date less than or equal to the effective date, the extract engine will execute the "not found" condition.

Join Optimization

I think the idea was probably Jay's, but I don't think I know for sure where it started. It was that we could add another step into the SAFR Scan engine process to analyze the logic table and remove certain joins which had been performed by a view earlier in the process. For example if view 3261 did a join to the account master table, and 3262 required the same join, there would be no reason to go build the look-up key again; the results of the join were already known and the results of the join could already be known.

It was such a simple idea, but the word "simplistic" might be a better description. It started a process of work that continued part time for probably a year. We kept running into technical problems every step of the way. When we finally got it to work, the results ended up being remarkable. As we put the new process into production after making the code permanent and more testing, we found that we could reduce the CPU time on some already very efficient, join intensive processes by 60 and 70%. It was nearly unbelievable.

The result is a process whereby the more views that are resolved in one SAFR execution, with greater numbers of lookups to shared table, the greater the efficiency is for each join.

Next, let's consider how the data is prepared for joins by understanding the Reference File Phase.

Chapter 42. Reference File Phase

Another of my early memories with Doug was one day during the large retailer project when Doug happened to be in the office in Sacramento. I am sure he was under a great deal of pressure to add features to SAFR to support the project. I went into his office and somehow complained about the workload Randall and I were carrying trying to finish up the software on our own. He looked up and said very quickly something to the effect of, "Life is pretty hard for everyone." I understood what he meant immediately. Stop feeling sorry for yourself and get back to work. So I did.

Core Image

There are always resource constraints. The concept of a "core image" file used for in memory processes has been around for decades and was developed to get around computer memory constraints.

Computer programmers have always known that memory access is much faster than disk access, but memory is much more expensive than disk. So probably to solve some problem whereby a lot of data (for the day) had to fit into memory for rapid access, someone suggested that those parts of data known to not be needed be removed from the data in a preprocess before the data is actually loaded into memory for use.

SAFR performs this process in the reference file phase process. The reference file phase analyzes the logic table to determine all joins that will be performed, what the keys to the reference tables are, what effective date keyword constants need to be translated, and the resulting data fields on each table that will be use. It then reads the actual reference data and creates a copy that can be loaded in memory which is as small as possible. It also builds a control file and control report that tells the extract phase what memory will be required to load the data.

Logic Table Phase

The reference file process begins actually in the Logic Table phase. Think back to the extract only view we created above. Remember that it read the event file, and extracted only those columns of data that were required into the extract file. When any of the views need to perform joins, the Logic Table program dynamically creates similar views.

First, after the VDP Builder selects views that are required for this run, the Logic Table program creates a logic table we have been analyzing, called the XLT for Extract Logic Table, for these views.

The Logic table program then reads this XLT. Every time it sees a logical record that is not the event file, it knows a join is needed.

The Logic table program then creates a JLT, or Join Logic Table. For each new LR, it creates an extract only view, which is to read the look-up LR as an event file. The Logic Table program looks at the logical record definition to determine what the keys are to the target LR. For each key field, it creates a column, a DTE, that will extract that key data and place it in the reference file phase extract file for that reference file. It puts the start date field if the LR is effective dated as the first column after the key.

It also keeps track of all the fields that are required as data, or answer fields by the views from that reference file, for example, the customer name or an account description. In other words, each "L" field in DTL or CFLC in view 3263 would be another column in this generated extract only view. In the JLT each of these fields are DTEs.

Reference File Phase

The same program that executes the XLT is used to execute the JLT, GVBMR95. The event files for this phase are the reference files. There are no lookups performed in this phase of processes, each column is a DTE. When the JLT is executed, the outputs from these views are a set of files known as the RED, Reference Extract Data. These are the core image files.

Here is an example of the RED for the Account Title Master reference file.

```
................111checking account
................121automobile
................122Personal property
................123home
................211credit card payable
................222mortgage payable
................411salary revenue
```

Figure 107. Sample RED File

The RED is prefixed by 16 bytes (four full words) of data that are used in the Extract Phase after the data is loaded into memory. So the key begins in position 17. On this reference file, the key is 3 bytes in length. The values used in CFLC or DTL functions begin at position 20, the "checking account" on row 1.

The reference file phase also builds a view to produce a control record for each reference file. This view only puts out one record per reference file LR. Each of these views is also in the same JLT; they read the same event file, just like views 3261 and 3262. This view accumulates the number of reference file records that have been written to the RED. The Logic table contains a counter, including a DIM4, to define a four byte binary field, an ADDC to add a constant of 1 to the counter for each reference file record read, and a SETC to set the accumulator to zero before the next file is processed. The extract file containing these records is called the REH or Reference Extract Header records.

A small program produces a control report from these records to show what the memory utilization will be in the extract phase for loading the reference files.

```
REPORT ID: GVBMR71                         GENEVA DEMO                          PAGE:              1
BUILD    : 04001        SAFR Reference File Creation Control Report   RUN : 09/18/09 10:49

  LR                            FILE  INPUT       RECORD    KEY KEY EXTR   ---INTERNAL TABLES---
  ID   LR NAME                   ID   DDNAME      COUNT     LEN OFF FILE#  ROW LEN   TOTAL BYTES
----- ---------------------- ----- -------- ----------- --- --- -----  ------- -------------

 1258 ACCOUNT_TITLES          1285 ACCTIT              7   3  16     3       56           392
 1262 CC_DESC                 1286 CCDESC              3   5  16     4       56           168
 1263 LEGAL_ENTITY_DESC       1287 LEDESC              2   9  16     5       56           112
                                                 -----------                        -------------
                                                          12                                 672
                                                 ===========                        =============
```

Figure 108. REH Report

The following is the GVBMR95 control report for the reference file phase.

```
MR95 - PARALLEL THREADS EXECUTED.............                          1
MR95 - VIEWS PER  FILE PROCESSED.............                          6
MR95 - TOTAL NUMBER OF LOGIC TABLE ROWS.......                        74
MR95 - SIZE  OF GENERATED LOGIC..............                      1,320
MR95 -        EVENT  FILE  RECORDS  READ.......ACCTIT                  7
MR95 -        EVENT  FILE  RECORDS  READ.......CCDESC                  3
MR95 -        EVENT  FILE  RECORDS  READ.......LEDESC                  2
MR95 - TOTAL EVENT RECORDS    READ.....................               12
MR95 - TOTAL PIPE  RECORDS    READ.....................                0
VIEW DEF:    3265/ACCTIT     F:             0 NF:         0            7(GREF003)
VIEW DEF:    3264/           F:             0 NF:         0            1(GREFREH)
VIEW DEF:    3266/CCDESC     F:             0 NF:         0            3(GREF004)
VIEW DEF:    3264/           F:             0 NF:         0            1(GREFREH)
VIEW DEF:    3267/LEDESC     F:             0 NF:         0            2(GREF005)
VIEW DEF:    3264/           F:             0 NF:         0            1(GREFREH)
MR95 - TOTAL LOOKUPS PERFORMED.......................                  0
MR95 - TOTAL RECORDS WRITTEN TO FILE..........GREFREH                  3
MR95 - TOTAL RECORDS WRITTEN TO FILE..........GREF003                  7
MR95 - TOTAL RECORDS WRITTEN TO FILE..........GREF004                  3
MR95 - TOTAL RECORDS WRITTEN TO FILE..........GREF005                  2
MR95 - TOTAL EXTRACT RECORDS WRITTEN.................                 15
MR95 - TOTAL PIPE    RECORDS WRITTEN.................                  0
MR95 - EXTRACTION  ELAPSED TIME (IN SECONDS).........                  0
```

Figure 109. Reference File Phase GVBMR95 Control Report

It shows that the program read three different input files, the ACCTIT, CCDESC and the LEDESC files. Two views executed against each for a total of six views. It read 12 records and wrote 15: 12 reference file records and 3 REH records.[123]

Custom Processes

The format of the RED and REH files are open formats. Other processes could be used to build these files and present them to the extract engine. In fact, in some instances with voluminous reference files, specific views could be built and maintained that output these record structures. Unlike the standard SAFR processes where every record in the reference file will be written to the output RED (albeit likely shorter with fewer fields and the key and effective date at the front), these views could include selection logic, or join together data in preprocesses before executing the main SAFR extract process.

Additionally, Doug created a small subroutine, GVBUR45, containing the SAFR lookup algorithm. This routine can be called from any program to perform lookups. It accepts an REH file, and multiple associated REDs. It must be called once to initialize the process, and once to clean up at the conclusion. The parameters passed to it during mainline processing look much like the values passed by a join and the LK functions. In this way, the SAFR lookup capabilities can be used outside of SAFR.

Our next step in the process will be to understand the Extract Files.

123. Note that the reference file phase is executed in single thread mode, noted by the number of parallel threads executed message. This is because the REH views must not write their data until after all RED record have been written. The REH views contain a counter of the RED records, and must wait to be executed after the RED views are complete. This can most easily be accomplished by running in single threaded mode.

Chapter 43. Extract Files

I remember one day when Doug was in the office in Sacramento asking him a question, and him needing to go look at the source code. So we walked into his office and he booted up his PC. At the time, before Windows 95, our PCs had Windows 3.1 which ran on top of DOS. I was a bit surprised after the machine completely booted up with the Windows graphical interface to watch Doug go to the top of the screen and close the graphical user interface. He wanted to get back to the DOS prompt so he would be able to work. This fact speaks a great deal about removing layers between him and the machine.

The Format phase program is a generalized control break engine, a very different kind of program than the extract program. Control break logic is what performs a "group by" function in a database, or a “sum fields” function in a sort utility. It collapses a set of records with the same key together to produce a subtotal of some kind, and then performs the same function on the next set of rows.

The Extract Record was created to support this control break logic. It is vital to understand it's structure before understanding the remaining logic table functions, and the remaining processes of the SAFR Scan Engine.

Extract Record Overview

I have created view 3264 and specified that it use the Format Phase. This changes some of the function codes that are used in the extract phase.

The extract records are written to Extract Files, temporary files between the Extract Phase and the Format Phase. The Extract Record has the following general layout.

Figure 110. Extract Record Structure

- The control area contains values that describe the rest of the record, like the number of SAFR view columns on this record, and the length of the sort key. The last field in the control area is the view number. We'll explain why later.
- The Sort Key or SK area contains the values the user has specified the output file should be sorted and/or grouped by.
- The Data Transform or DT area contains alphabetic and alphanumeric and numeric column data that is not used in a format time calculation, including sub-totaling, or format time selection logic.
- The Calculated Transform or CT area contains column data that is either used in a format time calculation, including sub-totaling, or format time selection logic.

With this understanding, let's look at the logic table for a view requiring the format phase.

Logic Table Phase

VIEW ID: 00003264 FILE ID: 00001284

LOGIC ROW	GOTO ROW1	GOTO ROW2	FUNC CODE	SEQ NUM	LR ID	FIELD ID	POS	SOURCE LEN	SOURCE FM	SOURCE CN	SOURCE D	TARGET LEN	TARGET FM	TARGET CN	TARGET D	OTHER DATA CMP	OTHER DATA LEN1	OTHER DATA VALUE1
55			NV		1264													
56	59	74	JOIN		1263	2890	1		1							001	0001	1
57			LKE		1264	63311	1	9	3			9	3			001	0000	
58	59	74	LUSM															
59	60	74	CFLC		1263	63316	1	30	1							001	0018	K & N jone
60	63	65	JOIN	1	1263	2890	1		1							001	0001	1
61			LKE	1	1264	63311	1	9	3			9	3			001	0000	
62	63	65	LUSM															
63			SKL	1	1263	63316	1	30	1			30	1			001	0000	
64	66		GOTO															
65			SKC	1	1264		1	30	1							001	0004	NULL
66	69	71	JOIN	2	1258	2888	1		1							001	0001	
67			LKE	2	1264	63313	15	3	3			3	3			001	0000	
68	69	71	LUSM															
69			SKL	2	1258	63318	1	30	1			30	1			001	0000	
70	72		GOTO															
71			SKC	2	1264		31	30	1							001	0004	NULL
72			CTE	3	1264	63315	26	5	4		2					001	0000	
73			WRXT	1														

Figure 111. Format Phase View Logic Table

This logic table has an SKL function, a build sort key from looked-up values. It also has a SKC, build sort key from constant in case the lookup fails. It also has a CTE, a calculated transform from an event file field. It also has a WRXT, a write the extract record, rather than the WRIN for the input record, or WRDT for just the DT section of the extract record.

The following graph shows these additional functions.[124]

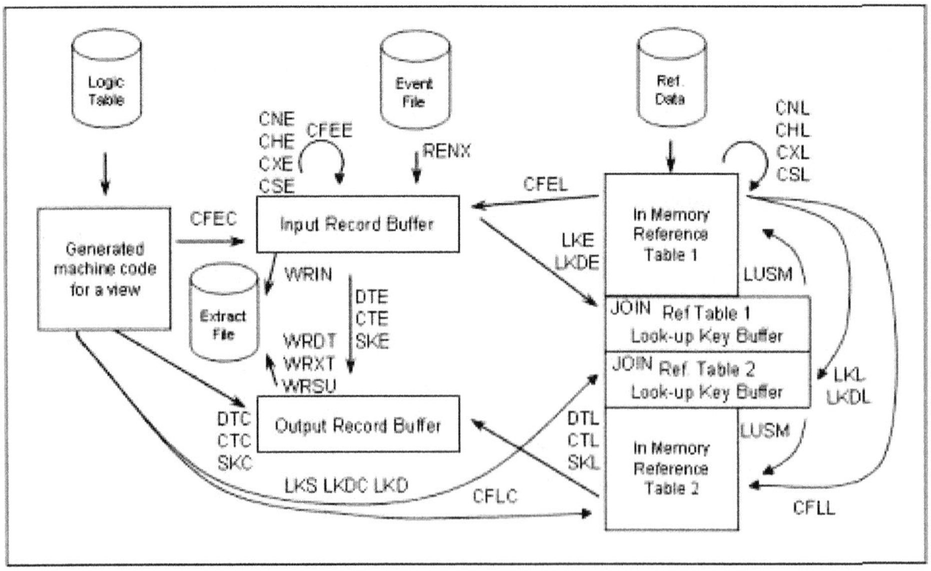

Figure 112. Format Phase Logic Table Functions

124. Additional class tests are also shown. CNE is Class Test Numeric in event record, CHE is Class Test High-values (hex Fs) in event record, CXE is Class Test Null (hex zeros) in event record, and CSE is Class Test Spaces (hex 40)in event record.

Extract Phase

The following is the Extract Phase Logic Table Trace for view 3264 for the first event file record.

```
  EVENT      EVENT          VIEW       LOGIC        SEQ
  DDNAME     RECORD       NUMBER        ROW         NUM *****VALUE-1*******
  Display  Filter  View  Print  Options  Help

EVENT                1 V:    3264 LT:      55 NV
EVENT                1 V:    3264 LT:      56 JOIN
EVENT                1 V:    3264 LT:      59 CFLC  000 K & N jones      K & N jones
EVENT                1 V:    3264 LT:      60 JOIN
EVENT                1 V:    3264 LT:      63 SKL   001 K & N jones family
EVENT                1 V:    3264 LT:      64 GOTO
EVENT                1 V:    3264 LT:      66 JOIN
EVENT                1 V:    3264 LT:      69 SKL   002 checking account
EVENT                1 V:    3264 LT:      70 GOTO
EVENT                1 V:    3264 LT:      72 CTE   003 [hex value '000603970C']
EVENT                1 V:    3264 LT:      73 WRXT  001
```

Figure 113. Format Phase View Logic Table Trace

CT data in the extract file are stored in packed format in order to save CPU cycles converting the data into and out of other formats. z/OS, the mainframe operating system, performs numeric calculations most efficiently on data in packed formats. Since all CT data is used in a calculation of some kind, it is converted into packed format as soon as possible. To see the CT values in the trace, you must display the output in hex mode to read the packed numbers.

The following is the first extract record for this view shown in hex format:

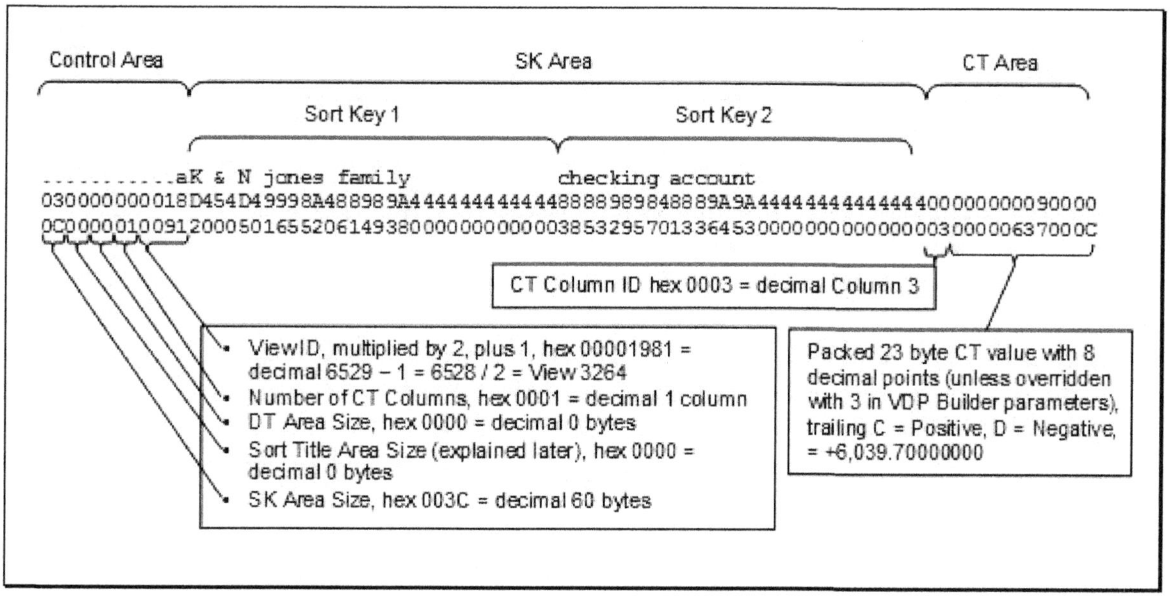

Figure 114. Sample Extract Record

The following is the GVBMR95 control report for all the views we have constructed so far, run in one pass.

```
MR95 - PARALLEL THREADS EXECUTED.............                              1
MR95 - VIEWS PER  FILE PROCESSED.............                              4
MR95 - TOTAL NUMBER OF LOGIC TABLE ROWS.......                            75
MR95 - SIZE   OF GENERATED LOGIC..............                         2,104
MR95 -        EVENT  FILE  RECORDS  READ.......EVENT                      18
MR95 - TOTAL EVENT RECORDS   READ....................                     18
MR95 - TOTAL PIPE  RECORDS   READ....................                      0
VIEW DEF:    3261/EVENT      F:            0 NF:           0         13(F0003261)
VIEW DEF:    3262/EVENT      F:            0 NF:           0         18(F0003262)
VIEW DEF:    3263/EVENT      F:           54 NF:           0         17(F0003263)
VIEW DEF:    3264/EVENT      F:            0 NF:           0         14(EXTR001 )
MR95 - TOTAL LOOKUPS PERFORMED.......................                     54
MR95 - TOTAL RECORDS WRITTEN TO FILE..........EXTR001                     15
MR95 - TOTAL RECORDS WRITTEN TO FILE..........F0003261                    13
MR95 - TOTAL RECORDS WRITTEN TO FILE..........F0003262                    18
MR95 - TOTAL RECORDS WRITTEN TO FILE..........F0003263                    17
MR95 - TOTAL EXTRACT RECORDS WRITTEN.................                     63
MR95 - TOTAL PIPE     RECORDS WRITTEN.................                     0
MR95 - EXTRACTION  ELAPSED TIME (IN SECONDS)..........                     0
```

Figure 115. Extract Record Example GVBMR95 Control Report

View 3264 extracted 13 of the 18 event records read. But any view sent to the Format phase also receives a Header Record for each thread (each input file) processed, with control information about that view. Thus the total record count of 14 records, written to EXTR001 DD Name includes one header record from reading a single input file.

Only one view wrote to EXTR001. But each extract file also receives a Control Record which has a count of all the records written to the extract file. This record is the last record written to the extract file. Thus the total records written to the extract file is 15.[125]

At the conclusion of the Extract Phase, the following extract records are contained in the file, plus the header and control records.

125. Also, note that view 3264 performed no lookups, although the logic table contained Join functions. This is because these same joins were performed in view 3263, and thus did not need to be repeated for view 3264, in this case saving the CPU time for 18 joins. This is join optimization at work.

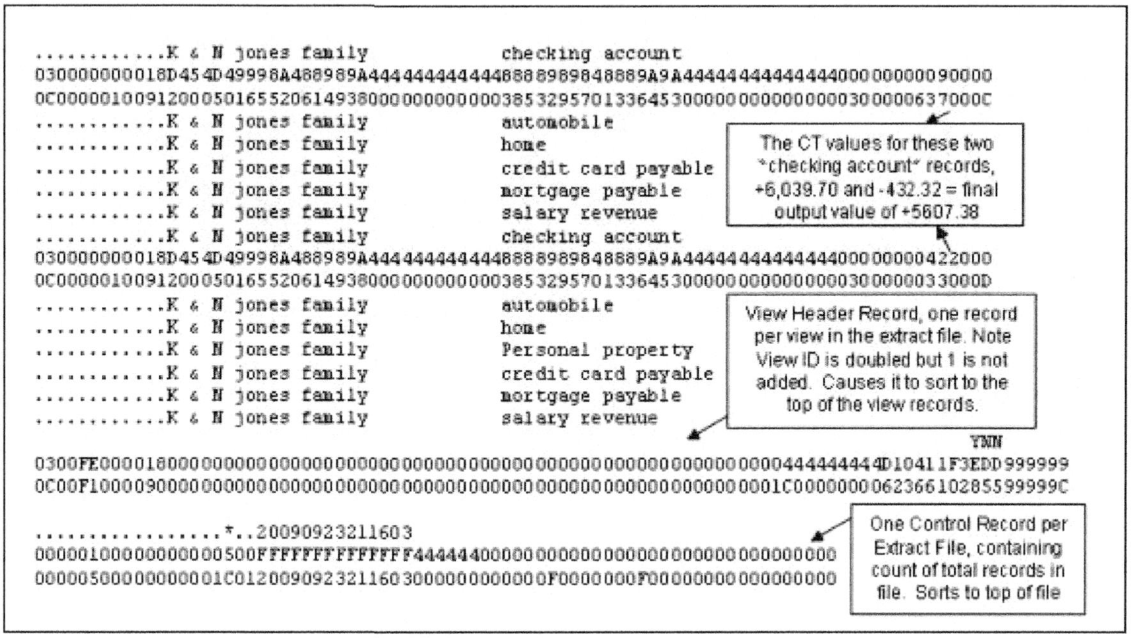

Figure 116. Sample Extract File

Note that these extracted records are in random order. All are for K & N jones family, because our view only selected those records. But the account name, the second sort key is not in alphabetical order, and the rows with the same sort keys have not been collapsed, as shown in what will be the output from the format phase below.

```
K & N jones family  automobile             42,270.00
K & N jones family  checking account        5,607.38
K & N jones family  credit card payable       800.00
K & N jones family  home                  185,001.00
K & N jones family  mortgage payable          876.25
K & N jones family  salary revenue            543.00
K & N jones family  Personal property      15,245.00
```

Figure 117. Sample Format Phase Output

And that brings us to the next step in the process, the need to sort the extract file.

Chapter 44. Sort

We performed a benchmark for an airline, and in that process Jay (I suspect) outlined a way of reducing the amount of data in the extract files that turned into a feature called extract phase summarization. We'll discuss that below. But before that feature was available, I remember many hours of babysitting SAFR processes only to see the sort portion of the process fail.

Remember in Chapter 19, "Select, Sort, Summarize," on page 89, we reviewed the challenges of sorting data. Sorting data can be the longest process in general business computing, particularly in reporting. High volume sort processes can challenge and even exceed two of the three parts of our compute environment, memory and disk for even the largest compute environments. Memory is challenged because that is where all the work takes place. Disk is challenged because the file must be at a minimum copied, in most cases nearly tripled, before the process is through. Only CPU capacity is typically not challenged in sort processes.

Sorting data is the one part of the SAFR batch process that uses other companies' software products. Sort utilities have existed for years on mainframes, and are highly tuned through years of development and testing. But because it is such an important part of the reporting process, it is important to understand some basics about sorting large files.

Sort and Merge Basics

Before describing sorting large files, let's first understand what a merge process looks like. Sort utilities can merge multiple files that are already in sorted order. Merging requires reading the first record from each of the files, comparing those records to determine which record to write out next to the output file. Only one record from each file needs to be in memory at any point in time.

Back to sort. Like any other program, sorting utilities only work with data in memory. That doesn't mean that files which can't fit into memory can't be sorted. If the data is too large to fit into memory, sort utilities bring as much data into memory as they can, sort those records, and then store that set of records onto disk in temporary files. They then bring in another section of the file, and do the same thing. After the utility has read and sorted into a temporary file the last record in the file (which might end up needing to be the first record written to the output file), it then performs a merge process. It opens each of the temporary files, reads the first record from each, and writes the first record to the output file.

Note here, though, that a record was read from disk (1st IO), sorted into a temporary file and written to disk (2nd IO), read from disk (3rd IO) and finally written to the output file (4th IO). For this one reason, sorting large files can be very, very, very slow.

Business Event Based Sorts

The need for extreme care is even more acute when attempting to implement a business event based reporting architecture. Consider why by examining the views we have built and run thus far. Suppose all of the views we have constructed were Format Phase views, they all had no general selection criteria, so every event record read is written to the extract file[126], and they all wrote to EXTR001. If that were the case, then the GVBMR95 control report would look like this.

126. They may have different sort criteria, columns, calculations, etc., thus all the outputs may be different, but the total record count would not change.

```
MR95 - PARALLEL THREADS EXECUTED.............                          1
MR95 - VIEWS PER  FILE PROCESSED.............                          4
MR95 - TOTAL NUMBER OF LOGIC TABLE ROWS.......                        75
MR95 - SIZE  OF GENERATED LOGIC..............                      2,104
MR95 -        EVENT  FILE  RECORDS  READ.......EVENT                  18
MR95 - TOTAL EVENT RECORDS   READ.....................                18
MR95 - TOTAL PIPE  RECORDS   READ.....................                 0
VIEW DEF:     3261/EVENT       F:            0 NF:        0           19(EXTR001 )
VIEW DEF:     3262/EVENT       F:            0 NF:        0           19(EXTR001 )
VIEW DEF:     3263/EVENT       F:           54 NF:        0           19(EXTR001 )
VIEW DEF:     3264/EVENT       F:            0 NF:        0           19(EXTR001 )
MR95 - TOTAL LOOKUPS PERFORMED........................                54
MR95 - TOTAL RECORDS WRITTEN TO FILE.........EXTR001                  77
MR95 - TOTAL EXTRACT RECORDS WRITTEN..................                77
MR95 - TOTAL PIPE     RECORDS WRITTEN.................                 0
MR95 - EXTRACTION  ELAPSED TIME (IN SECONDS)..........                 0
```

Figure 118. Multiple View Impact on Sort Phase GVBMF95 Control Report

Note that from reading an event file with only 18 records in it, we have created the need to sort 77 records (18 x 4 views, + 4 header records, + 1 control record). It becomes clear how reports which perform a significant summarization of business events can have performance issues.

Extract File Sorts

Think for a moment about the order of the records in the extract file if we had executed the above set of views. GVBMR95 Logic Table Trace would show event file record 1 being read by view 3261, and written to the extract file. Then that same record would be processed by view 3262 and written to the extract file. Then on to the next view, and the next view. At the end of the processes, each event file record would be written four times into the extract file. Except for putting the sort keys on the front of each extract record, extracting the data does nothing to put them into the right order[127].

When GVBMR88 runs, it needs all the records for view 3261 to be next to each other, in sorted order by the sort key so it can perform sub-totaling and calculations. Because SAFR shares the extract files, to reduce operational complexity by having every view written to a separate file, SAFR precedes the Sort Key Data with the View ID, as the last field of the control area. The Extract Program creates the sort control cards--the commands to the sort utility--for each extract file. The start position always starts with the view ID in the control area, but the length of the data to be sorted is the longest SK area for any view writing to that extract file.

The control record and header records are constructed in such a way that they sort to the top of either the file or the view respectively. In this way, sort places the control record, then header for view 3261 then all the extract records for view 3261 in order by their sort criteria at the top of the file, followed by the header record for 3262, etc.

Typically, one has to instruct the sort utility about specific fields by position and length that are needed to be sorted in descending order. But because all the data is in one file, sorting data in descending order requires a bit of a trick. The Extract program converts the data into a form called "two's complement" which is similar to creating a reverse image of the data. The data can then be sort ascending, and the Format program then converts it back into the original form, thus creating a descending order to it. We'll show an example below.

Extract Phase Summarization

Jay recognized in the airline benchmark that we had to create a single record which summarized the entire file to be used in another pass of the data as a reference file key. Perhaps the problem was one

127. This need not be the case, if each view's outputs are assigned to a unique extract file. Thus the extract program by segregating the data has furthered the sort process.

where we had to calculate the percentage of total for the individual rows. He asked Doug to create a special process at the end of the Extract engine that, instead of writing the record to the extract file, kept the record in memory until the next extract record came along. When the process saw the next extract record, it would compare the sort keys; if they were different, then the first record was written to the extract file; if they were the same, the process would accumulate all CT columns immediately, and no record was written to the extract file.

The impact of this process was that a very large file with one value on all records for collapse was reduced to a single row containing the total of all the records in the file at the end of the extract process. Instead of having to replicate every record into the extract file, sort them, and then reduce the answer to one row, SAFR arrived at the answer at the end of the extract phase.

This is great, but what if the event records had multiple values that needed to be collapsed? One approach considered was sorting the event file before execution of the Extract. But requiring the input event file to be in a sorted order reduced the application of this technique to a broader set of views. The idea behind the event based architecture was the ability to produce many views of the business events with access to all the business event attributes. Having the event file in sorted order was the same as requiring definition of indexes on the file, which reduced the type of access that could be gained. If the records came in completely random order, the extract file may end up with just as many records with no extract phase summarization.

Doug realized this, and could see that with a small change, the technique could be broadened to apply to many more views. What was needed was to keep a stack of output rows, a thousand or so for each view, rather than just one row, and keep those rows which had the most activity against them in memory, allowing the least used rows to drop into the extract file. Thus as an extract record was ready to be written to the extract file, a simple index of the view's sort keys pointing to the proper record would allow collapsing that record. Let's use an example to show how this works.

Extract Phase Summarization Example

I have created view 3265. This view reduces our 18 journal entries by the family name into two categories, working capital and other. I have used the following logic text to convert the accounts into constants that are then used in collapsing the data as the second sort key.

```
If {ACCOUNT} = 111 Or {ACCOUNT} = 211 Then
 COLUMN = "Working Capital"
Else
 COLUMN = "Other"
EndIf
```

The view generated the following logic table.

```
VIEW ID: 00003265      FILE ID: 00001284
-----------------------------------------------------------------------------------------------
LOGIC  GOTO  GOTO FUNC SEQ     LR  FIELD        SOURCE            TARGET      OTHER DATA
  ROW  ROW1  ROW2 CODE NUM     ID     ID  POS  LEN FM CN D   LEN FM CN D CMP LEN1 VALUE1
-----------------------------------------------------------------------------------------------

   74             NV          1264
   75    78    80 JOIN  1   1263  2890    1        1                     001 0001 1
   76    77    80 LKE   1   1264 63311    1    9   3         9  3        001 0000
   77    78    80 LUSM
   78             SKL   1   1263 63316    1   30   1        30  1        001 0000
   79    81       GOTO
   80             SKC   1   1264          1   30   1                     001 0030
   81    83    82 CFEC  2   1264 63313   15    3   3                     001 0003 111
   82    83    85 CFEC  2   1264 63313   15    3   3                     001 0003 211
   83             SKC   2                31   30   1                     001 0015 Working Ca
   84    86       GOTO
   85             SKC   2                31   30   1                     001 0005  Other
   86             CTE   3   1264 63314   18    8   3                     001 0000
   87             WRSU  1
```

Figure 119. Extract Phase Summarization Logic Table

Note that his logic table contains a WRSU function, a write summarized extract record. When turning this feature on, knowing the event data as I did, I told SAFR to make a stack of four extract records; I knew there would be no more than four records in the final output, so no memory would be wasted, but the sorted file would be as small as possible.

The following is the Logic Table trace for records 1 and 2. Note that the comparison on record two failed the "IF" selection criteria above, so the "else" condition was executed. After these two rows, there were two records in the stack, both for the "K & N jones" family, one "Working Capital" and one "Other".

```
 EVENT     EVENT        VIEW      LOGIC       SEQ
 DDNAME    RECORD       NUMBER    ROW         NUM *****VALUE-1*******
EVENT            1 V:    3265 LT:       74 NV
EVENT            1 V:    3265 LT:       75 JOIN
EVENT            1 V:    3265 LT:       78 SKL   001 K & N jones family
EVENT            1 V:    3265 LT:       79 GOTO
EVENT            1 V:    3265 LT:       81 CFEC  002 111                                111
EVENT            1 V:    3265 LT:       83 SKC   002 Working Capital
EVENT            1 V:    3265 LT:       84 GOTO
EVENT            1 V:    3265 LT:       86 CTE   003
EVENT            1 V:    3265 LT:       87 WRSU  001 00000088

EVENT            2 V:    3265 LT:       74 NV
EVENT            2 V:    3265 LT:       75 JOIN
EVENT            2 V:    3265 LT:       78 SKL   001 K & N jones family
EVENT            2 V:    3265 LT:       79 GOTO
EVENT            2 V:    3265 LT:       81 CFEC  002 121                                111
EVENT            2 V:    3265 LT:       82 CFEC  002 121                                211
EVENT            2 V:    3265 LT:       85 SKC   002 Other
EVENT            2 V:    3265 LT:       86 CTE   003 00007994
EVENT            2 V:    3265 LT:       87 WRSU  001
```

Figure 120. Extract Phase Summarization Logic Table Trace

The following is the extract file.

```
............c wheeler                        .*Ï:Ä××××××××××××××××××××××××
030000000001884A888989444444444444444444444425776BBBBBBBBBBBBBBBBBBBBBBBBBB00000004890000
0C0000010093306855359000000000000000000000009C7A6FFFFFFFFFFFFFFFFFFFFFFFFFF030000048 0000C
 --------------------------------------------------------------------------------
............c wheeler                        .ÑÄ_Î¦Î×.=ÇÎ*=¼××××××××××××××
030000000001884A888989444444444444444444444416667678376757 6BBBBBBBBBBBBBBB000000000030000
0C000001009330685535900000000000000000000000996D6A8FCE86CECFFFFFFFFFFFFFFF030000009 0000C
 --------------------------------------------------------------------------------
............K & N jones family               .*Ï:Ä××××××××××××××××××××××××
0300000000018D454D49998A488989A44444444444425776BBBBBBBBBBBBBBBBBBBBBBBBBB000000000480000
0C0000010093200050165520614938000000000000009C7A6FFFFFFFFFFFFFFFFFFFFFFFFFF0300000860000C
 --------------------------------------------------------------------------------
............K & N jones family               .ÑÄ_Î¦Î×.=ÇÎ*=¼××××××××××××××
0300000000018D454D49998A488989A4444444444441666767B3767576BBBBBBBBBBBBBBB000000002150000
0C00000100932000501655206149380000000000000996D6A8FCE86CECFFFFFFFFFFFFFFF0300000990000C
```

Figure 121. Extract Phase Summarization Extract File

I have made the second sort key, the "Working Capital" and "Other" values, descending. The extract program has therefore translated these values into two's complement; thus the values are not readable in the extract file. But it is clear there are only four records in the extract file, and there are two sets of the same unreadable characters, "other" and "working capital". The numbers in the CT area for column 3 (the two byte binary value on the front of the CT column) match the final output after sorting and running the Format phase (remember they have 8 decimals places). Note that the records aren't yet in sorted order; they appear in the extract file in the order they first appeared in the event file.

Here is the final output from the Format phase.

```
c wheeler           Working Capital           93
c wheeler           Other                 44,889
K & N jones family  Working Capital       29,195
K & N jones family  Other                  8,468
```

Figure 122. Extract Phase Summarization Output

Now, if I changed the stack count so that the extract program only keeps 3 records, I know that the stack will overflow; there won't be enough records in the stack to summarize all the event records. Here is the extract file having done so (and making the sort key ascending so it is now readable).

```
............c wheeler                        Working Capital
030000000001884A888989444444444444444444444E9998984C898A89444444444444444000000000010000
0C000001009330685535900000000000000000000006692957031793130000000000000000030000090000C
 --------------------------------------------------------------------------------
............K & N jones family               Working Capital
0300000000018D454D49998A488989A444444444444E9998984C898A89444444444444444000000002150000
0C00000100932000501655206149380000000000006692957031793130000000000000000030000990000C
 --------------------------------------------------------------------------------
............c wheeler                        Other
030000000001884A888989444444444444444444444DA889444444444444444444444444444000000004890000
0C00000100933068553590000000000000000000000638590000000000000000000000000030000480000C
 --------------------------------------------------------------------------------
............c wheeler                        Working Capital
030000000001884A888989444444444444444444444E9998984C898A89444444444444444000000000020000
0C0000010093306855359000000000000000000000669295703179313000000000000000003000000000C
 --------------------------------------------------------------------------------
............K & N jones family               Other
0300000000018D454D49998A488989A444444444444DA889444444444444444444444444444000000000480000
0C00000100932000501655206149380000000000006385900000000000000000000000000030000860000C
 --------------------------------------------------------------------------------
```

Figure 123. Extract Phase Summarization with Smaller Stack

See that there are two "c wheeler/Working Capital" rows in the file that will be collapsed by the Format engine. The first record was the least used set of keys, and so when the fourth record showed up, this one was dumped to the extract file. Later on, another record with this key showed up again, and so the next lowest record, likely the "K & N jones family/Working Capital" record was dumped to the file, leaving the last three records in the stack until the end of the event file was reached and they were written to the extract file as well.

In this way the memory used for the stack can be efficiently used; we don't need to know exactly what results we will get at the end of summarization, but we can still gain the benefits in reducing the sort file size. Typically, a few thousand records are kept in the stack by default for each view which uses extract phase summarization. If per chance, one knows that the extract file will not significantly be reduced (it has a lot of sort keys or very large number of possible values per sort key), then it is best not to use extract phase summarization. The cost of the CPU cycles to test to see if things can be summarized may be less efficient than simply allowing sort to do its job.

It is difficult to overstate the importance of the extract phase summarization innovation, and I don't think anyone saw how far reaching it was when created. Overnight, the long running sort jobs went away because the extract files were now measured in hundreds and thousands of rows, not millions. Beyond that, it highlighted exactly the right place to perform the function of collapsing records.

The act of summarization is the act of building an index, and extract phase summarization builds an index based upon the intersection of the event data and the view definition at exactly the right point in the process. As we noted in Chapter 14, "Reporting," on page 67, reporting by and large is the act of accumulating business events to an understandable level, and that level almost always has a high degree of summarization with it. Thus millions and billions of business events are reduced down to thousand, or hundreds, or sometimes even tens and single digit numbers of rows. The computer has sufficient memory to maintain hundreds of these small summaries while passing through the event file.

Chapter 45. Sort User Exits

While in Sacramento I started working on the mainframe before I had been on the Internet, and before I had my own e-mail account. I vaguely remember one day when Randall showed that it was possible to send a message to another user on the mainframe with the TSO "Send" command. You could only type 115 characters, and the message was only displayed on the screen when the message recipient hit enter. We used this simple way of communicating when working on projects from hotel rooms. We had to dial into the network on the hotel phone, and cell phones were very uncommon.

I mention this because I remember thinking when I saw instant and text messaging and twittering that they really aren't any different than the TSO send command. There really are very, very few innovations in computing, because the machines do basically the same things today that they did when they were invented. I have often said, "There are no new verbs in COBOL."

A similar concept is the idea of an application programming interface or API. An API is the ability to call an external program to do functions. On the mainframe, applications had defined points when they could call "user exits". An exit would be a program written to do a function which an application, like sort, could not do itself.

Sort has a number of possible points when it can be instructed to call a custom program, but for our purposes we will focus on only two: feeding data to sort, and reading data from sort. We'll deal with the second of these first.

Write Exits

During the period when we had huge extract files, before extract phase summarization, SAFR would typically perform significant IO to:

1. Read the event file and
2. Write the extract file in the Extract Phase,
3. Read the unsorted extract file and
4. Write the sorted extract file in the Sort phase, and then
5. Read the sorted extract file to produce the summary report in the Format phase.

Doug recognized that using the sort user exit concept we could eliminate an entire write and read of these files by having the format program, GVBMR88, called by sort as a user exit. In this way, as the sort utility prepared to write the data to the output file, it would call and pass this record to GVBMR88. GVBMR88 would then process this record as if it had read it from disk. When GVBMR88 completed, it would instruct the sort utility to delete the record rather than write it. The Sort utility didn't need to know that the record had already been used for its intended purpose; it would simply continue on to the next record. In this way IO steps 4 and 5 of the process were completely eliminated.

This became the standard configuration for running GVBMR88, even after the advent of extract phase summarization, even though the extract files now tend to be significantly smaller. GVBMR88 is run as a "write exit" to Sort, since it is called by sort just before it writes a record to disk.

Read Exits

The other applicable exit is a read exit, which effectively passes data to the sort utility to sort. In early 2000, I think it was, at about the same time Doug and I were trying to finish the logic table optimizer, we did an experiment one evening. We wanted to see if we could eliminate the 2nd and 3rd types of IO.

I had learned about the sort parameters to control the amount of memory it tried to use, the names for its sort work or temporary files, and to allow it to be run in parallel with other instances of sort running at the same time in the same task. Doug then created a process to call sort in the midst of extract processing instead of writing the records to the extract file. Sort would then be keeping all these records in memory if it could, (and if not writing them to temporary files on disk), until GVBMR95 said it was done handing its records. Sort would sort the records and then call GVBMR88 when it wanted to start writing records to disk.

To our surprise, after a couple of hours we made the process work. Without writing any data to disk, we went from the event data to the final output. I don't remember if we tried calling sort from multiple views (for example, view 3264 and 3265), which would have required having multiple copies of sort and GVBMR88 running simultaneously under GVBMR95 (one sorting the records for view 3264, independently from the other sorting the records for 3265). I suspect we didn't get that far, but we thought it was possible to do but likely would have required changes to the way GVBMR88 performed its file allocations.[128]

In the end, because of extract phase summarization, this feature didn't become a standard configuration and has never been used in a production SAFR process. The extract files became small enough that the time to write and read them between GVBMR95 and Sort became trivial. On the other hand, the added complexity of making multiple sort processes run in parallel, with multiple GVBMR88 executions as well, in a chain of programs calling each other as exits, and contending for memory and file names, and everything else, provided little benefit. The simplicity of the process made the cost of the IO worth while. If needed for a particular instance, a SAFR Extract phase write exit, described in a later chapter, could be written to call sort (which is actually how Doug accomplished the work that night in the first place).

Sort Permutations

SAFR has the ability to generate summary files from event files. We've noted over the years that many of the views have the same selection criteria, because the outputs are simply different cuts or dimensions in data warehousing terms, of the same event data. We also found that many of these cuts of data are in a similar "family" in a sense; they are permutations of the same set of keys. For example, some need access to a financial summary by the account number (123) while others would prefer to access the data by the account title (home).

This grouping of data has generated a class of tools that create "cubes", groups of these cuts of data all stored and grouped together. We'll deal more with this concept in the next chapter on SAFR cubes. At this point though, I should explain about a special sort read exit call GVBSR01 written by Jerry Canterbury in 2003 as part of a project that created a reporting dashboard for IBM. The goal was not only efficiency, but also maintenance. Using this feature, the development team had to develop many fewer views. The additional cuts of data provided by other views were generated in the batch process. Efficiency came by eliminating the 2nd and 3rd IO types above for these sets of views.

First, parameters which are input to the Logic Table process tell that program to generate a number of additional views, similar to the process it undertakes when it creates the JLT for the reference file phase. The parameters point to a view that has all the sort keys of interest. It then tells the program to create copies of that view, but with only specified sort keys, and in particular order. The Logic Table program puts these additional views in the VDP, but not in the logic table. Thus only the data needed for the first view is extracted from the event file by the Extract program.

The next step in the process was to invoke GVBSR02 (Sort-exit/Read program number 2) as a read exit to sort. Sort actually read the file, but before doing anything, it would give the record to GVBSR02. GVBSR02 would look at the VDP and detect which views needed generated extract records from the base

---

128. GVBMR88 used a fix set of DD Names to its outputs to different file types. Multiple instances of it would attempt to open the same files at the same time, which isn't allowed by the operating system. Parameters can be passed now to GVBMR88 which tell it which files names to use, so this configuration is now possible, although not tested.

view. It would then generate new records for these new views by simply changing the control area view ID to match the view in the VDP, and then giving the additional records to sort to include. It appears to sort, and to GVBMR88, as if these records were in the extract file, but the 2nd and 3rd IO types above are eliminated.

This process moves the potential explosion of event records needed for each view from MR95 back to sort input. GVBSR02 creates the additional records needed for each view, rather than GVBMR95. These records only exist in memory, and are never written to disk as sort passes them to GVBMR88 which produces the final output. Thus in one execution of SAFR entire cubes can be created very, very efficiently.

SAFR has multiple exit points as well, as discussed in Chapter 51, “Exits,” on page 267. But first let's actually talk about the Format program.

Chapter 46. Format Phase

Remember in Chapter 43, "Extract Files," on page 221, we outlined that the Format Phase is a control break program which performs the "group by" or "sum" function. Our focus in this chapter is upon the functions that can be performed in this phase.

In early 2003, as part of developing Version 4 of SAFR, I volunteered to sit in front of the computer with Doug and to recreate each defect in the debugger to speed up Doug's time coding. Over the course of a couple of months we had closed out most of the significant defects we had in the extract engine, GVBMR95. However, there were a pile of defects for the Format engine, GVBMR88, that we hadn't seriously attacked. I remember telling Doug one night, "I don't think we have any other defects right now for GVBMR95 that we can productively work." Doug reluctantly responded, "OK, pull up GVBMR88 in the debugger, and let's get started." I could tell Doug loved MR95, and tolerated MR88.

Format Time Logic

Our focus on the extract thus far has focused on performing functions against business events, for the most part. As we noted in Chapter 27, "Find More Detailed Events," on page 131, the syntax of building logic text which is turned into logic table functions uses fields from the event file. Fields on the event file can be used for selected values and making keys for joins, etc. that are not passed into the extract file in any way, or included in the final output.

We can't ignore the need, though, to perform some of the same functions after summarization. These needs are much less frequent, but they exist nonetheless. For example, certain reports would be extremely long if all the zero values were shown in the report. Many accounts may not have any activity against them, or after all the activity is summarized, it nets to zero. Extract time logic can be used to eliminate *event records* with zero balances, but excluding *zero balances* that are the result of netting has to ultimately be performed after summarization is complete.

The format phase logic uses columns in the workbench, not field names. This is because data going into the format phase no longer matches an LR. For example, the extract program may have "created" a new field by inserting a constant in a column, similar to what was done with words "Working Capital" or "Other" sort constants were used above. In this case, there is no "field" to use in the logic text during the format phase. As another example[129], the input to the format phase may not come from just one event file.[130] Views can combine data from multiple event files into the same extract file. Thus GVBMR88 is limited to working with data in the extract file, no matter where that data came from.

To repeat, GVBMR88 has a number of the same functions as GVBMR95. The difference is, the logic text executed in GVBMR88 specifies columns, view columns, and it only operates against numeric fields. In other words, the 'Event File' for GVBMR88 is the extract file, and its 'fields' are the columns of data in the extract record.

Although both selection and calculations can be performed in GVBMR95 or GVBMR88, originally calculations were only available at Format time in GVBMR88, and selection was only available in GVBMR95. Even now, more functionality for each of those functions is available in the original respective engine.

The format time logic text for GVBMR88 record selection looks like the following:

```
SELECTIF (COL.4>200 and COL.5 > 200.00)
```

129. As discussed in Chapter 27, "Find More Detailed Events," on page 131.

130. It may be profitable to review Figure 59 on page 134 - Extract and Format Phase Differences.

This will only select summarized rows where column 4 (record count) and column 5 (amount) are greater than 200.

As another example the following performs a calculation.

```
If COL.5 > 200 Then
 COLUMN = COL.5 /100
EndIf
```

It tests column 5 (amount) and if it is greater than 200, it makes the column equal to the value in column 5 / 100.

All format time logic text causes the numbers involved to be CT columns in the extract record. This is because CT format, packed with a standard number of decimal points, is the most efficient format for doing calculations, including summarization.[131]

Hardcopy Output

The SAFR Scan Engine is neither solely an ETL tool, nor truly a reporting tool, but it began life, with the Alaska implementation, as more of a reporting tool. The Format program, GVBMR88 began as a print formatting engine.

The following is a sample of a SAFR hardcopy report still produced by GVBMR88.

```
REPORT ID: GVBMR88                      SAFR DEMO                            PAGE NO:       1
VIEW   NO:     3436          Format Phase Hardcopy Example                  09/28/09 12:03

                                   RECORD COUNT          AMOUNT
                                  ---------------  ---------------
LEGAL_ENTITY 522349731 c wheeler
 COST_CENTRE CC218 CHARLES
  ACCOUNT 111 checking account                 91        58,655.43
  ACCOUNT 121 automobile                       76        15,567.00
  ACCOUNT 123 home                         44,803       387,000.00
  ACCOUNT 211 credit card payable               2         1,000.00
  ACCOUNT 411 salary revenue                   10             0.00
                                  ---------------  ---------------
 COST_CENTRE CC218 CHARLES                 44,982       462,222.43
LEGAL_ENTITY 522349731 c wheeler           44,982       462,222.43

LEGAL_ENTITY 522349999 K & N jones family
 COST_CENTRE CC110 DAD
  ACCOUNT 111 checking account                 88         6,039.70
  ACCOUNT 121 automobile                    7,994        23,985.00
  ACCOUNT 123 home                             10       185,000.00
  ACCOUNT 211 credit card payable          28,004           200.00
  ACCOUNT 222 mortgage payable                 87           309.25
  ACCOUNT 411 salary revenue                   41             0.00
                                  ---------------  ---------------
 COST_CENTRE CC110 DAD                     36,224       215,533.95

 COST_CENTRE CC111 MUM
  ACCOUNT 111 checking account                603          -432.32
  ACCOUNT 121 automobile                      172        16,285.00
  ACCOUNT 122 Personal property                70        15,245.00
  ACCOUNT 123 home                              1             1.00
  ACCOUNT 211 credit card payable             500           600.00
  ACCOUNT 222 mortgage payable                 32           567.00
  ACCOUNT 411 salary revenue                   61           543.00
                                  ---------------  ---------------
 COST_CENTRE CC111 MUM                      1,439        34,808.68
LEGAL_ENTITY 522349999 K & N jones fam.    37,663       250,342.63
GRAND TOTALS                               82,645       712,565.06
```

Figure 124. Sample Format Phase Hardcopy Output

131. Extract phase calculations result in another set of logic table functions, including ADD, SUB, MUL, and DIV, as well a DIM function to declare and initialize accumulators, and SET functions to move values to them.

Sort Titles

In recent years, there are few customers using this type of SAFR output. But it is instructive to investigate this format a bit, not only because the tool still produces these outputs, but also to understand the functions they performed. Such functions are done in different ways now, but the principles involved are the same.

One feature of this report is that the report is sorted by the code values for Legal Entity, Cost Centre and Account, but next to each of these code values is a description. The report is not sorted by these descriptions. These descriptions are called sort titles. In many reporting applications today code descriptions are embedded in or referenced by dimension attributes.

When creating SAFR Version 4, I argued that the process of creating these titles should be called aggregation phase look-ups or joins. I didn't win the day, but thinking of them that way may help understand how they are produced.

The following is the logic table for this view:

VIEW ID: 00003265 FILE ID: 00001284

LOGIC ROW	GOTO ROW1	GOTO ROW2	FUNC CODE	SEQ NUM	LR ID	FIELD ID	SOURCE POS	SOURCE LEN	SOURCE FM	SOURCE CN	SOURCE D	TARGET LEN	TARGET FM	TARGET CN	TARGET D	OTHER DATA CMP	OTHER DATA LEN1	OTHER DATA VALUE1
113			NV		1264													
114			SKE	1	1264	63311	1	9	3			9	5			001	0000	
115			LKLR	1	1263	2890	1		1							001	0004	
116			LKE	1	1264	63311	1	9	3			9	3			001	0000	
117			KSLK	1	1263	63310	10	30	1							001	0000	
118			SKE	2	1264	63312	10	5	1			5	1			001	0000	
119			LKLR	2	1262	2889	1		1							001	0004	
120			LKE	2	1264	63312	10	5	1			5	1			001	0000	
121			KSLK	2	1262	63308	6	30	1							001	0000	
122			SKE	3	1264	63313	15	3	3			3	5			001	0000	
123			LKLR	3	1258	2888	1		1							001	0004	
124			LKE	3	1264	63313	15	3	3			3	3			001	0000	
125			KSLK	3	1258	63304	4	30	1							001	0000	
126			CTE	4	1264	63314	18	8	3							001	0000	
127			CTE	5	1264	63315	26	5	4		2					001	0000	
128			WRXT	1														

Figure 125. Sort Title Keys Logic Table

This view has three sort keys, the SKE functions above. It also has two columns of data, the CTEs. We know the output is sent to the Format phase because of the write extract record, WRXT function at the bottom.

In the middle there are a number of build Look-up Keys from Event file, LKE functions, but these aren't preceded by JOINS. They are followed by KSLK, which stand for Key Save, Look-up Key.

At the end, the SK area of the extract record is a section of the record for Sort Title Keys. GVBMR95 performs all the functions to prepare the keys for doing the Look-up to Summary Structure, or LUSM function, but it doesn't do that last step in the lookup. The actual look-up is done in the Format phase, by GVBMR88.

The Reference Phase actually prepares two sets of files. It creates the RED and REH for Reference Extract Data and Header. It also prepares a similar set of data called the RTD and RTH, for Reference Title Data and Header. The RTD and RTH are used by GVBMR88 to do this last stage of look-up.

So GVBMR88 only does one step look-ups, the last step of the lookup. If a multiple step look-up is required to get the title, the beginning joins will all be performed by GVBMR95. Only when a LUSM function is about to be performed to get the actual sort title data will GVBMR95 be instructed to save the key it was about to use, for use in GVBMR88.

GVBMR88 performs the join after summarization. So this process can perform many less look-ups (less CPU time) if there is a high degree of summarization in the extract file.

Sort Keys

Also, while developing version 4, I suggested to Doug we should create an option to simply show the sort fields as columns of data because people seem to be more comfortable with this nowadays through familiarity with spreadsheets. The following output is what I had in mind, and which Doug agreed we could do.

```
1REPORT ID: GVBMR88                    GENEVA DEMO                          PAGE NO:        1
 VIEW   NO:     3444            Format Phase Sorts As Columns               09/28/09 12:03

LEGAL ENT   LE TITLE      COST CE  CC TITILE ACC  ACCOUNT TITLES        REC COUNT      AMOUNT
---------  ------------  -------  --------- ---  --------------------  ----------  -----------
522349731  c wheeler     CC218    CHARLES   111  checking account              91    58,655.43
522349731  c wheeler     CC218    CHARLES   121  automobile                    76    15,567.00
522349731  c wheeler     CC218    CHARLES   123  home                      44,803   387,000.00
522349731  c wheeler     CC218    CHARLES   211  credit card payable            2     1,000.00
522349731  c wheeler     CC218    CHARLES   411  salary revenue                10         0.00
---------  ------------  -------  --------  ---  --------------------  ----------  -----------
522349731                CC218                                             44,982   462,222.43
522349731                                                                  44,982    62,222.43

522349999  K & N jones   CC110    DAD       111  checking account              88     6,039.70
522349999  K & N jones   CC110    DAD       121  automobile                 7,994    23,985.00
522349999  K & N jones   CC110    DAD       123  home                          10   185,000.00
522349999  K & N jones   CC110    DAD       211  credit card payable       28,004       200.00
522349999  K & N jones   CC110    DAD       222  mortgage payable              87       309.25
522349999  K & N jones   CC110    DAD       411  salary revenue                41         0.00
---------  ------------  -------  --------  ---  --------------------  ----------  -----------
522349999                CC110                                             36,224   215,533.95

522349999  K & N jones   CC111    MUM       111  checking account             603      -432.32
522349999  K & N jones   CC111    MUM       121  automobile                   172    18,285.00
522349999  K & N jones   CC111    MUM       122  Personal property             70    15,245.00
522349999  K & N jones   CC111    MUM       123  home                           1         1.00
522349999  K & N jones   CC111    MUM       211  credit card payable          500       600.00
522349999  K & N jones   CC111    MUM       222  mortgage payable              32       567.00
522349999  K & N jones   CC111    MUM       411  salary revenue                61       543.00
---------  ------------ -------  --------  ---  --------------------  ----------  -----------
522349999                CC111                                              1,439    34,808.68
522349999                                                                  37,663   250,342.63
GRAND TOTALS                                                               82,645   712,565.06
```

Figure 126. Sample Hardcopy Output with Sort Fields as Columns

Although I was more successful in arguing this feature, Doug protested mildly saying that the indented format was much more elegant. It caused me to pause for a moment. I hadn't recognized the function the indenting did in the report until then. But the indenting was a form of indexing, indexing for human eyes to find the appropriate row on the report. One can scan the report quickly to find changes in Legal Entity, whereas in this second report one has to look for repeating lines or subtotals.

Note that what we typically experience in a spreadsheet is fundamentally different than what is shown in this report. Most spreadsheets do not have multiple levels of summarization within them. People like to copy formulas across a lot of rows, and placing the report above into a spreadsheet requires different formulas when sub-totaling the cost center or legal entity. Typically, the cost center summary would be on a separate tab, and not include the account column, and the legal entity summary would be on another spreadsheet tab as well, and not include cost center or account.[132]

132. This discussion ignores the fact that often additional sort breaks are needed for understanding balances at differing levels within the account, cost center or legal entity hierarchies. These would add additional tabs to the spreadsheet.

Each of these tabs could be produced as a separate view; they would only have the sort keys of interest for that tab. The problem is, the extract file that must be sorted to produce these three views would have more data in it than the data needed to produce this one report which has all the same information on it. Again we see the proliferation of outputs needed from one set of business events.[133]

Alternatively, a pivot table can be created from one spreadsheet with all the columns in it, and by including or excluding columns, the subtotals change. But very large spreadsheets can take a long time to update the pivot tables. Again, the balancing act is apparent between function and performance for reporting processes, whether on a large machine or a PC.

Subtotaling and Calculations

There are times when the level at which calculations are performed is important. In some cases, calculations must be performed on the detailed records. For example, it isn't possible to summarize the cost of different items and the number of items selected and then multiply the summarized numbers to produce a total cost. Math dictates performing multiplication first, before addition; summarization is a form of addition. Before the advent of extract phase calculations, a different set of codes was available in GVBMR88 to tell MR88 to do the calculations at the detailed level. These functions can be used, or extract phase calculations.

Additionally, in some cases, like in calculating percentages, the calculation must be re-performed at each level of the subtotal break. There is no value to calculate a percentage at the account level (for example record count / amount for a percentage of amount per record) and then add up these percentages for the cost center level. The division must be performed at each level of summarization. A different type of subtotal code is available for this function.

GVBMR88 also has the ability to add the value of the prior line to the current line, thus creating a running total on the report.

All these features are still available in GVBMR88, but used much less frequently than they were when it was much closer to an end user reporting tool. With the advent of spreadsheets and proliferation of database reporting tools, such functions tend to be performed there, after the hard work of summarization of business events is performed by SAFR.

File Format Output

These hardcopy and spreadsheet type outputs were the only outputs from GVBMR88 in the earliest days. It was likely Jay who suggested the format phase should also be able to simply produce sequential files, sometimes called flat files. These types of files have no index structure to them; they are basically a dump of data. Adding this feature moved SAFR from being purely a reporting tool to having more characteristics of an ETL tool. It could now put out data that can be used in subsequent processes. And often those subsequent processes ended up being additional SAFR passes of the data to do more complex functions.

Later, the ability was created to create the copy and extract only views we first discussed was created, reducing the number of Format time File Format Output views that are created. If summarization is needed though, they have to go through sort and GVBMR88.

With respect to summarization, there is a key distinction that should be remembered about file format output though. In the same way spreadsheets don't deal well with having different levels of summarization in one tab—account subtotals, cost center subtotals, and legal entity subtotals—most other tools that would act upon file output do not as well. Therefore it was decided that GVBMR88 would simply produce the lowest summarized level outputs. For example, from the report above, it would only

133. An alternative is to use the Sort Permutation process to create each of these tabs from this base report.

write out the Account level rows, not the Cost Center or Legal Entity subtotals. This means many of the sub-totaling codes aren't applicable for file format output.[134]

Executive Information File Structure

The last type of output to be created by GVBMR88 actually demanded a new program be written. These are the SAFR Executive Information files or cubes. And although produced by another program, they are part of the Format Phase as well.

We introduced the SAFR Executive Information File output or XIF in Chapter 29, "Iteratively View Results," on page 145. Each XIF file is like one cut of a reporting cube. It contains all the data for one hardcopy report in it; in other words, subtotals for multiple levels of sort breaks are contained in the file. The first records in the file contain information that allows a program to interpret the rest of the file, including the view title (record type 0), the sort/subtotal fields (record type 1), descriptions of each column (record type 2), and an index as to where in the file the different subtotal breaks start (record type 3). The following is a representation of the version 1 XIF file, modified in some ways to make it more readable.[135]

134. The way this decision was implemented in GVBMR88 means that file format output cannot be effectively used by the GVBSR02. GVBMR88 examines the entire sort key area in determining break points, rather than inspecting individual fields within that sort key. Thus all the outputs from GVBMR88 sort permutations for file format output look exactly alike.

135. The file structure has been modified for this book, including adding dashes between fields, removing some space and values for formatting. The version 2 format is null delimited in a slightly different structure. The general relationship between records is the same.

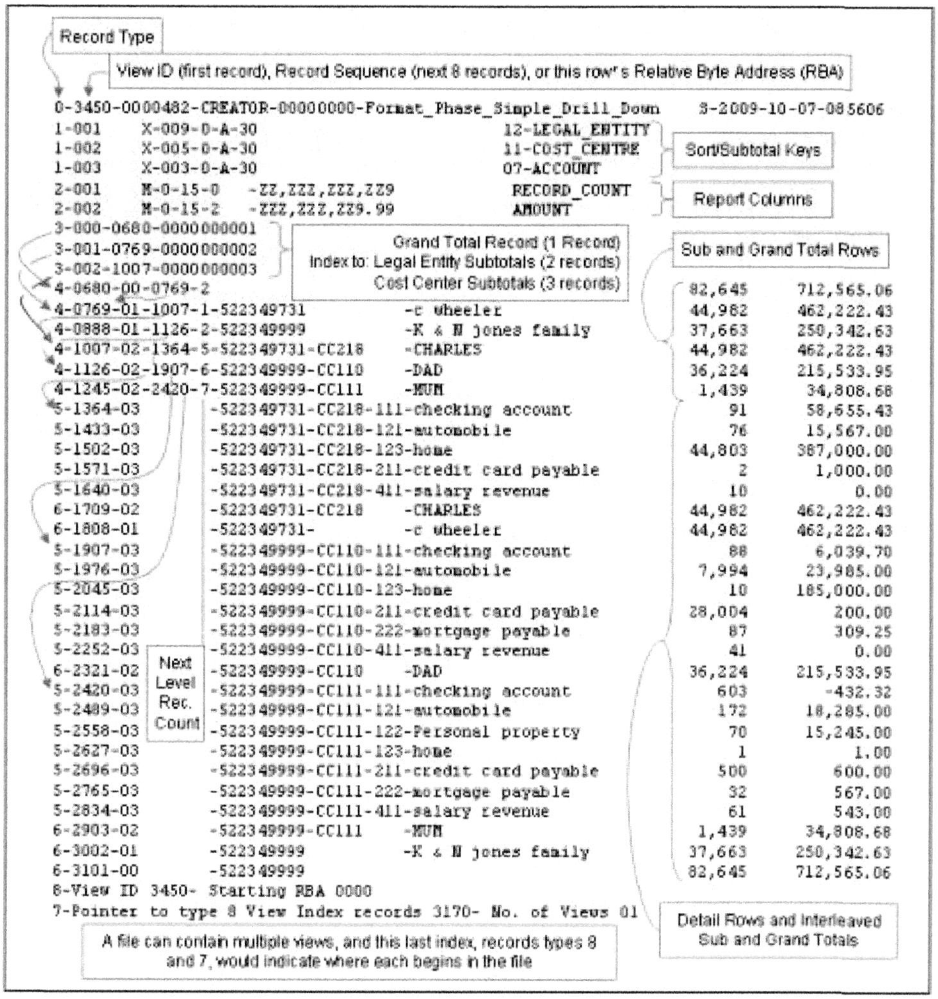

Figure 127. Sample Executive Information File (XIF) Layout

Although the file contains all the rows of the hardcopy report shown above, they are upside down order, in that the grand total record is at the top of the file. After the grand total are the other subtotals. The next section of the file contains the lowest level of detail in the file, the type 5 records. These have the same type 4 subtotal records interspersed within them. Thus a hardcopy report could be produced just by reading the type 5 and 6 records. The last records, the type 7 and 8 records, are used if a file contains more than one view's output. The type 7 record, always the last record in the file, says where the type 8 records start, and the type 8 records point to the various type 0 records for the views which might be contained in the file.

The file format allows a program to read the top part of the file, format the page layout for view title, sort fields and columns, and display the first grand total record. Then, when the user drills down on the grand total record, the RBA pointer and record count on type 4, 5, and 6 records tells the program to do a "seek" for an RBA, which moves the read-write head of the disk to the specific point where the next record exists, reads the number of records in the record counter, and display them to the user. This is incredibly efficient indexing method; exactly the right data is transferred into memory for display. Each of these new displayed records also has RBA pointers to allow for additional drill down to the next level.

GVBMR88 writes the different record types and levels to individual files. The type 0, 1, 2 and 3 records are written to the XIH, executive information Header file. The grand total record is written to the XIS00, summary level 00 file in our example. The Legal Entity subtotals are written to the XIS01, file, the Cost Center subtotals to the XIS02, and so on. The type 5, 6, 7 and 8 records are written to the XID, for detail, file.

After GVBMR88 runs, one additional major program, GVBMR49 runs. It simply assembles the XIF file from these different files, in order.

The Executive Information file replaced some of the earlier backend SAFR components, like CRP, Consolidated Report Production which accumulated the hardcopy reports, and reproduced sections of them and routed them to users. These relied on people to send printed papers to mail stops; we now rely upon computers and IP addresses to do the same.

The Executive Information File structure, and reporting tools that are built upon them, allow users to get to the data they need in a very efficient manner. The format is an open format; any tool can be used to create an XIF file for use by the SAFR Insight Viewer.

Chapter 47. "Look At It Go"

Although the logic table codes and some of the features above have changed, most of the above I learned during the years I lived in Sacramento. At the conclusion of that time, I had a thorough understanding of how to apply SAFR to problems. I had concluded the pharmaceutical data warehouse, the cookie manufacturer, the computer chip manufacture and a year of work at the insurance company. I had been on the testing, technical support, project, sales, and documentation teams, and was starting to prove that I could contribute to the architecture team.

Yet the constant travel, the demands of the computer chip manufacturing job even though it was in town, three small children at home, and questions about the real prospects of the tool becoming more widely known all combined to make me question if I was in the right job. After the chip manufacturing project was over, I returned to the insurance company. There, I had chances to work with Doug in the same location on a daily basis. I shared with him quite openly these questions on a two hour ride to the airport in March 1998.

The response I received from Doug that day was very consistent with the message I would receive over the next few years whenever I went to him for advice. Whenever I would ask something like, "What do you think I should do," I almost always received the answer, "It depends on what you want." I know I wasn't the only one who had this experience.

It wasn't that he left me feeling like I hadn't received good instruction at the end of the conversation. It was simply that he was very careful in steering in any one direction. In a sense, he often helped me uncover what I wanted by simply asking me questions and reacting to my responses. In this conversation, and another two months later, he perceived the fatigue and was sympathetic to the causes. He didn't have the answers for how to solve it, but expressed confidence that he knew I would find the right answers no matter what those answers ended up being. I always left feeling that his friendship wasn't dependent in any way on what I chose to do.[136]

That summer I also had a chance to sit down with Rick for a couple of hours and talk, and I expressed the similar feelings to him. In a similar way, Rick was very understanding and supportive of whatever decision I wanted to make. I was very fortunate to have two mentors with such concern for me as a person; it allowed me to navigate some difficult personal waters over the next couple of years.

Looking back at what happened over the next few months, though, I have wondered if Doug, with Rick's support, wasn't a bit less passive in his response than I perceived at the time. As I have noted, SAFR at the time had a character based user interface which was completely functional, but not at all technologically hip in any way. I think Doug perceived that to keep interest of the younger team members and attract more customers, it was time to invest in the tool to change that. Two months later I found myself in Dallas for two days to work with Sherwood Daniels, a PricewaterhouseCoopers (PwC) consultant Doug had met on that project, to mock up a different kind of user interface.

A few weeks later I worked at home, and I decided to simply use Excel macros to mock up some of my own ideas. I did so over about two days. I shared them with Doug. I was a bit surprised at how positive his reaction was to it. I don't believe it was because he wanted me to feel good, but rather he thought they were very interesting and he was impressed how quickly something could be put together. I think

136. The two exceptions to his reluctance to steer directly are first, the story I have already told about day he told me life was tough for everyone, and second a few years later when at lunch I had been thinking I needed to get back to some of my school and auditing business skills rather than continue to dive so deep technically. The conversation wasn't longer than 10 minutes. I could tell he thought the idea of not doing technical things so boring he couldn't concentrate on the conversation; he wanted to get back to his computer. :-)

that experience might have been misleading about what the effort involved in building such a user interface would be. He told me years later that he had been warned by another consultant that it was a massive effort, and it turned out to take years to complete.

A few weeks later, he sent me out to Philadelphia to meet Troy Deck, owner of Wingspan Technologies. One of the team members in Dallas had suggested Troy to Doug as someone who was in the business of developing the kinds of user interface we were thinking of. I enjoyed the creativity.

This work went on to become part of a large investment bank SAFR project that created the UNIX version of SAFR, with the new user interface. Having put down this foundation, I concentrated on innovating with the scan engine.

In the fall of that year, I felt I had to finally make a decision about what way to go with my work. I was looking for some sort of external validation as to the approach to take when one morning I met with Lloyd Jackson, IT employee with a deep history with an insurance company with whom I had been working for months now. After the meeting Lloyd told me, "Kip, every project has its formal leadership, and its informal leadership. You need to be the project leader on this, and we will continue to make progress. We need your leadership to get this done." His words hit me right between the eyes. It felt like it was exactly what I should be doing.

My wife agreed to move again so I could eliminate the 8 hour one-way commute. This meant I could better balance the demands of the project with being with my family. For the next few years, I helped create SAFR processes which did what we thought were pretty incredible things. It stretched the machine and software in some pretty amazing ways.

A couple of months after Doug created the SAFR feature called piping, I remember we tested for the first time SAFR's ability to run a massive set of views simultaneously for the allocation process. The team had constructed programs to generate SAFR views. The way the rules were defined and the programs interpreted those rules resulted in 26 thousand views. I don't remember for sure, but I suspect the record for views run in a single execution of SAFR was in the hundreds, perhaps low thousands. I set up the JCL for the GVBMR95 execution while Doug stood behind me and watched. We ran the process. SAFR read the logic table and generated the machine code. It then attempted to execute the machine code, but we received an operating system error. Each view called a user exit multiple times to perform a special allocation function that SAFR didn't do natively. The operating system would only allow 32,767 instances of a single program in a single address space; somewhere in the operating system there was a binary half word containing a counter of the number of instances of the program and we had exceeded what that counter could hold. We were trying to create over 67,000 instances of the program.

To get around this, I took the user exit load module and copied it two other times, and gave each a unique name. I then went to the logic table and edited it, causing less than 30,000 calls to each one of the newly copied load modules. I kicked off the extract program again. It ran to completion. Because the event file only had 5,000 records in it, it took only a moment to complete. I remember Doug commenting, "I can't believe it worked." To think that the arrays, length of pointers, and other elements of the program had allowed that many views to be generated amazed him.

I looked at the GVBMR95 control report and noted that the logic table of 3 million rows had caused the program to generate 3 megabytes of machine code. I remember going to the insurance company production load module library, where all written programs over all the years for all mainframes in the company were compiled. The total library size of all those programs was less than 3 megabytes. We had generated a lot of machine code.[137]

137. GVBMR95 control report in author's possession.

On another occasion, I don't remember the specific set of views, but Doug and I were doing some performance tests. I was responsible for setting up the tests after the views had been created and Doug was perhaps finished with some feature, a SAFR exit, or in other cases just observing. I would adjust GVBMR95 parameters like the `READBUF` and `WRITEBUF` parameters which specify how much memory is allocated to reading and writing. Sometimes in doing these types of performance tests I would go so far as to make sure that the input files and output files were on separate disks and controllers so that we wouldn't get IO contention.[138]

I had set up the test, and for some reason Doug and I were back in our individual rooms at the hotels late in the evening when it was time to run it. That might have been because the machine utilization was very low so we wouldn't be impacted by other processes on it. Again, this was before cell phones and we might have been in different hotels so we had to dial into the system on the hotel phone line and talk to each other with 115 character messages using the TSO "send" command a little like using instance messaging. Doug could watch my job run at the same time I did. It showed us things like how much CPU time it was taking, how many IOs had been requested, etc. I remember the CPU utilization was shown as a set of asterisks in a row, each asterisk representing the processes was using 10% of the machine capacity or something. The machine was a fairly powerful machine for the time, with 8 or 10 processors in it.

I kicked off the job and went to watch it process. I suspect I sent Doug a message saying, "Job nnnn is now running." GVBMR95 starts pretty slowly as it loads the logic table, the VDP, and the reference files into memory and generates the machine code. I remember Doug once watching with me and telling me when it was generating the machine code because all the IO stops for a few seconds as it makes multiple passes through the logic table that was in memory. It then began parallel processing, where multiple event files are read in parallel all at the same time. Doing so means that multiple CPUs can be used as well.

Parallel processing was not a very common thing at the time. Typically non-parallel programs, like COBOL, might use 5 to 10% of the CPU at any one time. As the GVBMR95 kicked in, the percentage of the CPU started to climb, 30, 60, 80%. These weren't single spikes in processing, but sustained rates for a number of minutes. As it bounced between 80 and 90% and periodically spiked at nearly 100%, I got a message from Doug saying, "Look at it go!!!!!!!!!!!" For all of his experience, I am not sure Doug had ever seen a mainframe utilized like that by one process. GVBMR95 was nearly consuming an entire mainframe for perhaps 10 to 15 minutes.

---

138. In other words, ensuring that the input "binder" and output "binders" were different, and were written to and read by different people so there was no turning pages between reading and writing.

Figure 128. Southern Pacific Engine 4294

When I was living in Sacramento a couple of times during lunch I went over to the California State Railroad Museum near the office. The last exhibit is one of the largest steam engines ever built. It was a cab forward Southern Pacific engine 4294[139] built in the late 1800's. It was built to haul the trains over the incredibly steep Sierra Nevada mountains on the cross-continent journey. The cab forward design was created because it passed through very long wooden snow sheds, more like tunnels, built to keep the snow off the tracks. With the cab at the back of the engine, the smoke and ash from the boiler would fill the cab and nearly choke the engineers. The solution was to put the cab on the front of the engine, which must have given the engineers very dramatic views through the mountains.

It is a massive engine, and for its time was the height of complexity and power. As I sat and looked at it, I would think of those engineers, with their hands on the controls and the wind rushing through their hair as they controlled this combination of thousands of parts all working in harmony in rapid succession hour after hour after hour.

Through those years, at times I was privileged to be the engineer at the controls of this incredibly powerful data processing engine Doug had constructed. As I have contemplated that night and thought of the incredible harmony of billions of machine instructions like those engine parts, independent parallel processes utilizing an entire mainframe over a sustained period of time like the drive wheels of the engine, performing millions and billions of joins similar to pistons firing, and mile after mile of event data in front and extracted records in the rear, with a hint of virtual wind as they passed by, I am grateful to Doug, Rick, the team and my family for allowing me to experience it.

139. Photo by Carl Morrison. Used by permission.

Chapter 48. Multi-Threading

I have heard Rick advocate using all available means to solve it. He meant we should not rule any approach out. Certain computing problems require the same approach. High system performance means being able to apply all available computing resources. One of the most perishable computing resources is a CPU cycle. Unused CPU cycles perish with the passing of each nanosecond.

Almost all modern computers have multiple CPUs in them, including many PCs. Such computers are capable of parallel processing. To utilize a box with 10 CPUs at 90% requires that 9 of those processors all be used at the same time. Although I don't believe the terminology is precise and is somewhat platform and language dependent, for purposes of our discussion we'll say parallel processing can be either multi-process parallelism or multi-thread parallelism. SAFR used both approaches.

Multi-process Parallelism

The format engine, GVBMR88 and associated programs are executed in a parallel process mode; in other words multiple "meetings" are started and held in separate "rooms." In mainframe terms, we simply submit separate jobs; and they don't share memory in any way. The extract engine, GVBMR95 is a multi-threaded parallel processing engine. A thread might be thought of as one of our sub-meeting with its own agenda meeting in the same room as all the other sub-meetings but sharing the white board and binders. One particular "meeting agenda" is being worked by each CPU while the main or initially started program (what Doug calls the Mother Task) waits and watches. The following diagram shows both types of processes.

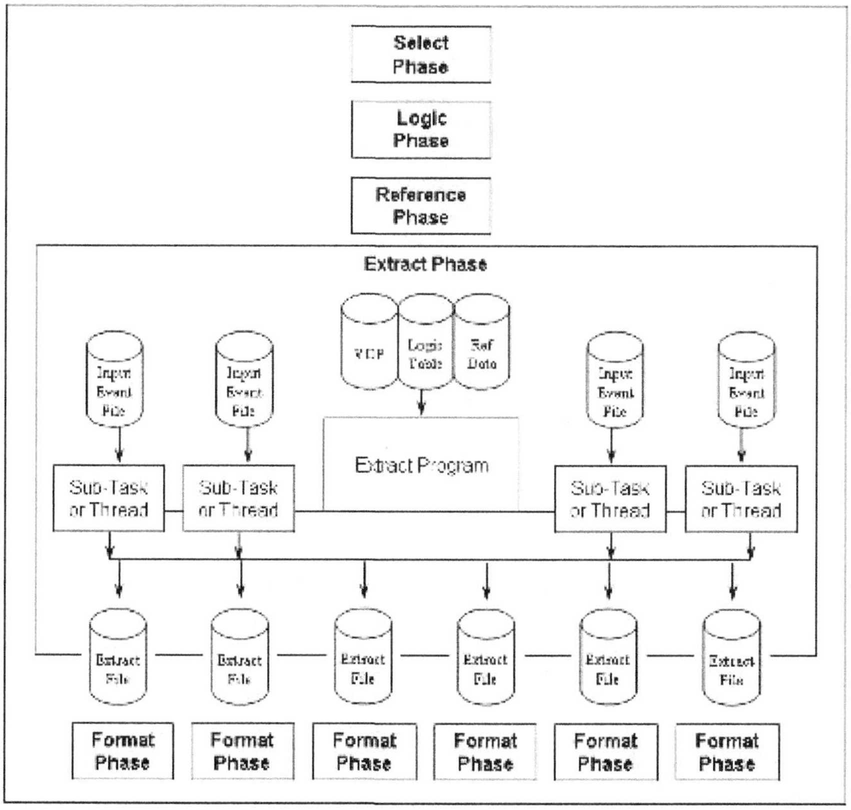

Figure 129. SAFR Parallelism

The first three steps of the Scan Engine are executed essentially once in serial mode. They produce three outputs, the VDP, Logic Table, and Core Image Reference Data files.

The extract engine takes in these three files. Thus far in describing GVBMR95, we have only executed a single SAFR thread. Thus the view processing has primarily demonstrated the ability to minimize IO; the data was read once to produce all the outputs. CPU use has also been minimized by generating efficient machine code, optimizing lookups.

We also executed only a single Format Phase job, which sorted the extract file containing all the data extracted for all the views which required the format phase. Each row was prefixed by the view ID, so when the sort was complete, all rows for that view were in sorted order together.

However, GVBMR95 can write output to multiple files. In the early days of the system, typically a standard set of extract files were established for a SAFR run and views were assigned to use an extract file in a round robin fashion by the select phase. Thus view 1, 7, 13 would be assigned to extract file one, and 2, 8, 14 to extract file two and so on. The format phase is now used much less frequently because of extract only views, etc., so Format Phase configuration tends to be much more customized.

We could cause each view to write to a different extract file, and multiple Format Phase processes could then be executed: If the views running in the extract phase shown on Figure 118 on page 228 were modified so each would write to its own extract file, then the control report would look like the following:

```
MR95 - PARALLEL THREADS EXECUTED.............                        1
MR95 - VIEWS PER  FILE PROCESSED.............                        4
MR95 - TOTAL NUMBER OF LOGIC TABLE ROWS.......                      75
MR95 - SIZE  OF GENERATED LOGIC..............                    2,104
MR95 -       EVENT  FILE  RECORDS  READ.......EVENT                 18
MR95 - TOTAL EVENT RECORDS   READ.....................              18
MR95 - TOTAL PIPE  RECORDS   READ.....................               0
VIEW DEF:    3261/EVENT       F:           0 NF:          0         19(EXTR001 )
VIEW DEF:    3262/EVENT       F:           0 NF:          0         19(EXTR002 )
VIEW DEF:    3263/EVENT       F:          54 NF:          0         19(EXTR003 )
VIEW DEF:    3264/EVENT       F:           0 NF:          0         19(EXTR004 )
MR95 - TOTAL LOOKUPS PERFORMED.......................               54
MR95 - TOTAL RECORDS WRITTEN TO FILE..........EXTR001               20
MR95 - TOTAL RECORDS WRITTEN TO FILE..........EXTR002               20
MR95 - TOTAL RECORDS WRITTEN TO FILE..........EXTR003               20
MR95 - TOTAL RECORDS WRITTEN TO FILE..........EXTR004               20
MR95 - TOTAL EXTRACT RECORDS WRITTEN..................              80
MR95 - TOTAL PIPE    RECORDS WRITTEN..................               0
MR95 - EXTRACTION  ELAPSED TIME (IN SECONDS)..........               0
```

Figure 130. Parallel Format Phase GVBMR95 Control Report

Note that the DD Name on the end of each view is different. After the extract phase, four format phases would be executed, one to process each extract file.

Multi-process parallelism is not very unusual. Similar to running many meetings simultaneously in separate conference rooms, it is used quite frequently with fairly unsophisticated tools to solve particular problems more quickly.

The down side with multi-process parallelism is that memory cannot be shared between processes. Data must go through the operating system or much more frequently written to disk, to be shared among processes. Thus even within SAFR, the core image reference data used in creating sort titles in GVBMR88 must be loaded into each Format Phase. Thus multi-process parallelism allows application of more CPU resources to a problem, but isn't the ultimate in efficiency.

Partitioned Event Files

Suppose we make one change to the last set of views we ran in our example, and we split the input journal entries into two files instead of one file. We place all the journal entries for one legal entity (family) in one file and the others in another file. Thus the data in both files has not changed, and if we concatenated the files together (in other words, told the operating system to present both files, one right after the other, to the program as if they were one file) the views would process without any other adjustments.

No change is required to the views to cause GVBMR95 to perform multi-threaded parallel processing. Views read Logical Record/Logical File combinations. The only change required is to define another Physical File under the existing Logical File in the SAFR metadata.

If this is done, GVBMR95 generates machine code for each file. After generating the machine code, GVBMR95, the mother task, instructs the operating system to execute these two programs and tell it when they have finished. The GVBMR95 control report for this execution is shown below.

```
MR95 - PARALLEL THREADS EXECUTED..............                    2
MR95 - VIEWS PER  FILE PROCESSED..............                   18
MR95 - TOTAL NUMBER OF LOGIC TABLE ROWS.......                  324
MR95 - SIZE  OF GENERATED LOGIC...............                8,320
MR95 - 64-BIT EXT SUM   MEGABYTES  USED.......                    2
MR95 -       EVENT  FILE  RECORDS  READ.......EVENT1              5
MR95 -       EVENT  FILE  RECORDS  READ.......EVENT2             13
MR95 - TOTAL EVENT RECORDS   READ.....................           18
MR95 - TOTAL PIPE  RECORDS   READ.....................            0
VIEW DEF:    3261/EVENT1    F:          0 NF:          0          0(F0003261)
VIEW DEF:    3262/EVENT1    F:          0 NF:          0          5(F0003262)
VIEW DEF:    3263/EVENT1    F:         15 NF:          0          5(F0003263)
VIEW DEF:    3264/EVENT1    F:          0 NF:          0          1(EXTR001)
VIEW DEF:    3265/EVENT1    F:          0 NF:          0          3(EXTR001)  IN:     5
VIEW DEF:    3434/EVENT1    F:          0 NF:          0          6(EXTR001)
VIEW DEF:    3436/EVENT1    F:          0 NF:          0          6(EXTR001)
VIEW DEF:    3437/EVENT1    F:          0 NF:          0          6(EXTR001)
VIEW DEF:    3450/EVENT1    F:          0 NF:          0          6(EXTR001)
VIEW DEF:    3261/EVENT2    F:          0 NF:          0         13(F0003261)
VIEW DEF:    3262/EVENT2    F:          0 NF:          0         13(F0003262)
VIEW DEF:    3263/EVENT2    F:         39 NF:          0         12(F0003263)
VIEW DEF:    3264/EVENT2    F:          0 NF:          0         14(EXTR001)
VIEW DEF:    3265/EVENT2    F:          0 NF:          0          3(EXTR001)  IN:    13
VIEW DEF:    3434/EVENT2    F:          0 NF:          0         14(EXTR001)
VIEW DEF:    3436/EVENT2    F:          0 NF:          0         14(EXTR001)
VIEW DEF:    3437/EVENT2    F:          0 NF:          0         14(EXTR001)
VIEW DEF:    3450/EVENT2    F:          0 NF:          0         14(EXTR001)
MR95 - TOTAL LOOKUPS PERFORMED........................           54
MR95 - TOTAL RECORDS WRITTEN TO FILE..........EXTR001           102
MR95 - TOTAL RECORDS WRITTEN TO FILE..........F0003261           13
MR95 - TOTAL RECORDS WRITTEN TO FILE..........F0003262           18
MR95 - TOTAL RECORDS WRITTEN TO FILE..........F0003263           17
MR95 - TOTAL EXTRACT RECORDS WRITTEN..................          150
MR95 - TOTAL PIPE    RECORDS WRITTEN..................            0
MR95 - EXTRACTION  ELAPSED TIME (IN SECONDS)..........            0
```

Figure 131. Parallel Processing GVBMR95 Control Report

The first line shows how many threads have been executed in parallel. Note now that the results of each view are shown by physical event file, including lookups found, not found, records written (including a header record for each physical file read per view) and which extract file the data was written to.

Making this one change means we may allow the operating system to process our data twice as fast, if it assigns our threads to different CPUs at the same time, and both CPU's perform the same amount of work. This one change might cut the time of the process in half.[140]

140. Note that in the example given, the time would be nowhere near half because the thread processing is almost instantaneous due to the small size of the event files. The start up time for reading the logic table, VDP and reference data files, code generation, and the shut down time of closing extract files and printing the control report is always single threaded.

The two files above both have the same kinds of records in them; the resulting generated programs to read each of the files would be nearly byte for byte the same. This is because we simply defined a new physical file under the logical file. The views are exactly the same. But multi-threading isn't limited to reading multiple files containing record described by the same LR. In Chapter 27, "Find More Detailed Events," on page 131, when discussing sort/merge processes, we described a multiple source view. A multiple source view can read different logical files, defined by different LRs, and combine the data into a single output, particularly when the two LRs include a common set of fields for sorting and summarizing. The two files may be read in parallel in GVBMR95.

Thus partitions can be assigned for various reasons. They may have no meaning, and are simply to increase parallelism like the example above. The partitions might have meaning as well, such as containing event data from history or containing a different record type. The generated code in each thread may be unique, because some views might read two different logical files, while other views in a thread do not. Each thread is effectively a custom developed program for extracting data from that event file.

Parallelism can get out of hand though, as shown in the next chapter. Next let's turn to understanding how to control performance, and really get the most out of parallelism when needed.

Chapter 49. Control and Contention

Doug is fond of repeating a conversation he had one day with another consultant that was an expert on a different hardware platform. They were talking about the procedures of replacing failed CPUs within a computer, and Doug was impressed with how well-versed the consultant was in these procedures. Doug asked, "How often do they fail?"

"All the time," was the response.

I have heard statistics about the amount of down time for some large organizations for specific mainframes, and was impressed that in the course of a whole year it was measured in seconds totaling a few minutes. I wouldn't be surprised to learn there are mainframes that have run continuously for years. Mainframe crashes are very rare. I have tremendous respect for the operating system.

Those results haven't come by accident; a lot of thought over a long time has created that ability. And the thought isn't just by those who design and write the operating system and create the hardware. It also comes from those who make the systems run routinely at specific companies. They tend to be a careful lot, wanting to know something of the way the tools will impact the machine.

That's why on every project, as we have explained how SAFR works to the project team members, we always anticipated the meeting with systems people. As we outlined the potential performance of SAFR someone always says, "We better meet with so and so." We would begin by being grilled on what impact it can have and how it can be controlled.

Oops

Those concerns aren't without merit. There is a very small group of people I know who have mistakenly found ways of impacting various mainframes running SAFR. I am one of them, but am not going to share that story. I will share Mukesh Patel's story, a long time consultant with SAFR. He once created some custom programs called read exits that would run under SAFR. SAFR executed in parallel mode, each thread calling these programs. Unfortunately, he or someone else created a condition that caused an infinite loop in the exit program, not in SAFR itself.[141]

Mukesh knew the test he needed to run required reading a large amount of event data to test the new program functions. So he started the job and left for the day. After the jobs had been running for hours, and the infinite loops had kicked in, the monitoring operator, who didn't know anything about the jobs or Mukesh, decided he would help GVBMR95 finish. So he issued an operating system command to give it a higher priority effectively allowing it to use more CPU time.

When it was explained to me, I was told the operator mistyped the command and gave it the highest priority on the box, higher than the operating system. This meant that no other process or program on the computer would cause the SAFR threads to be swapped off the CPU. In addition to the infinite loop, SAFR also required no IO. The threads would run forever. There were enough threads so that every processor was fully utilized. SAFR, the infinite loop exits, abetted by the operator, took over the machine. The machine had to be IPLed[142], the mainframe term for rebooted.

141. SAFR itself has only one looping construct, that of the Event File read in the RENX statement. The user cannot assign "goto" row values; they are all determined by the SAFR View Complier. With the exception of the possibly codependency of views reading and writing to the common key buffer, users cannot create infinite loops.

142. IPL stands for Initial Program Load.

Control Parameters

In our meetings with the systems people, we would begin by explaining that the primary means of controlling GVBMR95 is the JCL parameters. SAFR is subject to all the typical system controls, including job classes, which indicate how long a job can execute and its priority relative to other jobs, space allocation, region size, which indicates how much memory can be used, and others. These parameters have always proven adequate in preventing SAFR from doing things it should not. And for most installations, these parameters are adequate for tuning SAFR runs so that SAFR is used to solve the problems required of it while using the resources that the organization allocates to it.

Additionally, other parameters have been developed over time to allow additional control. These include parameters that indicate how many threads should be executed. The Thread Governor, as it has come to be called, allows whoever defines the SAFR pass (an execution of a set of views reading a set of event files) to say how many disk threads and how many tape threads can be run simultaneously, up to 999 threads each.

The thread governor was developed because of tape drives. The actual number of tape drives available on a machine limited how many event files could be read. Tape is a particularly low cost medium for storage of event files. Because SAFR reads event files serially, reading from and writing to tape is completely acceptable. There is no need for direct or random access which disks provide. But typically the number of tape drives in an environment is substantially lower than the number of disk drives. So, on some projects, a SAFR developer would unwittingly submit a SAFR job that wanted to read 10 tape event files in parallel, when there were only 8 tape drives for example. The job would sit and ask the operator to allocate additional tape drives he would have had to go buy and install to satisfy the request. Finally he would cancel the job saying "Sorry, can't do that."

If the logic table contains views which are reading more event files than the thread governor allows, SAFR will begin executing the number of governed threads. When a thread is complete, the next waiting thread is started. Thus the SAFR GVBMR95 processing loop is:

```
Loop until end of threads
 Loop until end of event records
  Loop until end of views
  Next view
 Next event record
Next thread
```

GVBMR95 accepts additional parameters to control various debugging and run time parameters.

Having established control of the process, we need to understand the other extreme of what is possible. Simply breaking up event files into a lot of small files to be processed in parallel may not produce any performance gains. It is possible that although GVBMR95 executes parallel threads, that effectively because of system or process configuration, they effectively run serially.

A Parallel Processing Example

Over the years, I have seen Doug explain the details of parallel processing with the following chart.

143. The statistics on this chart are from approximately 1997.

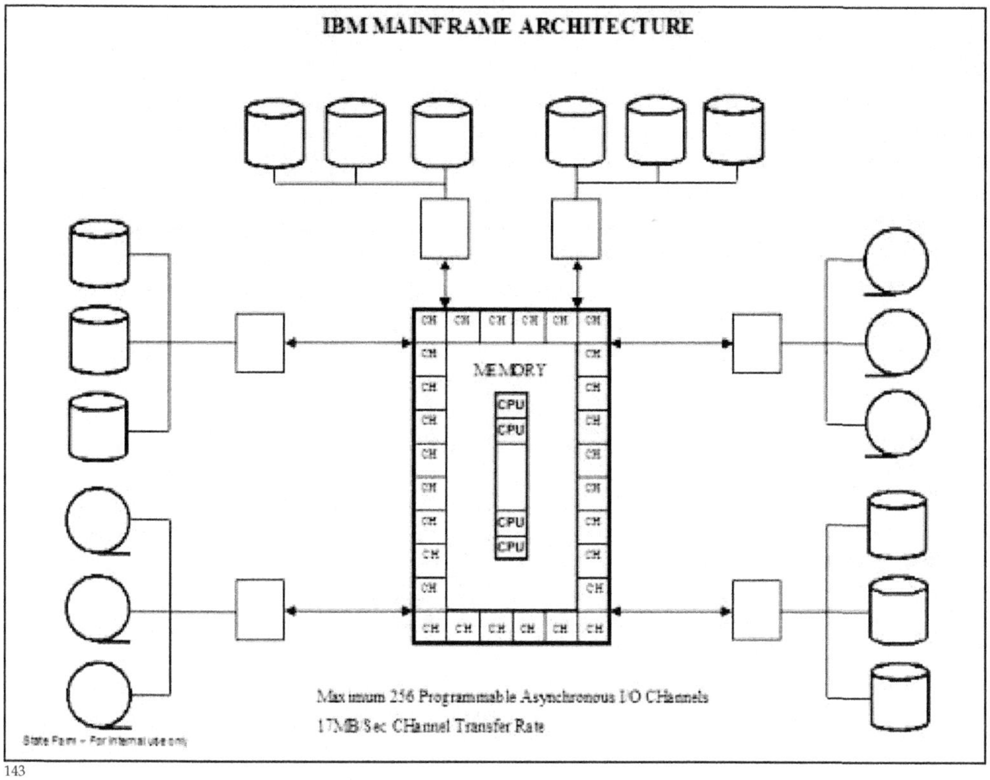

143

Figure 132. IBM Mainframe Architecture

When parallel processing starts, depending upon the other programs being run by other users and the control parameters assigned to SAFR, the operating system will assign threads to individual CPUs, shown in the middle of the picture. Let's suppose that we execute two threads in parallel, and both are assigned at the same time to individual CPUs. Almost immediately the threads will require event file data to be read from disk.

On many computers, the CPU plays some role in transferring data from disk, but not on mainframes. Instead, mainframes have a set of specialized CPUs called channels, represented by CHs around the sides in the diagram. These limited function CPUs only transfer data from disk into memory. Because the threads require data from disk, they are "swapped off" the main CPUs to wait for the data to be made available by the channels. The CPUs move on to other programs.

As discussed in "Block Sizes" on page 90, data is stored on disk in what is called a block. A block is a fixed size for the disk. The event file records might be 100 bytes long, but the block might be 32760 bytes in length. The channels know nothing of the 100 byte record length. They transfer one block, 32760 bytes, for each event file into memory. If two files are on the same non PAV disk (parallel access volume), then the same channel must do the work for both files serially. After a block is in memory, the channels instruct the operating system it has retrieved the data. The operating system then assigns the threads to a CPU. If only one CPU becomes available, only one thread begins processing, by reading the event file data. Thus if the file shares a channel or disk, or there is only one CPU available, we have had no parallelism.

Our potential road blocks to parallelism aren't through yet. A moment later, perhaps, another CPU becomes available and the other thread is assigned to it. Because each block contains 3,270 records in our 100 byte LR example, for a few milliseconds they might both read data, do lookups, transform fields into sort keys, DT and CT columns, and write records to an area of memory reserved for the output file. If both threads need to write to the same extract file at the same moment, one of the threads will be given permission by the operating system; the other will be told to wait. It may be swapped off the processor if the wait is very long. Again, no parallelism.

Supposing each extract record is also 100 bytes long, at some point one of the threads might attempt to place the 3,277th record into the extract file buffer, the space of memory allocated for the output file. The record won't fit; it would make the block too large to store on disk. This triggers a call to the operating system to transfer the filled buffer out to disk; to write a block. The thread needing to write the record is swapped off the CPU. The assigned channel takes over and actually writes the block to disk. The other thread might continue processing if it doesn't require this extract file.

Again, perhaps we have no parallel processing when the last block of the last running thread is transferred into memory, and the thread has read all event records in the input buffer and created all the extract records in the output buffers, the threads can then shut down. GVBMR95 writes a message to the JES Message Log when each thread finishes processing, as shown below:[144]

```
J E S 2  J O B  L O G  --  S Y S T E M  B M S 2  --  N O D E

13.43.04 JOB07140 ---- TUESDAY,   20 OCT 2009 ----
13.43.04 JOB07140  IRR010I  USERID KIPT     IS ASSIGNED TO THIS JOB.
13.43.04 JOB07140  ICH70001I KIPT      LAST ACCESS AT 13:43:02 ON TUESDAY, OCTOBE
13.43.04 JOB07140  $HASP373 TTDEMOE1 STARTED - INIT 2    - CLASS A - SYS BMS2
13.43.04 JOB07140  IEF403I TTDEMOE1 - STARTED
13.43.04 JOB07140  -                                      --TIMINGS (MINS.)--
13.43.04 JOB07140  -JOBNAME  STEPNAME PROCSTEP    RC   EXCP    CPU    SRB  CLOCK
13.43.04 JOB07140  -TTDEMOE1          PSTEP695    00    111    .00    .00    .00
13.43.04 JOB07140  -TTDEMOE1          PSTEP696 FLUSH      0    .00    .00    .00
13.43.04 JOB07140  -TTDEMOE1          PSTEP700    00     95    .00    .00    .00
13.43.05 JOB07140  + ** GVB002I GVBMR95G - 002 threads started
13.43.05 JOB07140  + ** GVB007I GVBMR95G - Thread 001 finished EVENT1
13.43.05 JOB07140  + ** GVB007I GVBMR95G - Thread 002 finished EVENT2
```

Figure 133. JES Message Log Thread Messages

It is possible, therefore, to execute multiple threads, but for those threads to almost never run in parallel. To avoid this, we need to think about contention.

It is difficult to represent parallel processing in a book, but we can see the results of it in the extract program trace. Parallel processing means the extract file record write-order becomes completely random. The records written to the trace output are equally random. Now, looking at the event file DD name in trace becomes important. Note that below, record 5 is being processed in one thread, Event1, and then record two begins being processed in the Event2 thread. Reading the trace requires looking at the thread in addition to the record number and view ID.[145]

144. The threads do not issue the command to write the last block of the extract files, because the GVBMR95 mother task must add the control record to the standard extract files, those being sent to the Format phase, with a record count of the total records in that extract file. Thus the mother task issues the last write statements and closes the extract files.

145. Writing the trace records to Sysout is also a shared file and requires single threading. Because Sysout is just a file, it can be edited, and using the "Sort," "Find Exclude" and "Find Include" commands, one can more effectively analyze the trace. Alternatively, using trace parameters can control what data is written to the trace.

```
 EVENT      EVENT          VIEW       LOGIC          SEQ     FILE    RECORD     FIELD
 DDNAME     RECORD         NUMBER     ROW            NUM     ID      ID         ID
EVENT1               5 V:   3263 LT:     26 CFLC 000          0     1263     63316|
EVENT1               5 V:   3263 LT:     35 JOIN           1286     1262         2
EVENT1               5 V:   3263 LT:     36 LKE  001          0     1264     63312|
EVENT1               5 V:   3263 LT:     37 LUSM           1286     1262         2
EVENT1               5 V:   3263 LT:     38 DTL  001      83277     1262     63317|
EVENT1               5 V:   3263 LT:     39 GOTO
EVENT1               5 V:   3263 LT:     41 JOIN           1287     1263         1
EVENT1               5 V:   3263 LT:     44 DTL  002      83278     1263     63316|
EVENT2               2 V:   3437 LT:    306 WRXT 001
EVENT1               5 V:   3263 LT:     45 GOTO
EVENT2               2 V:   3450 LT:    307 NV
EVENT1               5 V:   3263 LT:     47 JOIN           1285     1258         3
EVENT2               2 V:   3450 LT:    308 SKE  001      84352     1264     63311|
EVENT1               5 V:   3263 LT:     48 LKE  003          0     1264     63313|
EVENT2               2 V:   3450 LT:    309 LKLR 001       1534     1263      2890|
EVENT1               5 V:   3263 LT:     49 LUSM           1285     1258         3
EVENT2               2 V:   3450 LT:    310 LKE  001          0     1264     63311|
EVENT1               5 V:   3263 LT:     50 DTL  003      83279     1258     63318|
EVENT2               2 V:   3450 LT:    311 KSLK              0     1263     63310
EVENT1               5 V:   3263 LT:     51 GOTO
```

Figure 134. Parallel Processing Trace

Contention

Parallel processing only happens when there is no contention between threads; when the threads do not need to share a resource, such as a portion of memory, or a channel to read the event files sitting on the same physical disk or an extract file.

This is a key point; memory or disk can only be updated by one process or one thread at a time. The operating system provides controls to make sure this happens. In our meeting example, confusion would reign if two people were trying to write to the same spot on the white board at the same time. This fact is what can create contention. Read only access to memory, such as searching the core image reference data, does not require single threading and does not create contention.

Doug has taken pains, and over time the team has discovered places where additional efficiencies can be gained by not sharing resources. For example, Doug made the in memory extract summary buffer unique per view within a thread. Thus the stack of records kept is actually by view by thread (event file). Randall found that significant CPU time can be removed from jobs if extract files are not shared by threads. The threads do not have to test and request access to extract files.[146]

Here are a few rules of thumb developed over the years. Obviously if a free CPU cannot be used to process a thread, then the machine will not be fully applied to solving the problem. And because threads typically require some IO and are not on a processor all the time, a ratio of three possible threads to each CPU usually allows for sustained parallelism.

There is a constant act of balancing CPU to IO. Some processes end up being CPU bound. In other words, there are not enough CPUs to run the process any faster; the amount of time on each CPU is much longer than the time needed for IO. For example, if a thread read in one record from disk, generated multiple gigabytes of data in memory from that one record, performed many calculations against that data, then summarized it down to write out a single record to the output file, there would be almost no IO involved. More CPUs would be necessary to run the process faster. The extreme of dividing the input records, each to its own file, so that we have one CPU for each input record would not even be enough to make the process run faster.

On the other hand, I have seen processes where the views scan millions of records, but only select a handful; sort of a needle in a haystack problem. Testing each record for inclusion in the output requires

146. Although not often configured this way, the sort utility can read concatenated Extract files. GVBMR88 can handle multiple control records in one execution. Thus the greatest efficiency can be gained if each view within each thread writes to its own extract file, and then files for particular views are concatenated together as input to the sort job.

very little CPU time. These types of processes are IO bound. Additional files, and channels can be added but at some point the operating system overhead for controlling the number of parallel threads consumes more and more CPU time. So one might achieve a balance between CPU and IO on these kinds of problems, but only because the CPU usage has become inefficient, total elapsed time may decrease, but CPU time may increase to a wasteful extent.

We should note that the threads aren't the only level of parallelism happening in GVBMR95. GVBMR95 also has overlapped IO. GVBMR95 actually allocates multiple buffers in memory for any one file it is reading or writing. Instead of waiting for the channels to operate against one large portion of memory, either reading it or writing it, GVBMR95 can begin reading data from one buffer while the channels are operating against other buffers. The same is true for writing data; the channels can begin to transfer extract file data to disk while MR95 is writing to other buffers.[147]

Next we'll learn about additional techniques to eliminate IO.

147. The number of these buffers is controlled by two GVBMR95 parameters, `READBUF` and `WRITEBUF`. After a typical point, the number of buffers typically is not a constraint inhibiting parallel processing. Doug has suggested that it takes about three times as long to write a record as it does to read a record. Thus he has suggested there should be a ratio of 1:3 for read verses write buffers. The default values of 5:15 are typically adequate.

Chapter 50. Piping, Tokens, and the Write Verb

I noted earlier in Chapter 36, "Optimize For Performance," on page 183 how the concept of piping came to be. It is useful when data needs to be passed from one or more views to one or more additional views. Tokens are another method to accomplish this function for special purposes. The Write statement is often used in conjunction with piping or other advanced SAFR processes.

Piping

Piping isn't too difficult a concept. Without piping, one or more views in a SAFR thread read an event file and write to an extract file. Another execution of GVBMR95, often called another pass of the data, allows one or more additional views to read that extracted data. By defining the output extract file from the first set of views as a pipe, and then reading that file as an input to the next set of views allows SAFR to connect the two processes and run them in one GVBMR95 execution.

Doug accomplished this quite quickly. When a program requires data from disk, it calls an operating system module, called a system service, access method, or something in the PC world akin to a DLL, to get that data from disk. This program on a mainframe talks to a channel. So reading data is really just a subroutine call to another program.

When piping, SAFR simply calls a very simple little module that keeps track of the reading status and the writing status between the two threads. When the pipe "reader" thread starts up, it calls the little program to tell it to get data. The module knows that the pipe "writer" thread has to execute to fill up the buffer, so it simply says, "OK, I'll be back in a bit with the data." The pipe reader gets swapped off the CPU waiting for data, and as the pipe writer executes.

When the pipe writer has filled an output buffer and it is ready to be written to disk, instead of SAFR calling the BSAM access method to write the data to disk, it calls this same little module and tells it to write the data. The module says, "OK, be back in a minute" and the pipe writer is swapped off the CPU. This module then posts to the pipe reader that it has data for it to read. The pipe reader wakes up and begins processing the data.

This little dance continues until the pipe writer says to write the last buffer, and the pipe reader has read what was written. There is a small degree of parallelism occurring because of the overlapped IO, whereby the pipe reader is reading buffers that are different from the buffers being written by the pipe writer. But this parallelism is only as long as it takes to process one buffer of data in either of the threads. The little module in the middle is said to be emulating an access method.

The pipe reader views must use an LR that matches the output from the pipe writer views to interpret the data, just the same as if they were reading a physical file. This often means that the views writing to the pipe are extract only views, only writing the DT fields to the pipe, but this isn't a requirement. Because extract phase summarization accumulates values in the CT columns, it isn't very common to use it in the midst of piping processes. Rather, typically the last set of views reading the last piped data are "reporting" type views which would use extract phase summarization.

One purpose for piping is to consolidate logic that would need to be applied in many views in one view, the pipe writer. The pipe reader views becomes like a sub or called module that only acts on the output of the first view, not the original input data. This simply improves the maintainability of the views so logic isn't replicated in multiple places; it doesn't necessarily improve performance.

Note that if more than one view is writing to the extract file, the record count in the extract file will likely not equal the record count in the original event file. Selection criteria, filtering out certain event records, will certainly change it. Alternatively, if the same event record is selected and written by the more than one pipe writer view, the same event record will be duplicated in the pipe. Thus one input event record can become multiple output records.

Piped Allocation Process Example

This fact was used to allocate event records to lower levels of detail for the insurance company. Programs were created that generated SAFR views which wrote to pipes. Thus an expense record for, say, the CEO of the company, could be turned into many new records each ultimately representing the portion of the CEO's salary attributable to an insurance policy, an extreme example. This would be done by allocating to lower and lower levels of detail in successive pipes.

For example, the first pipe writer views would have a column with the division number in it. There would be one view per division. They would each select the CEO's salary record, and multiply it by the value of that division to the total divisions. These records would be written to a pipe. In the next to last pipe, each insurance policy could have a column with the insurance policy number as a column, and have another column with a calculation multiplying the allocated salary records for the division by the proportion of that insurance policy's value to the total of all insurance policy values.

The last pipe reader thread would have reporting views within it. These would almost all use extract phase summarization because no one really cared how much of the CEO's salary was attributable to an individual policy. But they were interested in accumulating the total cost per insurance policy in different ways. These different summaries were the only things written to disk.

Thus there is a huge record explosion occurring in memory, but never going to disk, as one input event record is turned into thousands of allocated records, that are then collapsed into scores of summarized output records. It was quite a remarkable design.

The following is a sample GVBMR95 control report showing view 3459 writing to a pipe, and view 3458 reading from the pipe. This is done by looking for linkages between DD Names and numbers of records written and read for threads. View 3459 writes to the DD Name F0003459. This is the file handle for the output side. At the bottom of the control report, we can see that the total records written to this DD Name, 18, are written to a pipe. The total records written are the same as the total records read in the top of the report from the pipe DD Name, EVNTPIPE, the file handle of the reading thread. In the middle of the report, View 3458 is shown reading from EVNTPIPE DD Name.

```
MR95 - PARALLEL THREADS EXECUTED..............                        3
MR95 - VIEWS PER  FILE PROCESSED..............                       21
MR95 - TOTAL NUMBER OF LOGIC TABLE ROWS.......                      343
MR95 - SIZE  OF GENERATED LOGIC...............                    8,704
MR95 - 64-BIT EXT SUM    MEGABYTES  USED.......                       2
MR95 -          EVENT  FILE  RECORDS  READ.......EVENT1               5
MR95 -          EVENT  PIPE  RECORDS  READ.......EVNTPIPE            18
MR95 -          EVENT  FILE  RECORDS  READ.......EVENT2              13
MR95 - TOTAL EVENT RECORDS     READ.....................             18
MR95 - TOTAL PIPE  RECORDS     READ.....................             18
VIEW DEF:   3261/EVENT1     F:            0 NF:          0        0(F0003261)
VIEW DEF:   3262/EVENT1     F:            0 NF:          0        5(F0003262)
VIEW DEF:   3263/EVENT1     F:           15 NF:          0        5(F0003263)
VIEW DEF:   3264/EVENT1     F:            0 NF:          0        1(EXTR001)
VIEW DEF:   3265/EVENT1     F:            0 NF:          0        3(EXTR001)
VIEW DEF:   3434/EVENT1     F:            0 NF:          0        6(EXTR001)
VIEW DEF:   3436/EVENT1     F:            0 NF:          0        6(EXTR001)
VIEW DEF:   3437/EVENT1     F:            0 NF:          0        6(EXTR001)
VIEW DEF:   3450/EVENT1     F:            0 NF:          0        6(EXTR001)
VIEW DEF:   3459/EVENT1     F:            0 NF:          0        5(F0003459)
VIEW DEF:   3458/EVNTPIPE   F:            0 NF:          0       13(F0003458)
VIEW DEF:   3261/EVENT2     F:            0 NF:          0       13(F0003261)
VIEW DEF:   3262/EVENT2     F:            0 NF:          0       13(F0003262)
VIEW DEF:   3263/EVENT2     F:           39 NF:          0       12(F0003263)
VIEW DEF:   3264/EVENT2     F:            0 NF:          0       14(EXTR001)
VIEW DEF:   3265/EVENT2     F:            0 NF:          0        3(EXTR001)
VIEW DEF:   3434/EVENT2     F:            0 NF:          0       14(EXTR001)
VIEW DEF:   3436/EVENT2     F:            0 NF:          0       14(EXTR001)
VIEW DEF:   3437/EVENT2     F:            0 NF:          0       14(EXTR001)
VIEW DEF:   3450/EVENT2     F:            0 NF:          0       14(EXTR001)
VIEW DEF:   3459/EVENT2     F:            0 NF:          0       13(F0003459)
MR95 - TOTAL LOOKUPS PERFORMED.........................              54
MR95 - TOTAL RECORDS WRITTEN TO FILE..........EXTR001               102
MR95 - TOTAL RECORDS WRITTEN TO FILE..........F0003261               13
MR95 - TOTAL RECORDS WRITTEN TO FILE..........F0003262               18
MR95 - TOTAL RECORDS WRITTEN TO FILE..........F0003263               17
MR95 - TOTAL RECORDS WRITTEN TO FILE..........F0003458               13
MR95 - TOTAL RECORDS WRITTEN TO PIPE..........F0003459               18
MR95 - TOTAL EXTRACT RECORDS WRITTEN..................              163
MR95 - TOTAL PIPE    RECORDS WRITTEN..................               18
```

Figure 135. GVBMR95 Piping Control Report

The following is a portion of the trace output showing the end of the pipe writer thread, which contained view 3459, and the beginning of the pipe reader view 3458. Note the WRDT function in view 3459, an extract only view, writing records to the pipe.

```
 EVENT      EVENT        VIEW       LOGIC      SEQ    FILE    RECORD    FIELD
 DDNAME     RECORD       NUMBER      ROW       NUM     ID       ID        ID
EVENT2          13 V:    3459 LT:    338 DTE  003    84403     1264    63313|  1
EVENT2          13 V:    3459 LT:    339 DTE  004    84404     1264    63314|  1
EVENT2          13 V:    3459 LT:    340 DTE  005    84405     1264    63315|  2
EVENT2          13 V:    3459 LT:    341 WRDT 010
EVNTPIPE         1 V:    3458 LT:    171 NV
EVNTPIPE         1 V:    3458 LT:    172 CFEC 000        0     1264    63311|
EVNTPIPE         2 V:    3458 LT:    171 NV
EVNTPIPE         2 V:    3458 LT:    172 CFEC 000        0     1264    63311|
EVNTPIPE         3 V:    3458 LT:    171 NV
EVNTPIPE         3 V:    3458 LT:    172 CFEC 000        0     1264    63311|
EVNTPIPE         4 V:    3458 LT:    171 NV
EVNTPIPE         4 V:    3458 LT:    172 CFEC 000        0     1264    63311|
EVNTPIPE         5 V:    3458 LT:    171 NV
EVNTPIPE         5 V:    3458 LT:    172 CFEC 000        0     1264    63311|
EVNTPIPE         6 V:    3458 LT:    171 NV
EVNTPIPE         6 V:    3458 LT:    172 CFEC 000        0     1264    63311|
EVNTPIPE         6 V:    3458 LT:    173 WRIN 011
EVNTPIPE         7 V:    3458 LT:    171 NV
EVNTPIPE         7 V:    3458 LT:    172 CFEC 000        0     1264    63311|
EVNTPIPE         7 V:    3458 LT:    173 WRIN 011
```

Figure 136. Sample Pipe Trace Output

Tokens

All threads run asynchronously. That means when they will and won't be executing is unpredictable. There are certain problems where coordination between the views or, more often, between the pipe reader views and other data in the original event file is needed (see next two chapters). Piping can't be used for this. Tokens can be used to solve this problem. They are not often used, but we will describe how they work.

Tokens can be thought of as a working storage or temporary variables. The token writing view creates the variable that can be used by other views within the same thread. Unlike piping, which passes data between threads, tokens only are available within threads.

Similar to piping, there are token writer views, and token user views. Let's deal with a single token writer view first. The token writer operates upon event data like any other view, but its output is a token. A token record is simply written to memory. The output must match an LR that will be used to interpret the record similar to a pipe output. Any view that writes a token is moved to the top of the thread, so its output can be used by any other view in that thread.

Similar to piping, the token reader views can read the token output instead of the regular event file. This is accomplished by a little slight of hand in the thread. GVBMR95 simply changes the address of the event record to point to the single token record (always a single record) written. Thus there will never be more tokens written in a thread than there are event file records. Unlike pipes, tokens do not accomplish the data explosion needed for an allocation process. If selection criteria caused the token writer to not write a record, then the token reader will read one less record from the event file.

In addition to *reading* a token, the token can also be used as a look-up. Thus a view might still read the event file record as its input, but form a key of some kind to "join" to the token. This isn't a true lookup in the sense of searching for many records to find the one with a matching key. There is always only one record available—the record written as a token. If no record is written as a token, then the lookup is treated as not found.

There can actually be multiple token writers, even though there is only one token record in a thread. All token writers are moved to the front of the thread. They are executed in order by their view ID. The last token writer to write a record wins; that record will be used by all token using views.

Thus logic can be consolidated in token views, similar to the purpose of piping. Any token user views can also be aware of all the other aspects of the thread. Tokens are most often used in conjunction with user exits, discussed in the next chapter, which have visibility to the aspects external to the thread. Tokens, though, accomplish no parallelism. The token writers and token readers execute serially.

In the following example, view 3460 is in the pipe reader thread. It performs a number of look-ups to create a single record that is pre-joined by the pipe writer view. This might be done because it is expected that doing all the joins up front in the thread will make the logic in the using views easier to understand. View 3461 looks up to the token, and view 3462 reads the token, both in the same pipe reader thread.

```
MR95 - PARALLEL THREADS EXECUTED..............                     3
MR95 - VIEWS PER  FILE PROCESSED..............                    25
MR95 - TOTAL NUMBER OF LOGIC TABLE ROWS.......                   393
MR95 - SIZE  OF GENERATED LOGIC...............                10,160
MR95 - 64-BIT EXT SUM   MEGABYTES  USED.......                     2
MR95 -        EVENT  FILE  RECORDS  READ.......EVENT1              5
MR95 -        EVENT  PIPE  RECORDS  READ.......EVNTPIPE           18
MR95 -        EVENT  FILE  RECORDS  READ.......EVENT2             13
MR95 - TOTAL EVENT RECORDS   READ......................           18
MR95 - TOTAL PIPE  RECORDS   READ......................           18
VIEW DEF:   3261/EVENT1    F:        0 NF:          0              0(F0003261
VIEW DEF:   3262/EVENT1    F:        0 NF:          0              5(F0003262
VIEW DEF:   3263/EVENT1    F:       10 NF:          0              5(F0003263
VIEW DEF:   3264/EVENT1    F:        0 NF:          0              1(EXTR001
VIEW DEF:   3265/EVENT1    F:        0 NF:          0              3(EXTR001
VIEW DEF:   3434/EVENT1    F:        5 NF:          0              6(EXTR001
VIEW DEF:   3436/EVENT1    F:        0 NF:          0              6(EXTR001
VIEW DEF:   3437/EVENT1    F:        0 NF:          0              6(EXTR001
VIEW DEF:   3450/EVENT1    F:        0 NF:          0              6(EXTR001
VIEW DEF:   3459/EVENT1    F:        0 NF:          0              5(F0003459
VIEW DEF:   3458/EVNTPIPE  F:        0 NF:          0             13(F0003458
VIEW DEF:   3460/EVNTPIPE  F:       54 NF:          0             18(F0003460
VIEW DEF:   3461/EVNTPIPE  F:        0 NF:         17             17(F0003461
VIEW DEF:   3261/EVENT2    F:        0 NF:          0             13(F0003261
VIEW DEF:   3262/EVENT2    F:        0 NF:          0             13(F0003262
VIEW DEF:   3263/EVENT2    F:       39 NF:          0             12(F0003263
VIEW DEF:   3264/EVENT2    F:        0 NF:          0             14(EXTR001
VIEW DEF:   3265/EVENT2    F:        0 NF:          0              3(EXTR001
VIEW DEF:   3434/EVENT2    F:        0 NF:          0             14(EXTR001
VIEW DEF:   3436/EVENT2    F:        0 NF:          0             14(EXTR001
VIEW DEF:   3437/EVENT2    F:        0 NF:          0             14(EXTR001
VIEW DEF:   3450/EVENT2    F:        0 NF:          0             14(EXTR001
VIEW DEF:   3459/EVENT2    F:        0 NF:          0             13(F0003459
VIEW DEF:   3462/EVNTTOKN  F:        0 NF:          0             18(F0003462
MR95 - TOTAL LOOKUPS PERFORMED........................           125
MR95 - TOTAL RECORDS WRITTEN TO FILE..........EXTR001            102
MR95 - TOTAL RECORDS WRITTEN TO FILE..........F0003261            13
MR95 - TOTAL RECORDS WRITTEN TO FILE..........F0003262            18
MR95 - TOTAL RECORDS WRITTEN TO FILE..........F0003263            17
MR95 - TOTAL RECORDS WRITTEN TO FILE..........F0003458            13
MR95 - TOTAL RECORDS WRITTEN TO PIPE..........F0003459            18
MR95 - TOTAL RECORDS WRITTEN TO FILE..........F0003461            17
MR95 - TOTAL RECORDS WRITTEN TO FILE..........F0003462            18
MR95 - TOTAL EXTRACT RECORDS WRITTEN..................           198
MR95 - TOTAL PIPE    RECORDS WRITTEN..................            18
MR95 - EXTRACTION  ELAPSED TIME (IN SECONDS)..........             0
```

Figure 137. GVBMR95 Token Control Report

The following is a sample of the trace for these two views, with descriptions of the functions in the logic table for each.

```
 EVENT      EVENT         VIEW       LOGIC         SEQ
 DDNAME     RECORD        NUMBER      ROW          NUM    DESCRIPTION
EVENT2            13 V:    3459 LT:     387 WRDT 011    View to write last record to pipe
EVNTPIPE           2 V:    3458 LT:     165 NV          View to copy pipe data to file
EVNTPIPE           2 V:    3458 LT:     166 CFEC 000    Selection criteria for view failed
EVNTPIPE           2 V:    3460 LT:     168 NV          View to create token in Pipe Reader Thread
EVNTPIPE           2 V:    3460 LT:     169 DTE  001    View columns must match output token LR
EVNTPIPE           2 V:    3460 LT:     170 DTE  002
.............................................................
EVNTPIPE           2 V:    3460 LT:     190 WRTK 000    Write Token function
EVNTPIPE           2 V:    3462 LT:     390 NV          View reads & copies token record to output
EVNTPIPE           2 V:    3462 LT:     391 WRIN 007
EVNTPIPE           2 V:    3461 LT:     191 NV          View reads Pipe but looks up to token
EVNTPIPE           2 V:    3461 LT:     192 JOIN
EVNTPIPE           2 V:    3461 LT:     195 CFLC 000
EVNTPIPE           2 V:    3461 LT:     204 JOIN        Build Key to look-up to token record
EVNTPIPE           2 V:    3461 LT:     205 LKE  001
EVNTPIPE           2 V:    3461 LT:     206 LKE  001
EVNTPIPE           2 V:    3461 LT:     207 LKE  001
EVNTPIPE           2 V:    3461 LT:     208 LUSM        Look up to token record
.............................................................
EVNTPIPE           2 V:    3461 LT:     229 WRDT 013    Writes data from token and pipe to output
```

Figure 138. Token Trace Output

Write Verb

The write verb allows a SAFR developer a finer level of control over when and where an extract record is written.[148] In all the examples thus far, the views have an implicit Write statement, telling GVBMR95 to write the extract record after it has built the last column of the view and tested for extract summarization. Where the extract record was written is controlled by the View Properties. For extract only views, the default DD Name is "Fnnnnnnn" where nnnnnnn is the view number padded with 0's to the left. Views can also be directed to write to a specific physical file in the SAFR metadata.

Suppose a single view may be able to satisfy multiple needs even though the output records are exactly the same. Two or more outputs may share many of the same output fields, but one requires another column or two. Inserting a WRITE function after the first record has been built causes GVBMR95 to write that record. Then additional columns can be added and another write verb inserted to write all the data from the first record plus the additional columns.

Thus the write verb allows multiple copies of the same extracted record for different purposes. One company actually makes on-site and off-sight backups in the midst of the business function SAFR process because it eliminates two additional IOs of the repository. It can also control the target file based upon a condition, or splitting one input record into many.

Another common use is in partitioning the output to continue parallelism through SAFR processes. Remember that the standard SAFR configuration is that the same view in multiple threads writes to the same extract file. When using piping or writing the output to the repository, it isn't desirable to collapse them into single partitions on output. No parallelism will be achieved in subsequent processes.

The write verb also allows conditional calls to a write exit, discussed in the next chapter. This allows for write exit parameters to be changed based on column logic. Another less used reason is to break up a multiple occurring segment of a record into individual records. This would be similar to a record containing an "occurs" clause in COBOL.

In the following example, view 3463 is a copy input view reading both the EVENT1 and EVENT2 physical files. It contained the following logic text:

---

148. I am indebted to Stephen Frobish and Andrea Orth for portions of this material.

```
If {LEGAL_ENTITY} =  522349731 Then
 WRITE(SOURCE=INPUT,DESTINATION=EXTRACT=02)
Else
 WRITE(SOURCE=INPUT,DESTINATION=EXTRACT=03)
EndIf
```

The file associated with DD Name DEST002 contains all the data for one legal entity and DEST003 contains all the data for the other legal entity. Note that because our input event files were already partitioned this way, the output files will be the same as the input files.

Let's suppose that these two files are the weekly files, and we have a third input file that contains the new records for the day, a mixture of legal entities. If our view also read this file, but only writes the two new versions of the weekly file, we have read the daily and weekly files, other views could have produced outputs from all of this data, while performed the weekly master file update process. This is a common approach and use of the write verb to update the master file, while maintaining partitioning.

The control report shows the results of using the write verb in view 3463.

```
MR95 - PARALLEL THREADS EXECUTED..............                              3
MR95 - VIEWS PER  FILE PROCESSED..............                             27
MR95 - TOTAL NUMBER OF LOGIC TABLE ROWS.......                            403
MR95 - SIZE   OF GENERATED LOGIC..............                         10,424
MR95 - 64-BIT EXT SUM   MEGABYTES  USED.......                              2
MR95 -        EVENT  FILE  RECORDS  READ.......EVENT1                       5
MR95 -        EVENT  PIPE  RECORDS  READ.......EVNTPIPE                    18
MR95 -        EVENT  FILE  RECORDS  READ.......EVENT2                      13
MR95 - TOTAL EVENT RECORDS    READ.....................                    18
MR95 - TOTAL PIPE  RECORDS    READ.....................                    18
VIEW DEF:   3261/EVENT1     F:           0 NF:          0               0(F0003261)
...
VIEW DEF:   3463/EVENT1     F:           0 NF:          0               5(DEST002)
                                                                        0(DEST003)
VIEW DEF:   3458/EVNTPIPE   F:           0 NF:          0              13(F0003458)
...
VIEW DEF:   3463/EVENT2     F:           0 NF:          0               0(DEST002)
                                                                       13(DEST003)
VIEW DEF:   3462/EVNTTOKN   F:           0 NF:          0              18(F0003462)
MR95 - TOTAL LOOKUPS PERFORMED........................                    125
MR95 - TOTAL RECORDS WRITTEN TO FILE..........EXTR001                     102
MR95 - TOTAL RECORDS WRITTEN TO FILE..........DEST002                       5
MR95 - TOTAL RECORDS WRITTEN TO FILE..........DEST003                      13
...
MR95 - TOTAL EXTRACT RECORDS WRITTEN..................                    216
MR95 - TOTAL PIPE    RECORDS WRITTEN..................                     18
```

Figure 139. GVBMR95 Write Verb Control Report

Note that view 3463 now writes to two different output files.

Next we'll examine what to do if SAFR native capabilities are not up to solving a specific problem.

Chapter 51. Exits

As we discussed in Chapter 45, "Sort User Exits," on page 233, exits are a common concept that allows software products to call custom coded programs at specific points to perform functions the tool itself does not do[149]. SAFR has four major points which can invoke a user exit. The first three are Extract Phase exits, and are used much more frequently than the Format Phase exit. They are:

- Read Exits, which present event file records to SAFR threads for processing. It is associated with an event LR and the REEX logic table function (Rather than a RENX function), and is called each time the event LR records in the input buffer have been processed.
- Lookup Exits, which accept join parameters and return looked up records in response to individual joins. These exits can also be used as simple function calls. It is associated with a lookup LR and a LUEX logic table function (rather than a LUSM), and is called each time a join to that LR is required.
- Write Exits, which accept extract records and can manipulate them before being written to extract files. It is associated with a view, or a write statement within a view, and the WREX logic table function (rather than WRIN, WRDT, or WRSU functions) creates the extract record.[150]
- Format Exits, the only GVBMR88 exit, accepts summarized and formatted Format Phase output records prior to being written to files. It is associated with a view that is assigned to the Format Phase. Format exits are very similar to write exits, except that the record being dealt with is the final output record, rather than the extract record. Because of its similarity to write exits and infrequent use, we won't describe this exit in any more detail here.

Read Exits

The first read exit I wrote read the SAFR Field Definition file and calculated the start position of each field based upon the lengths of the prior fields in the file, a field not stored on the file. It would detect a change in the logical record for the fields, and start the running position over at 0. This allowed SAFR to produce reports of its own metadata, including a field position on the input file.

I wrote this exit because this isn't a function well suited to SAFR. SAFR doesn't do many functions that look back at the prior event record, and none that look forward at the next event record.

In SAFR I created a logical record which matched the output from the read exit. That output was the 20 fields or so on the Field Definition file, plus my one new field. SAFR knows nothing about the input to the read exit. For all SAFR knew, my exit could have read 10 different files and combined them all together to make an event file, or not read any files and made up data to pass to SAFR.

The read exit emulates an access method; in other words instead of SAFR calling the system BSAM access method to get data from disk, it calls the exit. This means that the program must return the results that an access method would return.

Remember that access methods that read from disks don't know about the actual length of the data records processed by the program. Rather their record lengths are blocks.

My read exit read (using the standard COBOL QSAM access method) manipulated one record at a time. I could have defined my file to SAFR as if the block size was the length of one of my field definition records, perhaps 50 bytes in length. In other words, I could have made the block size equal the Logical Record Length (LRECL). However, this meant that SAFR would be calling my exit each time a new

149. See also "Extensibility" on page 149.

150. Although technically not a SAFR user exit, one could write a sort read exit to manipulate the sort input file in extract file format, but the same data would be available to the write exit, so I can't conceive of a reason to do so other than the GVBSR01 and 02 sort exits already described.

record was needed. The overhead for calling a subprogram is very high. SAFR has to save its register values before calling, and then they have to be restored before going back as well as a host of other functions.[151] This CPU time can really add up on a large file.

A more efficient method is for the read exit to process many records as if they had come from disk as one block, and then returning all of them as one block to SAFR. SAFR will parse the individual records according to the Logical Record Length, and only return to the read exit when a new "block" of data is needed.

This process can make a read exit more complex but is important for performance.

Look-up Exits

Look-up exits are probably the easiest to create. This is because they accept a set of parameters and return a record. The parameters passed to the lookup exit are whatever values are placed in the fields of the join key. These can be constants, fields from the event file, or fields from another lookup, including calls to other exits. The output from the lookup exit is a record that must match the LR for the "reference file" record it is to return. Although it appears to a SAFR developer as if SAFR has taken the keys and performed a search of a reference table to find the appropriate record, the exit may have done no such thing. In fact, it could do something as simple as reordering the fields passed to it and returning the record.

I think the first lookup exit I wrote kept a copy of the key it had been passed in the last call, and compared the key from the current call with that saved key. If the keys were the same, then it returned a "not found" condition. If they were different, it returned a "found" condition. I then called this exit in multiple views, and coded the selection logic to only include found records. This allowed me to only select the event record once, in the first qualifying view, no matter what views it qualified for.[152]

Lookup exits have been written to perform math calculations that SAFR didn't do natively. In fact, before SAFR had extract time calculations, a generalized user exit allowed passing two numbers and an operator. The resulting record contained the results of the math. Many SAFR functions have first appeared as user exits, and were later folded into the main code base.

Write Exits

Write exits are called whenever a view is to write an extract record. The write exit is passed the extract record, and the event record. It can evaluate these records and can

- Tell SAFR to write a record the exit specifies (could be any record) and continue with event file processing.
- Tell SAFR to skip this extract record and continue event file processing.
- Tell SAFR to write a record the exit specifies (could be any record) and return to the exit to do more processing.

The exit can manipulate the extract record; substitute a new record, table the extract record in some way and then dump the table at the end of event file processing, or any other number of things. Note, though,

151. I remember Doug noting that when the new version of COBOL was released, COBOL II to COBOL LE, the run times for the SAFR jobs at the insurance company significantly increased. So he created a dummy COBOL read exit that did nothing, and a little assembler program to call the exit one million times. He used the new and the old versions of COBOL and found that with no functional change, the CPU instructions for the new version of the language went up 2 or 3 times, or some large number. Calling programs is expensive in terms of CPU time.

152. Note that this type of exit cannot be optimized in the join optimization process. If the logic table calls to it were optimized, it would only be called once for each event record; every subsequent call would return the same "found" value. The need for a field on the user exit screen that indicated if an exit could be optimized (it is a stateless program, not remembering its prior state) was discovered in testing join optimization development.

that unlike read exits which do open and actually read files, write exits typically do not. They return records to SAFR to write to the extract file. They could do their own IO, but there is typically no benefit to doing so. SAFR's write routines are very efficient.

Write exits are inbetween read and lookup exits for complexity. This is mainly because of the complexity of dealing with extract records. The exit must know what the extract record will look like for a particular view. This might be easiest to determine by actually writing the view, and inspecting the extracted records to find positions and lengths. Any changes in the views can create a need to update to the write exit. Write exits outputs have no interaction or dependencies upon LRs.

Extract phase summarization made its first appearance as a write exit. The exit was called on each extract record. The exit allocated its own memory space, and built a stack of summarized event records. Only if the extract record caused the exit to overflow the stack did the exit tell SAFR to write a record. When the thread was finished processing, on the last call to the write exit the write exit would loop through the stack and instruct SAFR to write each record in the stack and return to it for additional processing until the end of the stack was reached.

Other Features

In addition to the above passed parameters, each exit receives a set of static parameters that do not change throughout event file processing. These can be used to further generalize an exit.

For example, I created the small lookup exit I described above accepted a set of static parameters that described how long the passed key was from the join. It would use this length to determine what length of data to store and compare. In this way, this same exit could be used on multiple joins with different keys, from 5 bytes to 50 bytes, regardless of whether the key was composed of 1 field or 50. This same approach was used by the calculation exit so that it could work with different sizes of numbers being passed to it.

Using this generalization approach has allowed the team to create a number of exits that can be used many different times.

Each exit is called once before event file processing begins so it can initialize memory and set up shop. They are also called one time after event file processing is complete to perform clean up. These calls are indicated to the exit through a status code.

The following picture shows all the logic table codes, including those for exits, tokens, and extract time calculations.

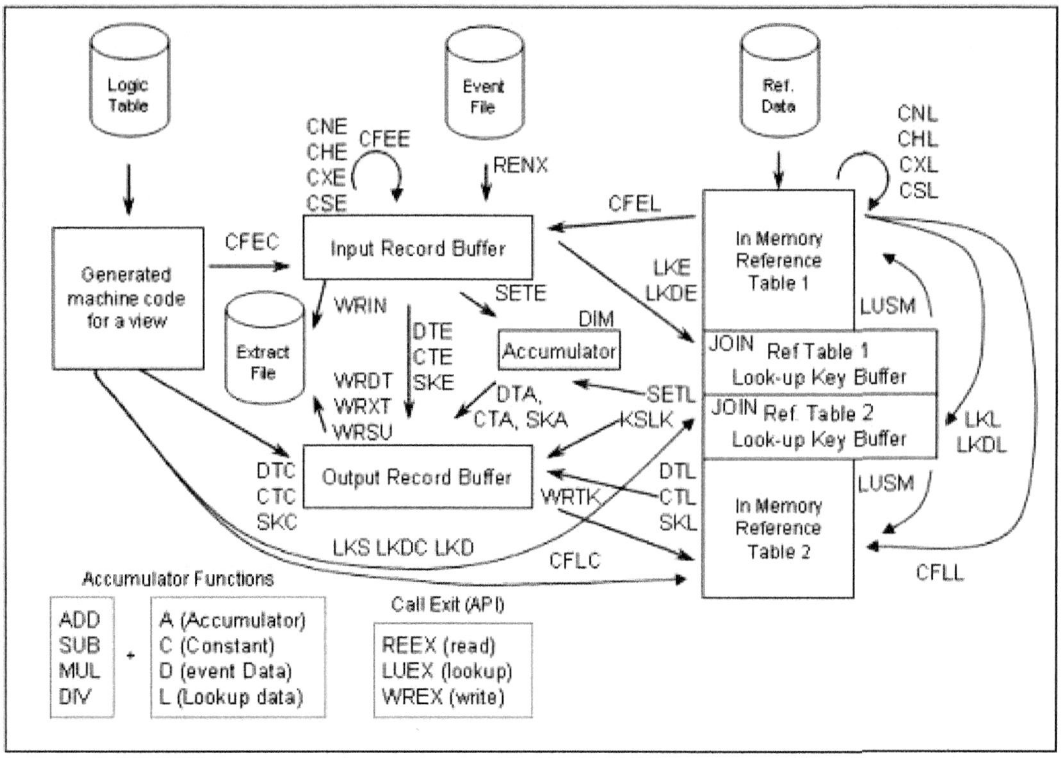

Figure 140. Exit and Other Logic Table Codes

All of these features bring us I guess to what I would call the *pièce de résistance* of SAFR configuration. It combines almost all of SAFR's capabilities in GVBMR95 into one process.

Chapter 52. Common Key Data Buffering

In Chapter 27, "Find More Detailed Events," on page 131, I described Doug creating the read exit for SAFR to read the Stacked Data Element file. The Stacked Data Element or SDE file contained many records of many different record types. In other words, one file needed multiple LRs to describe its records. Some of these records were "P" elements, for Policy level business events, like the ones Mark Kimmell used. Others were "L" elements for Ledger level business events. These are the ones Jim used in "show me the money." Other record structures were reference data, describing either the policy or company or ledger account attributes. The reason Doug had to write the exit was because the file didn't follow typical file structure rules. Doug's read exit made each element its own logical record; thus SAFR views could decode them.

Multiple Record Type Files

Thus far in our discussion, we have painted the picture that a single file can be described by a single LR. With the SDEs, though, this wasn't the case. Each SDE had a field in it that described the record type for that record, whether a P110 or something for the policy level transactions, or L103 for the ledger reference record. To read this file, each view had to have a record filter—the first record filter—which selected only records of a particular type which that view wanted to use as its event file.[153]

Thus in one SAFR thread, reading one SDE file, there could be different views each selecting a different type of SDE as its event file, and producing outputs from selected records of that file.[154]

Paired Look-up Exit

None of this was all that new to the tool. The break through that started the feature now known as Common Key Data Buffering was that Doug recognized, and there was a business need, to join from the business event SDE to the other reference data elements in the same SDE. A two-pass architecture could have been used, whereby views in the first pass would simply select and dump the desired reference data elements. These could then be put into the RED in the second pass and looked up as the SDE event elements were processed.

This approach was a loser when it came to performance. The volume of these reference elements was very high, because they could be on each policy transaction. This meant the IO was substantial for the first pass to just get the records out. They would take a lot of memory when loaded as reference files, and the search of them would waste CPU time in searching large tables unnecessarily.

Instead, Doug knew that the P element reference data would be in memory—in the read exit input buffer—at the same time the P business event came in, so Doug had an idea. He created a lookup exit that would be able to find the input buffer from the read exit, find any record in it of a particular type, and return that record as if it were the result of a lookup.

This approach worked because the elements in the SDE file that were related came at the same point in the file, so they would be in the read exit buffer at the same time. Doug recognized that this approach could be used to solve other problems.

---

153. Failure to make these record filters ends in views producing nonsensical outputs or, at worse, data exceptions.

154. In fact, the view described in Chapter 27, "Find More Detailed Events," on page 131 under "sort merge" was a multiple source view, but not in the typical sense we have described so far. Rather, it used this concept of each view selecting a particular type of record as its event file from the input file. Thus both "sources" were from the same file, just different LRs. One source read perhaps the "L110" elements to produce the ledger columns; the other read something like the P110 elements to produce the policy level columns. Both elements had the account key on them so that when the extract records were summarized, the results were collapsed into a single row.

For example, on the high tech chip manufacturer, we had to create views which joined from the event file to a reference file that was very large; larger than would fit in memory. The event file and the reference file were both in sorted order by the key that would be used to do the join. Doug had created a lookup exit which would read the reference file one record at a time as the event file was processed. This accomplished the join without loading everything into memory.

Then another problem came up which showed the limitations of this approach. A view needed to read the reference data file as an event file, to count records or something. It had to be read again just to produce this view. Again, this meant another pass of the data just to use some portion of it as a reference file.

Normalization

In Chapter 35, "Model the Repository," on page 179, we talked about modeling the data repository. It may be very useful to review the data structure example and description in that chapter. A common trade off in designing reporting applications is what level of normalization of the data is appropriate. For on-line systems, the process of storing a piece of information in only one place is important, so that update processes are efficient. Don't store the customer's name on every business event because if it changes you'll have a lot of records to update. Normalization also saves storage space because data is only stored once.

The problem with normalization is it requires joining data back together to make sense of it. If we want to report on many business events and summarize by single customer name, we have to put the data back together again. Thus I have heard Rick talk about "scatter and gather" whereby we spread everything out but then have to gather it all back together again for reporting. Joining takes CPU time.

As I said, for on-line systems, normalization is important. But once we have "cool data" as Rick calls it, records that aren't going to be updated any longer, we can "denormalize" it, putting certain well used fields on the business events that we would often need in reporting. Repeat the field on each record, so we don't have to do the join to report. This uses storage space to save CPU time.

Alternatively, dynamic denormalization is what is possible because of the exit Doug wrote. Instead of storing all the data in one denormalized file, as Greg and Doug worked together. Greg normalized all the tables; he stored each field only once. Then Doug made sure that the tables or files were in the form of a hierarchy, where the key to the top table, like Policy, was the high order key on all the other tables. The key for the next table down, Term, was repeated as the second key on all lower tables. Then Doug specified that the files be kept in sorted order by these keys.

Doug created a read exit to open all these files at once, the Policy, Term, Transactions, and read the first record from each file. It would continue reading records from these files until the Policy key changed. The data for one policy exists in memory at any one point in time, as shown in the Sample Insurance Input Buffer Figure 86 on page 181. This data looked just like the results of reading the Stacked Data Element file with many related records in memory at the same time. He then created a companion lookup exit to be used to search these records in the same way.

Now the data can be stored in a normalized manner, saving IO when reading it because there are fewer bytes (values aren't repeated on each transaction if they describe the same policy, for example), but the joins are very efficient because all the data needed for the joins exists in memory at one time. There is no additional IO to go find a reference data record and memory is not used for unrelated reference data.

Master File Update

What the project team did next was to turn SAFR from being a reporting system into a master file update process as described in Chapter 33, "Define Processes," on page 171. The team created views, one for each record type read by the exit, to write out a new updated version of that specific record type file. It contained a general select statement selecting only the appropriate entity records.

Because the data was presented by the read exit to the view, it appeared all records for that entity came from one specific file. But in addition to merging data from multiple entities, the read exit also merged data from multiple time partitions of the same entity.

For example, suppose we have a file that contains all the policy records the repository has ever seen. On a daily basis, we might receive a few updates to these policies from the source system. These come to the repository in their own file. The read exit can be configured to open both the history, and this new daily file, at the same time. It can merge records from these two entities into the same common key buffer, so that the policy record from yesterday (from the history file) and the updated policy record (from the daily file) for the same policy end up in memory at the same time.

The view which writes the new version of the repository history policy file can select both of these records. Thus at the end of the process, we have not only used the new policy record for any view which required it, we have also performed the update process to the repository by writing out a new history file.

This same approach was used to roll the daily records into the weekly file on a daily basis, the weekly file into the monthly file on a weekly basis, the monthly file into the annual file monthly, and the annual file into the history partition annually. Doing so meant that on a daily basis we don't have to write the entire history, annual, or monthly files; only the weekly files. This increases processing speed[155].

It is critical that all these files be created, and kept, in sorted order.

Let me make that point again. It is critical, for performance, that the process be defined to avoid ever sorting the files except perhaps the low volume daily input files. All other files must be written by SAFR in sorted order, preserving merge capabilities for the next execution.

Large Reference Files

The heart of the matter is the size of the reference files, and the processes to update them. At times, the reference data to be processed are larger in total than the event file containing the amounts to be summed.

Another common problem over the years was detecting changes in the reference data. Often systems present snapshots of the reference data; how a policy looks at a specific point in time. It is the responsibility of the repository to detect if any change in that policy has occurred by comparing it to the existing policy record.

Doug and the team recognized that they could also perform this function in the read exit, because the exit has both records available to it in the merge process. If the exit detected that the record in the daily file was exactly the same as the record in the repository, the exit could throw away the new record with no impact on any report. When a record was received in the new file that was different, the exit would place the processing effective date on the record. Thus the view writing the updated policy entity would write out both records, in sorted order by policy and effective date.

We found this model of processing so useful Doug was finding himself consistently writing these types of paired exits. He finally decided to generalize them, so they accepted parameters rather than having hard coded structures within them. The parameters specify which files should be opened, the start position and length of the merge keys on each file. This program and its related lookup exit are now part of the standard SAFR suite.

155. We used an alternative approach at the cookie manufacture, where we established seven daily files and each week we created empty versions of them. We then replaced an empty file with a real daily file each day. On a weekly basis, we accumulated all the daily files and rewrote monthly files I believe, eliminating the need to maintain weekly files at the cost of rewriting some data.

Paired Write Exit

The next development came with the creation of a companion write exit.

The first step in this development was when a project needed to use logic to generate additional event records. Instead of putting the logic into the SAFR module, Doug created the ability for the read exit to call other exits (programs which would emulate an access method for the read exit), to deliver records to it. These new records were simply inserted into the bottom of the common key input buffer, as if they had been read from disk.

On a later project, Doug recognized that often data is written by views in multiple pass processes and then needed for other views. Piping can be used for these purposes, but the pipe reader loses visibility and the ability to join to the other records in the read buffer. Rather than writing the data to disk, Doug created a companion write exit that was capable of inserting rows into the common key input buffer. These records looked as if they were read from disk, but they weren't; views downstream from the exit but in the same process created them.

Thus additional input records for a "virtual entity" could be created either by an exit or a view. An exit could be used if they were too complex for views, or views could do the work if control of the parameters in SAFR was easier for maintenance.

Results

This creates a very unique processing paradigm, something that I cannot think of an analogy for. It is almost as if a program is reading a file, and appending records onto the end of the input file; which records the program will see later as it continues processing. The truth of the matter is that the records aren't appended at the end of the input file, but rather in the middle of it, since the input files are sorted by policy, and that specific policy is being processed at the current moment and the records are inserted into the end of the input buffer.

As I have described this for people, they have wondered about the possibility of an infinite loop. There is a possibility if two views which create virtual output in the buffer are dependent upon each other for their input. The output from one view would create an output from the other view, which would then create output from the first view again. This would likely show up as running out of memory as the input buffer fills up and overflows. Understanding the dependencies between views to avoid creating this situation is important.

Most everything we have talked about came together in a most remarkable way in the spring of 2002.

Chapter 53. Spin-offs

While we continued to push the envelope with these kinds of software innovations, Rick also continued to try to find the right business model. PW had started a number of software initiatives in the early 90's including Activa II, an activity-based costing, budgeting and management software package, and Array, a COBOL system analysis tool, to build products, and at the end of the decade only SAFR was still around. Some had been sold, like Activa to Oracle, and the others had folded. Our sales experience showed PW did not have a software brand. Based upon the close connection with the mainframe, Rick decided to see if IBM was interested in buying the software. In the fall of 1999 after a couple of meetings they said no.

Next, having gained an inside look at the software, Troy Deck at Wingspan decided to take a shot at purchasing it. Troy worked very hard to raise capital, but couldn't raise the required funds, the amount of which seemed to me to inflate dramatically when ever someone showed up with a wallet. Raising significant capital was nearly impossible as well because PwC was an auditing firm. They couldn't engage in any type of investment activity with any audit client or anyone that invested in audit clients. With the size of PwC and the interconnected nature of capital, it probably seemed to Troy that only two little old ladies in Iowa qualified to provide funding and they weren't interested. Having successfully helped to build the new user interface and assisted in porting SAFR to client server, Troy finally gave up early in 2001.[156].

Somewhere in 2001 Rick got connected with Bob Beech and Digineer. The end of November they wanted to meet an existing customer to kick the tires so to say, so I hosted some of the employees at the Insurance Company. A joint venture was signed between PwC and Digineer in January 2002. The chip manufacturer was to provide some level of funding; the idea was to create a SAFR product that could work on a specially designed computer box. I remember Bob describing the self contained event repository with SAFR's ability to get through it quickly as a Hubble telescope beneath an employee's desk.

Soon thereafter I was invited by Bob to join Rick on a trip to Cincinnati, the company headquarters. The next day a coworker joined Bob and me to visit a professor at Vanderbilt University, a leading authority on Medical Informatics. Digineer's roots were in informatics and Bob wanted to validate that SAFR could be applied to the medical field.

It was exciting to have someone interested in the tool we had built, attempting to articulate its value, and to apply it to new subject areas. Yet launching a new business in the wake of the Internet bust was a difficult proposition to float; within a few months Digineer went out of business.[157]

In December of 2001 Enron failed, the largest US bankruptcy ever. The conflict within Arthur Anderson between auditing and consulting was partially blamed. I remember being amazed at the newspaper coverage in January when my business and even my firm were mentioned daily on the front page. The result was a set of new regulations that auditors could not consult with audit clients. Fear swept the PwC client base; the impact of the economy already weakened by the Internet bust and September 11th now started to hit very close to home.

156. The Wingspan web site notes: "Mr. Deck led the successful development effort to extend GENEVA technology to client-server." (http://www.wingspan.com/about/team.asp). Troy and Wingspan went on to develop a successful business and products supporting content management.

157. Bob went on to become a successful CEO of another life sciences company which was successfully purchased by a leading company in the space. He continued as the Senior Vice President, Corporate Development & Communications after the purchase.

PwC had considered selling the consulting division to HP for $19 billion, a year and a half earlier. Now with each passing day the value of the business dropped precipitously. It was a burning platform. Something had to be done immediately to avoid the same fate as Arthur Anderson. Leadership determined to spin off the consulting business through an IPO.[158] Even though PwC was an accounting firm, with experts at implementing every conceivable system, its own internal systems were woefully neglected. Because they weren't a public company, they had almost no external demands for investing in the systems. Suddenly the need for internal systems became critical.

As I drove to the airport when I left Digineer the afternoon of February 8th, 2002, Rick asked the team to join a conference call. He explained that he had been charged with building a reporting system to show PwC's revenue and costs by industry, a key aspect to understanding its business in preparation for the IPO S-1 filing. He recited a number of aspects of the problem that he was not responsible for with a certain sense of relief. The deadline was now July 1st. The S-1 had to be filed even earlier, so our team had even less time.

The race was on. We were to be tested to see how quickly we could build a reporting system using the concepts of a business event based architecture.

158. We later learned they had chosen the name of the company to be "Monday." I remember everyone trying to reconcile themselves to the name and a great deal of relief when it didn't happen.

Chapter 54. Crisis

The first few weeks of the project, I continued to work with Digneer while everyone else suddenly was immersed in the race. Monica Logan headed up the team organization, and Chris Stallman took on the project approach. In perhaps a week the team expanded to 20 people.

The first order of business was to deploy people to 12 different countries or processing regions that represented something like 80% of the global PwC revenues. These included the U.S., Australia, Belgium, Canada, Switzerland, Germany, Spain, UK, Japan, Netherlands, and groups of countries in both East Asia and South America. Rick outlined the instructions to the head executives in those countries, and used global executive support whenever resistance was encountered to following them. In three weeks, each finance department was instructed to provide the following data files from their systems for the current and two prior years:

1. General ledger balances or the journal entries, specifically identifying any manual adjustments
2. All the client billing detailed records from the billing systems
3. All the timesheet entries for billable staff.

Others began to work with the Global PwC Finance team. They learned that every month each country submitted a spreadsheet, called the MOR for Monthly Operating Report, of the financial results. These were consolidated into the global financial statements using a tool called TM1. Business team members obtained copies of these.

Note the pattern here: Find known numbers. Find the event file from the existing ledger. Establish the ability to recreate the numbers from the journals, and then drive to lower levels of detail in the transaction system files.

Build reference data was next. The reference data was listings of client code, with industry codes on them, billing rates, etc. They found, with time, that they needed to make these date effective, to account for changes in the reference data over time. So a small program was written to compare changed reference data. The team refined the reference data over time by producing many reports.

The firm had an existing data warehouse system that in summary showed the revenues by industry, be it consumer products, financial services, transportation and utilities, high tech, etc. However, there was a critical flaw in the data. The numbers were accumulated from the core financial system, the industry field representing the industry the consultant was assigned to, not the industry of the client. Each staff was assigned to an industry, say financial services, but if that staff worked on a consumer products client, the revenue showed up as financial services. There was tremendous sharing of resources, and so the numbers weren't accurate at all.

Rick knew that the financial numbers were the accumulation of the business events. In a consulting company the business events are timesheet entries of staff working on client engagements. Timesheets accumulate costs to projects. Costs are marked up, and turned into billing records to clients. So on the time and billing records the client would be identified in every case, and that client could be associated with an industry.

The files began to show up. The Global Financial Data Warehouse or GFDW architecture was very simple. The team guessed at a simple data model the records from all 12 countries would fit into. Because every country had different systems, SAFR views were created to transform in an ETL like manner the country source system specific formats into the standard layout. There were really three standard layouts, one for each of the file types.

The data volumes were not huge; there were a few hundred thousand employees worldwide, and they submitted timesheets weekly or so. There were fewer clients. However, the PwC mainframe was one of the smallest made. If we had to purchase and install hardware we never would have been able to meet the deadlines. As it was, because of the efficiency of SAFR we could make the system work within existing hardware.

Sequential generation data group or GDGs were used to partition the data by year and month for the larger countries. Using sequential files added efficiency by eliminating CPU cycles putting data into the database and pulling it out of the database. We also did not have to perform extensive data cleansing to prepare the data to load the database. If an extracted field was not used contained garbage, it was ignored through our entire process but not dropped. At times, as we did more data discovery, we found instances where fields we hadn't understood became useful. There was no additional work to use them since they were retained in the repository.

From Rick's phone call on February 20th, people were deployed to many of the countries starting February 25th. By the middle of March, data files from many of them were received, and the ETL views constructed to put them into the standard format. The MOR reports had been gathered, and control numbers identified. A simple set of balancing views against the standard files had been constructed.

I began to help out the second week of April or so as the team began to work to reconcile the data. By the 26th of April—2 months and 6 days after that phone call—the following reconciliation summary was produced.

Abbrv	Territory	MOR Net Revenue	Territory Net Revenue	Territory Net Revenue Adjustment	Difference Net Revenue (F)
		C	D	E	F = C-D-E
AUX	Australia	357,252,000.00	354,144,457.38	932,068.26	2,175,474.36
BE1	Belgium	245,947,000.00	245,207,164.01	(145,108.34)	884,944.33
CAX	Canada	544,124,000.00	544,124,601.94	0.00	(601.94)
CHX	Switzerland	279,700,000.00	263,349,165.91	30,722,377.09	-14,371,543
DEX	Germany	758,222,000.00	810,176,185.59	0.00	(51,954,185.59)
EAX	East Asia	229,951,000.00	226,261,901.54	0.00	3,689,098
ESX	Spain	256,775,000.00	262,901,055.31	(12,448,903.83)	6,322,849
GB1	UK	1,818,201,000.00	1,873,924,884.90	(17,221,477.66)	(38,502,407.24)
JPX	Japan	383,250,000.00	383,256,151.65	0.00	(6,151.65)
NLX	Netherlands	396,824,000.00	382,362,743.46	3,997,376.05	10,463,880.49
SAX	SOACAT	265,610,000.00	145,577,765.08	0.00	120,032,234.92
USA	US	6,545,120,000.00	6,339,507,591.39	99,377,802.00	106,234,606.61
		12,080,976,000.00	11,830,793,668.16	105,214,133.57	144,968,198.27
Percent of Total		100.00	97.93	0.87	1.20

Figure 141. Revenue Balancing Spreadsheet

The team had recreated from the detailed billing files (column D) and adjustments (column E) nearly 99% of the revenue numbers for three years of history to the globally reported financial statements (column C).[159] The team had also reconciled hours billed by staff to within 2.5% for the same 3 years.

Many of the regional finance people told Rick they had never reconciled the detail to their ledger numbers and they weren't sure it could be done. Rick asked if they were suggesting they wouldn't balance which would be a real audit issue. Immediately they all would say that it could be balanced, they just had never done it. When the auditors did arrive to test the S-1 schedule they signed off very quickly with no issues. They could easily test where the business events had come from, and recreate the summary numbers we had accumulated.

The first S-1 industry segmentation report was produced on April 17th, I believe. The schedule was a summary of the billing detail file joined to the client reference data, summarized by industry codes and countries. The outputs all fit in Excel, and Rick learned how to use pivot tables to change the dimensions easily. We would run the views to produce the S-1 data at the same time we balanced the files.

Rick had Mukesh Patel start a one man project completed in a few weeks. He used SAFR to allocate employee cost for the year to the projects the employee had worked on by hours worked. Mukesh did this with two or three passes of SAFR, and a handful of views. The outputs from the process then could be accumulated by project, to show the cost of the project, the revenue, and the gross profit.

Other team members enhanced the reference data, by creating mapping from local company IDs to global companies. In this way, the global project for General Motors or Nestle could be shown. Rick found that people inside the firm had never known the things he was discovering in the data. Because the event level data was gathered and accessible, it was an incredibly flexible reporting system. The following is the June 27th report ahead of the updated S-1 filing date. It is still incredible to me what the team could do, when using the right approach, with a system architecture that focused on capturing and reporting from business events.

159. The US was the most complex, because it also had the highest volume. In the next few weeks and months additional adjustments were identified for all the countries, which improved the reconciliation. Also additional countries were added, taking the system up to something above 90% of revenues, which were balanced to within about .2% of the total.

160. The MOR numbers cannot be broken out by industry because the attributes of the legacy financial system did not accumulate that attribute. Reporting from the event level data enabled viewing the data by the last two columns.

Fiscal Year	Industry Name	Total MOR Net Revenue	Total MOR Cost of Service	Total EMS Net Revenue	Total Allocated Cost of Service
2000	*****	5,125,870,220	2,876,086,638	9,269,428	2,922,462
	E&U	0	0	403,210,852	219,905,474
	FS	0	0	974,056,525	492,325,940
	G&S	0	0	1,124,232,882	710,280,987
	ICE	0	0	678,735,641	379,313,791
	Other	0	0	24,302,209	33,425,471
	Products	0	0	1,617,043,247	971,484,939
	TtI Adjustment	0	0	144,097,573	0
2000 Total		5,125,870,220	2,876,086,638	4,974,948,358	2,809,659,064
2001	*****	4,806,282,000	2,920,752,533	3,177,104	1,320,989
	E&U	0	0	462,810,688	260,397,809
	FS	0	0	877,039,918	494,027,638
	G&S	0	0	1,060,625,405	742,315,983
	ICE	0	0	578,963,719	380,403,947
	Other	0	0	12,428,928	6,279,747
	Products	0	0	1,725,318,201	1,035,996,170
	TtI Adjustment	0	0	79,810,569	0
2001 Total		4,806,282,000	2,920,752,533	4,800,174,533	2,920,742,283
9Mo FY02	*****	3,191,670,000	1,897,065,800	2,597,190	824,215
	E&U	0	0	333,275,813	195,917,955
	FS	0	0	483,485,583	273,373,184
	G&S	0	0	855,983,127	551,110,326
	ICE	0	0	373,024,275	228,005,012
	Other	0	0	2,360,185	6,846,366
	Products	0	0	1,115,202,985	640,982,335
	TtI Adjustment	0	0	27,786,142	0
9Mo FY02 Total		3,191,670,000	1,897,065,800	3,193,715,299	1,897,059,393
Grand Total		13,123,822,220	7,693,904,972	12,968,838,190	7,627,460,739

160

Figure 142. Industry Segmentation Report

I had a family vacation the middle of July and was pretty much completely cut off from the news media and the project. When I returned to work the following Monday, Lynn Groves Zuccala, the project manager, asked what I thought of the announcement. I asked what announcement. She couldn't believe I had not heard; IBM had announced they would buy the consulting division for $4 billion. What a radical change in plans.

Beginning in May and June the team turned the system into an operational system. Each country on a monthly basis would extract that month's data and send it over to the team to add to the warehouse. IBM used the results of the system to understand the business. Portions of it were used to convert the legacy data over to IBM's systems when the merger took effect on October 1st, 2002 and systems were converted in January.

About the middle of August I called Doug one night to talk about prospects and all the changes. In the course of the conversation he confided that he was being forced to retire prior to the merger with IBM. He asked me to keep the knowledge to myself. It concerned me. Over the next few days I vacillated between being worried and then at times I would feel that things would work out. I surely didn't know how, though.

About two weeks later we were together in the PwC office in Rosemont, Illinois. I suspect he could tell I was having one of the more worrisome days, and I think he changed his flight plans to spend a bit more time with me. It was a very kind thing of him to worry about and serve me at such a time, but very consistent with his nature.

He pulled me into an office and told me that we were still very good friends, and that would not change. He said he was very confident we would continue to have contact with each other. I knew that he was only a few months from when he would qualify for retirement, but he said he wasn't bitter, or really upset. He said that his ego was a bit bruised because he wasn't chosen to go forward into the new organization, but he wasn't really upset. He expressed faith that the right things would happen in the end.

I expressed affection for him, and I said that I wasn't really worried. Rather I felt comfortable with where things were going, but also felt bruised when he felt bruised. I did feel lightened after the discussion. We met for a few minutes multiple times throughout the day to coordinate how to handle his departure. He gave me approval to start telling selected individuals.

He left for the airport to fly home late in the afternoon. I walked to a conference room where Randall, Monica, Chris and Jim were talking. I said I had some bad news, that Doug was being forced to retire. I then said, "But there isn't any other group of people I would want to face this challenge with than this team."

Part 6. The Platform

All of the experiences over all the years have resulted in a platform that is radically different than today's financial reporting systems. Before we describe that system, let's review briefly the principles behind it, as outlined in Parts 2 and 3.

1. Business events are the stuff all business reporting systems are made of.
2. Answers to questions are most often contained in a single record of a report of some kind.
3. The reporting record and the business event are very different things; most often the reporting record requires passage of time, and accumulation of many business events.
4. As business expanded the use of IT, more and more attributes were captured on business events, with a corresponding demand to use them in reports.
5. Rather than scaling the posting processes to accumulate business events into reporting records by posting at lower levels of detail, IT chose to make multiple posting processes and reporting environments, each for a subset of attributes.
6. As reporting systems proliferated, the systems took short cuts with time and auditability, creating reporting systems which do not reconcile, adding to the confusion.
7. This proliferation of reporting systems with many different reporting models has caused:
    a. Increased IT cost in maintenance of systems,
    b. Increased cost in the business through reconciliation, inaccessible information, and poor decisions based on inaccurate information,
    c. Increased cost to society through poor transparency,
    d. Decreased flexibility to respond to new business, IT and societal demands.
8. These diseconomies of scale are most prevalent in the largest organizations.
9. The cost of financial and other types of reporting is enormous and, unless a different approach is taken to the problem, will become worse as we spend more money for the same solutions which are creating today's problems.
10. The alternative is to scale the posting process, moving the reporting function closer to the need and reducing the system proliferation.

The resulting platform, similar to a skyscraper, large factory or warehouse, consolidates many other functions into one location. This system demonstrates that greater scale is possible.

Chapter 55. Transition

The feelings of panic, followed closely by the feelings of euphoria, continued for a couple of years. Notwithstanding what happened to Doug, the prospect of being acquired by a technology company opened the possibility that SAFR might be more fully exploited as a software product. Even though IBM had taken a pass on purchasing SAFR by itself, they had now acquired it as part of a larger asset: all of PwC consulting.

Not long after the merger, we were introduced to people in the software group who were asked to determine if SAFR should be a "program product." There are many kinds of software products within IBM, but I take it program products are perhaps the highest designation with the highest requirements as well. There was a series of meetings with technical architects and business people. I remember getting the feeling that the business owner had been burned trying to turn a services developed asset into a product, and that the mainframe was being viewed as a non strategic platform.

The result of the reviews was that, yes, SAFR certainly had all the scale, weight, complexity, and feature set of a true product. However, there wasn't an easy way to integrate it with other products; for example, it doesn't use SQL, a common platform independent language that allows for different pieces to fit together. The second conclusion was that it didn't have the track record of sales to conclude that it could be supported financially on license revenue alone. This resulted in feelings of panic.

A/R Conversion and GSD

The reviews and other meetings opened up a lot of discussion with people inside of IBM, either in consulting or in the software area, that touched upon the problem SAFR solved. With the size and breadth of IBM, it seemed we could continually be introduced to new people to discuss the possibilities. So although by early 2003 prospects of being a program product dimmed, the opportunities for new uses of SAFR seemed very real. We were even able to start some internal IBM projects using SAFR.

Continuing the GFDW project, SAFR was used for conversion activities. Chris Stallman somehow was tasked with converting all of PwC's receivables into the IBM systems. Late in the project new requirements started to show up. Jim Hladyshewsky had been helping part time, and over night became more than double time.

Randall showed up and applied his ability to turn everything into a parallel process, and handle differences in processing for the numerous countries involved, simply by configuring his script generator. In the end he generated perhaps a million lines of code to make the system work. Chris and I thought an exit was needed, so one evening I took that assignment on as we sat around the conference table working. After a number of hours, I still couldn't get the very simple thing to work, perhaps not even compile. Chris then said something like, "You know Kip, if we did this in the view, we wouldn't need that exit." We all thought about it and agreed. I made a joke about feeling fairly useless.

Chris's success led to other internal projects. Another significant, if nearly unheralded application, was the Global Services Delivery project whereby SAFR was used to read IBM services ticket transaction repository and generate SAFR cubes. During this project Jerry Canterbury wrote the GVBSR01 and 02 Sort Exits to generate multiple permutations of a view. The actual constructed views covered 14 different dimension, for weekly, monthly, and quarterly views of the data; the generated views numbered around 1,000 views. The permutations would have been many times beyond that.

Rakesh Kant was key to the US data extracts on the GFDW project, the most complex country with the largest data. He and I had begun to talk about how to connect SAFR better to the downstream information delivery tools and he took the initiative to create a proposal about how he thought we might enhance SAFR to work with databases more effectively. He also took on a rewrite of the SAFR Insight Viewer, and created a very nice JAVA application.

Rakesh expanded this for the GSD project. He converted the SAFR Insight Viewer to work as a web service, wherein the custom browser interface built for users to select which cuts of data they wanted would request those cuts from the cubes. The SAFR Insight Viewer web service would perform the access to the correct cubes to satisfy the requests. Below shows the resulting web interface, fed with data from SAFR Scan Engine and the SAFR web service. This started Rakesh down the road of creating the SAFR Managed Insights and the Indexed Engine.[161]

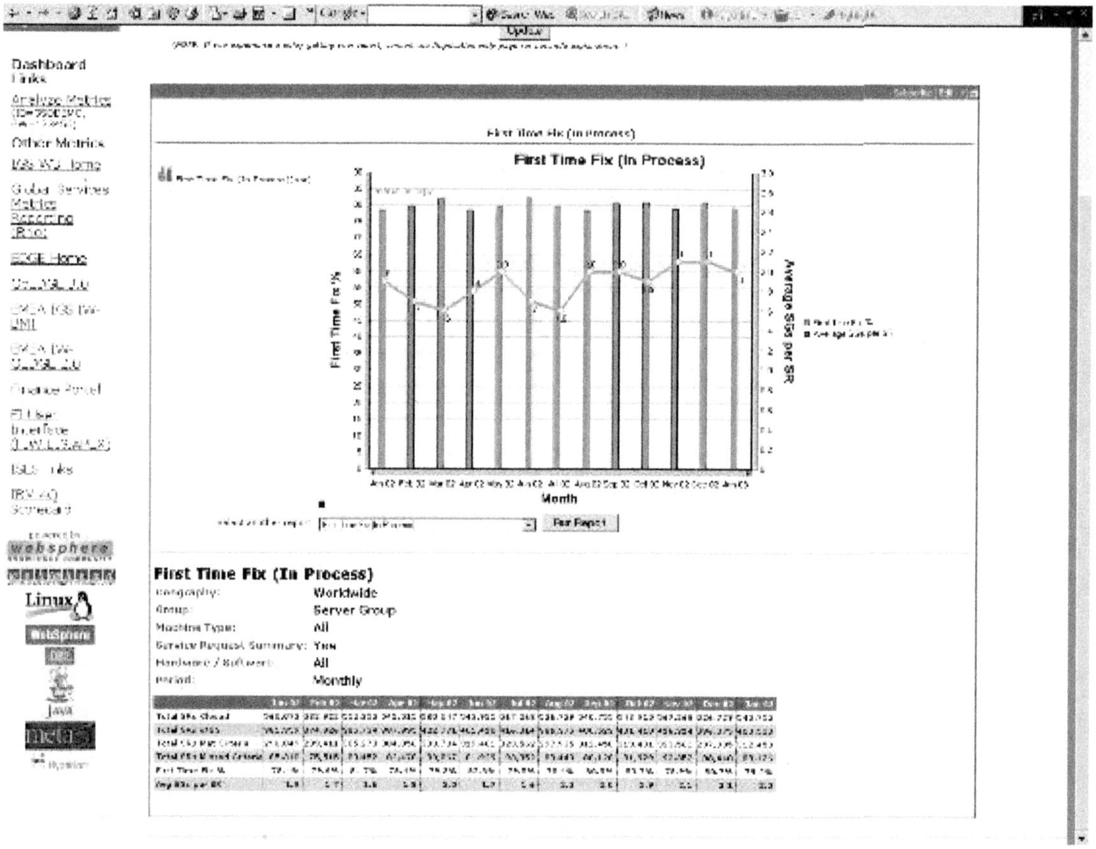

Figure 143. GSD System Sample Output

With this project, the difficulty in marketing seemed to ease dramatically: euphoria.

Version 4 Development

These projects were completed with either the CICS SAFR front end, termed Geneva Version 3.3 Viewbuilder, (initially developed in 1993), or used a limited set of the scan engine functionality and the new user interface, called the Workbench. The Workbench did not work completely with the mainframe versions of the Scan Engine, GVBMR95 and GVBMR88. There were two dependencies to finishing SAFR version 4 to hope to survive as a product: money, and people—specifically Doug: panic.

In the middle of January, Randall and I put together estimates of what it would cost to do various things with the software. On one extreme was the cost of just shutting the business down, which raised potential client relationship issues. At the other end was turning it into a full fledged product. In between

161. The story of this development is, in and of itself, likely worthy of an entire new part to this book.

were a couple of other options. I felt we really had a good story to tell about what could be done with the software. We reviewed it with Rick, and he agreed. He took it up the chain, and actually received approval to do one of the middle options. We had funding: euphor—OK, you get the picture.

The next part of the problem depended upon Doug. Similar to perhaps millions who have undergone the transition of a major corporate purchase, I could sympathize, undergoing feelings of frustration, anger, disappointment and fear myself. Fortunately, Doug had agreed to continue to work with us as a contractor.

The insurance company needed additional help with SAFR; they also wanted to use the new front end. With the funding provided by IBM, Doug and I started using their SAFR environment as a test bed to prove that the version 4 features worked the same. We had been working towards this goal for a while, but the need became more urgent. To set a measurable goal, I sent the IBM team the following e-mail on May 8, 2003:

> ...I propose that we identify a set of selected passes that we will convert to V4 in the next 3 weeks by May 30th and produce output files that we can compare byte for byte....
>
> A few years ago Blue Diamond Almonds ran a commercial with the tag line, "A can a week, that is all we ask." Well, perhaps we could name this our Operation Blue Diamond, and use as our motto, "A pass a week, that is all we ask."...

In the prior year we had become conversant with some debugging tools that actually were capable of managing the complexities of the parallel processing code generation environment. Most tools could not provide the insights needed. I had learned to do this with Randall's help.

Greg Forsythe and Michael Shapiro worked with the client team to identify areas we needed to focus, and to debug problems that were outside of the scan engine that could be handled by others. They would feed me the defects with the conditions that created them. I would then recreate them in the debugger, setting appropriate break points and doing the level of debugging I could do. I would call Doug over when I got to a particular point and he would analyze the problem. He might have me go on to other places, or go back and code a fix while I set up the next problem.

We worked very late most evenings. There was nowhere to get food inside the building, and once we left we couldn't get back in. The overhead lights would go off, and we would often sit with just our cubicle lights on as we worked for hours. By the time we left, there would often be only the local 24 hour diner open to feed us. I seem to remember earlier in the year taking Doug out to eat after 11:00 PM or so to the diner. It was his sixtieth birthday. What a celebration.

At the end of May, I was quite surprised when we could actually claim victory in our goal towards having three passes converted. That wasn't the end of the work; we continued working through the defect counts that summer and into the fall. But we had gotten over the hurdle; we had created version four of the software.

In February we held a second retirement dinner for Doug so the people at the insurance company projects could attend. After dinner he told me he spent a number of months feeling angry about how he had been treated. Yet one day he realized that he was getting to do the things he wanted to do, with the people he wanted to do them, and decided the anger wasn't what he wanted to feel on a daily basis. I found my own frustration subsiding that summer as well.

Chapter 56. Walkabout

The initial transition stage gave way to a period of reflection. The number of opportunities decreased as the organization converted from an accounting firm to a technology company with a very large sales force. I recognized in the Fall of 2003 that we weren't connected to that sales force in any meaningful way. Our funding was nearly used up and, given the Internet crash, no one was funding new IT tools. And prospects for new customers hadn't materialized.

Rick began in September of that year to work with a global universal bank, helping to outline a SAFR like financial reporting solution. They readily grasped the benefits of a business event based architecture. However, the entire IT strategic direction was to use UNIX.

In November, Rick went with the client to visit a strategic IT software partner. He was pretty impressed by what he saw, and told me he wondered how we could compete against a company with a 1 billion market capitalization, and 300 dedicated programmers. It threw me for a loop, but I didn't have a good answer.

At the end of the month, Rick asked if I would meet with a technician from that company and make my own assessment. I asked Monica to join me. It was a very interesting day. It led me to wonder as well if what we were trying to accomplish with SAFR couldn't be done another way. If that were possible, client investments in existing applications might be protected, and the benefits of the business event approach to reporting might be achieved much sooner, because the tools are already much more widely used.

Having consulted with a number of the team members about this sort of thinking, I asked Rick to let me contact IBM corporate development to investigate the possibility of an IBM divestiture of SAFR. This began a multiple month analysis of all aspects of the SAFR business. The corporate development people pushed us to explain the business model, the product, the market, the competitors, and the people. I remember one day being complimented for the thoroughness of our analysis.

We had a number of meetings with potential acquirers. One ETL vendor seemed particularly interested, which resulted in a number of onsite visits.

I came away with an understanding that SAFR wasn't solving the traditional ETL problem. As noted in Chapter 29, "Iteratively View Results," on page 145, those tools typically have many connectors to many data types.

With these insights while still in the midst of considering divestiture, I decided I needed to better articulate what was unique about SAFR. Our introductory meetings within IBM had emphasized what SAFR shared in common with other tools, in order to help properly classify it with other tools.[162]

I began making a slide presentation that explained the SAFR differences, that SAFR was about the convergence of ETL and reporting processes. Bill O'Connell, an IBM Distinguished Engineer in information management, was very helpful in encouraging my explanations. He gave me opportunities to present, and refine the deck to new IBM audiences. This generated another round of discussion, and interest in some quarters in pursuing a transfer of the tool.

Earlier in the winter, on the same day we had our first discussion with a potential acquirer, I had a good friend, whom I deeply respect and was then serving a five year assignment as the volunteer pastor of my church, contact me wondering if I would be interested in going to work with him. It would have been a

162. Parenthetically, I also had the idea to write this book.

complete career change for me. His call startld me evaluating over the next few months what I wanted to do for work. I analyzed, from top to bottom, what I did and did not like about my work, and considered if perhaps it was time for me to move on to something different.

In August all these divergent threads came together in some sense. I decided I should know for myself what this opportunity with my friend might be like. So I finally suggested I make an office visit and we discuss it. We went to lunch first, and he asked me a very unexpected question, but one completely in keeping with his concern for me as a mentor and friend. "Kip, if you somehow dropped out of the sky into a completely new place and had to find something to do for work, what would you do?"

I was speechless, which is not very common for me at all. Amidst all the turmoil, because I had this friend's potential offer of employment, I had not worried about what would become of me after the divestiture. It provided me tremendous emotional stability and objectivity. But amidst all my contemplation about what I liked and did not like about what I did for work, I had never thought to ask that particular question. What did I want to do? I remember stammering for what seemed quite awhile to me, and finally blurting out, "I think I would do exactly what I have been doing."

It was quite an insight for me. If I could, I would continue to do exactly what I have been doing. I still felt a real sense of mission.

The next day, I was in an IBM management training class. I was gaining a better perspective on what IBM really wanted me to be. That afternoon I left the class a few minutes early to have a discussion with the new CTO of IBM Information Management, Anant Jinghran. A month earlier in again reviewing the asset, he had felt he had misunderstood SAFR in prior discussions. He asked for more time, and this meeting was the result.

Also a month earlier, IBM had acquired the one ETL vendor who had shown the most interest in the tool. Instead of building from scratch on the base of SAFR, and capturing new white space at the same time, IBM had purchased a significant portion of the ETL market.

Anant listened as I and Randall explained the concepts behind SAFR more fully, the new insights on how SAFR was unique. I remember him asking about data cleansing, to which I responded with what's described in Chapter 29, "Iteratively View Results," on page 145. "What gets exposed through reporting is what gets cleaned up."

There was a slight pause, and he responded with, "Your and Randall's vision of this entire space is fascinating."

I was dumbfounded again, twice in two days. "Fascinating" he had said. There really was something to what we were doing, something fundamentally different than anyone else's approach. And what we were doing was exactly what I wanted to do for work, even though it was very challenging.

A few weeks later I called a team meeting. I titled my slides "Results of the SAFR Walkabout." A walkabout is "a short period of wandering bush life, engaged in by an Australian aborigine as an occasional interruption of regular work".[163] I explained everything that had gone on in the last year, and what the results were. There was still some small chance we might be made a software product, but similar to my feelings about me being in the right place, SAFR was also in the right place.

I decided it was time to stop thinking about what we might have been, and start being what IBM wanted us to be. I also decided to start pursuing every opportunity with abandon.

163. Merriam-Webster 11th Collegiate Dictionary sv "Walkabout".

Chapter 57. The General Ledger

On April 15th 2004, I flew to Buffalo, New York for the first time. I started on a project Rick had been working on for nine months, to build the next generation of the financial system for a very large, worldwide bank. I started by reviewing an existing reporting application, perhaps somewhat a test to see if I really knew anything, and was then assigned to install SAFR. The start of many large projects begins with attempting to gain traction. I think back to those days, as described by one man, with "...nostalgia for past days of obscurity." Those were days of obscurity, when few had any idea what we were really attempting to do, and the work effort that would be involved.

Let's start our analysis of the platform by examining the general ledger, and reviewing the basics of the posting process.

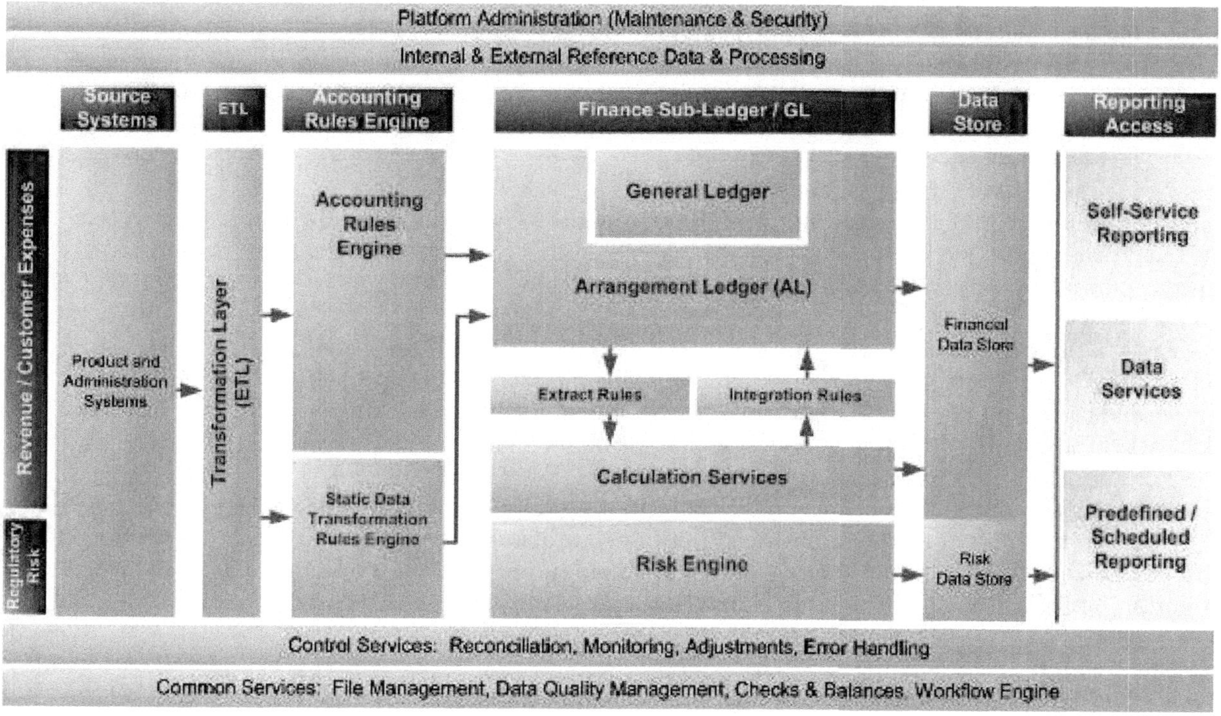

Figure 144. Financial Management Solution (FMS) Platform

The general ledger summarizes business events by those attributes called the accounting code block, and posts them to the ledger for some predetermined time periods, such as months, or now becoming more common, days. The major fields involved, which are also summarized on the general ledger, might be the following:

- Business Unit
- Ledger
- Account
- Cost Center
- Product
- Customer Type
- Affiliate

- Source
- Book Code
- Currency
- Date
- Period
- Amount

In addition to these fields, journal entries—effectively the transactions—typically also have a date and time stamp, a journal entry number/unique identifier, preparer and approver user IDs, and perhaps a description, particularly for manual journal entries.

Let's take a moment and properly orient ourselves with an example, one that includes scale.

Financial Services

Suppose we run a Financial Services company. Financial services includes banks, insurance, and financial markets. These types of institutions were at the forefront of developing modern accounting practices because the basic nature of their business is in many respects a general ledger. A portion of the money I deposit into an account (likely a name derived from its corresponding tracking device in the general ledger) is loaned to someone else, as represented in another account. The difference between the two accounts is the bank's capital.

One shift we will have to make is that from the banks' perspective, deposits aren't assets; loans are. Deposits mean the bank has to pay you, the account holder, when you ask for it, similar to accounts payable. Loans means the bank can ask you to pay when they want, an account receivable. As we consider our example at scale, we'll need to hold this in mind.

The reason a financial services company's financial systems deal with scale is because, now instead of keeping track of one person's financial statement, the company must keep track of thousands, hundreds of thousands, even millions of financial statements, or better said, financial position. Is that true you might ask? Consider the following.

Today's banking financial systems do not keep track of each individual's financial statement or position in total. Each portion of your personal financial position is broken up and held in different systems; or subsystems. The amount of your deposit on hand is held in one system; the Demand Deposit Account system (in the US). The amount of your home loan is held in the mortgage system.

Consistent with the subsystem architecture, in most cases your deposit account gets accumulated with lots of other deposit accounts, and one journal entry is sent to the general ledger system with all the activity—desposits or withdrawals—for today. The same happens with your mortgage. Your payment is accumulated with thousands or millions of others and sent to the general ledger system.

Thus the traditional financial system sits atop all these other subsystems and keeps track of the summary results. But as we have noted, the weakness of the subsystem architecture becomes clear as more and more attributes are needed for reporting. This need creates a proliferation of summary structures—effectively additional ledgers—to provide the answers. The accumulated affect becomes inflexible and unsupportable. An alternative approach is required. This is where the Arrangement Ledger comes in.

Chapter 58. The Arrangement Ledger

The bank I was working with recognized that they had numerous reporting systems dealing with the details of various customers. These details weren't in the General Ledger, but they were maintained in other, ancillary systems. And these other systems weren't built to the standards of a general ledger. Rather, often they were made to reconcile to some portion of the general ledger, perhaps after the fact, with adjustments made in numerous places. The finance organization had a single-minded determination to build a system capable of keeping these details.

With time, it became clear that the general ledger could not be expanded to keep all these details. Numerous discussions were had about the required form of the system. The technical team pointed out that any system that can maintain the details is capable of being the source for the summary. Yet to the finance team, the notion of a finance system without a general ledger, or a general ledger which is so radically different from anything owned by any other company, was just a bit too risky. Thus the idea of the Arrangement Ledger (AL) was born.

In a very similar manner to the General Ledger, the AL takes in journal entries, and posts them to the Arrangement Ledger. This might be done by simply adding an additional key, called the Arrangement ID, to the list of fields above to each journal entry and to the ledger.

Arrangement Defined

What is an arrangement ID? This could be a very lengthy discussion in some circles, but for our purposes, let's describe it as a specific customer contract. For example, if my company takes out a loan from the bank, that creates an arrangement. The arrangement ID might be simply composed of an ID from the source system that holds my loan details[164], and the loan number.[165]

By adding an arrangement ID onto the journals and the ledger, the balances accumulated now represent the balances for my loan. Within this same ledger, balances for any other loan are simply another set of rows.

Millions of "Ledgers"

The addition of this key has transformed the system from something containing a set of rows describing point in time balances for the entire company, or perhaps more accurately sets of rows describing each of the legal entities or companies, into a set of rows which describe an individual customer contract.

Let's be clear; there is not just one row for each customer contract. There are multiple rows for each customer contract because each customer contract is composed of multiple balances. There is a row that represents the principle of the loan, another for the interest payable, another for the fee revenue, another for accrued taxes. Typically, the General Ledger account, in combination with the arrangement ID would make each row of the Arrangement Ledger unique.[166]

Thus the Arrangement Ledger would contain millions even tens or hundreds of millions of tiny little ledgers, each reflecting the position of an individual customer contract as of a point in time.

---

164. This ID makes the arrangement ID unique across source systems.

165. In complex situation, many different banking "products" (a checking account, a loan, etc.) might be part of one contract. Although perhaps most arrangements are described by a contract, variations are possible. For complex contracts, multiple arrangements might be created and maintained on the system, to more closely reflect the way the systems are maintained in the source systems or aspects of a single contract that must be accounted for differently. In other cases, as discussed for retail systems, many arrangements might be aggregated (collapsed) into a single arrangement.

166. Ignoring other possible fields such as currency, dates, balance types, etc.

Transactions Versus Balances

But wait, you say; this sounds like a summary structure of some kind. And you would be right. Producing all the financial information from the transactions is unrealistic for a large bank. Insurance companies, even the largest, may be able to do so. This is because the business events with customers occur on average a few times a year. But banking transactions often occur multiple times each day, even each hour. In these instances, the volume is simply too high. Also, unlike insurance which requires tracking trends over longer periods of time, the value of the historical transaction data to banking is lower and diminishes very quickly.

Yet by creating an Arrangement Ledger, summarizing as an accommodation of the machine capacities, provides most of the benefits of the transaction data. Using the concepts explained in "Movements" on page 85 is critical to managing the size of the Arrangement Ledger data store. Maintaining arrangement details with a pure balance based approach for a large organization is likely impossible, and likely too expensive for any but the smallest organizations.

Additional Attributes

Remember that by summarizing by a selected set of attributes—like the accounting code block in the general ledger above—we eliminate other views of the data. Thus creating these tiny ledgers is not very transformative in itself. The additional attributes that describe the customer and the contract are the items of interest for so many other types of financial reporting.

If, in addition to the accounting code block we use in the general ledger, we attempt to summarize by all the other attributes, we (1) begin to store the same values on multiple records, because the contract and customer attributes describe the entire arrangement, not the individual balances, (2) we create a "reclassification" nightmare as the attributes change, needing to move balances between these attributes, (3) we destroy the ability to show the values historically.

Our choice of the customer contract level—the arrangement level—is not by mistake. Rather, by summarizing to his level, we have preserved the ability to capture and report all these metrics, every summarized balance, by any attribute which describes the customer or contract.

For example, if the following were the balances for a simple General Ledger:

Total By:	Arrangement ID	Business Unit	Ledger	Account	Cost Center	Product	Customer Type	Affiliate	Source	Book Code	Currency	Date	Period	Amount
GL		101	CA	60010	887	T	A	N	YS283	IH	US	09102009	3	984,309.82

Figure 145. General Ledger Summary Record

At the General Ledger level, data is at a summarized level; the arrangement ID is not meaningful. This shows us that for account 60010, cost center 887, and the rest of the values, the balances as of this 9/10/2009 is 984,309.82.

The arrangement balances that make up this single summary balance might be the following. Note that there are three different arrangements, each with the same set of attributes that make up this one balance.

Total By:	Arrangement ID	Business Unit	Ledger	Account	Cost Center	Product	Customer Type	Affiliate	Source	Book Code	Currency	Date	Period	Amount
Arrangement	234857274	101	CA	60010	887	T	A	N	YS283	IH	US	09102009	3	569,837.21
Arrangement	284756322	101	CA	60010	887	T	A	N	YS283	IH	US	09102009	3	138,094.67
Arrangement	265422713	101	CA	60010	887	T	A	N	YS283	IH	US	09102009	3	276,377.94

Figure 146. Arrangement Ledger Detail Balances

By just adding an Arrangement ID to the record, additional attributes can be stored in the arrangement ledger, without causing the balance to be shifted each time one of these other attributes changes. Because

Arrangement ID must be unique, they can be used to link to additional information as is shown below on the Standard Arrangement Layout, or SAL records.

SAL Records				
Arrangement ID	Interest Bearing Indicator	Origination Channel Code	Maturity Date	Renegotiated Indicator
234857274	Bearing	Branch	3/1/2011	Y
284756322	Non	Center	3/1/2011	N
265422713	Bearing	Center	7/1/2011	Y

Figure 147. Sample Standard Arrangement Layout (SAL) records

In this case, each arrangement has four additional attributes associated with it. The SAL can contain as many attributes as necessary to produce needed reports. Anything that describes either the customer or the contract can be stored on these records. As long as the attributes can be linked to the arrangement ID, such as customer information, they can be used in reports at a summary or detailed level. As these attributes change, new SAL records are created with effective dates on each. Thus at report time it can be decided which version of SALs should be used for the report.

Then it would be possible to combine the amounts in the arrangement ledger, and the SAL, and produce a view of the arrangement balances such as this:

Total By:	Value	Amount
Interest Bearing Indicator	Bearing	846,215.15
Interest Bearing Indicator	Non	138,094.67
Origination Channel Code	Branch	569,837.21
Origination Channel Code	Center	414,472.61
Maturity Date	3/1/2011	707,931.88
Maturity Date	7/1/2011	276,377.94
Renegotiated Indicator	Y	846,215.15
Renegotiated Indicator	N	138,094.67

Figure 148. Summaries by SAL attributes

The three arrangement records were summarized based on the values of the four attributes in the SAL giving a total of eight different summaries. We have just simply "pivoted" the core financial data by any of the SAL attributes. Because these reports are produced from the same base set of data, they can always be reconciled and are consistent. We have just added an incredible level of flexibility to the core financial system.

By organizing our arrangement ledger in this manner, we have created a single system capable of producing thousands of summaries from the same consistent, controlled set of numbers that feeds today's highly respected financial systems.

Chapter 59. Accounting Rules

Through the early period of the project, my role was mostly one of secondary support. I sometimes joked about being the office of "post decision support"; after a decision was made I could either give a thumbs up or thumbs down, but really was expected to be quiet during the deliberations.

One day, as I viewed the results of the performance test for a component called the accounting rules, I couldn't take it any longer. On February 1st, 2006 I came across a recent performance test of the accounting rules component. As I reviewed the results, I could tell the component was going to have significant performance problems when higher volume systems were used. I wrote an e-mail to Dave Willis about my observations, and stepped in the middle of a significant area of confrontation on the project. Dave told me later he wasn't sure he wanted to get my e-mail, but decided he couldn't ignore it once I sent it.

After a few months of serious debate about which course was the best, I was asked to give a presentation on accounting rules. The meeting was in a small room on a second floor of a rather old building in late June and I was assigned to present late in the afternoon. My slide deck was only 30 slides long, but later I was accused of having a 3,000 page deck. After 45 minutes, John Carr, the IT exec. at the head of the meeting, turned to someone sitting next to him and said "Pull him off the stage." I had carried the debate for my approach but was subsequently teased that if I were a doctor I would solve people's health problems by boring them to death.

Having made it this far in the book, I hope no one dies from reading the following summary of a paper I wrote in the midst of the debate.

Accounting Rules Engines and Accounting Rules are any automated facility that generates input data for the accounting systems. It performs many of the functions described in "Outputs" on page 172. They can be programs or the parameters programs use. A program in a product system, like a checking account system, that calculates accrued interest and creates a transaction could be considered an accounting rules engine. Many rules and engines are embedded in operational systems. Accounting environments usually contain processes between the source systems and the general ledger to modify and refine source system accounting transactions, and generate new transactions, e.g., to reflect offsets or reversals.

Transactions, Values and Journal Entries

Interest accrual records, for example, created in different bank operational systems have varying formats because source systems vary. Yet the general ledger classifies similar records from different sources in the same way. Therefore one function of the accounting rules is to change these records into a common or standard format before posting to the general ledger.

Doing so requires using values in the records produced by the operational system. For example, a value of "ABC" may mean "Deposit" in one current account or checking system, but "123" is used in another. Values from both records must be changed into journal entries, to reflect the credit to current account liability before posting to the ledger. Thus, the accounting rules for the first system must associate "ABC" with "credit current account liability" whereas rules must associate "123" with the same meaning for the other. Additionally, one source system may send the offsetting debit as an additional record, whereas the debit for the other might need to be generated.

Technical Transformations

In ages past, finance has been adequately served by writing specifications for IT functions and having IT write the programs. Changes required were specified by the business, and made by IT. However, with more frequent need for changes and greater familiarity with IT systems by finance, systems have become more and more parameterized. Finance can make changes to the systems by changing the parameters or reference data.

Finance could actually take responsibility for all aspects of the system, writing and implementing programming logic. However most finance departments do not desire complete control, including responsibility for very technical functions such as initializing data formats or error handling.

The architecture includes a Technical Transform Layer or TTL which can perform these functions. Effectively, any function that finance does not want to own specifically can be placed in this layer. If finance were comfortable with IT making all changes to all parameters and programs required to create accounting system inputs, the entire Accounting Rules Engine function could be placed in TTL.

Logic and Tables

Accounting Rules Engines (ARE) are programs. Accounting Rules are often expressed as parameters to those programs. They are mostly maintained in one of two ways: Tables or procedural logic.

1. Tables are easily thought of as spreadsheets, with rows and columns. They have one or more columns designated as the key. For example, if the "123" were a value in the first column of the table, the second column might contain "credit current account liability". The reference data described in Chapter 28, "Define Reference Data," on page 137 could be considered a list of parameters which act as rules. Values in one column—the key—are converted into values selected in the outputs—the answers.
2. Procedural logic is very close to program code. This logic might be presented to the user in syntax comparable to that used in Excel for conditional statements such as IF (A31 = "123", "credit current account liability"). This does not require that all valid values be listed, thus reduces the number of rules that must be maintained.

An accounting rules engine can be constructed completely of logic without the use of any tables, but the opposite is not possible. An ARE cannot be constructed purely of tables. Logic is necessary to string together and access tables. Said another way, someone could write all of the logic needed in an IF statement without using an Excel "Lookup" function, but simply creating a table within a spreadsheet does not highlight the row containing the answer.

Although an accounting rules engine can be constructed completely with logic, tables provide a distinct advantage: transparency. Values in tables can be easily searched, more quickly understood, and are simpler to update than values embedded in logic. As an analogy, the financial statements are also presented as tables, allowing simple search, rather than trying to find total interest expense in a management discussion document. Tables are easier to search and update than is logic. In most systems a combination of logic and tables is used.

Record Types

Source systems for financial services companies normally provide more than one type of record to the accounting environment.

1. Transactions. Records that reflect particular business events are called transactions. They are most often turned directly into journal entries, as discussed above.
2. Balances. Often systems also present end of day balance records, giving perhaps the end of day position for each customer's account. These can be used as either "post and reverse" type journal entries for some systems, or to reconcile the platform balances to the source systems.
3. Static data or Arrangement. They also can provide account details, describing customer account arrangement type, interest rate, and maturity date. These records are used primarily in reporting processes, to categorize the posted balances. The values on these records must also be standardized across the system, by product at least, to simplify the reporting processes.

All three records are used for financial and regulatory reporting processes.

The accounting rules bridge the source systems to the accounting functions. The functions they perform are tightly coupled with the source systems, but the outputs are standard across the enterprise. They can be expressed as either tables or procedural logic. And they can use information from multiple types of records to properly classify information.

Having expressed these concepts, I watched over the next few months as Dave "Murph" Murphy, Debbie Byrnes, and Jerry Canterbury proved that these thoughts were correct. I was very impressed with the simplicity of the architecture Murph defined to make this all real. What had been months of debate and contention simply washed away as the solution began to take form. It showed me how important it is to have the right idea and a team capable of making that idea reality.

Chapter 60. Reclassification

Creation of a General or an Arrangement Ledger fed by transactions from source or product systems means we now have two master files; the master file in the product system and a representation of those balances in the ledger. Care must be taken in creating the linkage between these two systems, similar in some ways to the care taken when connecting a trailer to a semi. If the connection is not strong enough, the trailer may become disconnected while in transit; the semi and trailer then having nothing in common. If connected too securely, the whole may not have the flexibility required to turn or handle rough roads.

Starting in August 2005 for an entire year, the size of the endeavor slowly dawned upon the team, with deadlines for interim deliverables starting to loom large. The "days of obscurity" were now past. The result of multiple proofs of concepts showed deeper analysis was required, particularly around the arrangement ledger. It became clear we needed to spend some significant time considering this connection, particularly because it would not be the same as a general ledger connection. I remember a brainstorming session with Sandy Peresie and Tata Rao to lay down the framework with which to comprehend the less intuitive nature of these behaviors.

Definition

Let's begin by defining reclassification. Finance processes typically include reclassification adjustments. These are usually fairly simple. For example, for most purposes a particular account might be classified as a "contra" account, like loan loss reserves, reducing the total asset value of the loans. It typically is a "negative" amount relative to the asset shown in the asset section of the balance sheet. However, being a negative amount, it could also be classified as a liability, which typically has a "negative" balance. Thus for some reports, finance might make journal entries to "move" an amount from one reporting category to another.

The problem with making this adjustment permanently is that the accounting rules for new transactions posting into this balance won't be affected by simply making the reclassification adjustment; they will continue to post to the "asset" account unless the system is changed in some way. Supposing this is not done, this reclassified balance becomes a "stranded" balance. It will neither increase nor decrease in an automated way. It will remain on the books until someone manually moves it back to the "asset" side, or changes the accounting process to post new entries to this balance.

This then is a different sort of business event. The act of commerce here may be as simple as adjusting the presentation of a report. This might be done because regulations require a certain presentation. Or it may be done simply for internal reasons. Nevertheless, these are valid business events.

However, if we construct an arrangement ledger, the need for manual journal entries to adjust millions of small ledgers might become overwhelming. It is probable that the work effort involved in maintaining, controlling, and adjusting millions of arrangements to reflect the change from "asset" to "liability" is simply too large for a finance function. A host of employees are involved in ensuring that balances in the source systems, the loan or deposit systems, for individual customers, are maintained correctly. To replicate that army in the finance area would be simply too costly. The reclassification processes must then be automated.

Reference Data Reclass

Suppose, for a moment, we performed no data design of any kind, as Steve Mongulla suggested was possible[167], and we simply placed on the front of the amount every attribute that would be used to classify that amount for any report. If we employed this type of architecture, and we had a change in any attribute, say state of residence for a customer, and wanted to see the entire customer balance at that time reported under the new state, we would have to create a transaction which reversed the old state and the entire balance, and an offsetting transaction which posts the entire balance to the new state.

If we created these types of records, it may have no impact on some reports. For example, a report which shows the balance as of today would show the entire balance under the new state, and the negating transaction would net the historical balances to zero—effectively it would be invisible in the report. This report is no different than a Recast view of the data, as discussed in Chapter 34, "Consider Complex Joins," on page 177.

However, if instead the report needs to show activity over time, then these new set of transactions should show the customer balance under the old state while it was there, then the negating record zeroing the balance out, and the entire existing balance posting to the new state. This is slightly different than a Switch view, which would never show the entire balance under the new state. A Switch report would show those transactions from the old state there, and the new ones under the new state.

Rather, this is a Reclass view of the data. This view requires the generation of reclassification journals for changes in any reference data attributes. Creating a system capable of performing this work can substantially increase the data volumes involved. Any change in a reference data attribute creates new business events or balance records. When to employ this view of the data must be carefully considered.

Anchor

The cause of reclassification, then, is the need to change attributes associated with balances. The assignment of attributes happens all along the data flow or data "supply chain" from source system to report. Any changes in rules or programs that assign attributes can cause a reclassification. Detecting in an automated way that a reclassification is necessary requires comparing the values assigned previously to the values to be assigned currently. Doing this requires a master key that does not change.

It is not typical to compare summarized journal entries output from a system one day to those output the next and determine if a reclassification occurred. The journal entries typically do not have any "anchor" or key by which to associate specific entries with other entries. Thus for a typical general ledger implementation reclassification detection must happen in the source system, where the program can see if the attributes assigned to a specific product system account number are different than those previously assigned using the product system master file. If they are different, then the product system program which generates accounting entries must create a reclassification entry to move the historical balance from one set of attributes to the new set.

An arrangement ledger, however, has a permanent key, an arrangement ID. Because of this, the reclassification processing can be moved from the product system to the finance system. This is the key to creating a stable yet flexible linkage between the product and the financial system.

Triggers

A "trigger" is required to allow the AL processes to detect when a reclassification is necessary. One trigger can simply be new transactions which have been turned into journal entries. As the AL attempts to post these journal entries to existing balances, it can compare if the attributes assigned in the new

167. See "Database Size" on page 84.

journal entries are consistent with the attributes assigned to the historical balances. If they are not, it can generate a new journal entry to move the balances to new attributes.

Using new source system transactions (formed into journal entries through the accounting rules engine) means that any accounting rules embedded in the source system posting process will be captured in the finance system. However, parameter or rule changes in the accounting rules engine may not be. If no transaction is presented to the system which uses the changed rule, the balance in the finance system may never change.

An approach to overcoming this limit is to broaden the set of possible triggers, by processing the end of day balances from the source system. These balances can be run through the accounting rules as if they were transactions. The resulting records, with finance system attributes rather than source system attributes, can be compared to the balances maintained in the arrangement ledger. Difference in attributes can be used by the arrangement ledger to trigger creation of reclassification entries to move the historical balances to the appropriate position.

This creates a flexible yet secure connection between the source system and the finance systems.

Backdating

If we are really serious about solving the finance system problem, though, we must not be simplistic about the required views of data that must be supported. One of the most important views is the ability to recreate historical views, how the balance sheet or other financial reports looked at some period of time. The problem with this requirement is that not all activity is recorded the day it happens. Business events, or acts of commerce, are discovered after the fact, and must be reflected through adjustments to the system. Product source systems miss cut-offs and provide automated feeds the day after the events took place.

If it were possible to simply summarize all transactions to produce reporting results as of a point in time, plainly including or excluding these late records can provide the desired perspective. But with high volume finance systems, this is not possible; balances must be created to reduce the input data volumes. This need complicates the posting processes. The posting processes must be able to update not only the back-dated period, but also walk forward the impact of those updates to subsequent periods. This also requires determining precedence for different types of back-dated updates. Again, using movements simplifies this problem.

Keeping these needs in mind while analyzing the requirements to perform reclassification processes can be very difficult. Having reconciled these needs, and created a system capable of performing these tasks, is a testament to the diligence of the team who created the first version of this system.

Chapter 61. Support Processes

On August 3rd 2006, Jeff Wolfers, a new project executive, sat down with me, said I seem to be central to a lot of what was going on with the project, and asked how I was doing. In response, I asked him where he had been four months earlier in the midst of the discussions about the accounting rules which really took a toll on me. He laughed. I noted that his question and the subsequent discussion did lift a certain amount of weight off my shoulders, giving me a feeling something on the project really could change.

This temporary relief quickly wore off a week later when Rick e-mailed me that Jeff had decided to put me at the center of fixing the project Jeff told me I could do whatever needed to be done to make the system work, but I had to make it happen quickly. As a postscript to his e-mail, Rick added "God help you." I sensed I would need that help.

This began a significant transformation on the project, with a very serious focus to get it done. I was overwhelmed with the amount of work there was to do. The team was reorganized, and attempted to construct every part of the system in parallel.

Surrounding the mainline posting process is a set of support functions, including reference data, adjustment and reconciliation processes. Working on these areas was very frustrating at times for the teams involved because we knowingly were breaking one of Rick's fundamental principles: do things in the right order.

Error Handling

For example, a team was deployed to build a system for error handling. The mainline flow of data through the system wasn't yet determined. The team responsible for error handling would schedule meetings with the mainline flow team and start with the same question every meeting: what errors do we need to handle? The mainline team would respond by saying they didn't know yet.

The number and types of errors that can be imagined are nearly unlimited. However, the number of errors that actual occur is much smaller; certain data conditions simply do not happen. Thus establishing mainline processes before attacking support processes is critical. Learning from preliminary testing what error conditions should be handled is the most efficient way of determining requirements for error handling.

In the end, the system employed a few simple principles for handling errors:

1. The vast majority of error conditions that can be handled in an automated way occur in the front end of the system, in either the Technical Transform Layer or Accounting Rules Engine. At the end of the ARE, data must be in a state that can be posted into the AL and GL. Detecting and preventing errors before posting is much easier than after posting. Once data is posted into the AL and GL, clean up processes are much more involved.
2. Large numbers of errors typically indicate the wrong file was processed. The most effective means of handling this condition is to obtain the right source system file and reprocess through the ARE.
3. Individual record errors typically are caused by accounting rules not updated for new values received from the source system. In these cases, preserving visibility to the values from the source system is critical to updating the rules to rerun the data. A reject handler system was used to store the records from the source and the rejects out of the ARE. These were recycled on a daily basis.
4. The end result of almost all automated error handling is to reprocess data through the front end of the platform.

Another set of errors have nothing to do with the source data itself. These errors are caused by incorrect reference data values. When these errors occurred, it resulted in wholesale reruns of the platform. Over time, the team constructed more and more validity checks on the reference data even before the sources were processed through the engines.

Reference Data

Trying to define all the reference data as an independent exercise was equally frustrating. I use the term reference data to encompass any parameter not maintained in IT script files which affects the way the system works. The problem with gathering reference data requirements is they are all completely dependent upon every other component of the system. The functionality must be defined in all other components, then that functionality broken down into what is configurable and what is not, before the total sum of reference data can be known. This is all true for reference data that is maintained on the platform; reference data maintained external to the platform is handled similar to a source system, which is interfaced to the platform.

That is not to say there are no major components to be built as infrastructure to manage reference data. In the end, the solution had the following major characteristics:

1. All rules related to the Ledgers (GL and AL) were stored in a set of tables called Reference Data Maintenance Facility (RDMF). This allowed the users to define the domain values for specific attributes in the system like the business unit, cost center, and nominal accounts. This also allowed them to specify various financial processing rules like revaluation and translation by organizing the accounts into trees. Other relevant information for ledger processing like the platform processing date, exchange rates, accounting period control tables were stored within the RDMF.
2. All rules related to accounting rules engine were grouped into a reference data component called Rules Table Maintenance (RTM). This was basically a repository that handled the table constructs (spreadsheet like structure) required to translate the source system attributes to the finance platform attributes. This repository had the ability to let finance maintain these rules in the form of 'keys' and 'answers'. This allowed them to enter the rules that formed the cornerstone of creating journal entries out of the business events.
3. All rules related to performing extracts (outbound) and inbound functions on the SAL records were stored in a special facility called Rules Maintenance Facility (RMF). This was again a user-facing repository that allowed the users to specify the input structures they would like to operate on and the rules that were needed to be applied on the platform structures in order to create the output structures required by downstream applications.
4. A publish/subscribe approach was used to introduce reference data changes into the production environment. As noted above, the parameters can fundamentally affect how data is processed in the environment, and thus need to be introduced in a controlled manner.
5. Particular care must be taken in designing the control of the platform processing date, a parameter used for consistency across all processes in the platform. Although a reference data component, it is not typically updated manually. Rather, its update cycle is carefully tied to the overall schedule of processes.
6. A hierarchy of maintenance facilities was created which published to lower level facilities that ultimately publish to individual processing instances. This allows for management of maintenance functions at higher levels (regional, corporate or global) of certain tables. The individual processing instances were tied to source system cutoff schedules. This allowed the system to run worldwide, rolling with the sun as periods were cut off.
7. Accounting and extract rules also have special characteristics because they connect values external to the system (both sending and receiving system code values) to platform values. Therefore the platform values must be validated against platform listings (in RDMF), but source system codes must be validated against external system listings. These systems also typically have a decidedly "local" flavor to them because they must be connected to local data sources and uses.
8. Changes to reference data must be date effective. The ability to recreate a view of the financial data as of a point in time requires retaining history, and the ability to do date effective joins. Certain reference data can be logically deleted only, because it is typically integral to the structure of the repository itself.

Adjustments

As noted in "Errors and Adjustments" on page 174, some would like to believe that all data should be captured correctly by source systems, and data in reporting applications or data warehouses should never be adjusted. The idea ignores reality and, if adhered to as a principle, means users will live with inaccurate and uncorrectable data. In a very simple sense, adjustments may simply be thought of as another source system; in fact certain business events are not automated because they happen infrequently or are of low value. The results of these acts of commerce may only be reflected in the reporting repository as manual "additions" in fact, rather than adjustments.

The adjustment facility becomes more useful if it has what might be termed a very simple reporting aspect to it, in that it allows users to select existing records from the repository as templates. The resulting process should not perform an update, but rather create new records, reversing the sign on the amount to back out from an existing location, and posting the amount to the correct set of attributes. Thus the output from the adjustment process is a new set of records, capturing the "business event" of adjusting the repository.

Although the outputs from the adjustment facility should simply be another set of records—more journal entries—that make marginal corrections to existing data by adding new records, these records do not go through all the steps of the accounting rules. Remember that the accounting rules translate from source system values into platform values. Adjustments are typically made in platform values; no translation is required. Special care must be taken in determining how these records relate to the accounting rules triggers for reclassification.

The facility should enable adjustment for any attribute in the repository. If constructed in a very forward thinking manner, a similar facility can be used for both reference data maintenance and adjustment. When I state any attribute should be adjustable, I include Standard Arrangement Layout (SAL) records as well, creating new date effective versions to reflect appropriate customer/contract attributes.

Having recognized the need for adjustment does not mean adjustments should be enabled anywhere in the architecture. The key to consistency is consistent inclusion of adjustments in any output that might be affected by them. Thus making adjustments in the AL, and allowing them to flow to the GL and any report or output necessary, means the business event of adjustment is made once, and reflected correctly everywhere.

This does not mean that every adjustment must be made at the lowest level of detail. The AL is capable of holding the summary level GL data, and adjustments can be managed in the same way. Certain attributes on adjustments are simply null, not being defined. There will always be adjustments which cannot be attributed to a particular customer/contract. For example, a portfolio of arrangements may be known, in the aggregate, to be less than the value of the individual instruments. Making an aggregated adjustment is completely acceptable. When including the entire portfolio in a report, this adjustment record should be included as well, even though it may only be shown under the attribute of "other" because is has no specific arrangement attribution.

Creation of an adjustment facility is creation of a limited use on-line transaction processing system. It should be approached as such.

Reconciliation

The last major support process is that of reconciliation. Reconciliation is necessary when two master files exist, two sources of the same data. If we had unlimited computing capacity and the ability to manage unlimited processing complexity, we would do all computer work in one system. We have neither of those, so we create multiple systems. We are then required to reconcile the systems to ensure data is not missing or inaccurate.

The first reconciliation that must occur is between the source system and the AL. As discussed under the accounting rules, if the source system provides end of day balances (or periodic cut off balances if the cycle is not daily), these balances can be processed through the ARE, thus being translated from source system values into platform values. These records can then be used to compare to the corresponding balances in the AL. Differences indicate an error in processing of some kind.

Another reconciliation point is between the AL and the GL. In this instance, the level of detail maintained in each is not the same. Thus the AL balances must be summarized to compare to the GL balances. If differences are found for any one record in the GL, all the corresponding detailed records from the AL are displayed. In this manner, evaluation of the causes of the out-of-balance can begin immediately. This same set of principles are used in multiple areas in the platform.

A couple years after the system went live I heard Dave Willis say that one of the smartest things done on the platform was building the automated reconciliation processes. Managing the detail involved in the platform is challenging, and not using the power of the machine to spot where and when differences occurred would make it nearly impossible. Until our ability is increased to scale to even higher amounts of data needed for analytical processes, reconciliation will continue to be an important function in maintaining the quality of the reporting environment.

Chapter 62. Calculation Engines and Reporting

With the tremendous pressure to make the project work, at times small arguments would break out, sometimes between the business and IT, sometimes between different parts of each of those teams. We developed a pattern of weekly meetings to make decisions and find resolutions as quickly as possible. Besides my technical team meeting about the architecture, Dave Willis and I met weekly with Pete Galbo and Mike Mann, from the business, to do almost nothing more than make decisions. We made those at what seems to me to be an amazing pace.

In the February of 2007 I reacted to a small prompting for an argument with a very caustic e-mail. Seeing my e-mail broadcast much further than I expected, I felt a need to apologize, so I left a handwritten note on Mike Mann's desk before leaving to catch my flight home. I quoted from Lincoln's first inaugural address. "We are not enemies, but friends. We must not be enemies. Though passion may have strained, it must not break our bonds of affection." The pressure cooker tested this resolve throughout the entire next year.

Engineering and Volume

Unfortunately, systems must be built from front to back, just like buildings must be built from the ground floor up. This means that the lion's-share of time is spent getting data into the system, and getting it out is always squeezed. The same was true for this system.

As if this weren't enough pressure, as we have noted, data loads increase through the layers of the system.

- The ancillary or support functions of the system have the lowest data volumes.
- The Technical Transform Layer and Accounting Rules Engine have more volume because they have to accept transactions and reconciliation balances from the source systems. But the number of transactions for a period—a day for example—is limited by the length of the period itself.
- The posting processes in the Arrangement Layer typically have more volume, because they must not only deal with the outputs from the accounting rules, including reconciliation balances, but also transactions that have now been turned into debits and credits. It must also take all these and apply them or compare them to yesterday's balances to create today's balances. This increases volume substantially.
- The highest volumes are with the reporting space, though, where the accumulated effect of history must be dealt with, not just today's transactions or today's balance, but balances for prior days, weeks, months and perhaps years. Not only this, but also these balances must be rolled up, summarized for the myriad of needed outputs, creating additional volume. This is an incredibly ambitious computer engineering challenge.

Data Stores

We constructed the system to use sequential master files for the Arrangement Ledger. This is because so many rows are touched in each update cycle that it is more efficient to read the entire master file and write an entirely new copy; and having the most efficient access method makes doing so possible in the shortest period.

The outputs from the master file roll-ups and the creation of a set of summary structures at the same time are stored in the Financial Data Store. These outputs facilitate the drill down from higher level summaries to lower and lower levels of detail, mimicking the basic financial reporting process of starting at summaries and gaining greater insight and transparency through drill down. The financial data store uses database technology as the basic access method for retrieving records. Achieving high performance load processes is a key to, again, making the system work in a reasonable time period.

Calculation Engines

Our engineering and volume discussion above ignored one more fundamental computing pattern: that of a calculation engine. As discussed in "Allocation Processes" on page 72, at times business events are generated using other business events or balances as input. Multi-currency translation, allocations, funding and analytical modeling are all examples of calculation engines. "Ledgers" tend to have a mix of receiving input records and posting them as well as generating new records, reflecting the passage of time as an example.

What to do with the results of these types of processes? It may be simple to think of these outputs as standalone, used in some set of reports. Thus they may be held in their own output area for use in reporting. It may be more efficient to place the results from these processes back into the Arrangement Ledger. The key question is do the outputs from these processes need be combined with other outputs to create meaningful reports. For example, do a significant number of reports need to include funding results with the original actual results to be meaningful? If they must be combined for one report, doing that at report time may be most efficient. If they must be combined for hundreds of reports, combining the resulting granular data in a high performance reporting environment may be the better answer.

Extracts

The finance systems typically are not the tail end of all processing. There are a lot of uses of finance data, and producing output files to be used in other systems is needed. A facility that allows the application of business rules, including translation of platform values into other code sets used for other purposes (a reverse Accounting Rules Engine in a sense) provides tremendous flexibility to answer questions from the information-rich environment provided. If constructed with an eye towards the calculation engine, great synergies are possible between these components.

Performance for this component must again be kept top of mind. Ways must be found to make use of the data when in memory. Mike Perez and Ravi Challagondla led a team that constructed a simplified front end to SAFR for use by the business called Rules Maintenance Facility (RMF), while still using the SAFR engine to produce the extract outputs. All the base SAFR capabilities become important in actually producing the outputs.

Managed Query

About the time Jeff Wolfers assigned me to be the Solution Architect , Rakesh Kant and Greg Forsythe were attempting to find a reporting solution with acceptable performance for the limited amounts of data that had been gathered through the Proof of Concepts (POCs) to that time. It proved very challenging, for many of the performance reasons discussed in this book. We determined that what was needed was an "on-line" version of SAFR, one that could be invoked and, each time the user clicked to either request a report or to drill down, perform all the steps of a reporting process—select, sort, summarize, format—rather than doing all those functions for all requests in one pass of the data. They used the database for basic record selection, sort and limited joins, but none of the other functions were required. They created a compiler, in Java, to perform the other tasks needed in very efficient manner.

I cannot do justice at this juncture to how the team went about doing this. I can say that having started last with the fewest usable components from the POCs, this team worked at break-neck pace to meet the implementation date, just a little over a year from the project restart date. Getting to the finish line proved very, very challenging for everyone involved.

Their work in this space was remarkable, and without it and the extract engine, all the efforts to capture and post the data would have been meaningless. Rakesh and Greg were joined by Sreenivasan Raghavan (who goes by just one name Raghavan, like all really cool people in the world) and a set of extraordinary people. They created the capstone of the system, and it was a very fitting capstone indeed.

Chapter 63. Go Live

At the end of September 2007, a little over a year from being empowered to really move things forward, I was in a weekly meeting when it became clear expectations were not aligned about how the system would perform the first day we tested it in parallel a month later. There was an expectation the system would run in one hour. I was a bit dumbfounded, knowing the pace we were running that such a schedule for the first run was no where near possible.

All testing to that point had been manually executed. The system had thousands of processes to be run, and it took multiple days to run the system through a test cycle. There simply had not been time in the race to meet the deadlines for analyzing which processes might be executed in parallel.

The race continued for another month. We ran the system in an abbreviated form to convert history for two weeks the end of October. But we could not end the history conversion processes and then start the first day of daily processing on the same day the source systems produced their outputs. So we started the daily schedule behind the source system, having to catch up to get on a daily schedule.

Doing so proved very difficult because the first part of the system could not be completely automated. The right files from the source systems had to be attached to the jobs manually, the jobs run, results verified, and errors corrected by rerunning. This work, plus the still barely automated sequential flow for many of the thousands of ancillary processes meant the system took 15 hours for the first day.

We also never had time to test rolling from one day into the next day. We had to determine on the fly what the key steps were in sequence for this process. Any mistake in developing these new procedures might mean we had to rerun an entire day, which would have been disastrous. We may not have been able to recover.

The business team was required to validate the results at intermediate points in the process at very odd hours. All of these factors added to the 15 hour run time in some measure. Because we had multiple days to catch-up, we could tell it was going to be a very long few weeks.

The teams worked around the clock. People would work as long as they could and then hand off to someone else. A week into it, I heard one team member explaining to another that he couldn't work the next evening because he had to attend his brother's wedding, but it would only be a couple of hours.

On November 9th, I woke up just after midnight and checked my e-mail. I'd received a message a few minutes earlier from Mike Blom who had run testing and was taking lead in keeping the schedule going in production. The only thing it said was "Somwthing went wrong" [sic]. From the spelling I could almost hear him hitting the floor as he hit the "send" button. I dialed into the ever open conference call number and picked up where he had "fallen" off. By 8:00 AM I wrote back, "Now that the problems are all resolved, I can confirm. 'Somwthing' did indeed go wrong."

Everyone on the project, IT and business, pulled together. Small improvements were made in the schedule every day, and the system began to run faster and faster. Within two weeks the system became quite stable, although additional tuning was necessary.

The plan had been to run the system for about 7 weeks, shut it down, implement more functions, convert history again and restart after the first of the year. As we analyzed the functionality the system was already providing, and what was required to hit the next major milestone, we determined we couldn't afford the additional conversion time. However, that meant we had to keep the system going through year-end: a whole series of processes we didn't think we needed to build for another 10 months had to be analyzed, designed, built and tested in three weeks. When January 2nd rolled around it all worked, to everyone's amazement.

There was never really a break for a great deal of celebration. I am also not sure our experience was all that unique: every large system implementation requires tremendous efforts by many people over a long period of time. Yet, I do remember thinking to myself, and perhaps even saying to a few other people on the team, that I was certain every team member would someday look back with fondness upon that time in some measure. I had a lot of team members expressed a deep sense of commitment to making the system work, and of accomplishment at overcoming the challenges in building it. The team work was terrific, and as the system was enhanced and greater and greater amounts of detail added to it over the ensuring years, it became a greater repository not just for finance but for a host of information needs. The business found immediate savings in its capital requirements because of increased understanding of its underlying obligations.

Over a year later, as the system began to be implemented in Hong Kong, I had lunch with Mike Mann who had taken a tour of duty there to help them implement the system. Three years earlier, January 2007, in our first project "summit" after the project reset, we had ended the day with raised voices and differing opinions. By May of that year, we had our second summit, and Mike approved clearing scores of issues from our path, as we raced to testing and then implementation.

Now here we were, another year beyond implementation, and both feeling we had succeeded in large part. At the conclusion of our day together, I gave Mike a copy of Lincoln's selected speeches and writings as a gift for his support through the project. Although all this is about reporting and computer systems, which in and of themselves aren't really that important, as Doug has told me over a lot of years, it is always good to be able to engage in good, honest work, regardless of what that work is. With that in mind, I had underlined this quote from the 2nd inaugural address, "With malice toward none; with charity for all; with firmness in the right, as God gives us to see the right, let us strive on to finish the work we are in."

Part 7. The Plan

Chapter 64. Promotion

Not long after my lunch with Mike, I began in earnest two "promotions". I was not very comfortable with either.

One was self-promotion. In the midst of the project Rick had become eligible for retirement. He found though that restrictions in agreements between PwC and IBM meant he could not continue any association with the project if he did so. My reaction to his potential leaving was not very positive; it also would have had a very disruptive influence on the project. He patiently continued to lead the way.

About that time it became clear to me that I must apply for partnership. I don't know why I had been reluctant to do so for so many years. Although I was very committed to my work (as if the preceding doesn't testify adequately to that), for some reason I was not interested in being a partner. I realized, though, that doing so was my duty; my duty to those I worked with, to the customers and to the ultimate good the solution could provide on so many levels. So one year into turning the project around, I began the process of promoting myself for partnership.

Somewhere along the path, I must have become confused. With the successful turn around of the project, the intense concentration and prospects of a successful implementation, I began to feel it was my right to be partner. Imagine my surprise, when one week before the system went live I learned I had been turned down. It made me question why I was going through everything I was; what was the point; and why no one outside the project appreciated the nature of what we were doing.

I spent a couple of months being angry about it. Glenn Finch and Sarah Diamond, executives within IBM, reached out to me in very personal ways. My wife Kari chided me for being so hostile to them in phone calls. Rick, as ever, was very temperate, understanding my anger and sympathizing without encouraging actions I would come to regret.

February 2008, despite tremendous continued pressure on the project to make the next deadline, I asked Rick if it would be OK if I took off early on Friday evening to take my two youngest children sledding. He approved. As we arrived home, while still in the car, I checked my e-mail, and noted the announcement about new partner promotions. I chose not to read it. My four year old son climbed in the driver seat, gave me a hug, and told me he loved me. I told him that I loved him too; that he was so important to me. He then said, "I am more important than your work, huh Dad?" and he ran off. "Out of the mouth of babes..." I thought.

Later that night, while watching TV with my wife I had a fairly strong feeling that, if in some way I did become a partner, I would likely use this experience a number of times in discussions with others. It would be difficult to buy this sort of experience, but would likely become something I would never want to give up. I learned much more from the failure than I ever would have learned from the success.

I wasn't promoted the next year either, although I made it further through the process. Everyone around me seemed quite surprised, and some were angry. Rick and others were quite fearful of how I would react. I mostly laughed, having adequately learned that my anger didn't help much at all. So in the spring of 2009 I began the process again.

The project of building the financial management solution began with the premise that standard off-the-shelf software would be used to build all components. But as time went on, the requirements for managing the voluminous data caused one component after another to fail. At most of these turns, the company chose to use SAFR to build the replacement components.

At some point, Rick realized it was not right to continue to do this work if SAFR was not going to be a going concern. He approached IBM leadership and explained the situation: If we are going to use this tool on the project, then we must be committed to growing the entire business. The response was an enthusiastic yes.

So the second promotion I undertook that spring was to attempt to explain better the principles outlined in this book. As noted above, I had recognized in 2003 what Rick had always said, our engineering was ahead of our marketing. It was clear that my partnership application was dependent upon demonstrating I could effectively sell the solution. I also recognized that an honest salesperson simply connects people with a problem to the solution for that problem.

I began in earnest to finish this book. I also began explaining the message in a lot of different settings.

Chapter 65. Start with Finance

The Order

Recently, I was asked to participate in the response to a mock request for proposal for a consulting rating agency. They wanted to see what we would propose they do to solve a fictitious company's many analytics, business intelligence and reporting problems. They listed a set of seven issues, in no particular order, that needed to be addressed.

I was asked to draft a summary of the issues, and how IBM would respond. As I analyzed the issues, I was surprised at the pattern I saw emerge. The following was my response:

As part of our proposal to assist your company, IBM has developed a series of viewpoints, insights gained through its experience and research. These viewpoints, aligned to the issues your company has identified, will serve to expedite insight derived through the project, either being validated or adjusted through the project approach as informed by the IBM Analytical Framework.

Similar to using multiple instruments to effectively monitor a complex machine, working across the range of issues is important to arriving at the desired destination. Insight gained from analysis on one issue informs direction on other issues. Our diagnostic approach provides this type of assessment. However, in the longer-term the desire to solve all issues simultaneously can lead to ignoring critical dependencies, resulting in missing significant opportunities and business benefits. Clearly understanding how each issue builds upon foundational premises leads to the highest levels of performance.

Issue: People & Organization

"The company is unsure about who should drive this strategy, what team should manage it, who should support this within the organization, what key processes must be managed, which methodologies and best practices should be used. To this end they are thinking of a competency centre."

IBM Point of View: IBM believes, based upon the issues identified, that the evolving role of the CFO in the last ten years positions him as critical to successful resolution of these challenges. IBM's CFO Study – based on input from over 1,900 CFO's and senior Finance leaders worldwide – attest to the emerging role of the CFO and how their influence reaches throughout the organization and into the Boardroom. The results show that the role of Finance goes beyond traditional Finance and is enterprise focused.

Certainly the CFO is not alone in responsibility nor capable of single-handedly resolving all the company's issues. The traditional finance systems were not designed for today's information explosion, and the traditional finance work force is not trained for today's analytical needs. However expanding upon the infrastructure and capabilities in the CFO organization will provide the shortest path to success.

Issue: Data Warehouse

"The company currently uses a mix of tools both at the HQ and in the business units. There is little standardisation of metadata and each business unit uses its own different reporting terms and definitions. The reporting is fragmented by both business unit and business function (Manufacturing, Wholesale & Retail). Furthermore, there is a range of complex and difficult to maintain data integration processes that support operational and management reporting. The group CFO and CIO desire an enterprise data warehouse and want to standardise on data integration, data quality, meta data and reporting standards across the group."

IBM Point of View: Analytical processes begin with data. Sophisticated models based upon faulty inputs produce meaningless outputs. Consistent with the emerging role of the CFO, a trend emerging in BI is recognition of the consistent value of the finance data. The underlying premise of finance systems are data driven, (1) accepting inputs from every source system capturing financial events, (2) creating an enterprise view of those events, at least in a limited financial sense, (3) with increasing pressure to provide insight into risk, strategic revenue planning, and business model innovation/reshaping as well as their traditional areas of focus such as cost reduction and selection of key performance indicators.

However, limits in the finance system architecture historically employed dropped the full breadth of attributes of interest to others outside finance. With advances in technology, it is possible to create data warehouse environments that provide very granular levels of detail, including individual customer, material and salesperson views yet with the reliability of the finance system: consistent, controlled, reliable information meeting the highest audit standards.

Approaching the data warehouse from the potential uses of the data alone fails to identify the commonality of the underlying business events. The combinations and permutations of source system business events used for analytical and reporting purposes change rapidly. Fundamental acts of commerce—business events—change much less frequently. This fact is a much more stable organizing principle; capturing and organizing source system business events, then providing capabilities to roll-up, summarize, transform and analyze data for a myriad of purposes which change much more frequently according to business needs and capabilities.

Issue: Financial Reporting

"The financial close, consolidation and reporting processes are both time consuming and resource intensive. The organization does not have a standardised chart of accounts or standardised report packs. Each of 10 regional production sites are run as independent business units and have a regional financial controller who produces financial reports for local requirements and also submits data for group consolidation. The Group controller is responsible for the consolidated financials and reports to the CFO responsible for all financial and management reporting. Lack of responsiveness to changing business conditions, poor transparency and inability to meet future compliance demands are identified concerns."

IBM Point of View: The world is awash in data, and more is created every day. Yet less of this newly created data is accumulated into meaningful outputs. And accumulating data is something very different than enabling an internet type search for a specific piece of data. The consolidated financial statements of the organization are, by definition, enterprise wide, although perhaps only for a handful of attributes. Yet this "supply chain" of data in summary is well respected if not adequate.

Working to expand this supply chain, in terms of (1) depth providing greater transparency to underlying business events, (2) breadth of attributes supporting a broader range of financial reporting processes, and (3) frequency to support more timely analysis, efficiently guides efforts to located trusted sources of data. This focus attacks the core issues of financial reporting in the most efficient manner.

Locating underlying business events source system by source system that tie in total to today's reported financial results provides a step-wise approach to expanding data within the data warehouse while at the same time providing greater business benefits immediately in reporting.

Issue: Sales and Management Reporting

"Currently the business functions provide their own reporting and analysis using (in one case) [a common reporting package], and for other BUs home-grown solutions and Excel. This is considered inadequate, costly and has been made a key priority by the COO. The sales group want a comprehensive reporting platform to enable much greater degree of self-sufficiency whilst increasing analytical functionality."

IBM Point of View: Historically, finance controlled a very small set of attributes—the accounting code block. Reporting on other attributes required creating separate "supply chains," sourcing business events to reporting processes. With the expansion of computing and increasing digitization of information, the number of data "supply chains" has expanded dramatically.

The company's work on ERP implementations over the years have likely captured many of the benefits of supply chain consolidation, concentrating resources and processes on fewer, high-value low-cost suppliers. Similar benefits will accrue to organizations that manage information as an asset, recognizing the data "supply chain" from capturing business events in source systems to aggregating and analytics in the end.

Organizing the data warehouse around business events, maintained at a granular level to retain customer, manufacturing, sales and other attributes, through a controlled and secure supply chain enables "pivoting" the financial numbers by hundreds to perhaps thousands of critical attributes. This approach enables sales and management reporting perspectives on top of the established finance data backbone, with a consistent set of tools and processes supporting an ever wider scope of reporting and analytical processes for the organization.

Issue: Budgeting, Planning and Forecasting

"For budgeting, the company relies upon on spreadsheets and manual processes. There is a disconnect between strategic plans (long-term), financial plans (fiscal) and operations (S&OP) which are run in silos. Budgets cannot easily be flexed to reflect changes in strategy and business conditions. The budget cycle is too long and there are concerns over the disconnectedness of the existing solutions as well as an inability to forecast or scenario plan for different outcomes. Furthermore, there are issues to link operational plans, between distribution and manufacturing and links between operational and financial planning. In addition they are considering some more sophisticated merchandise & store planning capabilities."

IBM Point of View: Next attacking the budgeting, planning and forecasting process bridges the company from gaining confidence in measurement of actual, meaningful results for broader and broader sets of functions, with greater transparency and limited breakages, to beginning to harness the power of those insights to drive achievement in the organization.

Implementing the budgeting, planning and forecasting process next creates the infrastructure for measurement of fundamental measures of effectiveness, again starting with the foundational financial processes. Having first established the data and analytical infrastructure capturing granular results of operation provides two key benefits: (1) the infrastructure expedites many aspects of the summary level functions of budgeting, planning and forecasting, allowing focus on the new process aspects of these functions, and (2) creating the foundational data supply chain with granular levels and expansive attributes provides tremendous flexibility when defining which dimension of data to use in budgeting, planning, and forecasting. The first question when plans and forecast are not met is "why?" Without granular, transparent data of actual results, these questions cannot be answered.

Establishing foundational analytical processes enables the higher order functions of scorecard or dashboards, and advanced analytical processes.

Issue: Scorecard or Dashboard

"The senior management team have identified the need for a scorecard or dashboard to deliver KPIs to the BU heads and the management group. They want to focus on measures related to high level financial and non-financial performance (such as customer and quality measures) and to help align daily activities with the more long term aims of the company. Furthermore, at the functional/process level, the sales, marketing and production functions are looking for operational dashboard/KPI reporting."

IBM Point of View: Scorecard and Dashboards provide a very effective means of establishing, publishing, monitoring and then driving change in the organization. By having established the information rich repository and foundational performance measure processes, KPI's can be defined for a broad set of measures, both financial and non-financial, using traditional finance attribution or customer, material or sales views. Similar to expanding the foundational financial reporting environment to non-financial data, scorecard and dashboard initiatives can expand the budgeting, planning and forecasting activities to non-traditional metrics, powerfully motivating, monitoring, and measuring achievement of objectives.

Issue: Advanced Analytics

"Currently the company lacks any comprehensive capabilities for advanced analytics such as data mining, predictive and descriptive engines, traditional statistical techniques, scoring, integrated visualization and reporting for solutions such as product, supplier, customer and market analysis."

IBM Point of View: A process of continuous innovation in reporting and analytics becomes possible, finding patterns, relationships, and insights in the business events of the organization, and using those insights to refine organizational analytical processes. This becomes possible by having established the data backbone, refined the content by use in core business processes, broadened the views it represents, and created an analytics culture which is fact-based and informed by the results of actual business events. Advanced analytics really becomes possible when the input data is accurate and accessible. The entire journey begins with capturing and keeping business events.

Chapter 66. Expand to Risk

Through interactions with multiple people in explaining these concepts, I have realized that in some measure what I am talking about might be called a data "supply chain." One of the big trends of ERP implementations for manufacturing organizations was supply chain consolidation. The systems allowed creating a very efficient process to procure materials for manufacturing goods and then distribute the finished products, providing significant savings. The systems did so by integrating with key vendors and significantly streamlined processes.

The same is possible in reporting and analytical processes. As we have noted in Chapter 13, "Business System Architecture," on page 63, we have traditionally built a new, single-use supply chain for every reporting need, taking the business events—transactions or acts of commerce—to the reporting use for them. The cost of IT is driven by the number of components that must be maintained: Systems, programs, scripts, copies of data, processors, disk farms, network devices, etc. Each time we write a new program and do not retire an old one there is a good chance we have increased the IT budget in some way, even if only marginally[168]. Each time IT creates another data supply chain, feeding the results of the same business events to another reporting application, we increase the cost of IT.

Establishing entire new supply chains is much more expensive than adding just a new reporting output. An entire new supply chain requires a data acquisition layer, a target repository, and posting processes of some kind (even if only in the database), as well as a reporting layer. Then there are business processes such as reconciliation and adjustment that must be performed for systems with high data standards.

An alternative, of course, is using the finance data backbone discussed above to reduce the data acquisition, target repository, posting and some portion of the reporting processes. The cost of establishing the data backbone is more than a traditional reporting "supply chain", but the per-unit cost of processing each business event through all the differing supply chains is less.

The Risk Supply Chain

One of the major supply chains built in financial services firms over the last few years supports risk reporting. Risk reporting started much later than the basic financial reporting. In many cases it has established a much newer supply chain of business events, and this supply chain continues to be enhanced as additional regulatory requirements emerge, like those issued as from Basel, Switzerland known as Basel Accords.

Because the attributes needed for risk analysis are many more than those traditionally kept by the finance system, the risk supply chain requires much lower levels of detail. Longer periods of history for account details are also typically desirable. Thus it has been even more challenged in its use of the basic reporting or subsystem architecture. This need for detail is mitigated because the risk system does not need to capture all financial events, but rather focuses much more on the originating product system postings, ignoring the offset side of the accounting system and financial events occurring in other systems which are not financial product related. The risk system also does not typically deal with some aspects of time, such as accruals processing.

In my discussions, some have suggested that instead of re-mediating the finance supply chain, we should switch and use the newer risk supply chain. If someone were to determine to use the principles outlined in this book to build the risk system first, it might be a simple thing to change the system components to have the following names.

168. Additional automation of the IT functions itself can mean less cost per item than in times past, but it is unlikely to ever be zero.

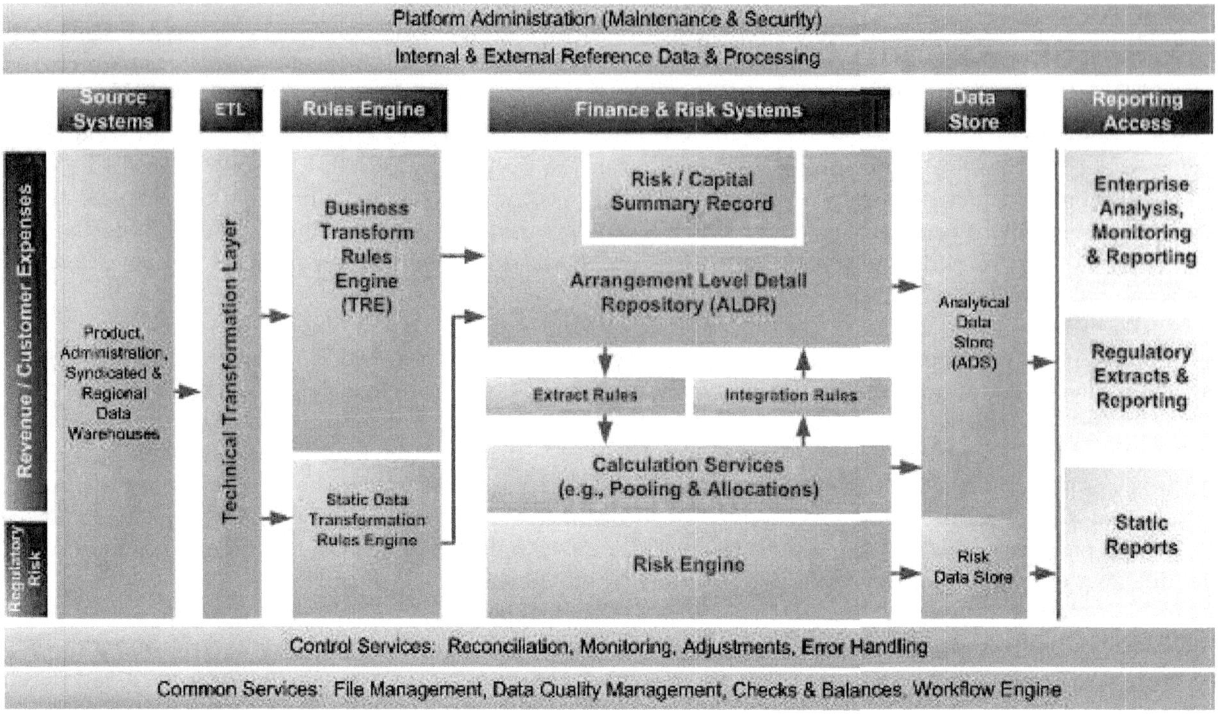

Figure 149. Risk Management Platform

Building out the risk system first, I believe, should still follow the approached outlined in the SAFR method:

- Locate the summary level financial feed from the originating system;
- Determine those portions of the feed that relate to both the finance and risk systems;
- Drive the risk portions to lower levels of detail ensuring details balance with the summary level finance feed.

If this approach is not taken, the risk system and the finance system will never be truly reconcilable. Following this method is likely still the right approach for the simple reason that in spite of all the shortcomings of the finance system, the risk systems are still reconciled to it rather than the other way around. The requirements are in the data.

When this risk-only system is turned on, it should be approached as a parallel run with the finance system, similar to when we start up the FMS solution. The FMS solution typically only runs in parallel for a short period of time before the legacy system is cut off in some way (perhaps through tranching, as described in Chapter 27, "Find More Detailed Events," on page 131). The risk solution may run in parallel for years before it is determined to add to it the remaining finance data, if they ever do.

Integrated Risk and Finance System

Alternatively, if the finance systems feeds are taken to the customer/contract level, and posted within the Arrangement Ledger, the risk system processes can use this data backbone as a source for its processes. The following picture represents a much more detailed view of the FMS platform, including risk analysis capabilities.

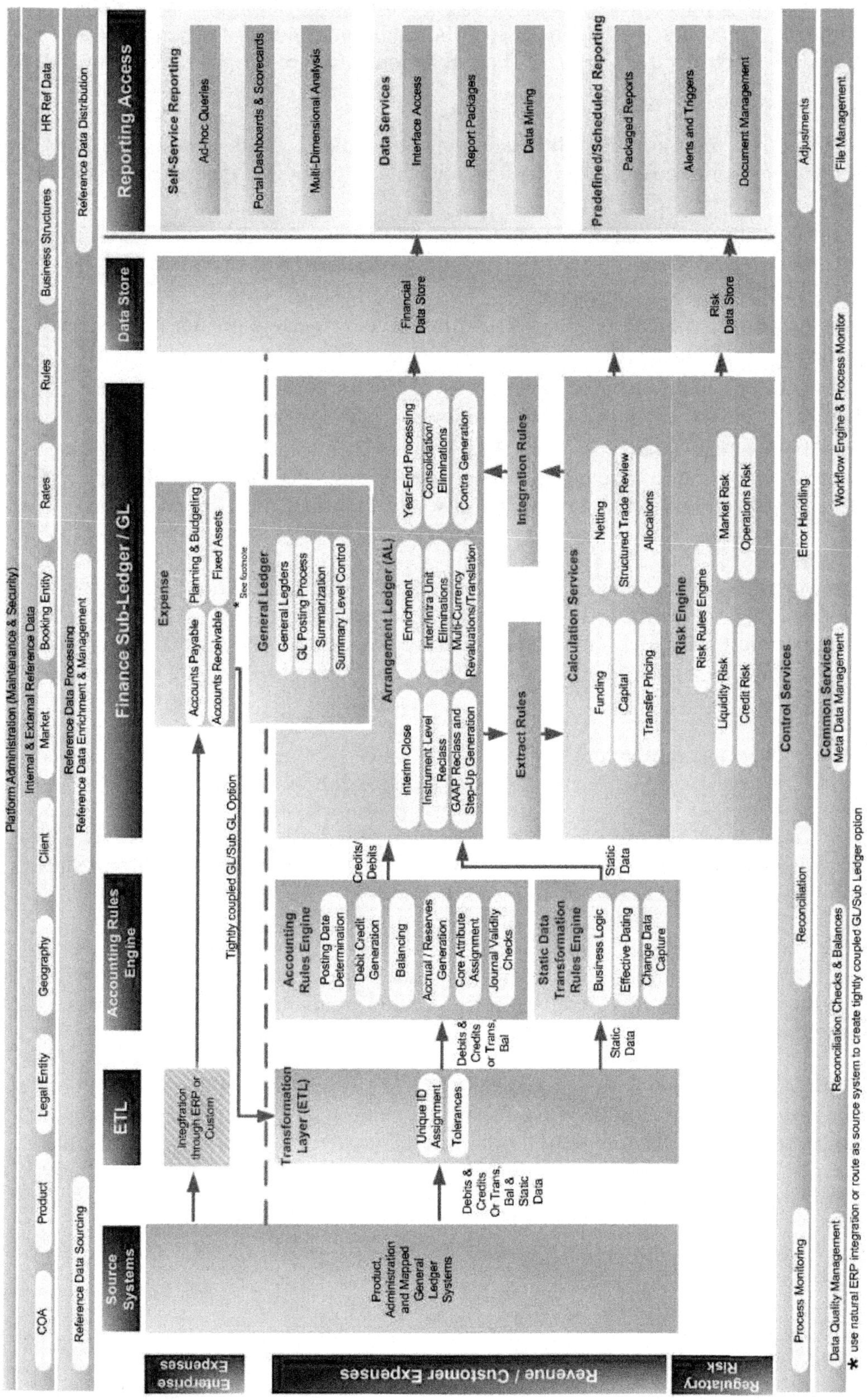

Figure 150. The SAFR Financial Management and Risk Solution

The picture contains more details of the source systems, TTL, Accounting Rules Engine, Data Store and Reporting Layers. Additionally, it clarifies the relationship of the traditional financial expense processes, such as accounts payable, payroll, etc. to the platform. These functions are typically handled by an ERP package of some kind.

In this respect, though, rather than the traditional integration of these modules with the GL, the GL is tightly coupled with the Arrangement Ledger, or AL. A few key aspects of the Arrangement Ledger are worthy of emphasis.

- Finance: The component is a finance owned component. It is not a transaction processing, settlement or other operational subledger system. Finance specifies the coding structures and processes. It is tightly coupled with the General Ledger.
- Detailed: It contains detailed data, often at a customer/contract level providing greater transparency for a greater set of purposes.
- Integrated: The AL is integrated with the source systems, but also with the integrated enterprise. Because its code structure starts with the General Ledger view, it encompasses the entire organization.
- Ledger: It is not a simple repository of source system data. It is not a simple data warehouse. Rather ledger functions are performed within it, like multi-currency processing, eliminations and consolidations, reclass and year-end processes. Thus drill down from any of the General Ledger balances is possible.

The use of on-platform or off-platform calculation services is reflected with the addition of the extract and integration rules processes. These would be used to extract that data from the AL needed for risk engine analysis. The outputs from that analysis may be used independent from the finance data. But as the diagram shows, there is only one supply chain of data into the platform, thus helping to ensure consistency.

The implications are much more than simply eliminating another set of systems or supply chain of the same business events to the risk systems. As I have watched the discussion on capital reserves funding that financial institutions must keep in wake of the 2007 financial meltdown, I have come to see that financial reserves are a question of risk, no doubt, and some portion of risk can be offset by knowledge. Increased transparency in reporting—visibility to the underlying causes of results and the current status of instruments—can significantly reduce the risk of default.

Undertaking building the type of system I have proposed is very expensive, as far as typical IT projects are concerned; it is a reworking of the entire information supply chain for organizations. I therefore have a proposal. I recommend that funding be provided by a corresponding reduction in capital reserves required for organizations that under take the initiative.

Extremely small changes in capital reserve laws can lock up—effectively consume—billion and billions of dollars. The changes in the systems needed are nowhere near that expensive. This is a reasonable approach, motivating the appropriate behaviors to build the new generation of reporting systems that will go much further to solving the financial reporting problems. It will be much more effective than focusing on indirect controls, or other types of regulation.

It may be possible, though, to take the solution even further, providing a greater base for the total reduction in IT costs.

Chapter 67. Beyond Finance and Risk

In 2001 I helped a reporting system strategy project for a regional bank. One day, the project manager and business expert, Lyn San got up to the white board and said, "Kip, why don't we suggest a system that looks like this?" She then began to draw boxes, each one representing a system component to perform some function in a fairly standard reporting or analytical system architecture.

As she finished, I asked, "Lyn, why would we suggest so many boxes?" She was a bit stumped and said, "Well, isn't that the way these systems are built?" I said, "Yes, typically, but why?"

I have since concluded that the simplest explanation is that we don't have unlimited computing capacity, and we can't manage unlimited complexity. Those two reasons are why we don't perform all processing in one big box—that big box being the operational systems.

Arrangement Ledger Performance

Yet the entire premise of this book is that if we discover the underlying fundamental computing patterns, and automate those efficiently, we can achieve much greater scale in analytical applications than we do today.

As an example of the most recent performance statistics for a large global bank's implementation of the platform, in one process SAFR was configured to read four files:

- 80 million SAL records
- 33.5 million AL key records (attributes which describe the balances below)
- 82.5 million AL daily balances
- 165.5 million AL monthly balances

For a total of 361.3 million total records. It then produced nine different outputs, ranging in size from 125,000 records to 248.3 million records[169] each of which summarized all of the input balances, writing in total 311.9 million output records. Using SAFR piping processes, it was possible to only perform one look-up from each daily and monthly record to the key and from the key to the SAL record. Thus the process performed a limited number of SAFR joins, 281.3 million joins.

This process was done in 120 CPU minutes. Thus if we take 361.3 million inputs, and 311.9 million outputs, for a total records processed of 673.2 million, SAFR processed on average 5.6 million records a minute combined input and output[170].

In a separate analysis, David Heap, a well-respected IBM System Z engineer, performed a detailed analysis of a SAFR process reading 11.186 billion input records, representing 1.551 terabytes of data. The process performed 19.709 billion lookups or in memory joins. It output 412 million output records for five different views. This required 4 hours and 45 minutes of elapsed time, and 20 hours 45 minutes of CPU time. After calculating total instructions available on this specific machine, David commented: "This is ...2,533 instructions per record—a VERY short instruction path-length!!"[171]

169. One extract reformatted each daily and monthly record with key values, thus the output for one extract equaled the two balance files combined.

170. Results spreadsheet in author's possession, unpublished.

171. David's full calculation was as follows: "This run ...started at 09:09 am on 5 May 2010. Elapsed clock time was 4 hours 45 minutes. CPU hour consumption was 20 hours 45 minutes. This was the equivalent of 4.37 fully loaded CPUs on the z9 EC 730. (The 30 CPU z9 can deliver approx 11,376 MIPS [millions of instructions per second]. If running at 100% capacity, so 4.37 CPUs

In other words, substantially more processing is possible than we typically think can be done.

Search Engines and Scale

The problem, in a nutshell, is one of accumulation of history. As noted in Chapter 2, "The Problem," on page 5, Internet search giants have solved the problem of finding a needle in a haystack. Search technology allows us to do that very efficiently. But finding a needle in a haystack is not the same as updating yesterday's balance with today's activity, and then combining that updated balance with a host of other balances to create a picture of accumulated results. There is no substantial accumulation process in an Internet search.

The Internet search process is certainly applicable at the front end of the analytic supply chain to find customers or balances or other information. It is also critical at the far back end of the supply chain, to find the appropriate accumulated balance. But it has precious little to do with the process in the middle of turning business events into accumulated balances. This is a very different problem, but is performed in business computing systems all over the place. This process requires as much attention as the intense focus on the needle in-a-haystack search technology investments of the last 15 years.

I have recently been surprised by the number of companies beginning serious initiatives to overhaul the entire flow of data through their systems, from operational systems to reporting. Some are attempting to go so far as to completely eliminate any other data stores for any details except in one primary environment. Realizing what it takes to gain consistency of views of the data across a large enterprise, I find these efforts amazing.

Yet, as I analyze the direction of IT in this regard, such efforts seem to be consistent with where we must go. While some companies are working to make technology smaller and smaller and more and more distributed, the other end of the spectrum must also be progressing equally, driving down the per unit cost in consolidated environments through economies of scale and increasing the insights provided through that data. And as a company establishes the data backbone with the scale capable of tracking daily balances for individual customer-contracts, there is one further step we may be able to take to make the system cost effective.

Source System Integration

In a 30 minute conversation with Rick and Dave Willis in July 2010, Dave observed that the platform we had constructed was effectively reprocessing the entire bank's balances every day. I asked him if he thought it possible to remove the need for the balances to be maintained in the source systems altogether and simply have those systems refer to the finance system for balances throughout the day. He said that he thought that was possible, and it would dramatically simplify the source systems.

I think this may be possible particularly for financial services firms. As we noted in Chapter 57, "The General Ledger," on page 291, financial services firms systems by their nature are much more similar to a general ledger than others are. Some of the products keep track of amounts people have paid and what they have loaned, insured, or underwritten—these are simply forms of accounts. As money is digitized, the business is a digital business. So thinking about their source systems in that manner makes sense.

But it seems to me the problem has to be approached recognizing the difference in some of the traditional "boxes" we have placed on financial services data flow supply chain diagrams, as outline in the following chart.

= (4.37/30)*11,376 = 1,657 MIPS consumed. This gives a TOTAL MIPS burn of 1,657 MIPS * 4.75 hours = 7,871 MIPS-Hours for this [SAFR Extract] job step.... In this case, I get {7,871 MIP-hours * 3,600 seconds = 28.335 Million Mip-seconds} / {Total input records of 11.186 Billion records}. This is 28.335 Million instructions per 11,186 records, or 2,533 instructions per record." E-mail from David Heap to Randall Ness, May 30, 2010, in author's possession.

Processing Characteristics	Transaction Processing	Operational Ledgers	Integrated Finance Detailed Ledger	Thin General Ledger
Frequency	Real time (Market Hours or 24x7)	Intraday	Period Close (3x/day, daily, monthly, quarterly, yearly)	Period Close (3x/day, daily, monthly, quarterly, yearly)
Level of Detail	Trade, Deal or Transaction Level	Product, "Leg," Lot, Policy or Customer Account Level	Product, "Leg," Lot, Policy or Customer Account Level	Aggregated Product/COA Level
Aggregation/ Integration	None	Settlement, Lot, Policy or Customer Account	Financial reporting level	Financial Accounting reporting level
History Required	1 Day History	Multiple Days, Weeks or perhaps a Few Months	Multiple Years	Multiple Years
Perspective	Quantity & Amount for Customer/Agent/ Acct. Rep/Trader Focus or View	Quantity & Amount for Settlement/ Customer/Cash/ Statement Focus, Operational Efficiency	Primarily amount for Internal & External View of Financial Performance	Nearly exclusively Amount, Internal & External View of Financial Performance

Processing Characteristics of Typical Financial Services System Layers

These various categories show a daunting array of requirements if everything were to be done in one system. Yet if this is the goal, perhaps a more practical approach, I submit, is to analyze the entire life cycle of business event generation through to report processes as a supply chain, and execute the appropriate layer of consolidated functions at higher scales.

Taking Dave's example, the periodic posting process is now in multiple systems; we post the transaction detail in the operational systems, we post in the finance system, we "post" (in a sense) in the risk system, we post in reporting applications. All these posting processes could be consolidated into one posting engine (measured in minutes) working with the last master file and new transactions to produce a new master file. Interim transactions during the post process would need to be logged for the next cycle. When the new master file is available, all functions would cut over to use it

So if we are to undertake a consolidated operational and reporting environment, we must (1) consolidate the existing supply chain functional processes into single layers, (2) design the processes and data structures to preserve all business events, both customer facing events and journal and other reporting events, (3) optimize the indexed access required at both ends of the supply chain: transaction capture and report analysis, (4) perform each function at the appropriate time and with great efficiency. For the posting and aggregating functions, this would be done periodically, as close to analysis as possible, using many of the features of the SAFR architecture. In this way the data may be shared but complexity and capacity might be managed.

I am not sure what the results of this system would be. Does it turn McCarthy's idea on its head: Instead of dismantling the finance systems all together, does it make the finance system the center of all needs for balances in the organization? Or does it do exactly what he envisioned, and nearly eliminate the finance system master files altogether? It will be interesting to see where we go from here.

Chapter 68. Partnership

On Thursday, January 28th, 2010, Rick invited me to join him Buffalo. He had been told I would receive a call on Friday morning, and thought it appropriate I be in the same city where I had received two calls the prior two years. I hadn't been to Buffalo for 9 months or so. Everyone was very kind, and it was wonderful to see them all.

On Friday morning Sarah Diamond, the head of IBM Global Business Services US Financial Services Practice, called to tell me I had been made partner. I thanked her, and then told her a story I had heard of a bride on her wedding day who had told her mother, "Mom, I am at the end of all my problems," and the mother replied, "Yes dear, but which end?"

I understood pretty clearly which end of my problems I was at. I began working even harder than I had worked months before to explain these ideas appropriately, and to effectively lead the team.

It's funny, but on Monday, August 30th 2010, I dropped Rick off at his hotel after having had dinner. The next day would be his last day of work with IBM; he had decided to retire after 33 years of work with it and predecessor firms. As I shook his hand, he smiled and said, "Well, I know which end of my troubles I am at." I suspect he could tell I didn't feel real well; I don't really wonder why I didn't.

For dinner that evening, I had wanted to take Rick to a restaurant that no longer existed. We had gone there on Thursday, May 9th, 1996, the same day I called Eric Denna and he had told me to "Study history." I had prepared for that dinner with Rick for a number of months, and presented a chart with four quadrants on it.

Technical	Functional
Sales	Project Management

I said as I saw the world, these are the four major areas of interest for an IT professional. I asked him what I should focus on. He said I should focus on Sales. It was good advice. It took me a few years to take it to heart.

I am encouraged by the results as I have worked on promoting the solution. Through this last year, as I have explained these concepts to scores of people who work in these and related fields, they all nod their heads in agreement. In fact, Tony Venezia, a long time PW, PwC audit and then IBM consulting partner worked with me to explain the concepts to an investment bank. He told me that one day as he was telling the story about where finance IT systems would go he started to tell the story I have explained here. He then said, "I realized there was no other story; there is no other way in which the systems can progress. This is the only course possible."

I raised my hands and felt like shouting Hallelujah! I then said, "Now, if it will only happen in my life time, I can die a happy man."

I am certain that, given time, the world will come to better recognize the unique nature of financial, reporting, risk, and analytical systems and their relationship to the operational systems. As we do so, the systems will provide greater insight, more cost effectively, with greater stability, by employing the principles I have been taught and discovered. We still have a ways to go to turn McCarthy's vision of what is possible into reality. But there is no other possible course. Of this I have no doubt.

Part 8. Appendixes

Appendix 1: Accounting Model

The following outlines how the trial balance can be produced from our 31 rows of Resource Accounting Model data.

Notice that two different types of rows, Transfers and Events, are shown in column C: To calculate the income statement we use only the events. To calculate Salary Revenue on our income statement for example, we scan column F looking for the Salary Revenue Account, 411. When we locate a matching row, we multiple the amount in column H by -1. Doing this for each income statement account will produce the same number shown on the Sample Trial Balance figure for April 30th.

Calculating the April 30th balance sheet amount is a bit more complicated because both the Event and Transfer rows must be taken into account, so we have to scan columns D and F. Each time we match a Balance Sheet account in column D, we simply accumulate the amount. If we match on column F, we must multiply the amount by -1 because we are taking the amount "From" this account. Doing this will again produce all the Balance Sheet amounts shown in the Figure 11 on page 26 for April 30th.

Suppose we now move into May, and add new rows to those above. We noted earlier that using the journal entries as a way of calculating the financial statements meant we didn't necessarily need to record closing entries. Is that still true of this new system? Can I calculate the trial balances as of May 1st? Yes, it is possible, but the formulas or processes become a bit more complex.

It requires evaluating the date column as well. The Income Statement by definition has a "from" and a "to" date, the period covered by the Income Statement. As we evaluate each row in performing the same calculations above, we check if the date on the row is greater than the first date, and less than or equal to the end date. If it is, we include it. If not, we skip it.

Again, calculating the Balance Sheet is similar except the Balance Sheet is as of a particular date, so we only have one date we use in our test. Again, we perform the same calculations as above, but only for rows prior to or equal to the balance sheet date are included.

The Net Worth account on the Balance Sheet requires additional work. Net Worth reflects the impact of the income statement on the Balance Sheet. To calculate Net Worth we not only follow the same procedure for the Balance Sheet that we have just described, but we also do the same thing for the Income Statement accounts. Whenever we see a Salary Revenue record prior to or equal to our Balance Sheet date, we add that amount to the Net Worth line as well. Thus the Net Worth account reflects the accumulated effect of all Income Sheet accounts over time.

Note that this simple system does not have the balancing control built into it that the double-entry system provides. If the amounts on the rows I have proposed are summed, they equal 108,899.60 which equals the sum of the corresponding rows from the double-entry system, proving that no recording errors have been made in creating my example. If the Events alone are summed, they equal Net Income as calculated under the double-entry approach; again showing no recording error in the entries I have made. If the Transfer events are summed, they equal 110,790.29. This is composed of the total offsets of 108,899.60 plus net income of 1,890.69. Because the balance sheet is a point in time statement (rather than showing activity over time like the Income Statement) these offsets have a net effect of zero upon the balance sheet. The following shows the detail:

Journal Entry ID	Date	Account Number	Account	Debit/Credit	Amount	Description
JE0	01 Apr. 2008	300	Net Worth	Credit	(106,452.78)	Opening Balance
JE1	08 Apr. 2008	211	Credit Card Payable	Credit	(34.93)	Purchased gas
JE3	17 Apr. 2008	111	Checking Account	Credit	(474.93)	Automobile payment
JE4	17 Apr. 2008	111	Checking Account	Credit	(147.23)	Utility payment
JE5	20 Apr. 2008	111	Checking Account	Credit	(425.00)	Auto insurance payment
JE6	22 Apr. 2008	211	Credit Card Payable	Credit	(198.78)	Purchased new tires
JE7	22 Apr. 2008	211	Credit Card Payable	Credit	(278.95)	Replaced alternator
JE8	24 Apr. 2008	111	Checking Account	Credit	(966.28)	House payment
JE9	27 Apr. 2008	211	Credit Card Payable	Credit	(28.58)	Purchased gas
JE10	28 Apr. 2008	211	Credit Card Payable	Debit	200.00	Credit card payment
JE11	29 Apr. 2008	111	Checking Account	Credit	(574.00)	Various payments
JE13	30 Apr. 2008	112	Investment 401(k)	Debit	481.86	Gains on 401(k)
			Total offsets		(108,899.60)	
			Plus Net Income		(1,890.69)	
			Grand Total		(110,790.29)	

All this analysis was performed to prove that the system is in balance. In a double-entry system, the sum of all the journal entries is zero. Thus my system does not have this one type of internal check built into it. Again note that this check within a double-entry system does not ensure that completeness or accuracy of the entries, just that no rows have been dropped or amounts transposed. A different reconciliation mechanism would need to be constructed to provide a similar assurance for my proposed system. If that reconciliation method required recording all these additional entries, there would be no reduction in number of entries needed in my system.

Appendix 2: Event Driven Business Modelling

Kevin W. Young and Terry Magee took these concepts further in the PwC methodology Ascendant Section R0615 Event-Driven Business Modelling (Copyright IBM Corporation, used by permission). After summarizing the discussion presented in these chapters, they noted:

"The concepts of event-driven business modelling are also to ensure the development of an integrated enterprise data model that supports the business information needs of the enterprise. Specifically, they are applied in the following areas:

"Business Event Modelling: Business events are modelled to provide a basis for developing an organization's data models - the enterprise-level Entity Relationship Model (ERM), Conceptual Data Model (CDM), and Multi-dimensional Data Model (MDM). By modelling the essence of business events, various user perspectives of the organization's data resource can be supported. Specifically:

- "The ERM provides a high-level enterprise view of an organization's kernel entities and their relationships.
- "The CDM represents a transaction processing perspective of an organization's data resource. It expands the ERM by identifying the characteristic entities, associative entities, and supertype/subtype entities and is further refined through a process of data normalization.
- "The MDM is developed from a performance measurement/decision support perspective. It identifies the key business analytical dimensions and facts.

"Entity Relationship Model and Conceptual Data Model: A major weakness of many of today's enterprise data modelling efforts is to focus on a narrow, functional (vertical) view of an organization's business activities. This often leads to the artificial separation of data into business (operational) data and financial data and the subsequent proliferation of information systems that deal with only one kind of data. Event-driven business modelling aims at resolving this problem by forcing the integration of all data relevant to operating and managing an organization's business. With business events being the fundamental units of analysis, the enterprise data model represents an integrated view of the essential data of the organization's business rather than the individual views of information users (e.g., the financial statement view of an accountant or the production management report view of a plant manager).

"Business Analytical Multi-Dimensional Data Model: As an integral part of enterprise data modelling, a Multi-Dimensional Data Model is developed to support the business analytical or decision support information needs of an organization. Specifically, business analysis dimensions and informational facts about the organization's business are identified and modelled to provide a basis for developing a data warehouse supporting the organization's business analytical information needs. Multi-dimension data modelling is primarily based on an organization's performance measurement framework - the organization's value chain, the performance measurement categories and the specific performance measures. This analysis is supplemented by examining the essential data about business events - the resources, the agents, and the locations. By focusing on business events, an organization's business analytical information needs can be determined in terms of the capabilities to extract information relating to:

- "Any events of a business process by time, agents, resources, and locations
- "Any period of time by events, agents, resources, and locations
- "Resources by type of event, time, agents, and location
- "Agents by type of event, time, resources, and locations
- "Location by type of event, time, agents and resources

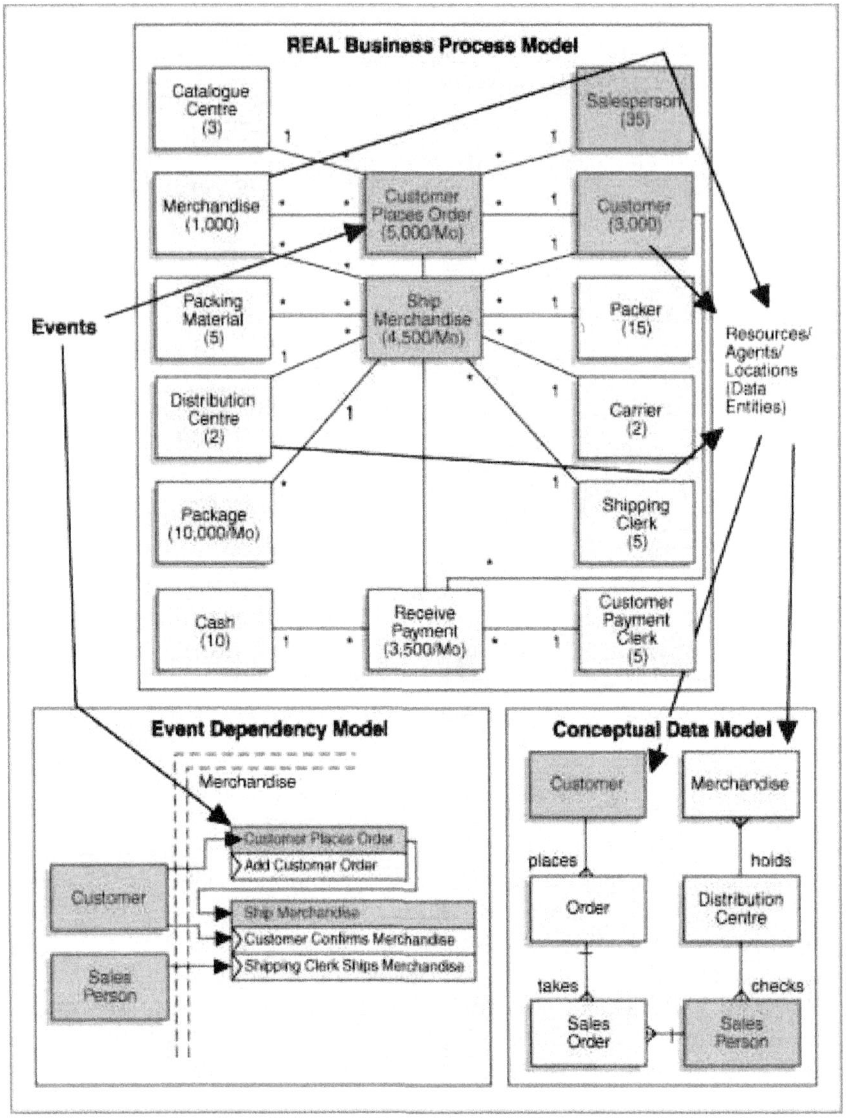

Figure 151. Exploring the Full Value of Business Events

"Taking the event-driven business modelling concept one step further, focusing on business events enables the development of information systems that can not only report in multiple ways on the current state of the business, but can also provide archival information on past events sorted by various criteria. Ultimately, this approach provides a mechanism for reconstructing the execution of a past event to identify not only the outcome of the event but also the conditions that existed within the business that dictated the result of the event (e.g., knowing that a customer order was rejected is important to many parts of a business, knowing why the order was rejected, such as because of a bad credit history or because the stock position was too low, may be even more important to the business).

"If all of the data relating to a business event is captured, including the conditions and values of any reference files accessed by the event, it should be possible to reconstruct the path of the event and repeat the outcome of the event at some future point in time.

"In practice, this is a major undertaking and requires that the technology (hardware and software) be sophisticated enough to capture all of the relevant data. Application software must be written to capture the data, as well as the data structures needed to store and allow retrieval of the data. However, once defined, the ability of the organization to manage the data at its disposal is almost infinite. It will effectively capture information that the business users may not even realize the importance of until some future point in time when they determine that they want to understand more about the business events with which they are dealing.

"The power that this approach brings is that it allows the business users to learn from their past experiences and interrogate business data to answer not just questions about "what happened to a specific business event on a particular day?" but also about "why did a business event result in a specific outcome?" or "what was the rationale behind the decision?"

"It is this power that information systems ultimately should embrace. As enabling technology becomes available, the development of information systems that utilize the full value of the business events should become the norm. The opportunity to take advantage of the event-driven approach should always be assessed for all current and future systems developments."

Authorship of material noted from discussion with Kevin Young, IBM Executive Consultant, June 9, 2009. Young noted that in the diagram presented "the lower left illustration of the Event Dependency Model, 'Customer Places Order' is the event and should be shown in the buff color below 'Add Customer Order'... which is the elementary process triggered by the Customer Places Order event."

Acknowledgements

Of course what is written in this book is not the work of only a few people. Building SAFR and implementing it against real world problems has involved hundreds of people. Some portion of those people have worked with the tool long enough to be listed on a team roster of some kind. Some continued for years; others only for the length of the project. I am appreciative of the hard work by these people. The following is a list of individuals from the Geneva System Group formation July 1993 through acquisition of the tool by IBM on October 2nd, 2002.

Early projects brought to the team Rick Roth and Doug Kunkel from State of Alaska of course as well as quite a number of future PW partners who were consistent boosters and supporters, Jay Poulos, David "Murph" Murphy, Mukesh Patel, Randall Ness, Julia Braun Roth, and William "Bill" Bengtson from State of Oregon, Renae Bell from State of Washington and Mike Tabb, Tony Talarico, and Jeff Gibbs from the State of Wyoming projects.

The development team in Sacramento included Brandy Smith, Clyde Simmons, Rob Clark, Monica Logan and Chris Stallman (both starting on the same day), Mona Breed, Cheryl Gentsch, Dave Haws, Spiros Velianitis, Barry Arabi, Mark Ashton, and for a few weeks in system testing with unforgettable first names: Nikki, Nicky, and Nicole. David Colpitts kept the mainframe running, and I always enjoyed calling Kip Powell for networking help.

A large US insurer independently came to the idea of an event-based architecture, and readily adopted the tool, folding in a very large set of capable team members through a number of projects, including Mike Schroeck, Peter Corbett, Lynnette Groves Zuccala, Anthony Boles, Sue Francis Fox, Greg Forsythe, Mark Kimmell, Mark Thyen, Laurie Lesniak, Wendy Lucas, Michael Shapiro, Jim Hladyshewsky, Mark Cederberg, Danielle Paquette Dulzer, Jerry Canterbury, Devin Brand, Tori Arnold McLaughlin, Fred Horwitz, Chad Williams, Michael Perez, Chandra Devarkonda, Michael Depodesta, Udayraj Nair, Paul Pace, Bill Garrison, Dean Lima, Matt Paliulis, Michael Vilhauer, Paula Shippee, Melissa Cox, Carrie Nisenholz, Michele O'Reilly, Ganesh Narayan, Choo Lee, Valerie Brown, Angie Degooyer, Denise Buchanan, Shannon Walker, Ann Randall, Amit Trehan, Tom Pozdol, Ravi Challagondla, Jeffrie Horner, and Vinod K Yada. And let's not forget Jeremy, although obviously we're beginning to.

Other projects included Paul Neary, Phillip Upton, and Gary Smith from Pharmaceutical Litigation Support Data Warehouse; Gary Spears, Kerri Meeks, Robert Frazier, Howard Joyce, Maya Davis, Robert Lippman, Rashad Khan and Steve Owens from the cookie manufacturer; Bill Ramsden, Dave Padmos, Mike Phelps, Linda Trieu from the computer chip manufacturer; Troy Deck and the Wingspan team, Al Sung, Tata Rao, Sherwood Daniels, Meri-Ellen Cain, Scott Pankoff from a Global Investment Bank; Rakesh Kant and Todd Topolski from a data integration company, Sam Kahng from the airline project, Bob Beech and the team at Digineer, Anthony "Tony" Minetti, Jr., Ben Yen, Bridgette Wage, Neil Cook, Mazen Mahmoud, Steve Graham, and Seth Weis from PwC's Global Financial Data Warehouse project.

Client team members may exceed the total of those listed above in implementing the system. Many ideas of how the tool can be applied and enhancements came from them. Many of them teased out significant architectural approaches to problems. The following are a selection of those team members who have been involved with the tool over multiple years. Don Wanie, Debbie Bump, Guy Warren, and Paul Diebels from Alaska, Doug Goldbach from Oregon, Charles Weber and Christine McDonald at proxy balloting processing company, Dimitri Kerrigan at the cookie manufacturer, Farrokh Sinai at a large regional bank, and Lloyd Jackson, Greg Michaels, Vanessa Menke, Lynn Kilhoffer, Kevin Bly, Byron Bordt, Andrea Orth, Scott Penland, Dan Vieth, and Steven Frobish from the insurance company, where Jim Dammeyer kept the mainframes humming.

The latest version of a financial management solution was built by a very large team on the FTP project. Thank you to Jeff Wolfers for empowering me to build the system, reading a very early draft of this work and encouraging me to explain the ideas more clearly. David Willis mentored me through leading a large team and taught me how to survive. Pete Galbo, Mike Mann, and John Pope at times challenged me to deliver on the promises of the idea, all the while fundamentally pulling for my success. I was supported by a tremendous set of individuals on the architectural team, including Dan Aminoff, Gary Kuechle and Greg Forsythe from the client and others, and a very dedicated management team in MaryAnn Kreamer, Dorrie Ihle, Andy Wells, Aileen Stewart and Mike Blom. It was painful enough that at times in the midst of it we all felt "somwthing went wrong [sic]."

The IBM team members on the FTP project and other SAFR team members in alphabetical order as of June 1 2009 include: Abhay Kumar, Al Sung, Amit Trehan, Amy Y Huang, Angela Liang, Ann Randall, Anoop K Sharma, Anthony "Tony" Minetti, Jr., Archana Dasar, Bharat Shah, Bill Lewis, Bill Yankowiak, Burt Phannemiller, Chandra Devarkonda, Chris Stallman , Daniel Cho, David "Murph" Murphy, Debarati Parui, Devin Brand, Devyani Sahasrabudhe, Dilip Sanchora, Doreen Rose, Doug Kunkel, Elana R Dunn, Eric Levy, Fred Horwitz, Greg Forsythe, Greg Halper, Greg Shipley, Hal Davis, Howard Reba, Ian Cunningham, Igor Urisman, Jason C Bryfogle, Jay Poulos, Jaydeep Marumale, Jeffrie Horner, Jennifer Wells, Jerry Canterbury, John Dravnieks, John Kaputin, John Buersmeyer, Jonathan Goffin, Jonathan Losh, Kanchan Rauthan, Kaushik Lala, Keith Barlow, Lan-Huong Nguyen, Larissa Razumovskiy, Laurie Lesniak, Manoj N Duse, Marjorie Galban, Megha Sethi, Michael Barrett-Lennard, Michael Perez, Michael Shapiro, Mihail Laftchiyski, Mohana Tenepalli, Monica Logan , Mukesh Patel, Mustufa Kasidwala, Neha Pardeshi, Neil Bloomfield, Nick Rimmer, Nigel Clark, Nikita Balakrishnan, Paresh Thatte, Patrick O Gan, Peter Cook, Pothalaiah Pasuluru, Pradeep Thirunagari, Priyamvada S Kale, Quinn Lui, Randall Ness, Ravi Challagondla, Rick Maynard, Richa Sinha, Rick Roth, Rob Saarva, Rohan Dhekane, Rushikesh Vyas, Sachin Khasgiwal, Sahn Nguyen, Sandeep Bs Gunjal, Sandeep J Gore, Sanjay Gulati, Santhosh Bhukya, Shailaja Khadilkar, Sherry Gola, Shruti Shukla, Sidharth Srivastava, Sreenivasan V Raghavan, Srini Murarisetty., Steven Brown, Suneetha Pampana, Susan McHugh, Tata Rao, Todd Topolski, Tom Pozdol, Uday Dixit, Vamshikrishna Asam, Varun Sharma, Vindisha Poojary, Vinod K Yada, and Yesh Tyagi.

Thank you to James Cortada and Barbara Nevergold for encouraging me to write and publish the work; Susan McHugh for assistance with footnote editing and graphics; Kevin Young for the references to the Ascendant Method material; and Devesh Nakra for developing the final *Financial Management and Risk Solution* graphic.

Laurie Lesniak's consistent encouragement, as well as acting as editor, typist, graphics processor and advisor pulled me though many weeks of doubt and discouragement.

The day I went to BYU to read McCarthy's paper again for the first time in years, I stopped by my consulting professor's office, J. Owen Cherrington who was in the prime of his life, but is now no longer with us. He kindly gave me a copy of his and Eric's textbook. I have thought of it as a symbolic act in passing on what he knew of these topics. I thank him for being a quiet mentor.

Finally, since this work is somewhat autobiographical, it might not be inappropriate to express sincere gratitude to my father, Bob, who taught me to work, my wife, Kari, my partner in it, and my brother, Lane, who told me to write about it.

Selected Bibliography

Academic Research

Of course, any additional study should begin with the fundamental source for this work, William E. McCarthy, *The REA Accounting Model: A Generalized Framework for Accounting Systems in a Shared Data Environment*. The Accounting Review, July 1982, 554-577, or at http://www.msu.edu/user/mccarth4/McCarthy.pdf. According to Dr. McCarthy's resume, "Professor McCarthy's 1982 paper on REA accounting systems was given the first Seminal Contribution to Accounting Information Systems Literature Award at the American Accounting Association meeting in Chicago in 1996."

An excellent review of the history of and related academic research leading to McCarthy's paper is found Cheryl L.Dunn and McCarthy, William E., *The REA Accounting Model: Intellectual Heritage And Prospects For Progress*, The Journal of Information Systems (Spring 1997), 31-51, or at http://www.msu.edu/user/mccarth4/DUNN&MC.htm.

McCarthy's own assessment of progress in understanding his work can be found at William E. McCarthy, *Semantic Modeling in Accounting Education, Practice, and Research: Some Progress and Impediments* Published in: Conceptual Modeling: Current Issues and Future Directions, 1999, 144-53, http://www.msu.edu/~mccarth4/chen-con.html (April 2008). There is a reference to the Price Waterhouse Geneva solution in this and various other academic articles as one of the few practical implementations of the theory. The Price Waterhouse Geneva solution is now the IBM Scalable Architecture for Financial Reporting (SAFR) product.

David P. Andros and Eric Denna published a paper in *Developing an event-based solution: The case of IBM's National Employee Disbursement System*, Journal of Information Systems, Vol. 10, No. 1 Spring 1996, 51 – 69. This system deals with the theory's implications on the capture of business events (on-line transaction processing) rather than the reporting problems focused on in this book.

Additional information on McCarthy and related academic work can be found at http://www.msu.edu/user/mccarth4/.

College Materials

Eric coauthored the following textbook after I left college, but it contains perhaps the best summary of his work. Anita Sawyer Hollander, Eric L. Denna, J. Owen Cherrington, *Accounting, Information Technology, and Business Solutions* 2nd ed. (© McGraw-Hill Companies Inc.: 2000). This work contains additional details about the methodological steps described for designing an REA business process model.

The call to arms against traditional accounting is best evidenced in Eric's volume: Eric L. Denna, et al, *Event-Driven Business Solutions, Today's Revolution in Business and Information Technology*, Homewood, IL: Business One Irwin, 1993.

The most important text book at school Eric had us thoroughly read and understand was Howard M. Armitage, *Linking Management Accounting Systems with Computer Technology*, published by The Society of Management Accountants of Canada, Hamilton, Ont. (September 1985).

The Financial Accounting Standards Board (FASB) *Statements of Financial Accounting Concepts: Accounting Standards 1997/98 Edition* (John Wiley & Sons, Inc. © 1997) is a very good summary of the conceptual underpinnings of accounting.

See John R. Alexander, *The History of Accounting*, Association of Chartered Accountants in the US (ACAUS), http://www.acaus.org/acc_his.html (May 2006) for a brief summary of the history of accounting. See also Alfred W. Crosby, The Measure of Reality: Quantification and Western Society, 1250 – 1600, [Cambridge University Press, © 1997]

SAFR and PwC Literature

Kevin W. Young, a coworker on the IEF project, and Terry Magee, my instructor for my introductory consulting class in Florida, summarized Eric's *Event-Driven Business Solutions* concepts in the PW methodology, later PwC's Ascendant R0615 Event-Driven Business Modelling section. Portions of this material remain in the IBM Method 7.2 as *Artifact: Business Event List (BUS 101) Copyright IBM Corporation.*. This material was also influenced by James Martin, *Information Engineering*, the theory behind IEF as a tool.

Price Waterhouse Data Warehouse Reporting Solution brochure, *State of Alaska benefits from data warehouse high-performance solution*, May 1996. Copyright IBM Corporation.

This book is directly based upon a number of published papers from Rick Roth as a partner with Price Waterhouse.

Richard K. Roth and Denna, Eric L. Ph.D. *Making Good on a Promise: Platform Assignment is the Key to Leveraging Data Warehouses* Manufacturing Systems, February 1996 (© Chilton Publications)

Richard K. Roth and Denna, Eric L., Ph.D., *Platform Assignment Principles For Decision Support Systems And Data Warehouses* Price Waterhouse White Paper, Nov 1995. Copyright IBM Corporation.

Richard K.Roth and Denna, Eric L., Ph.D., *A Summary of Event-Driven Systems Concepts* Price Waterhouse White Paper, undated (mid 1990's). Copyright IBM Corporation.

Richard K. Roth, *A Practical S/390 Parallel Processing Option for Data Warehouses* Price Waterhouse White Paper, undated (mid 1990's). Copyright IBM Corporation.

Richard K. Roth, *[ERP] High-volume Operational Reporting/data Warehousing Summary of Sizing Concepts and Architectural Alternatives* Price Waterhouse White Paper, September, 1996. Copyright IBM Corporation.

Computers

James W. Cortada has written a three volume history of computers and their impact upon various industries. I have used volume 1, *The Digital Hand: How Computers Changed the Work of American Manufacturing, Transportation, and Retail Industries* (Oxford University Press: © 2004)

W. H. "Bill" Inmon's *Building the Data Warehouse: Second Edition*, (John Wiley & Sons, Inc. © 1996) is probably the best work at understanding data warehousing and data base methods for responding to reporting problems.

The definitive work for understanding how a mainframe actually works is the IBM Enterprise Systems Architecture/390, *Principles of Operation* manual (IBM © 1990 – 1999). I have referred to the seventh edition (July 1999).

Index

About the Mentors

Eric L. Denna

ERIC DENNA is married to the former Lyn Hoggan and they are the parents of seven children and a growing number of grandchildren. Eric is a native of Northern California and now resides in Orem, Utah. Eric has a bachelor degree in accounting from BYU, a masters degree in information systems from BYU, and a Ph.D in Information Systems from Michigan State University where he was the Coopers & Lybrand Doctoral Scholar. Eric has worked for Ernst & Young, Price Waterhouse, and Coopers & Lybrand. He was associate professor of information systems at BYU's Marriott School of Management. After leaving academe he was chief information officer for Times Mirror Corporation, for BYU, and for The Church of Jesus Christ of Latter-day Saints. He was also Chief Operating Officer of The RBL Group (www.rbl.net) and SVP Operations and Global Process Design at Ascent Media (www.ascentmedia.com). He has served as a consultant to many organizations and is an experienced presenter at conferences, seminars, and symposia around the world. Eric is an advisor to Workday (www.workday.com), FlatworldKnowledge (www.flatworldknowledge.com), Proton Communications (www.protonc.com), and has been a research associate with The Research Board (www.researchboard.com). He has written five books and several scholarly and professional articles on the strategic use of information technology. He loves to hike, ski, garden, take long walks with his wife, sing with his wife, play with grandchildren, and hopes to return to writing some day.

Richard K. Roth

RICK ROTH retired from IBM in 2010 and is working as in independent consultant through his firm R.K. Roth LLC. He started his career as an instructor of accounting and finance at Iowa State University. He was with PricewaterhouseCoopers (PwC) for 25 years where he was admitted to the partnership in 1988. At IBM he was a Global Business Services (GBS) partner for 8 years after IBM acquired the PwC consulting practice in 2002. He has broad experience consulting with private and public sector clients. His primary area of expertise is design and implementation of high volume events-based financial and operational systems. He founded the Scalable Architecture for Financial Reporting (SAFR) practice at PwC in 1992 and remained the SAFR practice leader until his retirement in 2010. His primary emphasis has been on the systems aspects of financial transformation programs for some of the world's largest financial institutions. He graduated from Iowa State University with a Bachelor of Science in Business Administration in 1975 and the University of Iowa with an MBA in 1976. He grew up in Waterloo, Iowa and currently resides in Canyon Lake, Texas with his wife Julia.

Jay R. Poulos

JAY POULOS is the President of General Systems Solutions, Inc. He has over 35 years of experience in systems architecture and systems development project management. He has vast experience in implementing large-scale application systems in diverse industries including financial services, manufacturing, retail, transportation and government. His primary area of expertise is design and development of high volume transactional-based software systems. He is a patent holder for an enterprise-scale software system that has been successfully implemented in several Fortune 100 companies. Mr. Poulos graduated from Oregon State University in 1972 with a Bachelor of Science degree in Mathematics. He began his career with the Oregon Department of Transportation in the Information Systems Division. In 1985, he formed a consulting company and partnered with Price Waterhouse to develop and implement a financial management system for the State of Tennessee. He continued the partnership with PricewaterhouseCoopers and currently partners with IBM on large-scale financial systems development projects for large worldwide financial institutes. Mr. Poulos has lived in Oregon for 55 years and currently has a residence in Salem and a horse ranch in Sisters with his wife Janet. His daughter is an elementary teacher in the Seattle area, married to a soon-to-be CPA.

Douglas F. Kunkel

DOUGLAS KUNKEL specializes in custom mainframe software development for difficult performance sensitive applications. He is an independent consultant and retired PricewaterhouseCoopers Management Consulting Principal. During his 44 year career, he has provided services to large retail companies, financial services corporations, state governments, and universities. His diverse career began in 1966 with development of custom university Student Registration software for the new IBM 360/67 computers. This was followed by development of Library Automation software and a role as key architect for the Washington Library Network (WLN). Douglas then transitioned into database design before joining Price Waterhouse's Management Consulting State Government Practice. Employment with Price Waterhouse eventually lead to financial software development where he has remained for the past 20 years. Douglas holds a Bachelor of Arts degree in Mathematics and a Master of Science degree in Computer Science (1972) from Washington State University. As an Eagle Scout he has an ongoing connection to Boy Scouts of America having served as Scoutmaster on three different occasions. His ongoing service to his church community began with a 2 ½ year mission to Germany in 1962, and included a recently completed term as Bishop. Douglas was born in Ithaca, New York, and split his youth between Fort Collins Colorado, and Pullman Washington. Currently he resides in Oakland, California with his wife Kristin Carlsen of Yakima Washington. They enjoy their five children and eleven grandchildren.

Printed in Dunstable, United Kingdom

91343462R00205